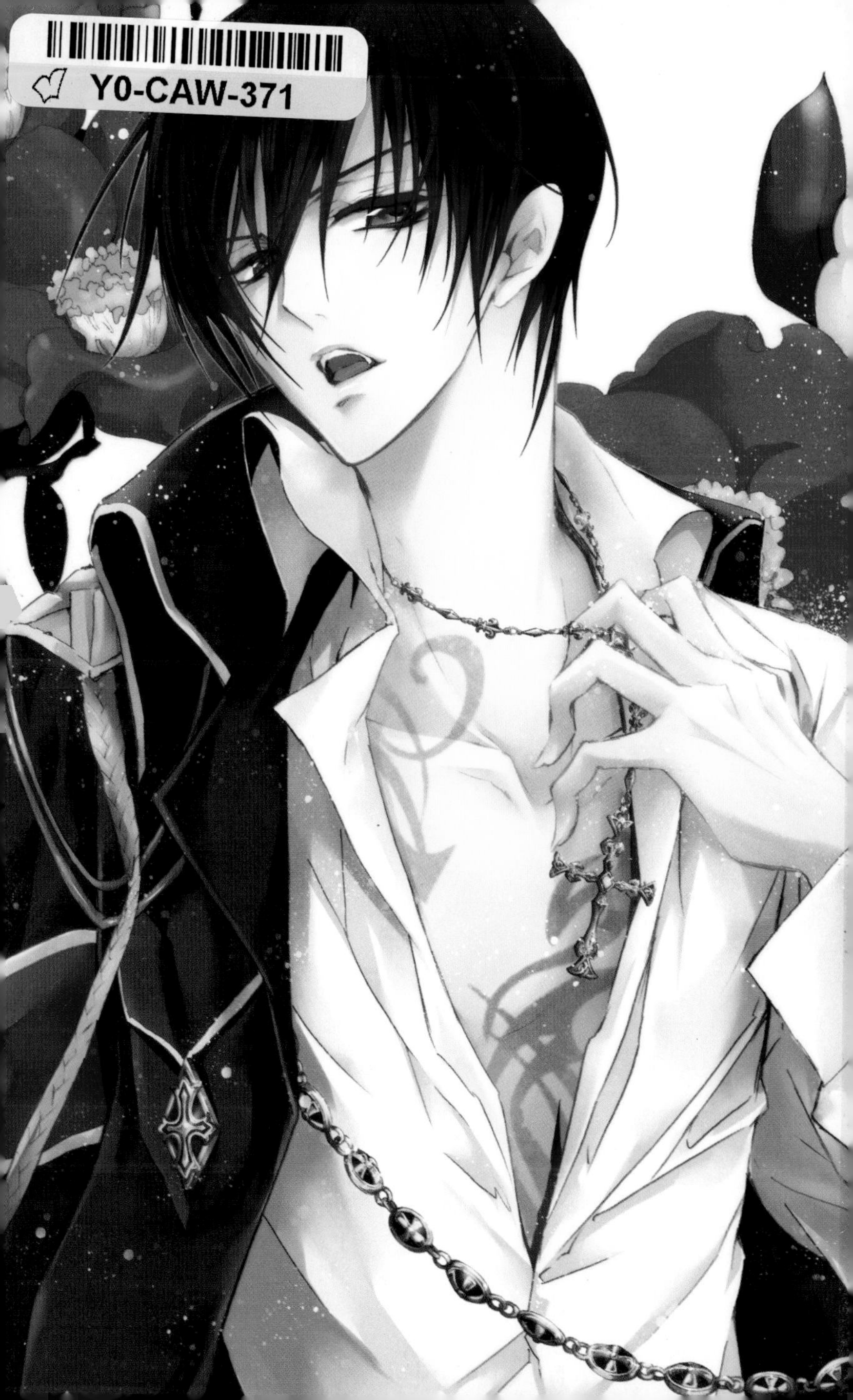

c o n t e n t s

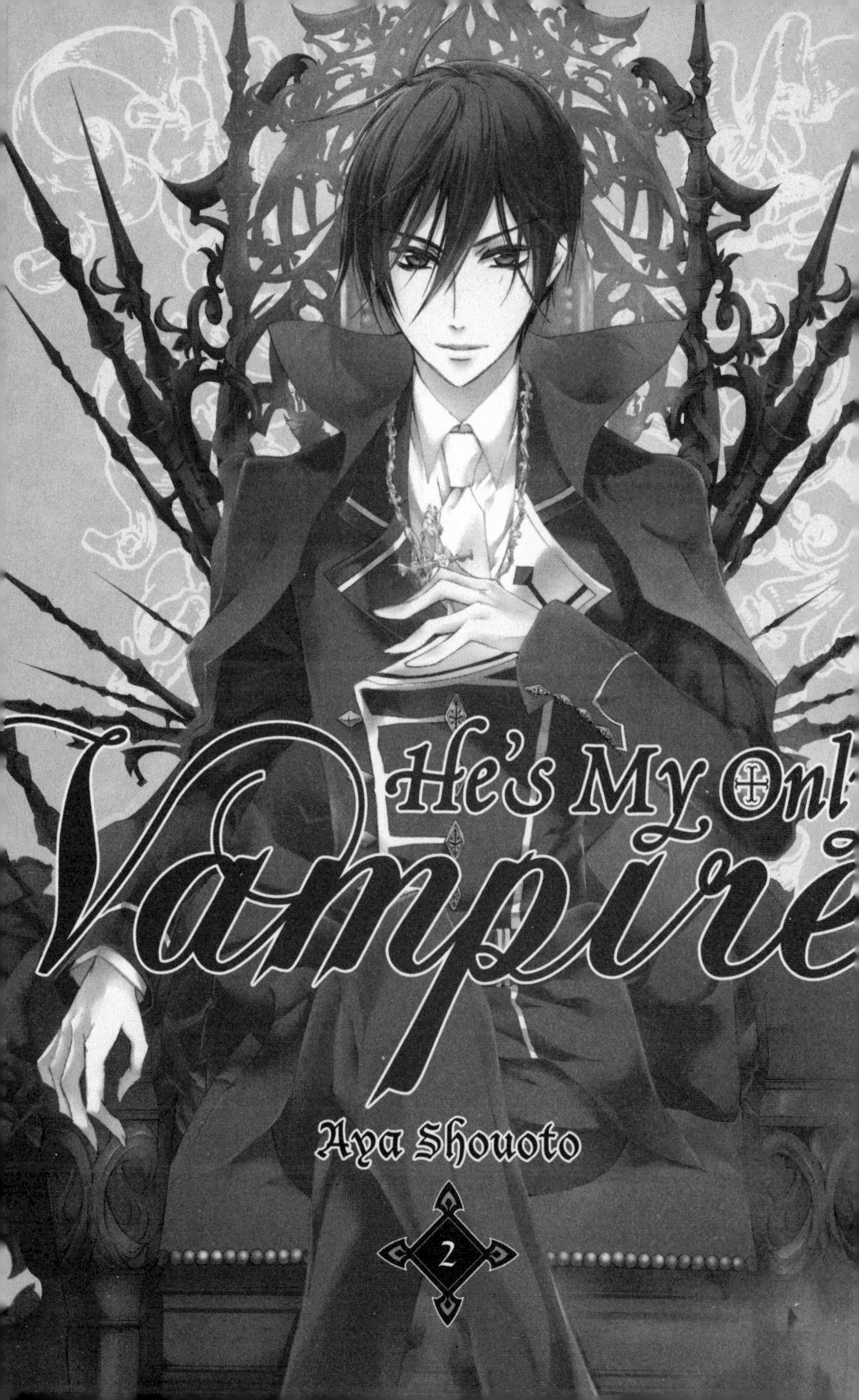
He's My Onl
Vampire
Aya Shouoto
2

Characters and Story

"Thrall"

One who is ageless and deathless and shall surrender the entirety of their being to their vampire master for all of eternity...

FORCED TO GIVE UP HER SPOT ON THE TEAM DUE TO AN INJURY, FORMER TRACK STAR KANA STARTS TO FIND HER DAILY LIFE AT ST. AGATHA ACADEMY A BIT UNFULFILLING. BUT ONE DAY, WHEN WALKING THROUGH TOWN, SHE SPOTS HER CHILDHOOD FRIEND AKI IN THE CROWD. WHILE ATTEMPTING TO CHASE AFTER HIM, KANA IS CAUGHT IN A TRAFFIC ACCIDENT THAT LEAVES HER ON DEATH'S DOOR. BUT WHEN AKI INTERVENES BY FEEDING HER HIS BLOOD, HE NOT ONLY SAVES HER LIFE, BUT ALSO MAKES HER INTO HIS "THRALL."

AKI HAS COME BACK TO TOWN TO COLLECT THE SEVEN STIGMAS AND GAIN THE POWER TO SAVE HIS YOUNGER TWIN BROTHER, ERIYA. HE DISCOVERS THAT JIN SHIRANUI, THE BOY WHO CAUSED KANA'S INJURY, IS THE OWNER OF ONE OF THESE STIGMAS. AS JIN, DRIVEN BERSERK BY HIS STIGMA'S POWER, RAMPAGES THROUGH THE TOWN, AKI PURSUES HIM IN ORDER TO TAKE JIN'S STIGMA FOR HIMSELF. HOWEVER, WHEN KANA PLEADS FOR JIN'S LIFE, AKI SPARES JIN, GIVING HIM A SMALL DOSE OF HIS PURE VAMPIRE BLOOD TO HEAL THE MADNESS, BUT IT TURNS OUT THAT SUCH AN ACT IS ACTUALLY FORBIDDEN—?!

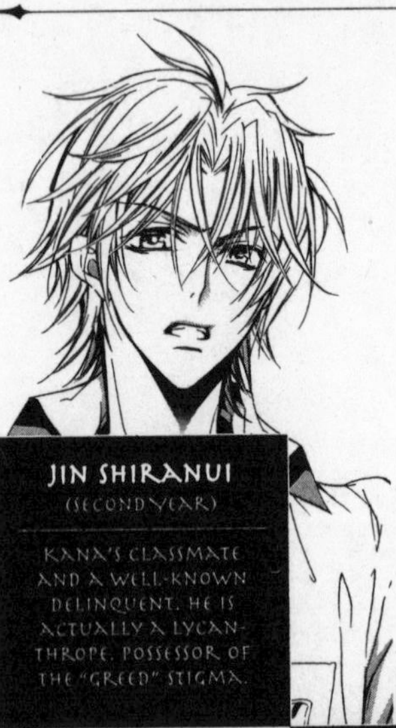

JIN SHIRANUI
(SECOND YEAR)

KANA'S CLASSMATE AND A WELL-KNOWN DELINQUENT. HE IS ACTUALLY A LYCANTHROPE. POSSESSOR OF THE "GREED" STIGMA.

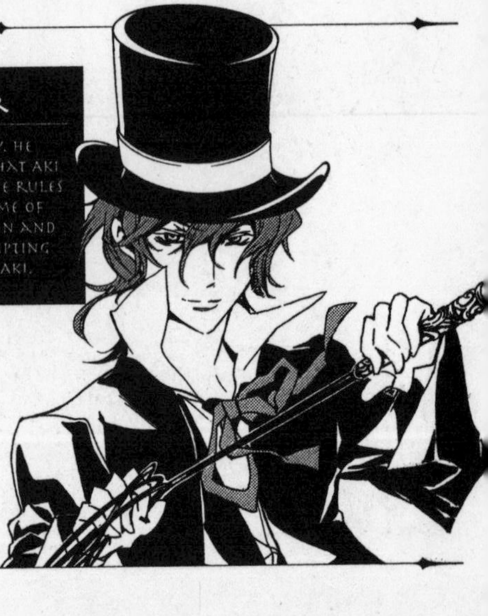

DEALER

AKI'S SENTRY. HE PROCLAIMED THAT AKI HAD BROKEN THE RULES BY GIVING SOME OF HIS BLOOD TO JIN AND IS NOW ATTEMPTING TO EXECUTE AKI.

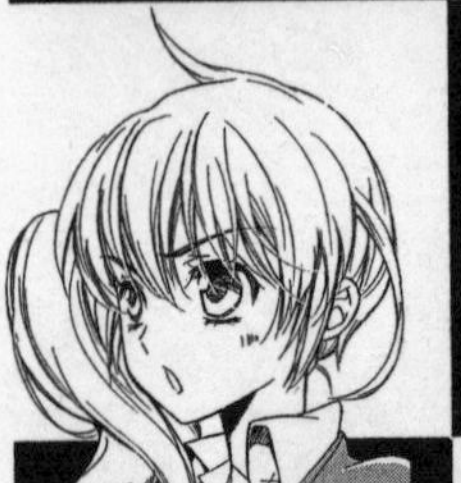

RIE KURUMIDO
(SECOND YEAR)

KANA'S FRIEND AND CLASSMATE. SHE HAS A BOLD PERSONALITY AND A STRONG CHARACTER.

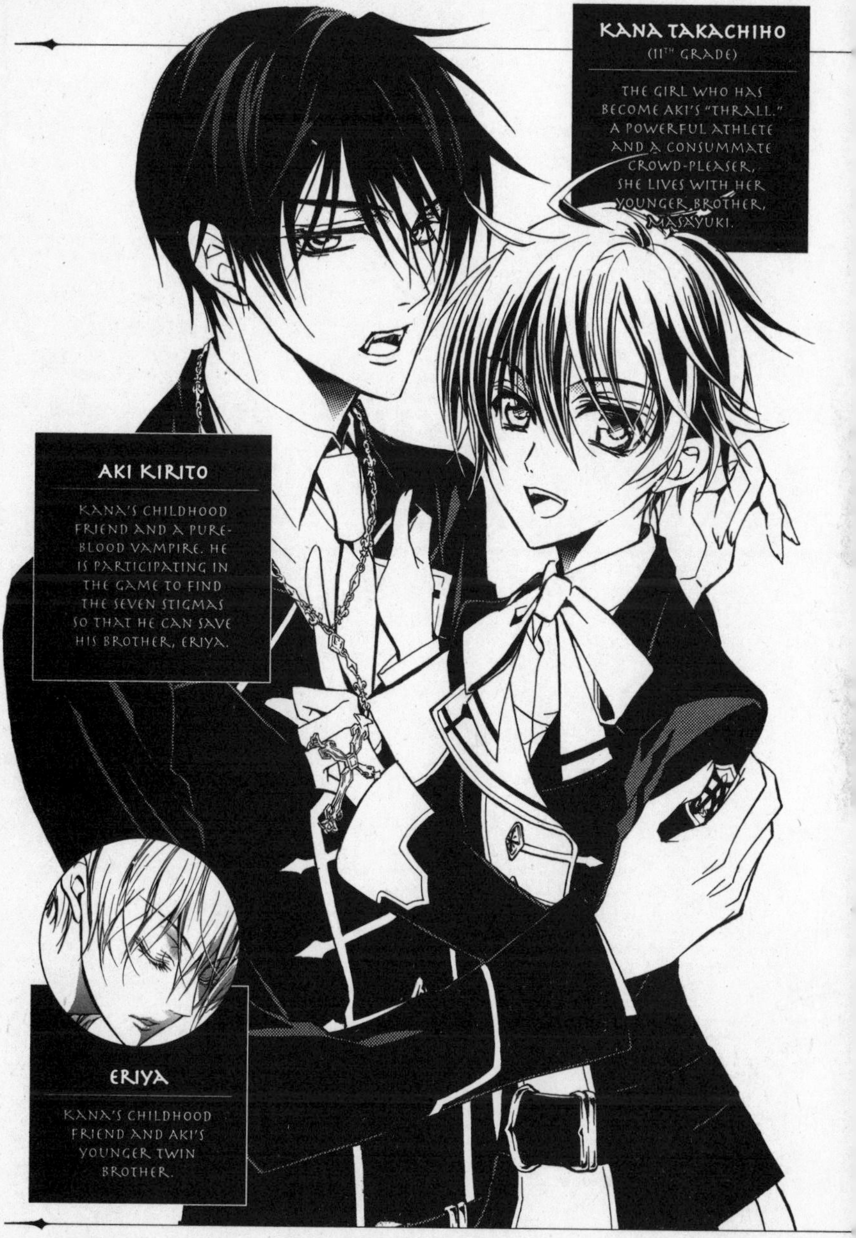
KANA TAKACHIHO
(11TH GRADE)
THE GIRL WHO HAS BECOME AKI'S "THRALL." A POWERFUL ATHLETE AND A CONSUMMATE CROWD-PLEASER, SHE LIVES WITH HER YOUNGER BROTHER, MASAYUKI.
AKI KIRITO
KANA'S CHILDHOOD FRIEND AND A PURE-BLOOD VAMPIRE. HE IS PARTICIPATING IN THE GAME TO FIND THE SEVEN STIGMAS SO THAT HE CAN SAVE HIS BROTHER, ERIYA.
ERIYA
KANA'S CHILDHOOD FRIEND AND AKI'S YOUNGER TWIN BROTHER.

He's my only vampire

Aya Shouoto

THOUGH YOU ARE, INDEED, A PUREBLOOD, BREAKING THE RULES ...
...CALLS FOR A SENTENCE OF DEATH.
HYOOOO (FWOOOOOO)
GAKU (COLLAPSE)
NOW ACCEPT DEATH AS YOUR ATONE-MENT.
...... GUH!
AKI!!
~moon phase~5

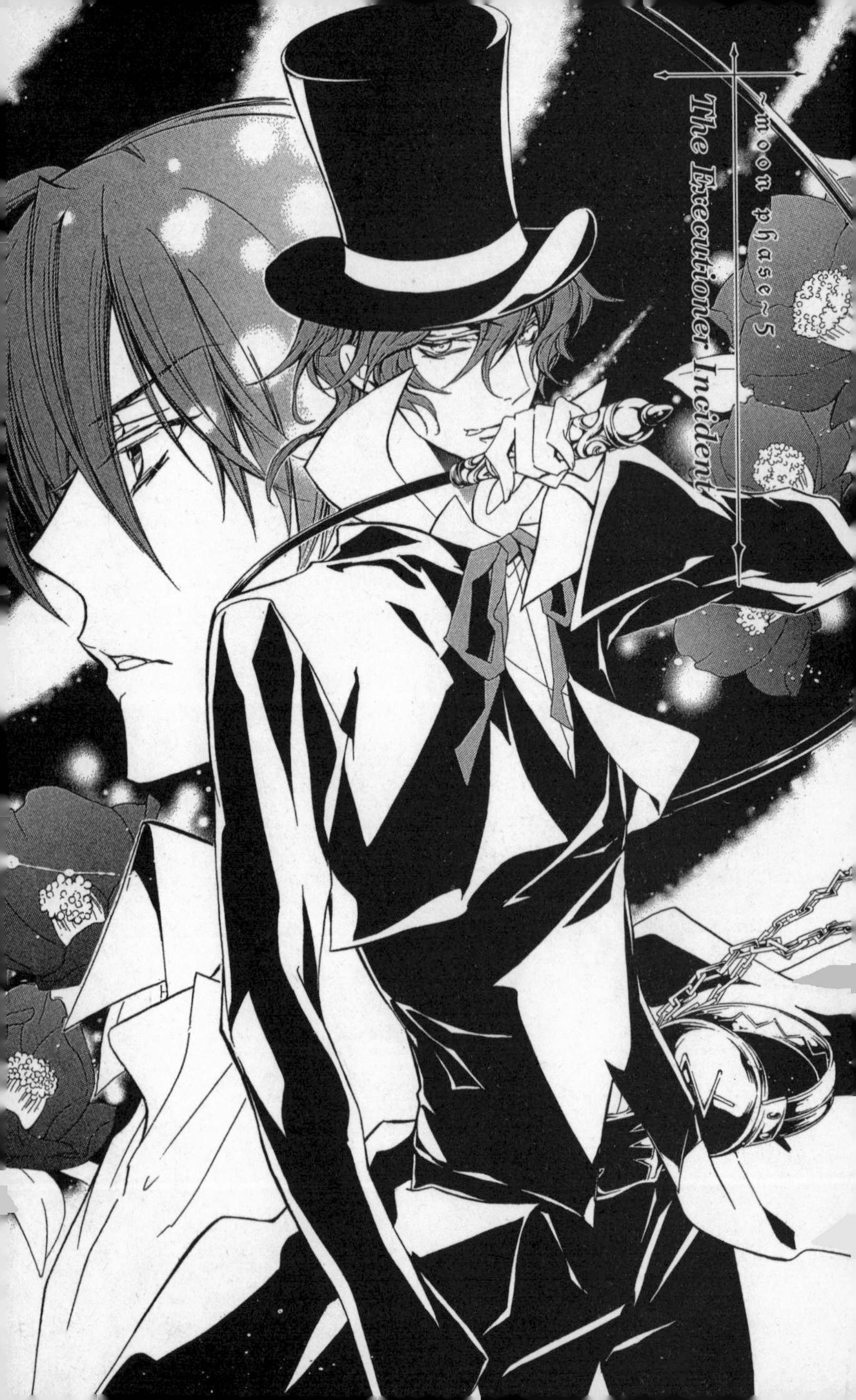
~moon phase~5
The Executioner Incident

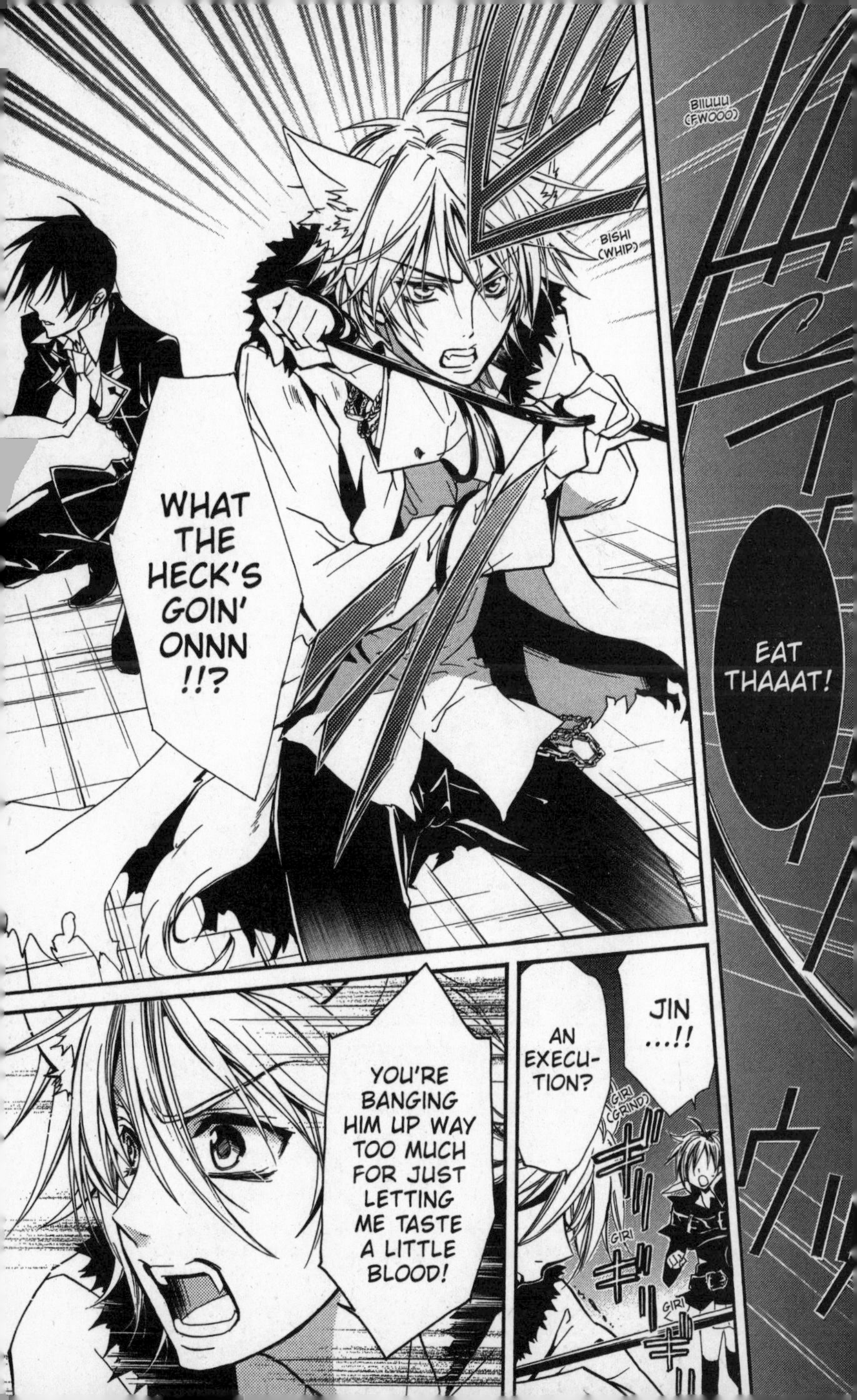
BIIUUU (FWOOO)
EAT THAAAT!
BISHI (WHIP)
WHAT THE HECK'S GOIN' ONNN !!?
JIN ...!!
AN EXECU-TION?
GIRI (GRIND)
GIRI
GIRI
YOU'RE BANGING HIM UP WAY TOO MUCH FOR JUST LETTING ME TASTE A LITTLE BLOOD!

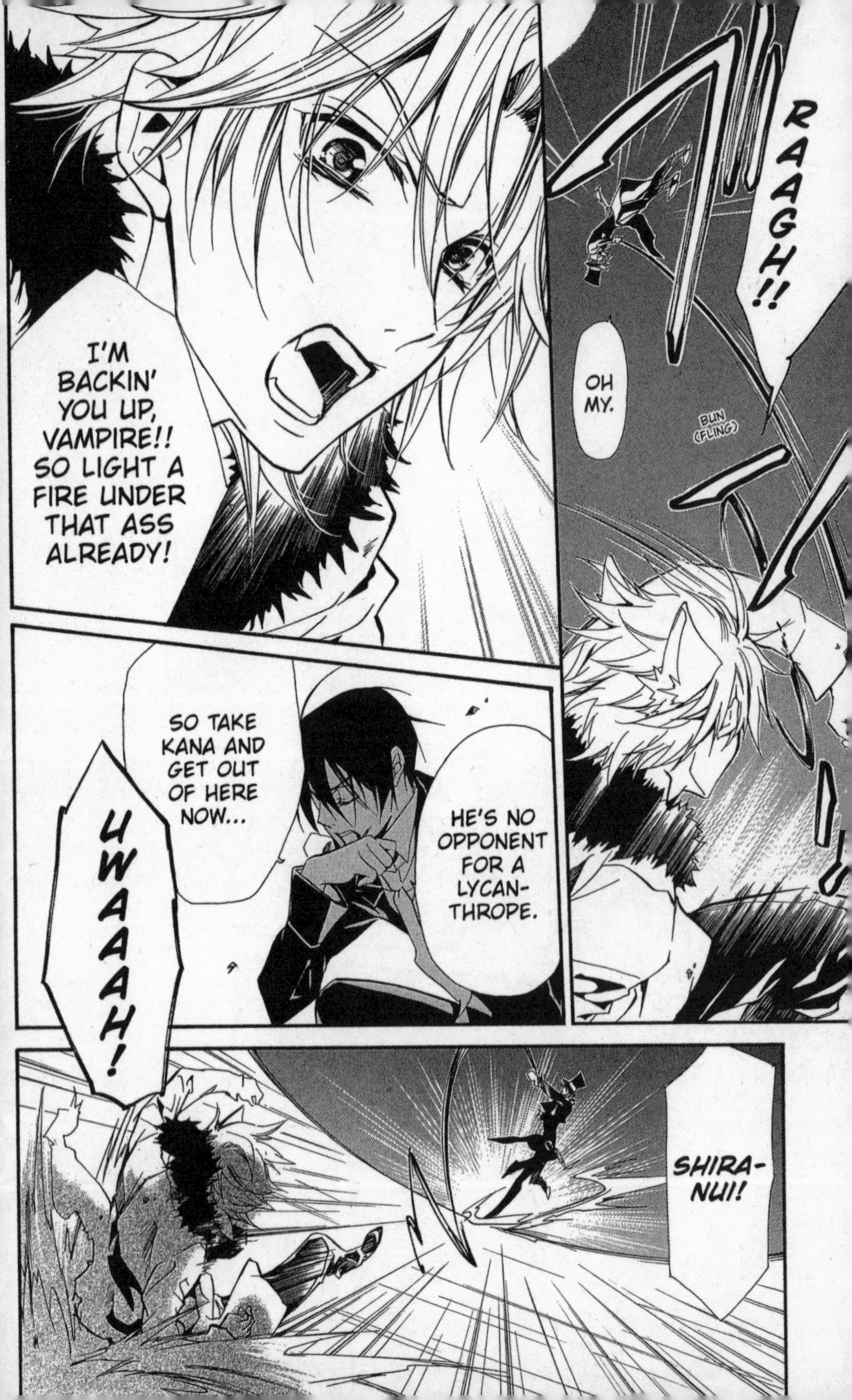
RAAAGH!!
OH MY.
BUN (FLING)
I'M BACKIN' YOU UP, VAMPIRE!! SO LIGHT A FIRE UNDER THAT ASS ALREADY!
HE'S NO OPPONENT FOR A LYCAN-THROPE.
SO TAKE KANA AND GET OUT OF HERE NOW...
UWAAAAH!
SHIRA-NUI!

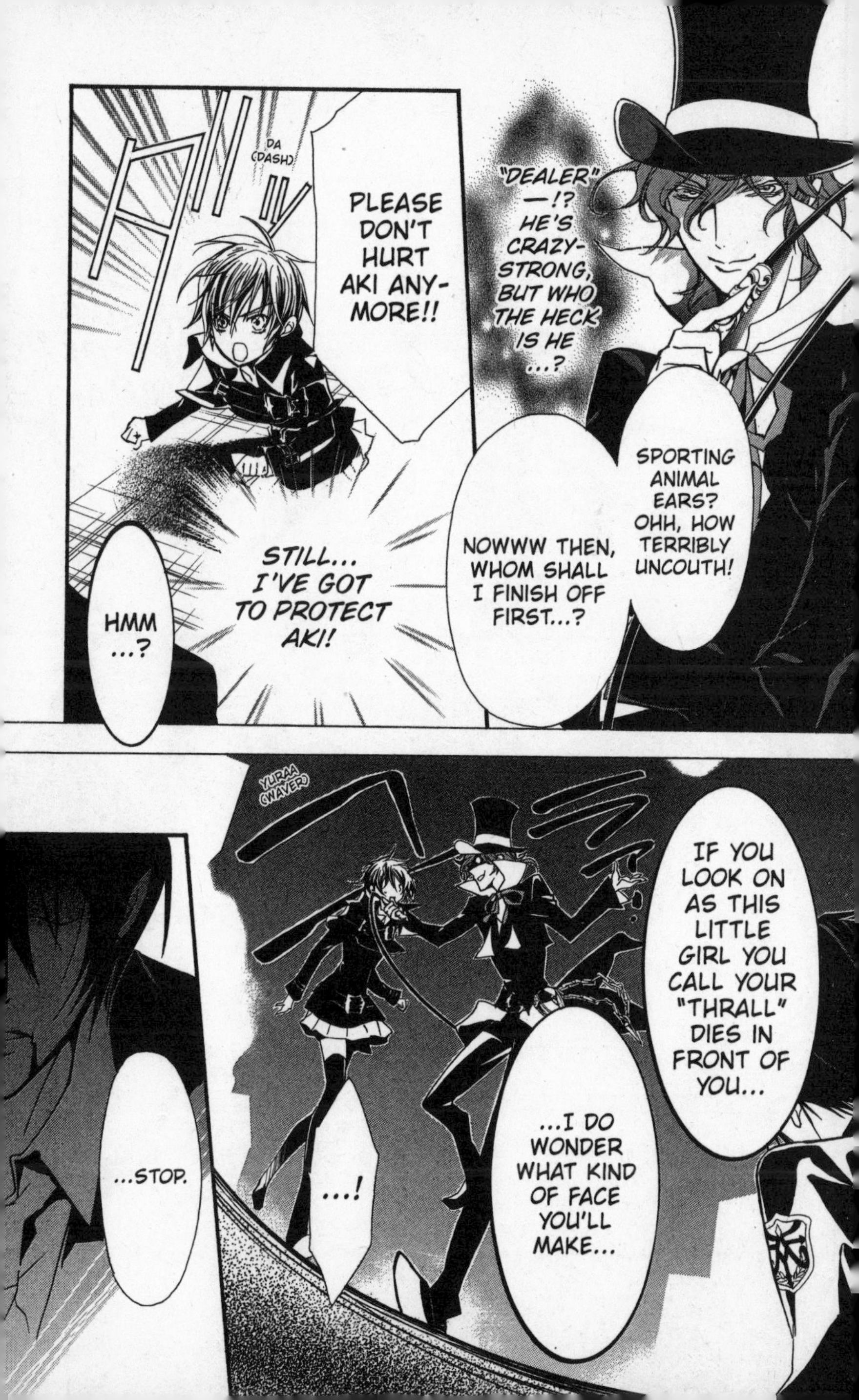
"DEALER"—!? HE'S CRAZY-STRONG, BUT WHO THE HECK IS HE...?
SPORTING ANIMAL EARS? OHH, HOW TERRIBLY UNCOUTH!
NOWWW THEN, WHOM SHALL I FINISH OFF FIRST...?
DA (DASH)
PLEASE DON'T HURT AKI ANY-MORE!!
STILL... I'VE GOT TO PROTECT AKI!
HMM...?
YURAA (WAVER)
IF YOU LOOK ON AS THIS LITTLE GIRL YOU CALL YOUR "THRALL" DIES IN FRONT OF YOU...
...I DO WONDER WHAT KIND OF FACE YOU'LL MAKE...
...!
...STOP.

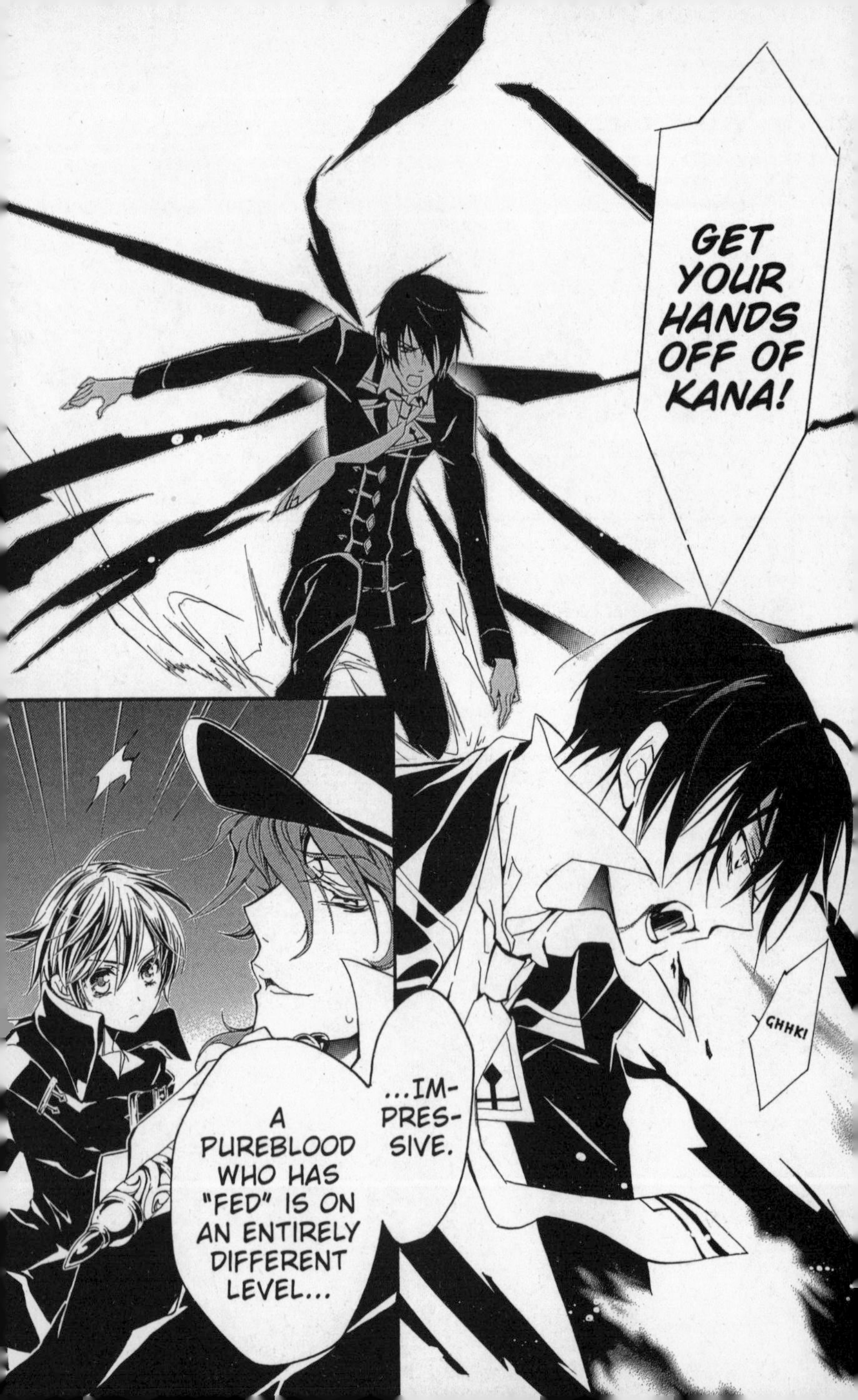
GET YOUR HANDS OFF OF KANA!
GHHK!
...IM-PRES-SIVE.
A PUREBLOOD WHO HAS "FED" IS ON AN ENTIRELY DIFFERENT LEVEL...

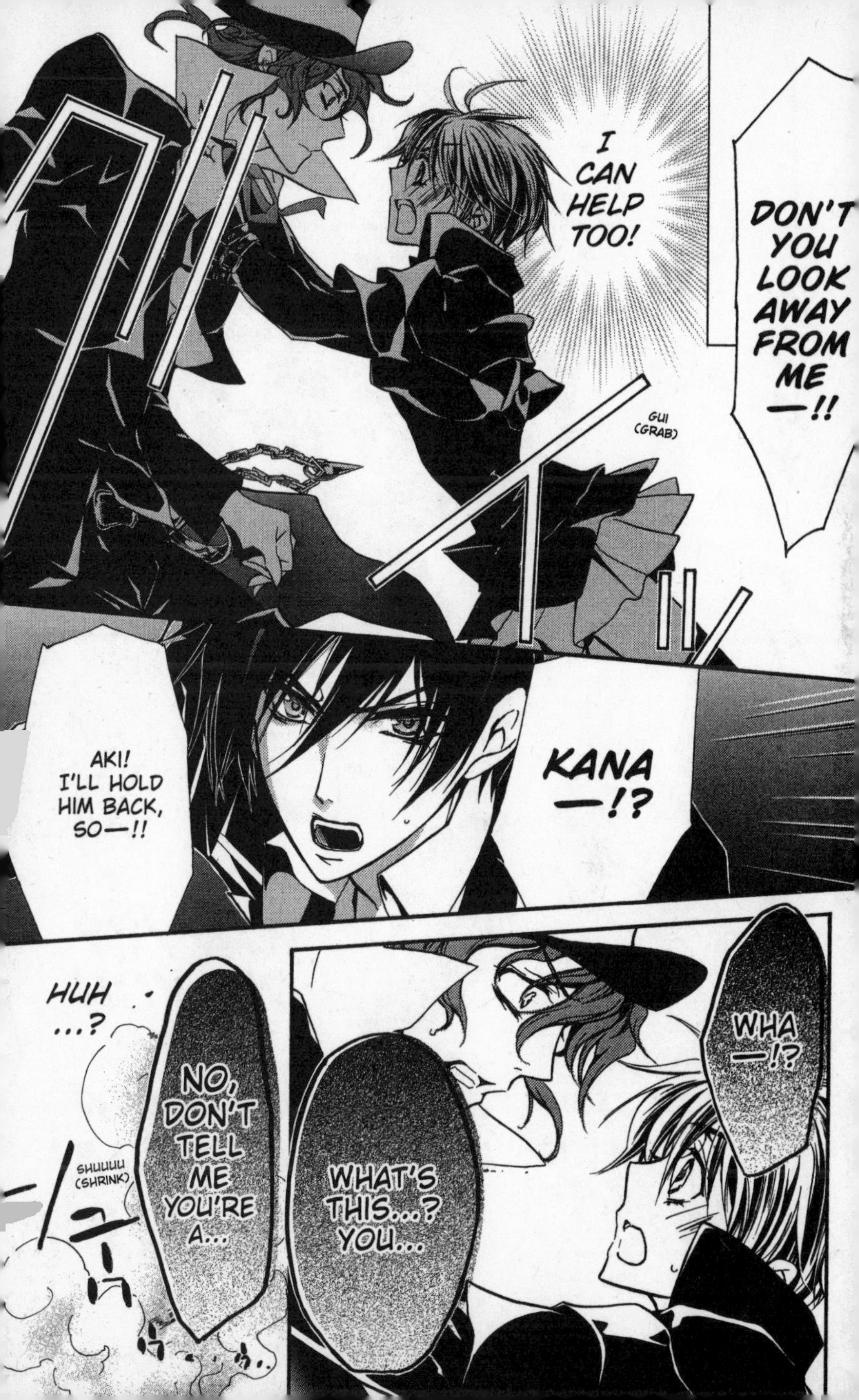
DON'T YOU LOOK AWAY FROM ME—!!
I CAN HELP TOO!
GUI (GRAB)
KANA—!?
AKI! I'LL HOLD HIM BACK, SO—!!
WHA—!?
WHAT'S THIS...? YOU...
NO, DON'T TELL ME YOU'RE A...
HUH...?
SHUUUU (SHRINK)

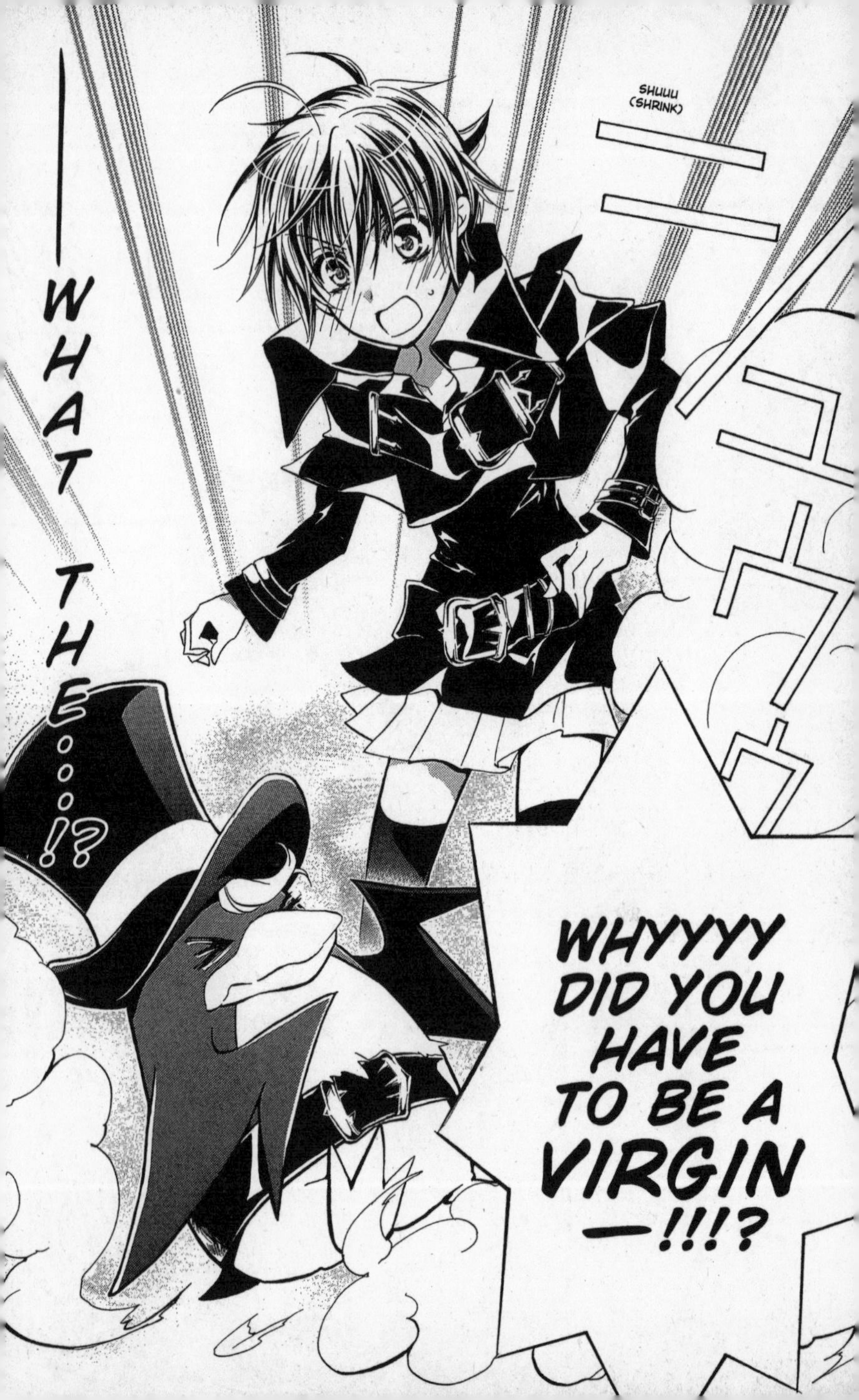
SHUUU (SHRINK)
—WHAT THE...!?
WHYYYY DID YOU HAVE TO BE A VIRGIN—!!!?

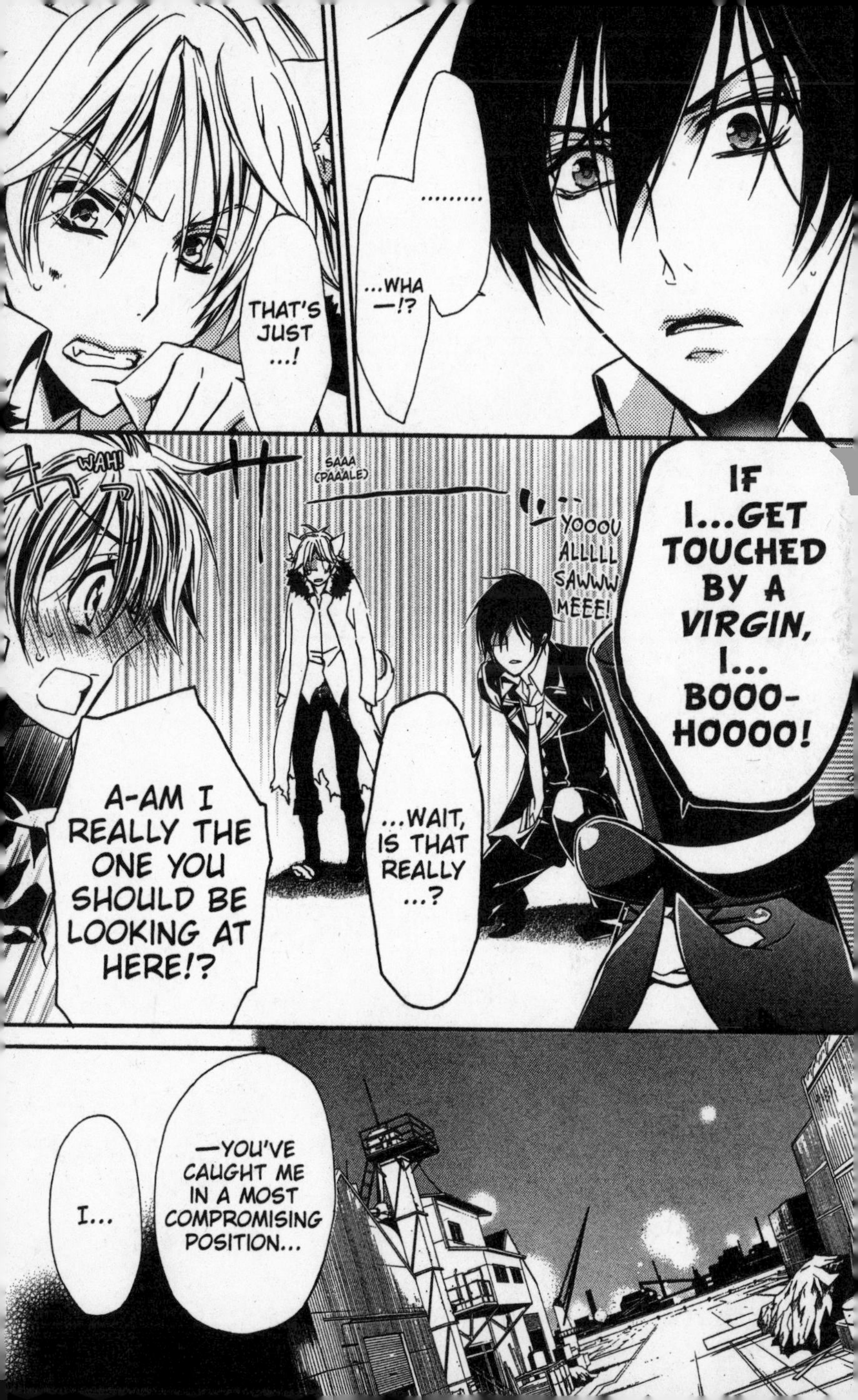
....
...WHA—!?
THAT'S JUST ...!
IF I...GET TOUCHED BY A VIRGIN, I... BOOO-HOOOO!
YOOOU ALLLLL SAWWW MEEE!
SAAA (PAAALE)
...WAIT, IS THAT REALLY ...?
WAH!
A-AM I REALLY THE ONE YOU SHOULD BE LOOKING AT HERE!?
—YOU'VE CAUGHT ME IN A MOST COMPROMISING POSITION...
I...

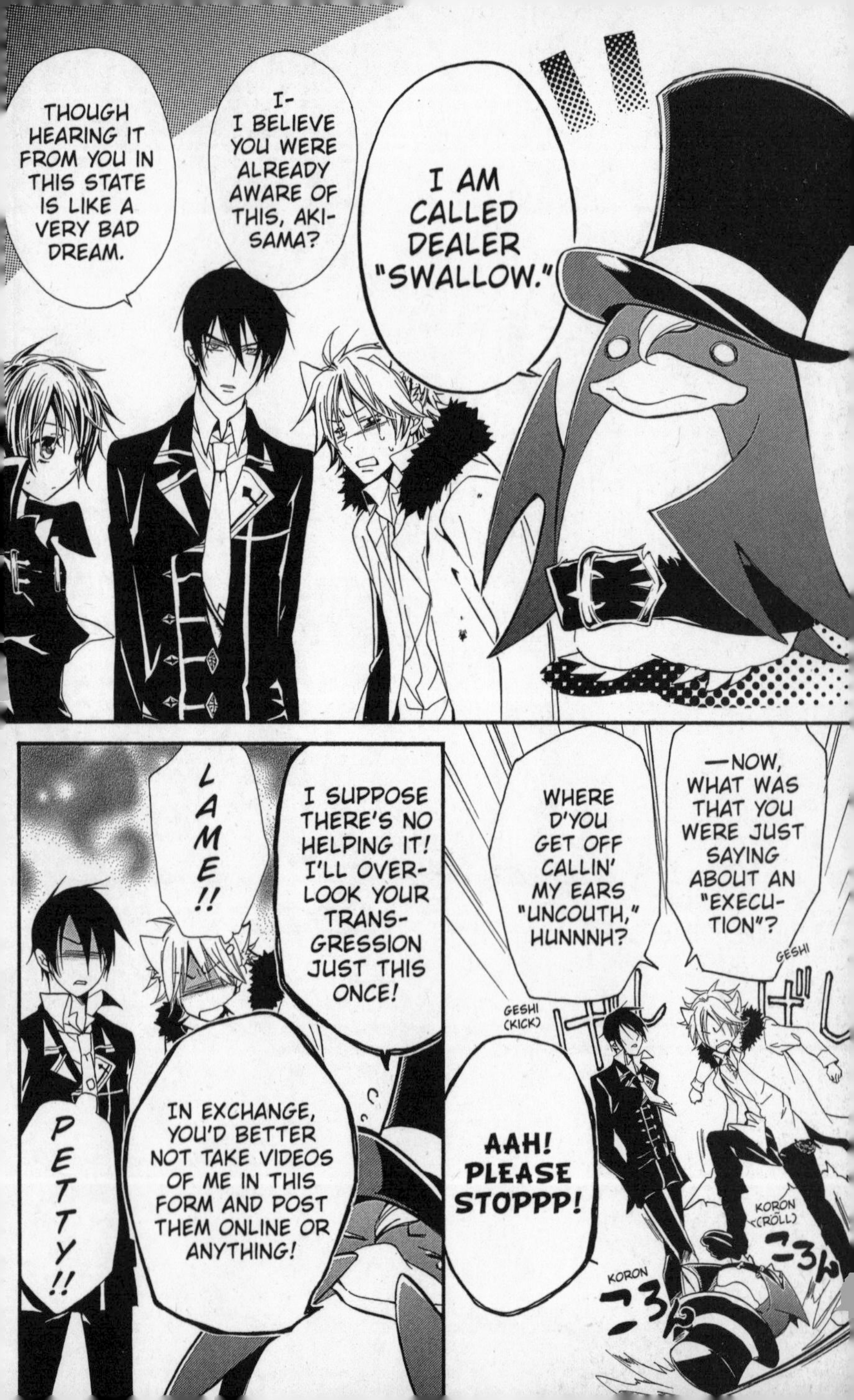
I AM CALLED DEALER "SWALLOW."
I- I BELIEVE YOU WERE ALREADY AWARE OF THIS, AKI-SAMA?
THOUGH HEARING IT FROM YOU IN THIS STATE IS LIKE A VERY BAD DREAM.
—NOW, WHAT WAS THAT YOU WERE JUST SAYING ABOUT AN "EXECUTION"?
WHERE D'YOU GET OFF CALLIN' MY EARS "UNCOUTH," HUNNNH?
GESHI
GESHI (KICK)
AAH! PLEASE STOPPP!
KORON (ROLL)
KORON
I SUPPOSE THERE'S NO HELPING IT! I'LL OVERLOOK YOUR TRANSGRESSION JUST THIS ONCE!
LAME!!
IN EXCHANGE, YOU'D BETTER NOT TAKE VIDEOS OF ME IN THIS FORM AND POST THEM ONLINE OR ANYTHING!
PETTY!!

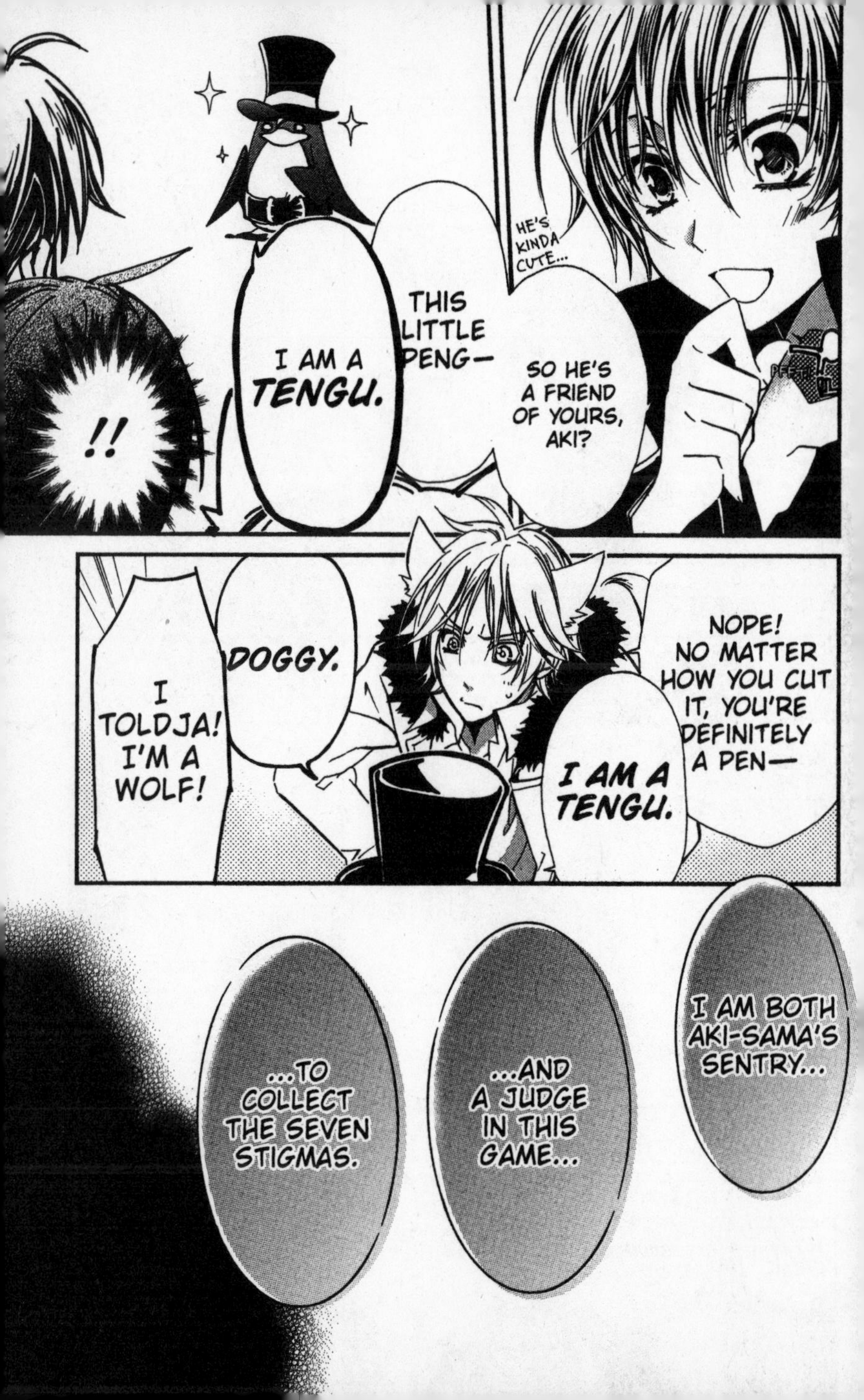
SO HE'S A FRIEND OF YOURS, AKI?
HE'S KINDA CUTE...
THIS LITTLE PENG—
I AM A **TENGU.**
!!
NOPE! NO MATTER HOW YOU CUT IT, YOU'RE DEFINITELY A PEN—
I AM A TENGU.
DOGGY.
I TOLDJA! I'M A WOLF!
I AM BOTH AKI-SAMA'S SENTRY...
...AND A JUDGE IN THIS GAME...
...TO COLLECT THE SEVEN STIGMAS.

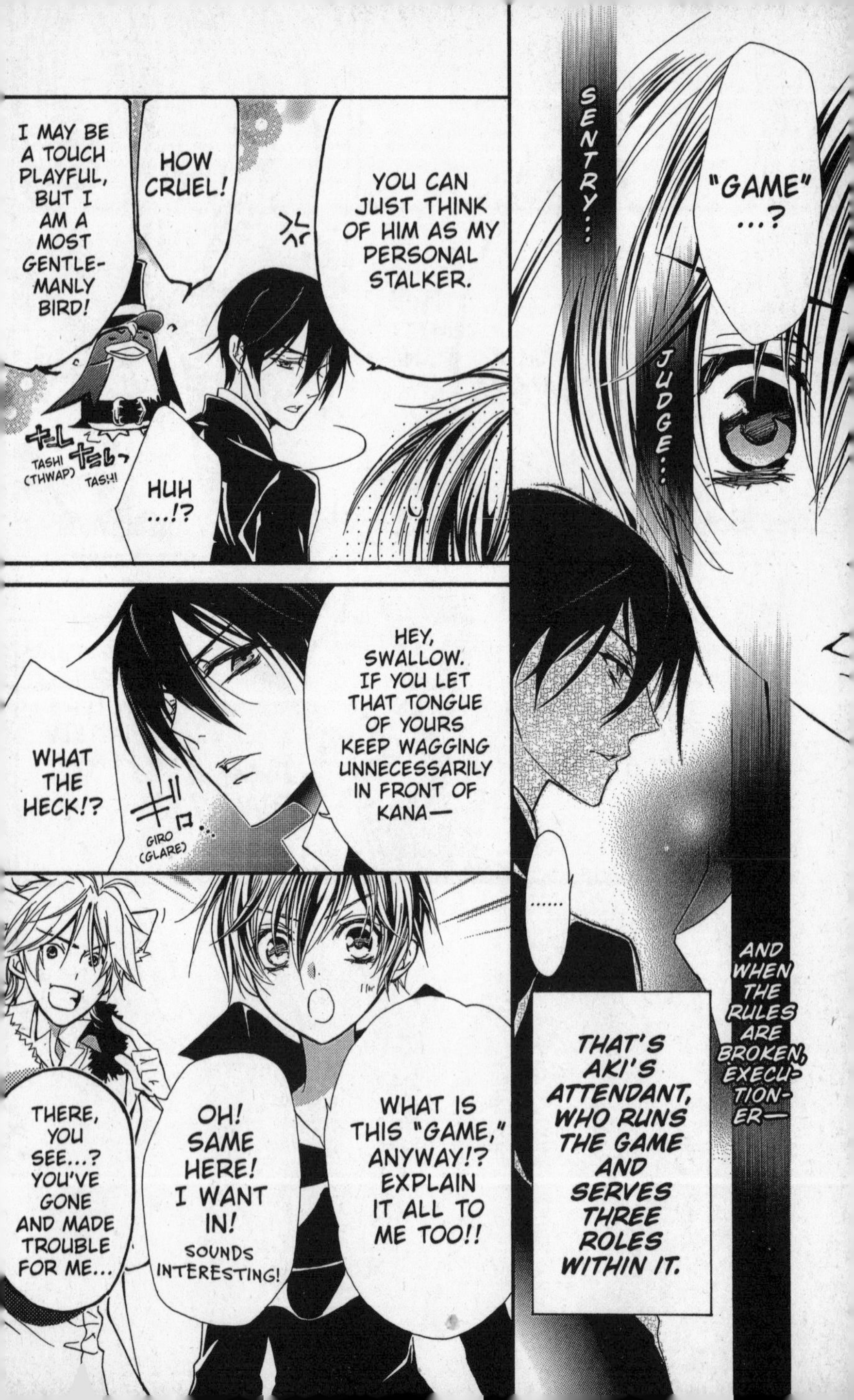
"GAME" ...?
SENTRY...
JUDGE...
......
AND WHEN THE RULES ARE BROKEN, EXECUTIONER—
THAT'S AKI'S ATTENDANT, WHO RUNS THE GAME AND SERVES THREE ROLES WITHIN IT.
YOU CAN JUST THINK OF HIM AS MY PERSONAL STALKER.
HOW CRUEL!
I MAY BE A TOUCH PLAYFUL, BUT I AM A MOST GENTLEMANLY BIRD!
TASHI (THWAP) TASHI
HUH ...!?
HEY, SWALLOW. IF YOU LET THAT TONGUE OF YOURS KEEP WAGGING UNNECESSARILY IN FRONT OF KANA—
GIRO (GLARE)
WHAT THE HECK!?
WHAT IS THIS "GAME," ANYWAY!? EXPLAIN IT ALL TO ME TOO!!
OH! SAME HERE! I WANT IN! SOUNDS INTERESTING!
THERE, YOU SEE...? YOU'VE GONE AND MADE TROUBLE FOR ME...

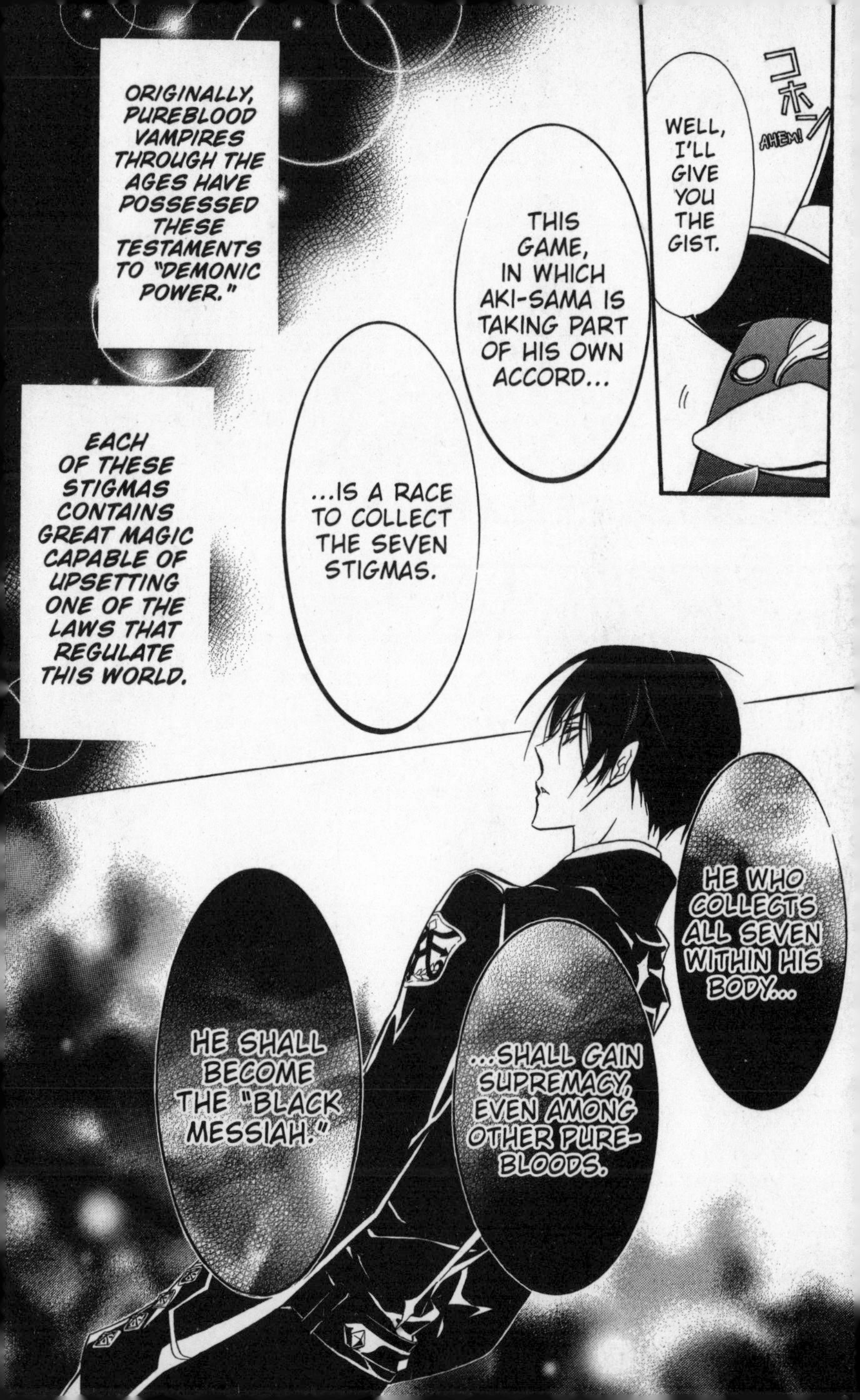
WELL, I'LL GIVE YOU THE GIST.
コホン
AHEM!
THIS GAME, IN WHICH AKI-SAMA IS TAKING PART OF HIS OWN ACCORD...
...IS A RACE TO COLLECT THE SEVEN STIGMAS.
ORIGINALLY, PUREBLOOD VAMPIRES THROUGH THE AGES HAVE POSSESSED THESE TESTAMENTS TO "DEMONIC POWER."
EACH OF THESE STIGMAS CONTAINS GREAT MAGIC CAPABLE OF UPSETTING ONE OF THE LAWS THAT REGULATE THIS WORLD.
HE WHO COLLECTS ALL SEVEN WITHIN HIS BODY...
...SHALL GAIN SUPREMACY, EVEN AMONG OTHER PURE-BLOODS.
HE SHALL BECOME THE "BLACK MESSIAH."

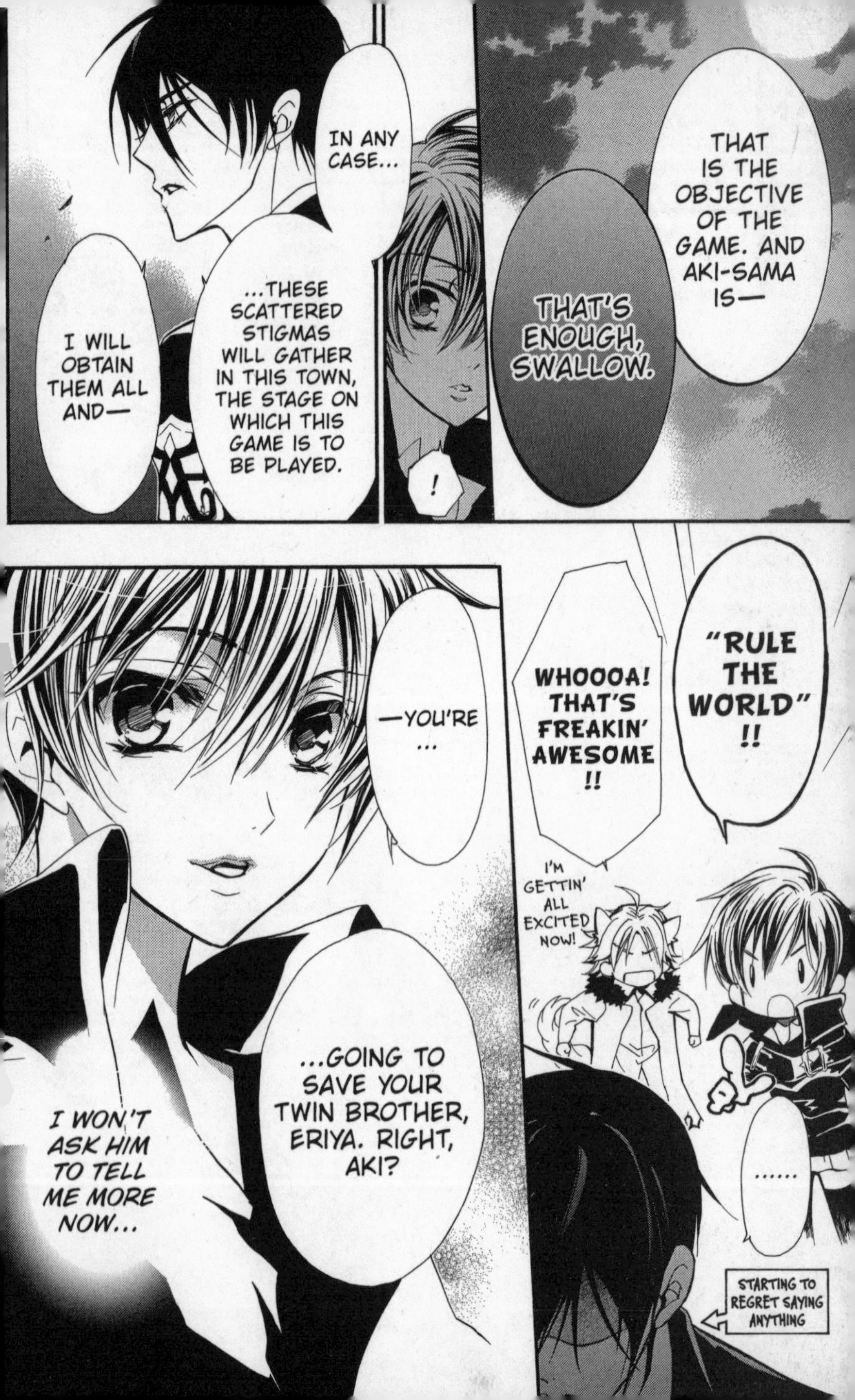
THAT IS THE OBJECTIVE OF THE GAME. AND AKI-SAMA IS—
THAT'S ENOUGH, SWALLOW.
!
IN ANY CASE...
...THESE SCATTERED STIGMAS WILL GATHER IN THIS TOWN, THE STAGE ON WHICH THIS GAME IS TO BE PLAYED.
I WILL OBTAIN THEM ALL AND—
"RULE THE WORLD"!!
WHOOOA! THAT'S FREAKIN' AWESOME!!
I'M GETTIN' ALL EXCITED NOW!
......
STARTING TO REGRET SAYING ANYTHING
—YOU'RE...
...GOING TO SAVE YOUR TWIN BROTHER, ERIYA. RIGHT, AKI?
I WON'T ASK HIM TO TELL ME MORE NOW...

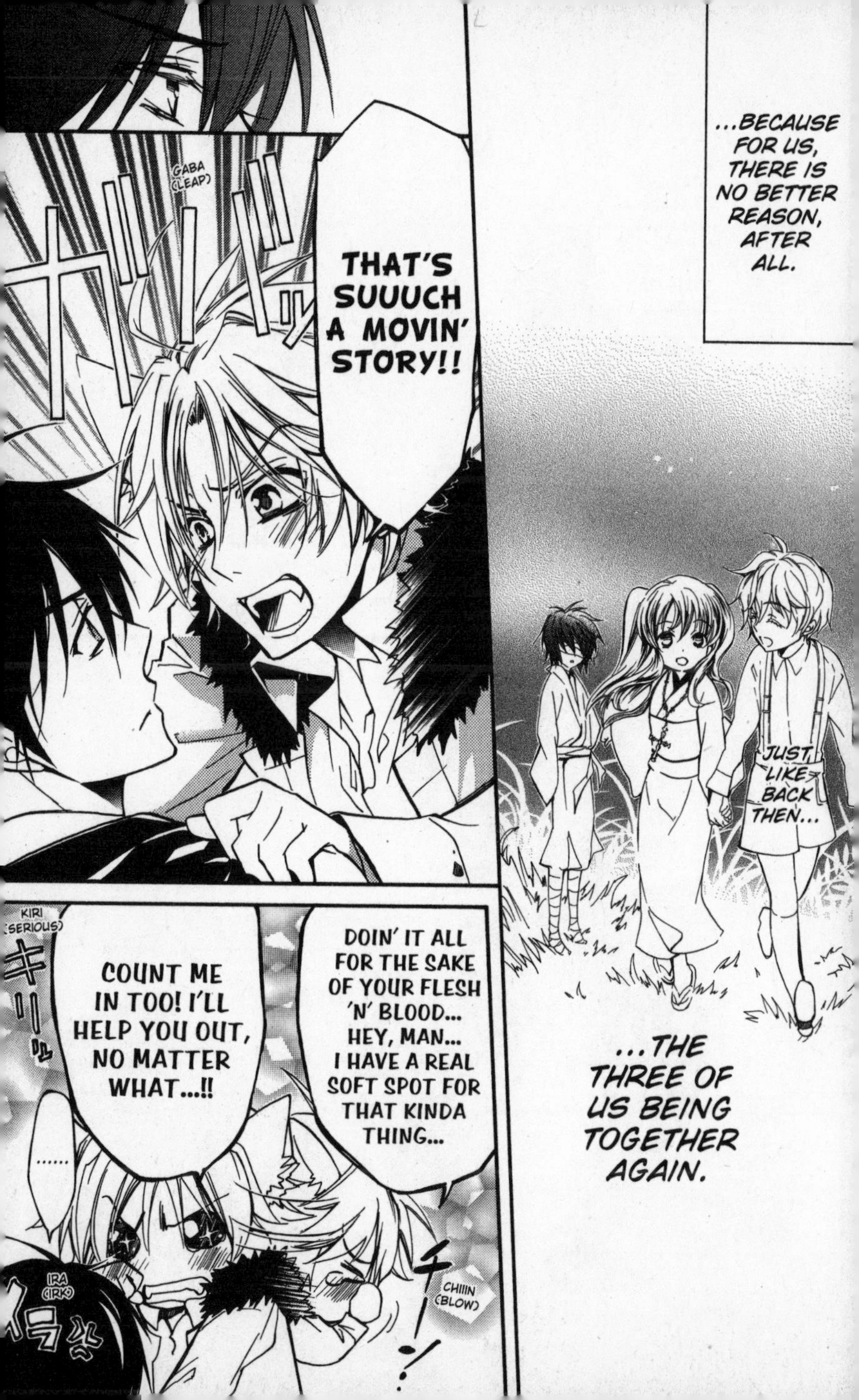
...BECAUSE FOR US, THERE IS NO BETTER REASON, AFTER ALL.
JUST LIKE BACK THEN...
...THE THREE OF US BEING TOGETHER AGAIN.
GABA (LEAP)
THAT'S SUUUCH A MOVIN' STORY!!
DOIN' IT ALL FOR THE SAKE OF YOUR FLESH 'N' BLOOD... HEY, MAN... I HAVE A REAL SOFT SPOT FOR THAT KINDA THING...
KIRI (SERIOUS)
COUNT ME IN TOO! I'LL HELP YOU OUT, NO MATTER WHAT...!!
......
CHIIIN (BLOW)
IRA (IRK)

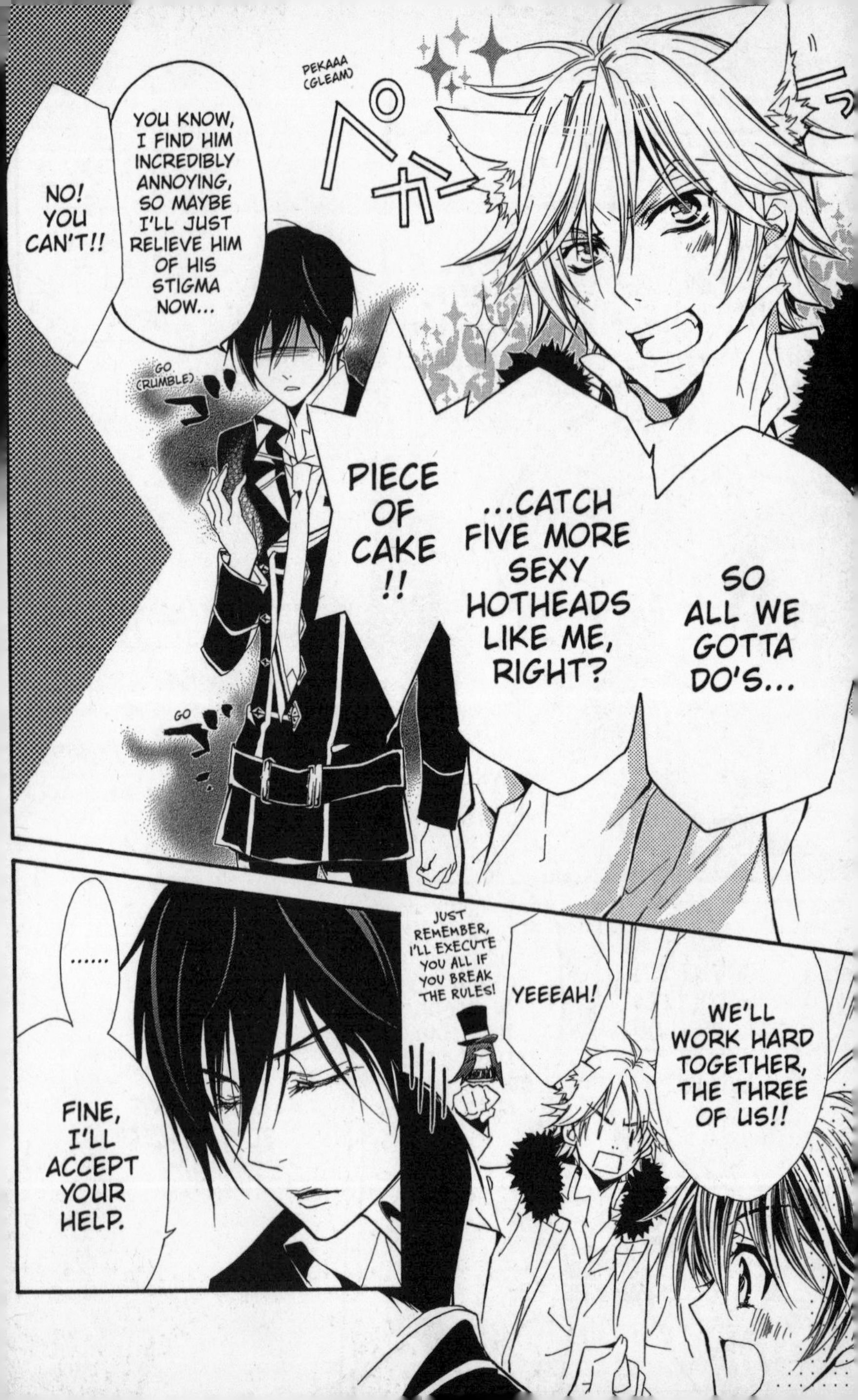
PEKAAA (GLEAM)
SO ALL WE GOTTA DO'S...
...CATCH FIVE MORE SEXY HOTHEADS LIKE ME, RIGHT?
PIECE OF CAKE!!
YOU KNOW, I FIND HIM INCREDIBLY ANNOYING, SO MAYBE I'LL JUST RELIEVE HIM OF HIS STIGMA NOW...
NO! YOU CAN'T!!
GO (RUMBLE)
GO
WE'LL WORK HARD TOGETHER, THE THREE OF US!!
YEEEAH!
JUST REMEMBER, I'LL EXECUTE YOU ALL IF YOU BREAK THE RULES!
......
FINE, I'LL ACCEPT YOUR HELP.

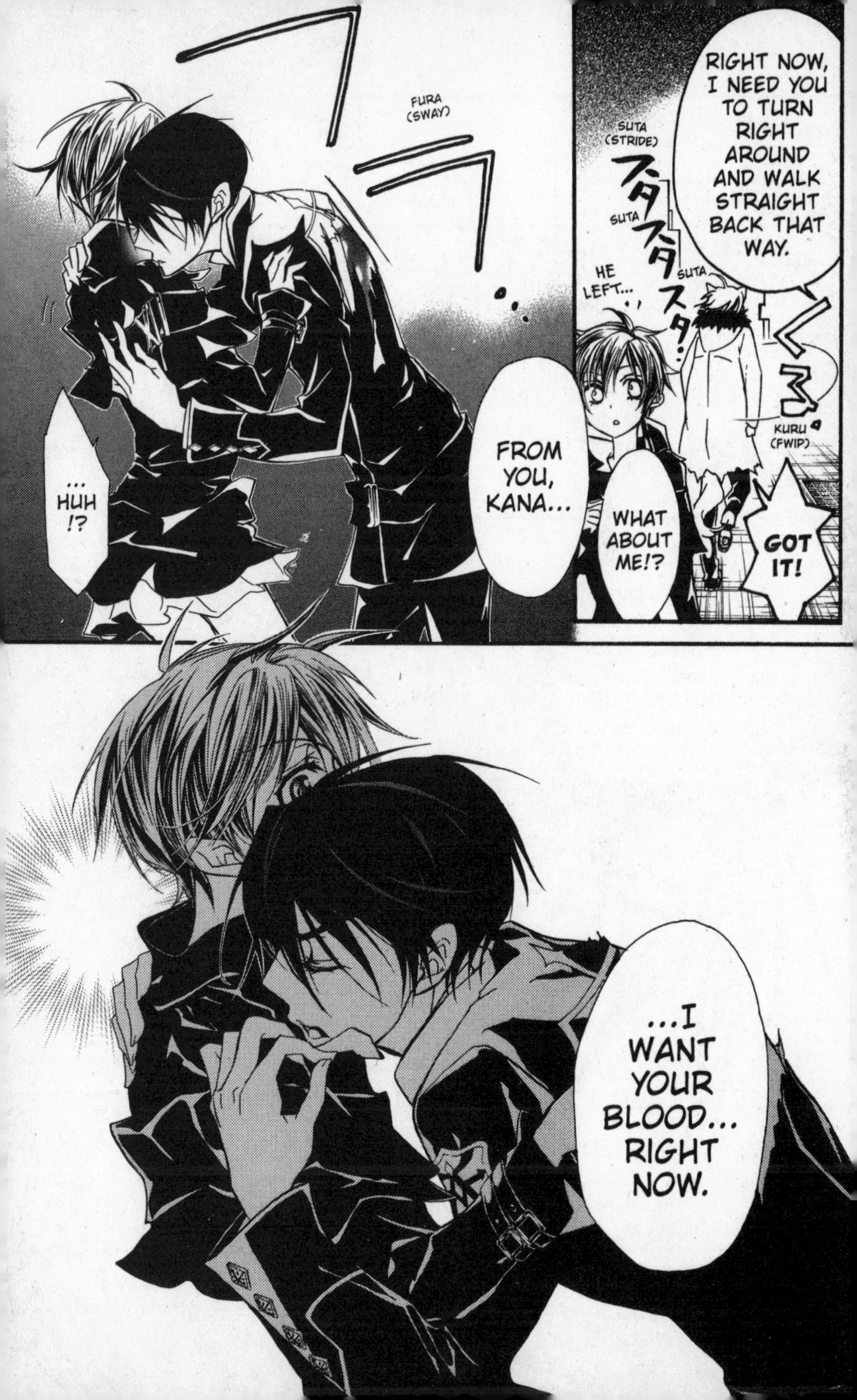
RIGHT NOW, I NEED YOU TO TURN RIGHT AROUND AND WALK STRAIGHT BACK THAT WAY.
KURU (FWIP)
GOT IT!
SUTA (STRIDE)
SUTA
SUTA
HE LEFT...
WHAT ABOUT ME!?
FURA (SWAY)
FROM YOU, KANA...
...HUH!?
...I WANT YOUR BLOOD... RIGHT NOW.

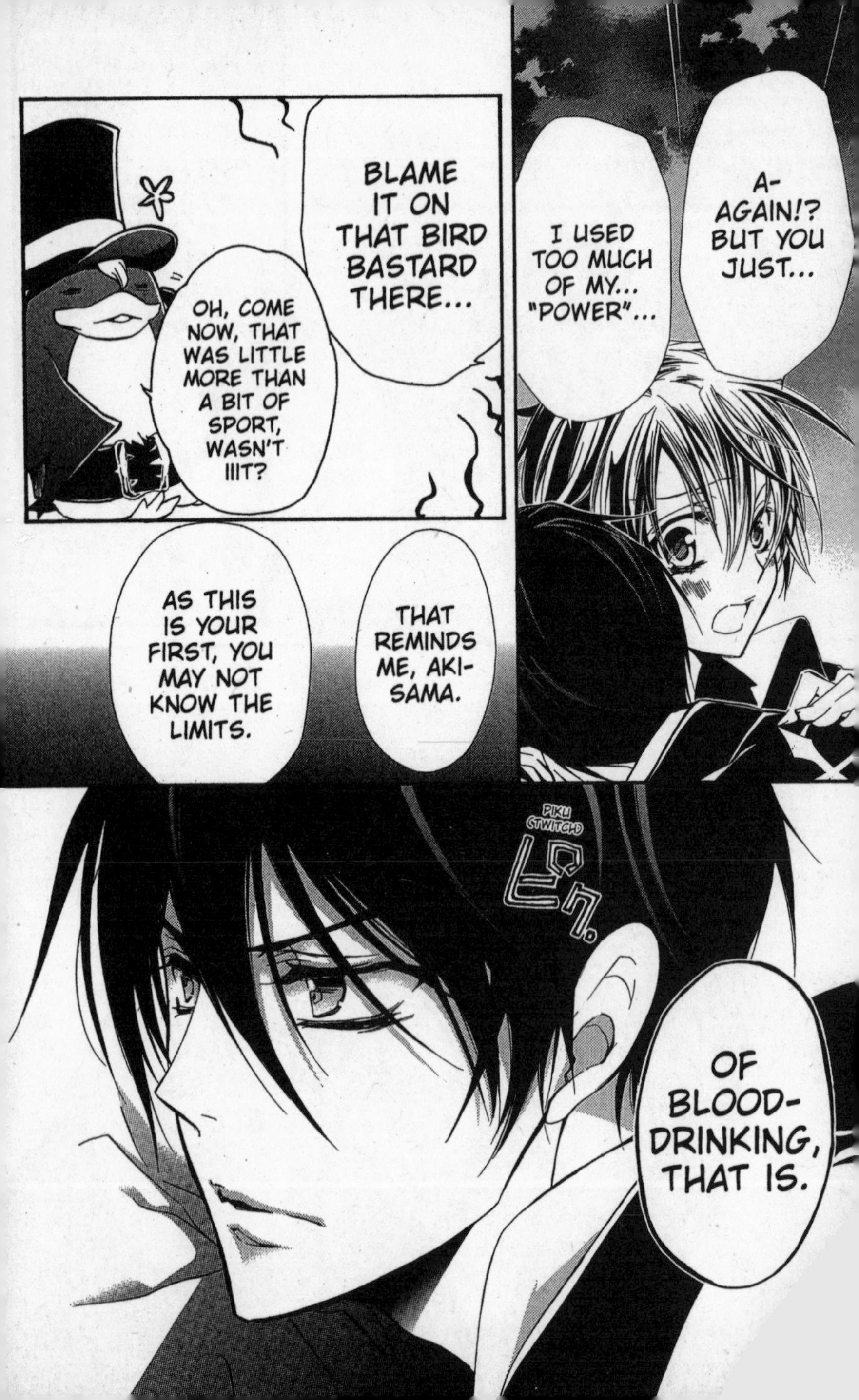
A-AGAIN!? BUT YOU JUST...
I USED TOO MUCH OF MY... "POWER"...
BLAME IT ON THAT BIRD BASTARD THERE...
OH, COME NOW, THAT WAS LITTLE MORE THAN A BIT OF SPORT, WASN'T IIIT?
THAT REMINDS ME, AKI-SAMA.
AS THIS IS YOUR FIRST, YOU MAY NOT KNOW THE LIMITS.
PIKU (TWITCH)
OF BLOOD-DRINKING, THAT IS.

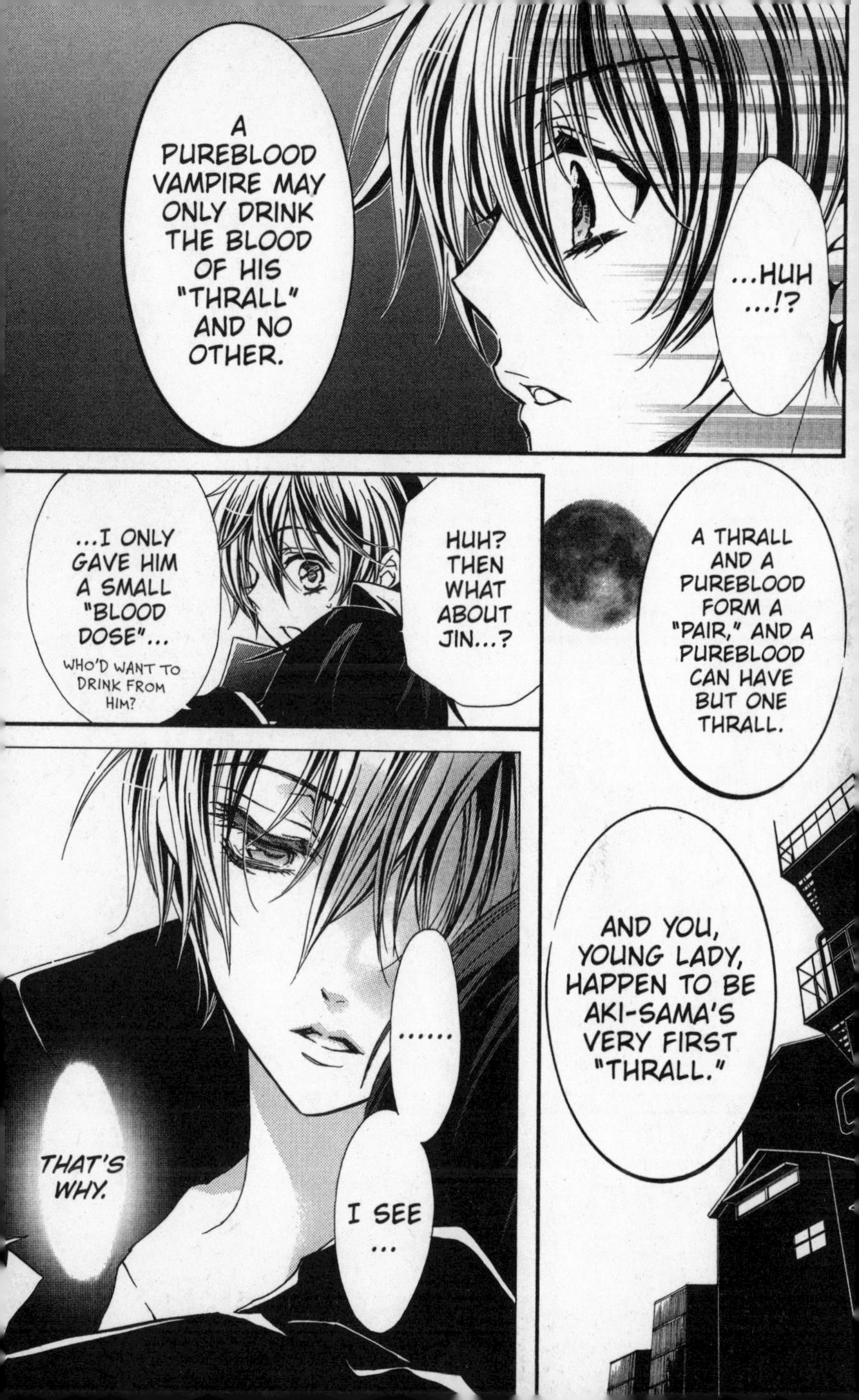
A PUREBLOOD VAMPIRE MAY ONLY DRINK THE BLOOD OF HIS "THRALL" AND NO OTHER.
...HUH ...!?
A THRALL AND A PUREBLOOD FORM A "PAIR," AND A PUREBLOOD CAN HAVE BUT ONE THRALL.
AND YOU, YOUNG LADY, HAPPEN TO BE AKI-SAMA'S VERY FIRST "THRALL."
HUH? THEN WHAT ABOUT JIN...?
...I ONLY GAVE HIM A SMALL "BLOOD DOSE"...
WHO'D WANT TO DRINK FROM HIM?
......
I SEE ...
THAT'S WHY.

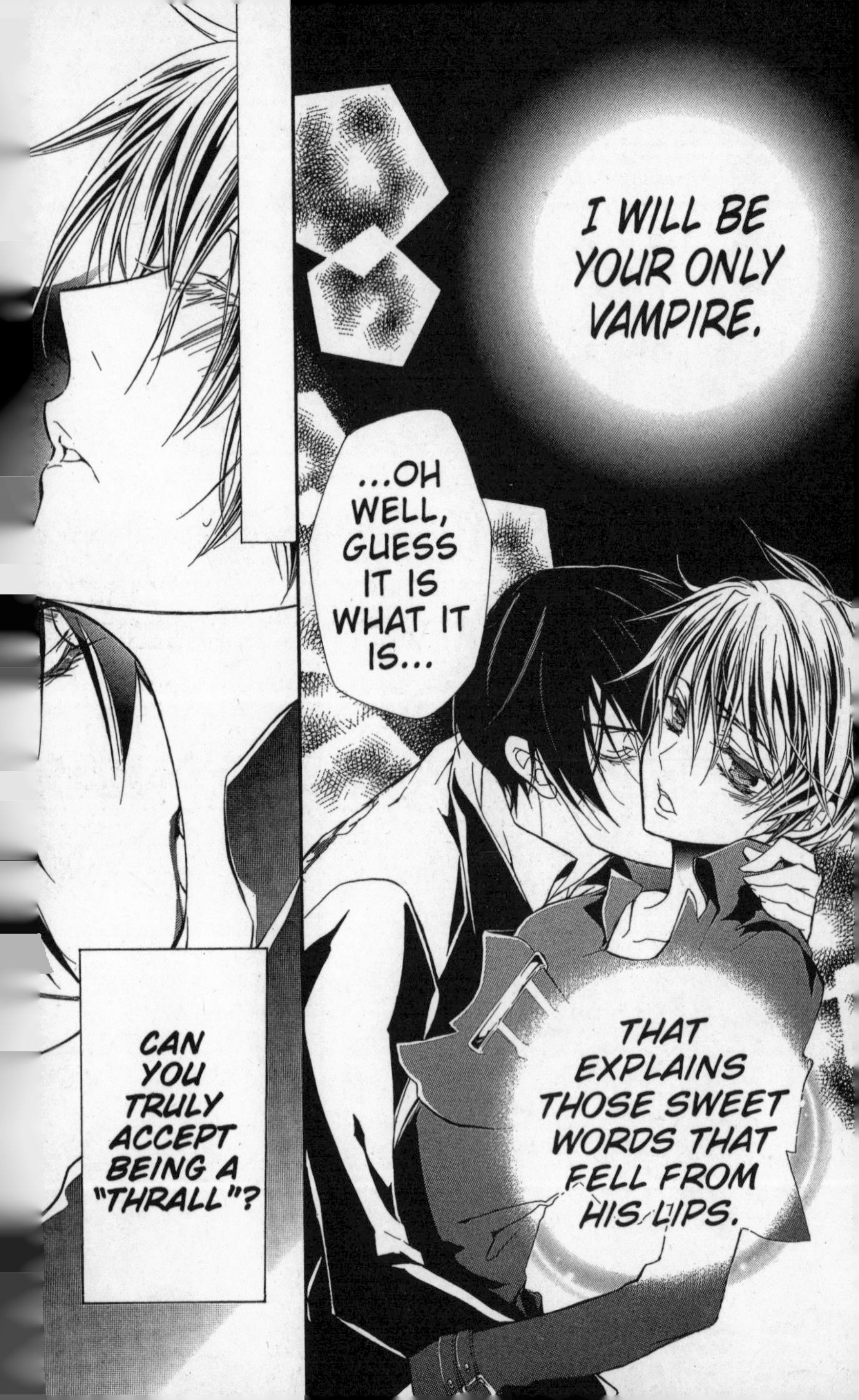
I WILL BE YOUR ONLY VAMPIRE.
...OH WELL, GUESS IT IS WHAT IT IS...
THAT EXPLAINS THOSE SWEET WORDS THAT FELL FROM HIS LIPS.
CAN YOU TRULY ACCEPT BEING A "THRALL"?

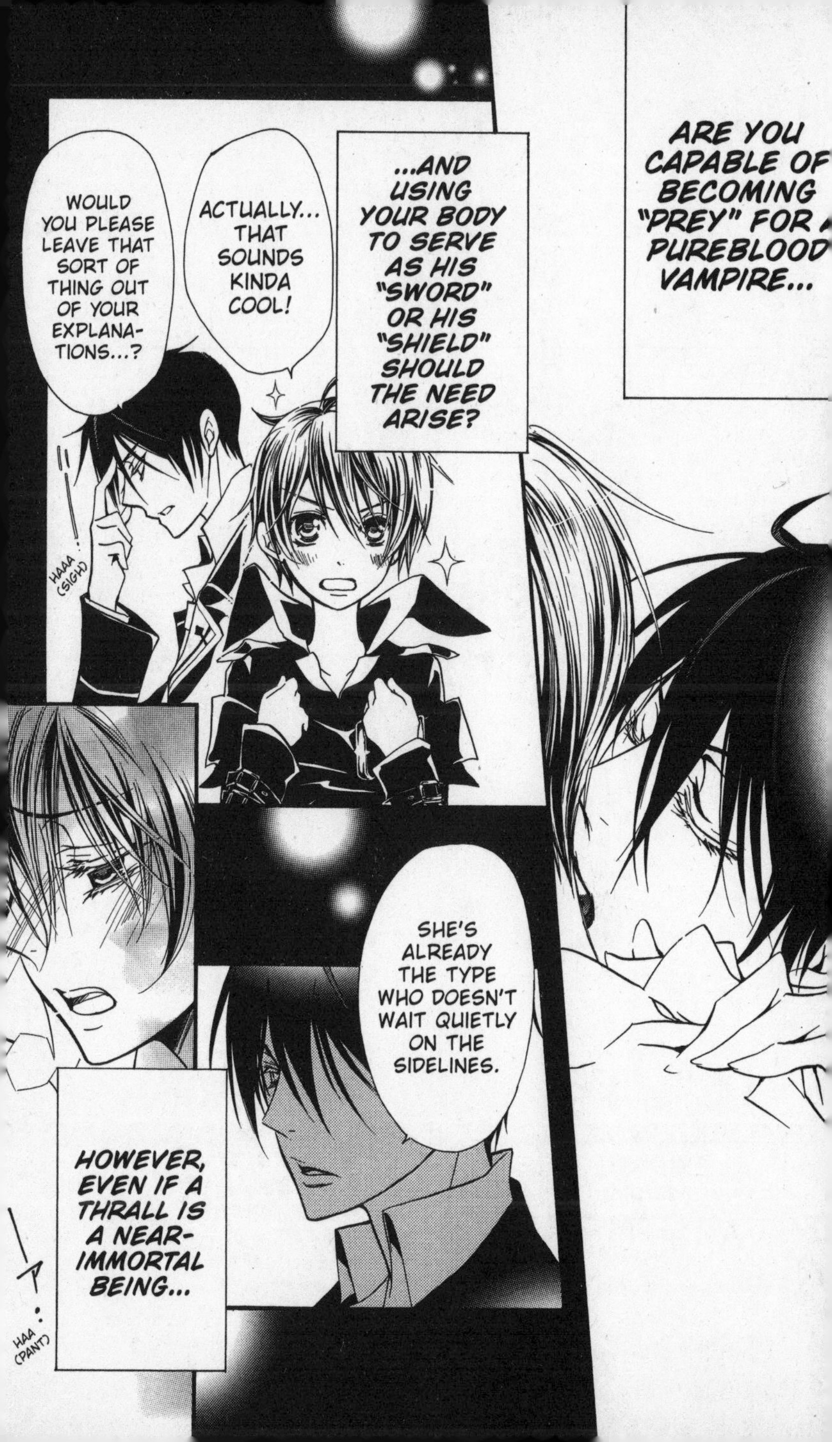
ARE YOU CAPABLE OF BECOMING "PREY" FOR PUREBLOOD VAMPIRE...
...AND USING YOUR BODY TO SERVE AS HIS "SWORD" OR HIS "SHIELD" SHOULD THE NEED ARISE?
ACTUALLY... THAT SOUNDS KINDA COOL!
WOULD YOU PLEASE LEAVE THAT SORT OF THING OUT OF YOUR EXPLANA-TIONS...?
HAAA (SIGH)
SHE'S ALREADY THE TYPE WHO DOESN'T WAIT QUIETLY ON THE SIDELINES.
HOWEVER, EVEN IF A THRALL IS A NEAR-IMMORTAL BEING...
HAA (PANT)

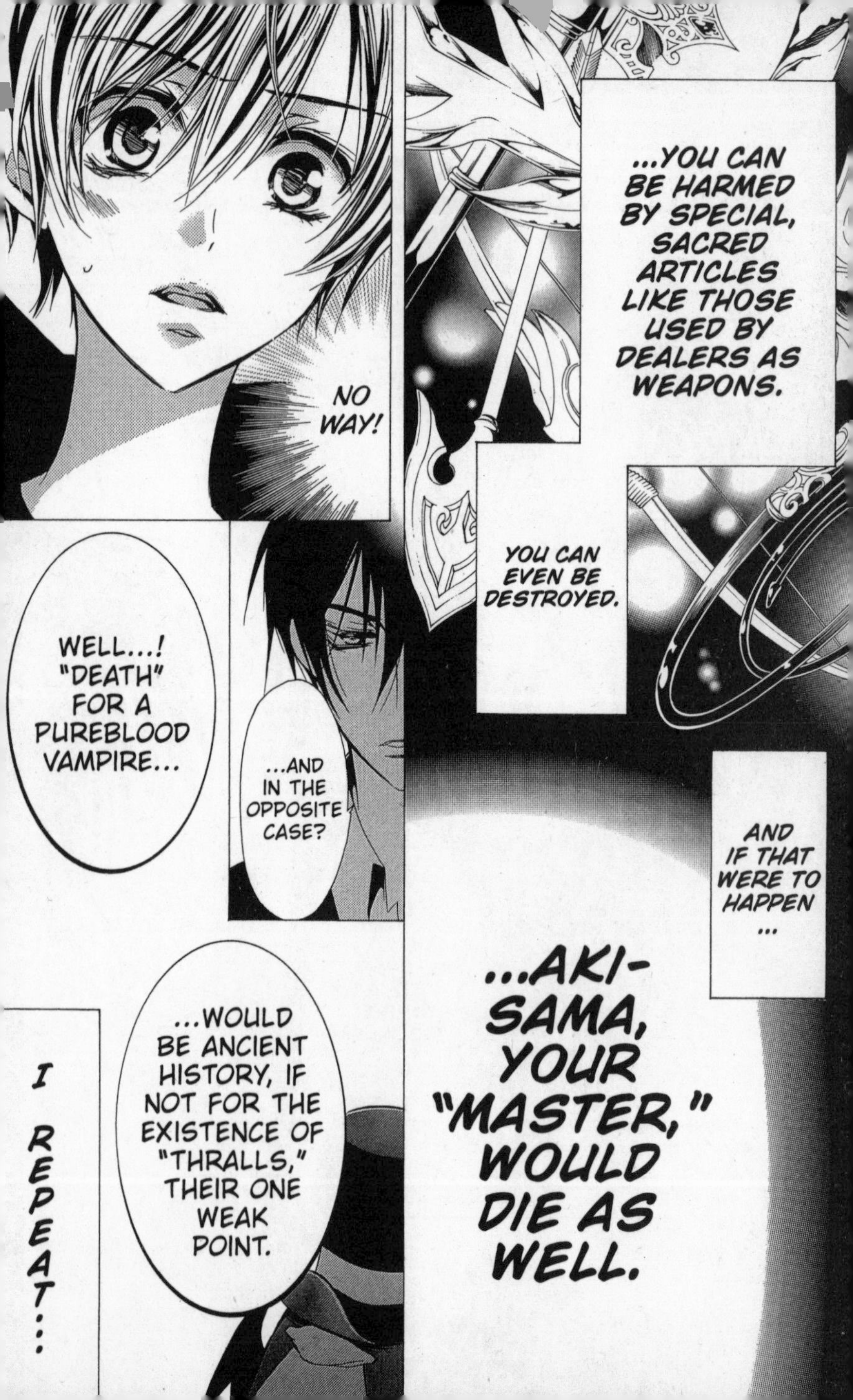
...YOU CAN BE HARMED BY SPECIAL, SACRED ARTICLES LIKE THOSE USED BY DEALERS AS WEAPONS.
NO WAY!
YOU CAN EVEN BE DESTROYED.
AND IF THAT WERE TO HAPPEN...
...AKI-SAMA, YOUR "MASTER," WOULD DIE AS WELL.
...AND IN THE OPPOSITE CASE?
WELL...! "DEATH" FOR A PUREBLOOD VAMPIRE...
...WOULD BE ANCIENT HISTORY, IF NOT FOR THE EXISTENCE OF "THRALLS," THEIR ONE WEAK POINT.
I REPEAT...

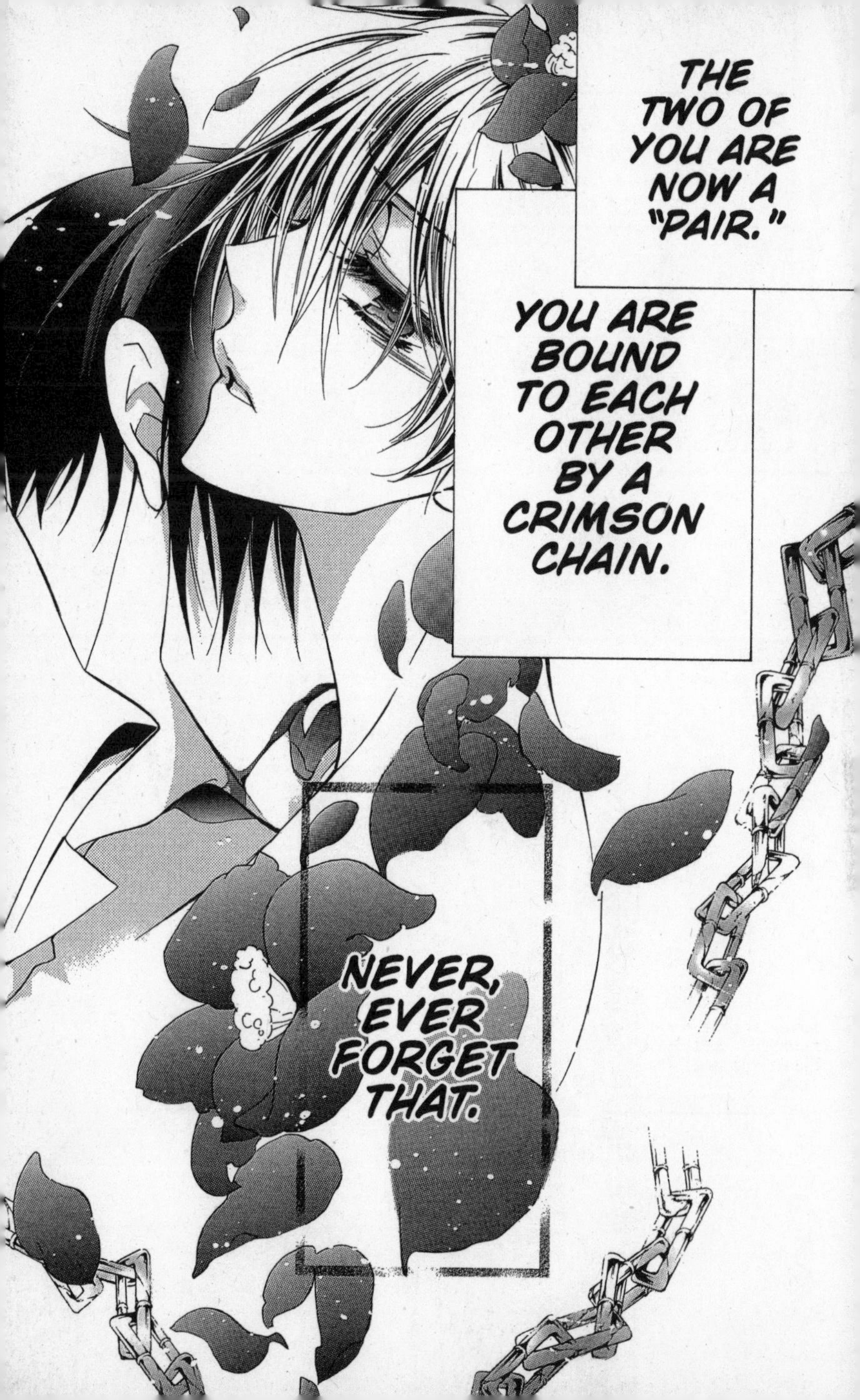
THE TWO OF YOU ARE NOW A "PAIR."
YOU ARE BOUND TO EACH OTHER BY A CRIMSON CHAIN.
NEVER, EVER FORGET THAT.

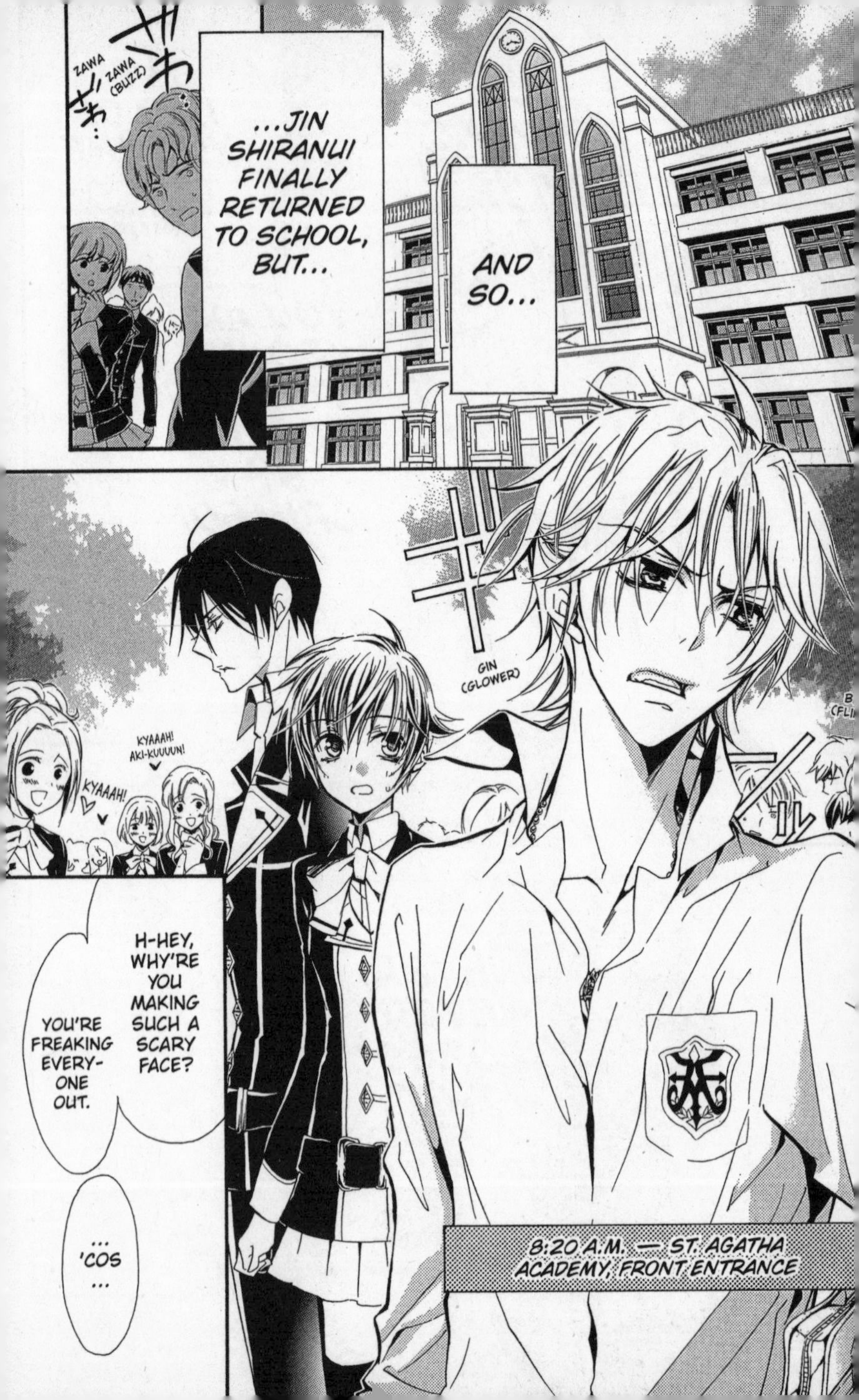
AND SO...
...JIN SHIRANUI FINALLY RETURNED TO SCHOOL, BUT...
ZAWA ZAWA (BUZZ)
GIN (GLOWER)
KYAAAH! AKI-KUUUUN!
KYAAAH!
H-HEY, WHY'RE YOU MAKING SUCH A SCARY FACE?
YOU'RE FREAKING EVERY-ONE OUT.
8:20 A.M. — ST. AGATHA ACADEMY, FRONT ENTRANCE
... 'COS ...

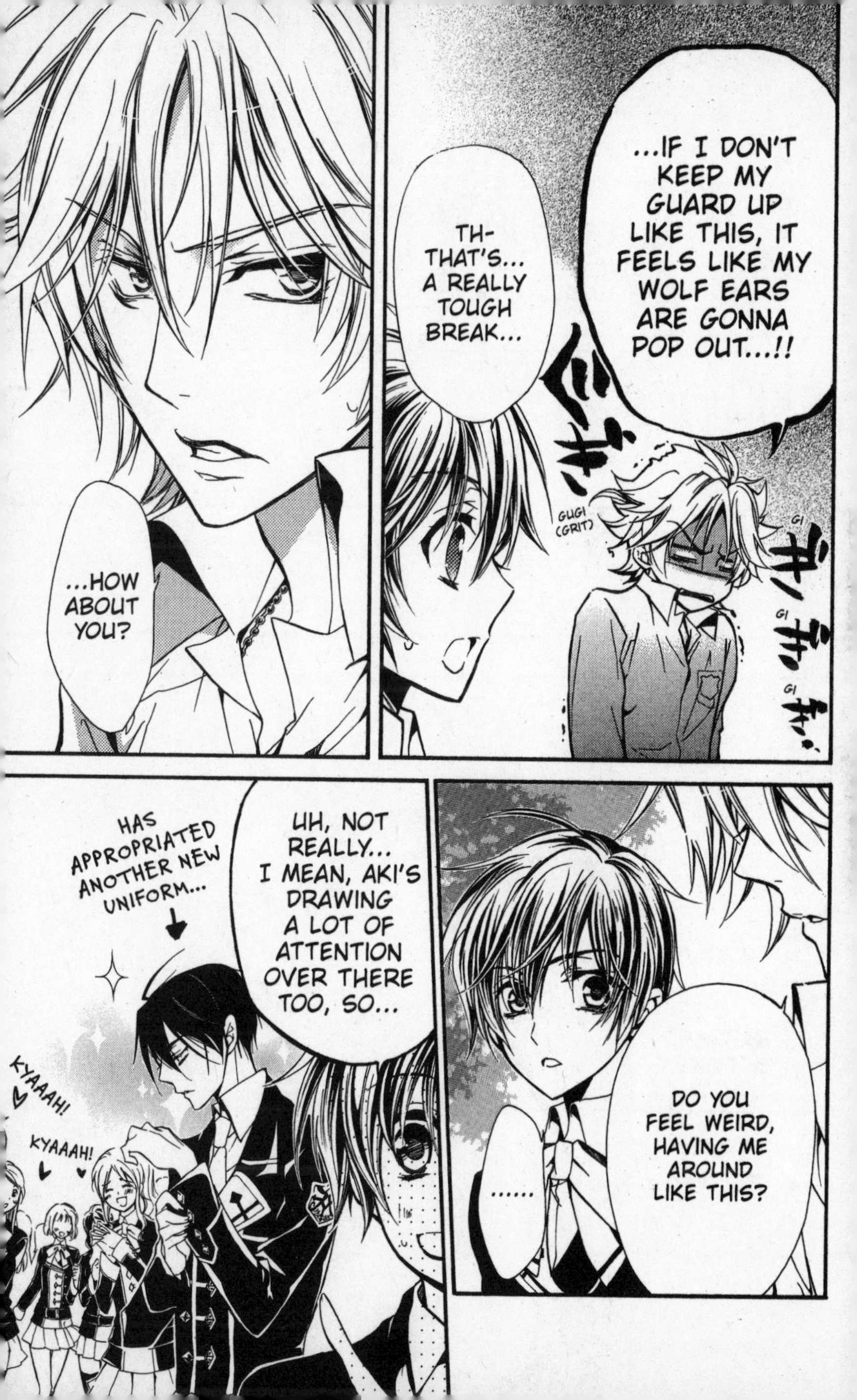
...IF I DON'T KEEP MY GUARD UP LIKE THIS, IT FEELS LIKE MY WOLF EARS ARE GONNA POP OUT...!!
GUGI (GRIT)
GI
GI
GI
TH-THAT'S... A REALLY TOUGH BREAK...
...HOW ABOUT YOU?
DO YOU FEEL WEIRD, HAVING ME AROUND LIKE THIS?
......
UH, NOT REALLY... I MEAN, AKI'S DRAWING A LOT OF ATTENTION OVER THERE TOO, SO...
HAS APPROPRIATED ANOTHER NEW UNIFORM...
KYAAAH!
KYAAAH!

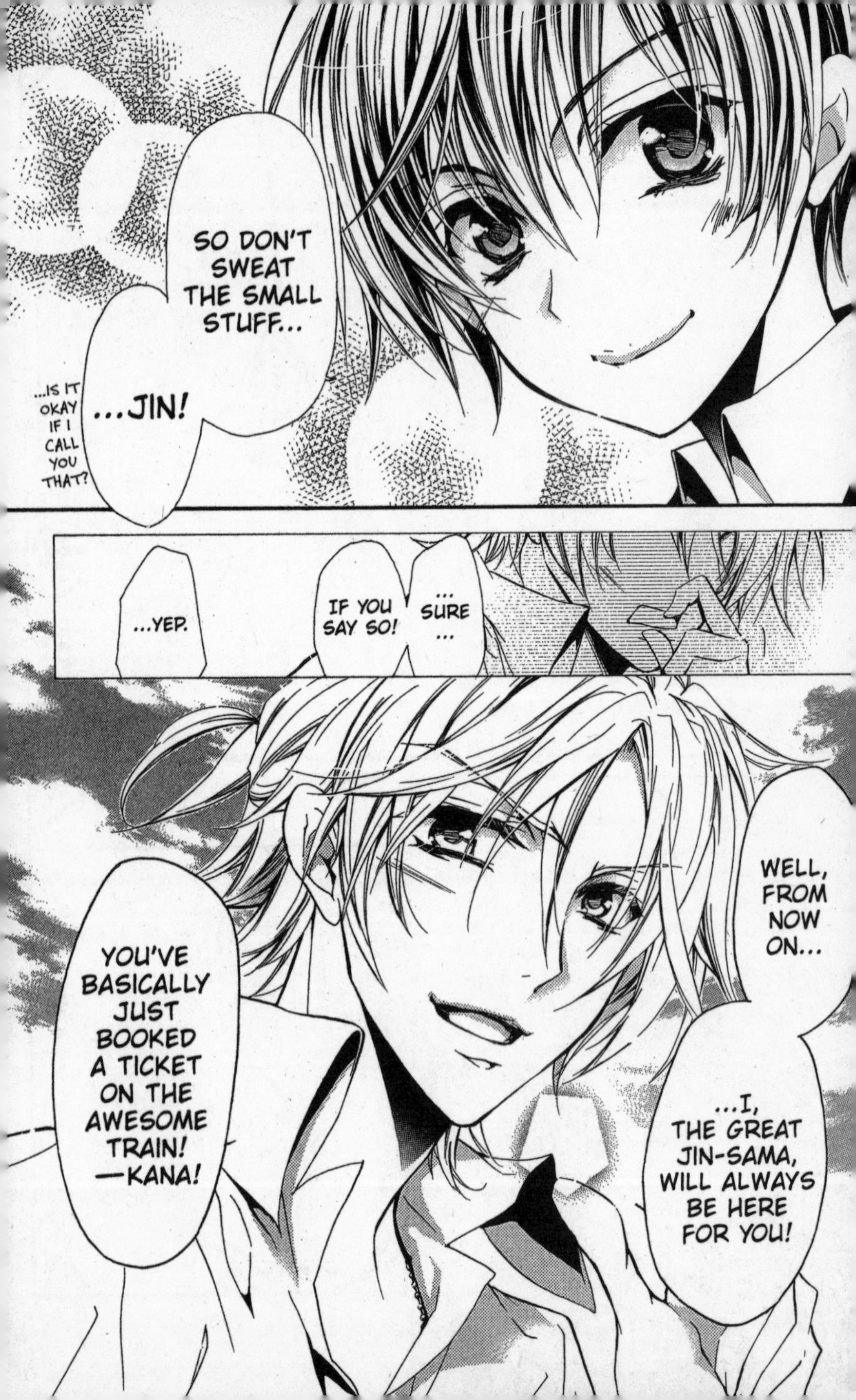
SO DON'T SWEAT THE SMALL STUFF...
...JIN!
...IS IT OKAY IF I CALL YOU THAT?
...SURE...
IF YOU SAY SO!
...YEP.
WELL, FROM NOW ON...
...I, THE GREAT JIN-SAMA, WILL ALWAYS BE HERE FOR YOU!
YOU'VE BASICALLY JUST BOOKED A TICKET ON THE AWESOME TRAIN! —KANA!

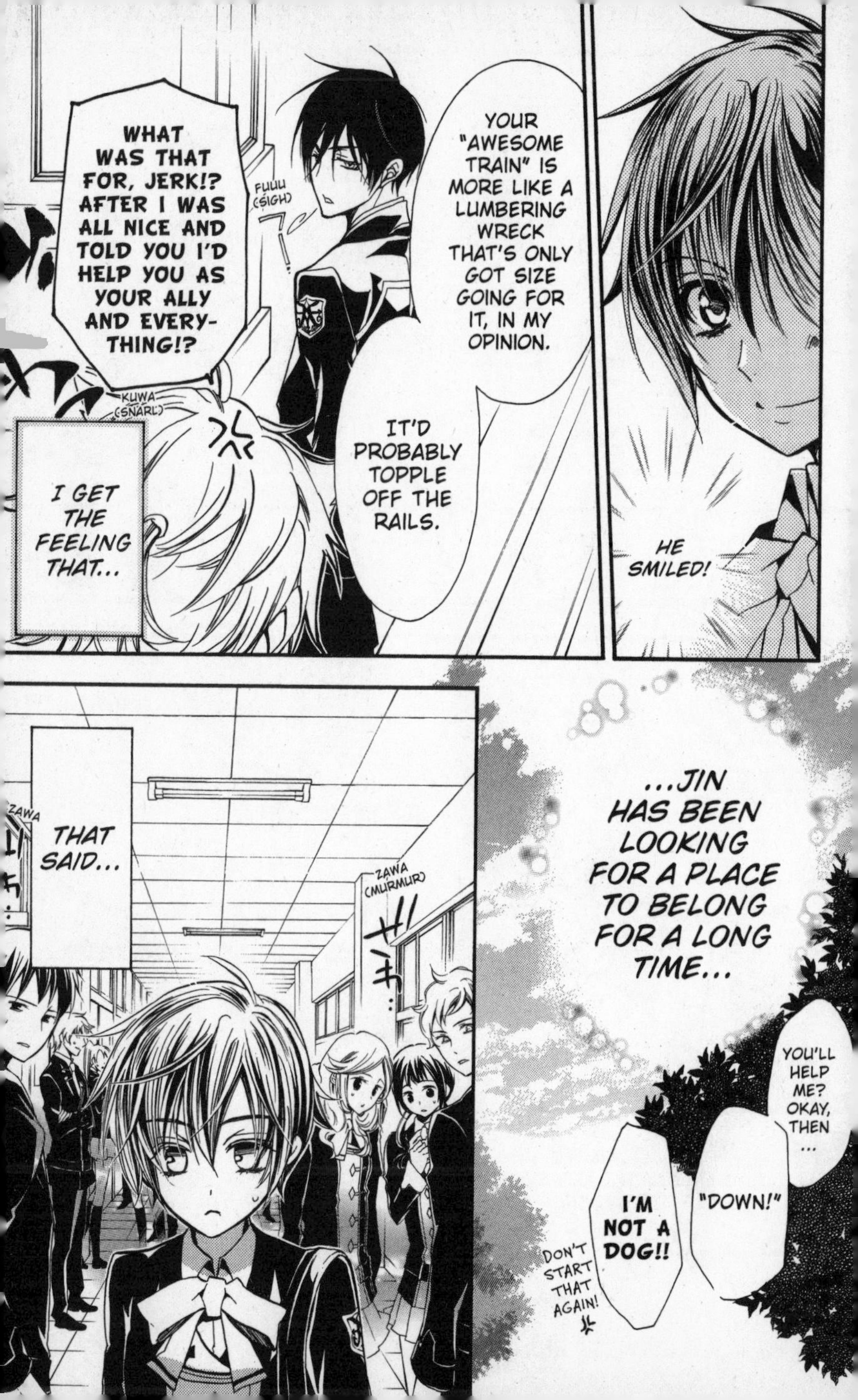
HE SMILED!
YOUR "AWESOME TRAIN" IS MORE LIKE A LUMBERING WRECK THAT'S ONLY GOT SIZE GOING FOR IT, IN MY OPINION.
IT'D PROBABLY TOPPLE OFF THE RAILS.
FUUU (SIGH)
WHAT WAS THAT FOR, JERK!? AFTER I WAS ALL NICE AND TOLD YOU I'D HELP YOU AS YOUR ALLY AND EVERY-THING!?
KUWA (SNARL)
I GET THE FEELING THAT...
...JIN HAS BEEN LOOKING FOR A PLACE TO BELONG FOR A LONG TIME...
YOU'LL HELP ME? OKAY, THEN ...
"DOWN!"
I'M NOT A DOG!!
DON'T START THAT AGAIN!
THAT SAID...
ZAWA (MURMUR)
ZAWA

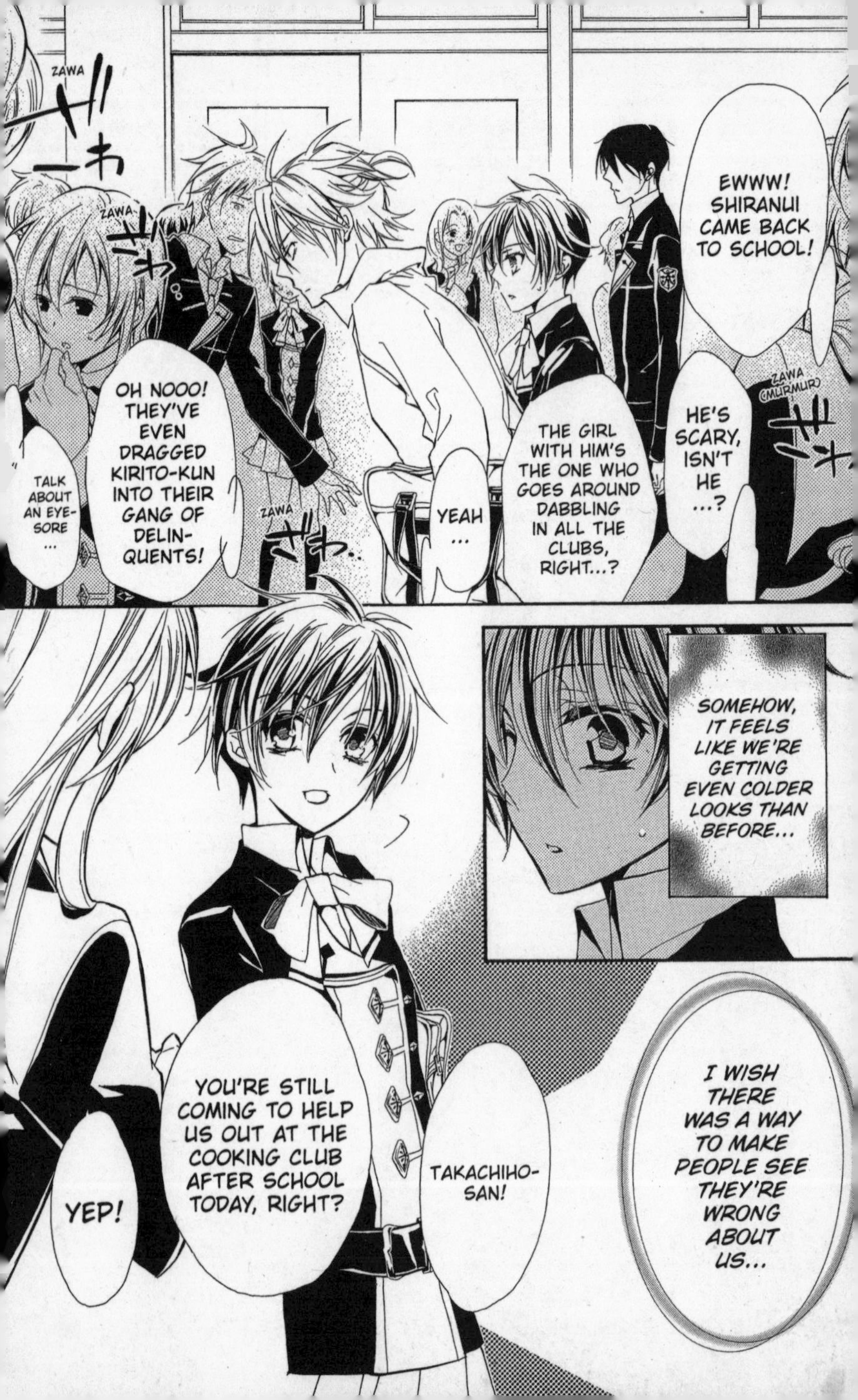

EWWW! SHIRANUI CAME BACK TO SCHOOL!
ZAWA (MURMUR)
HE'S SCARY, ISN'T HE ...?
THE GIRL WITH HIM'S THE ONE WHO GOES AROUND DABBLING IN ALL THE CLUBS, RIGHT...?
YEAH ...
ZAWA
OH NOOO! THEY'VE EVEN DRAGGED KIRITO-KUN INTO THEIR GANG OF DELIN-QUENTS!
ZAWA
TALK ABOUT AN EYE-SORE ...
ZAWA
SOMEHOW, IT FEELS LIKE WE'RE GETTING EVEN COLDER LOOKS THAN BEFORE...
I WISH THERE WAS A WAY TO MAKE PEOPLE SEE THEY'RE WRONG ABOUT US...
TAKACHIHO-SAN!
YOU'RE STILL COMING TO HELP US OUT AT THE COOKING CLUB AFTER SCHOOL TODAY, RIGHT?
YEP!

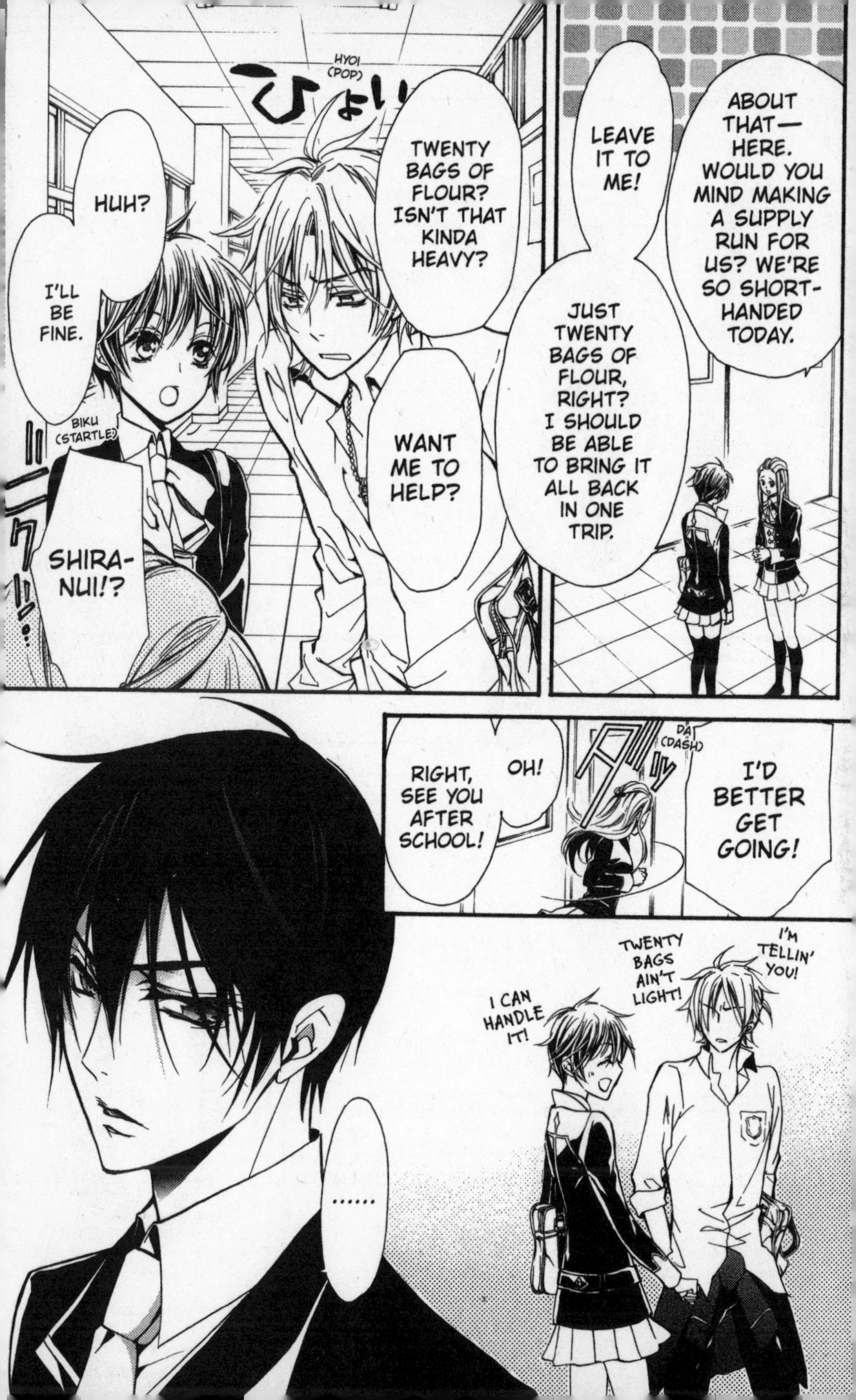
ABOUT THAT— HERE. WOULD YOU MIND MAKING A SUPPLY RUN FOR US? WE'RE SO SHORT-HANDED TODAY.
LEAVE IT TO ME!
JUST TWENTY BAGS OF FLOUR, RIGHT? I SHOULD BE ABLE TO BRING IT ALL BACK IN ONE TRIP.
HYOI (POP)
TWENTY BAGS OF FLOUR? ISN'T THAT KINDA HEAVY?
HUH?
WANT ME TO HELP?
BIKU (STARTLE)
SHIRA-NUI!?
I'LL BE FINE.
I'D BETTER GET GOING!
DA (DASH)
OH!
RIGHT, SEE YOU AFTER SCHOOL!
I'M TELLIN' YOU!
TWENTY BAGS AIN'T LIGHT!
I CAN HANDLE IT!
......

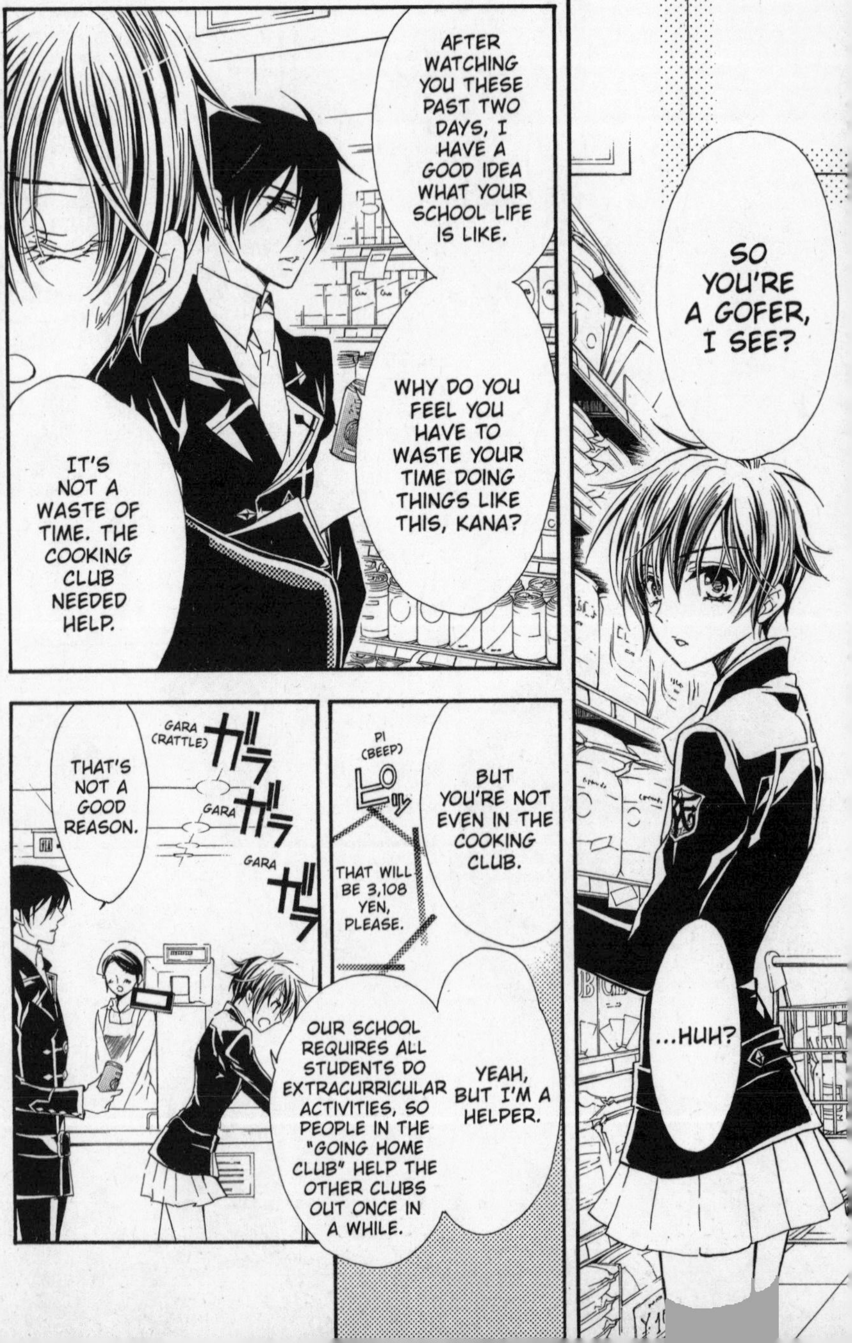
SO YOU'RE A GOFER, I SEE?
...HUH?
AFTER WATCHING YOU THESE PAST TWO DAYS, I HAVE A GOOD IDEA WHAT YOUR SCHOOL LIFE IS LIKE.
WHY DO YOU FEEL YOU HAVE TO WASTE YOUR TIME DOING THINGS LIKE THIS, KANA?
IT'S NOT A WASTE OF TIME. THE COOKING CLUB NEEDED HELP.
PI (BEEP)
ピッ
BUT YOU'RE NOT EVEN IN THE COOKING CLUB.
THAT WILL BE 3,108 YEN, PLEASE.
YEAH, BUT I'M A HELPER.
OUR SCHOOL REQUIRES ALL STUDENTS DO EXTRACURRICULAR ACTIVITIES, SO PEOPLE IN THE "GOING HOME CLUB" HELP THE OTHER CLUBS OUT ONCE IN A WHILE.
GARA (RATTLE)
ガラ
THAT'S NOT A GOOD REASON.
GARA
ガラ
GARA
ガラ

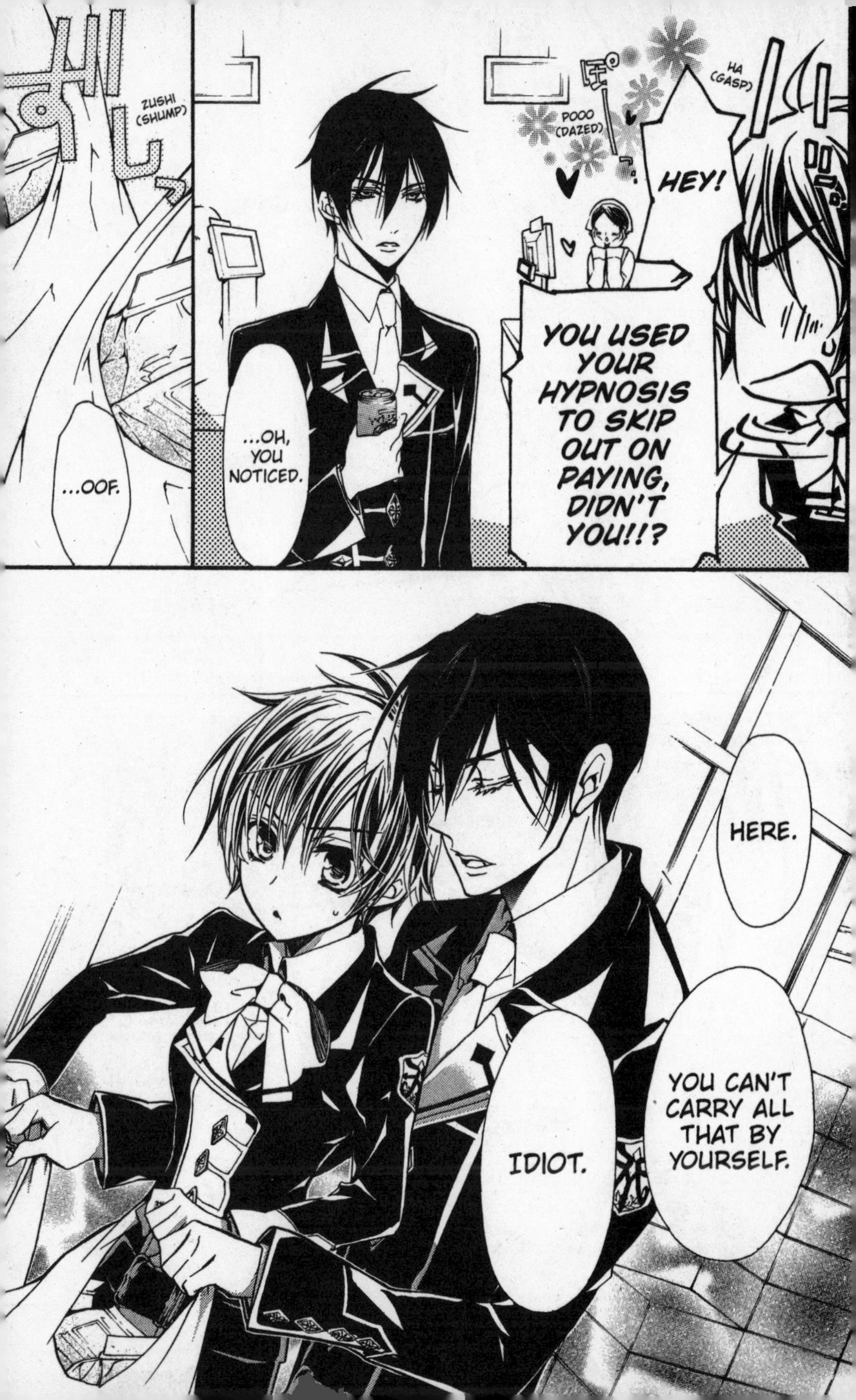
HA (GASP)
HEY!
YOU USED YOUR HYPNOSIS TO SKIP OUT ON PAYING, DIDN'T YOU!!?
POOO (DAZED)
...OH, YOU NOTICED.
ZUSHI (SHUMP)
...OOF.
HERE.
YOU CAN'T CARRY ALL THAT BY YOURSELF.
IDIOT.

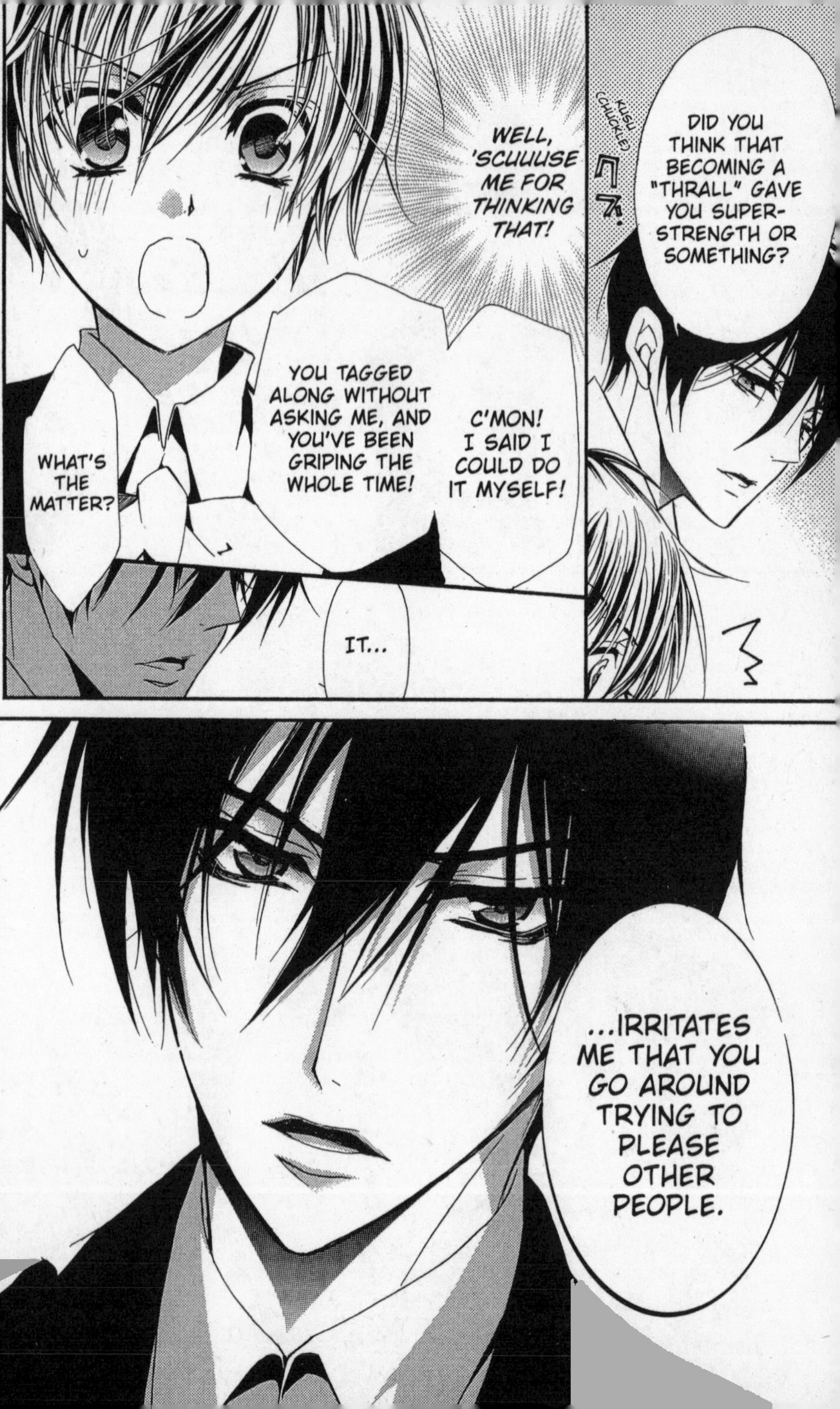
DID YOU THINK THAT BECOMING A "THRALL" GAVE YOU SUPER-STRENGTH OR SOMETHING?
KUSU (CHUCKLE)
WELL, 'SCUUUSE ME FOR THINKING THAT!
C'MON! I SAID I COULD DO IT MYSELF!
YOU TAGGED ALONG WITHOUT ASKING ME, AND YOU'VE BEEN GRIPING THE WHOLE TIME!
WHAT'S THE MATTER?
IT...
...IRRITATES ME THAT YOU GO AROUND TRYING TO PLEASE OTHER PEOPLE.

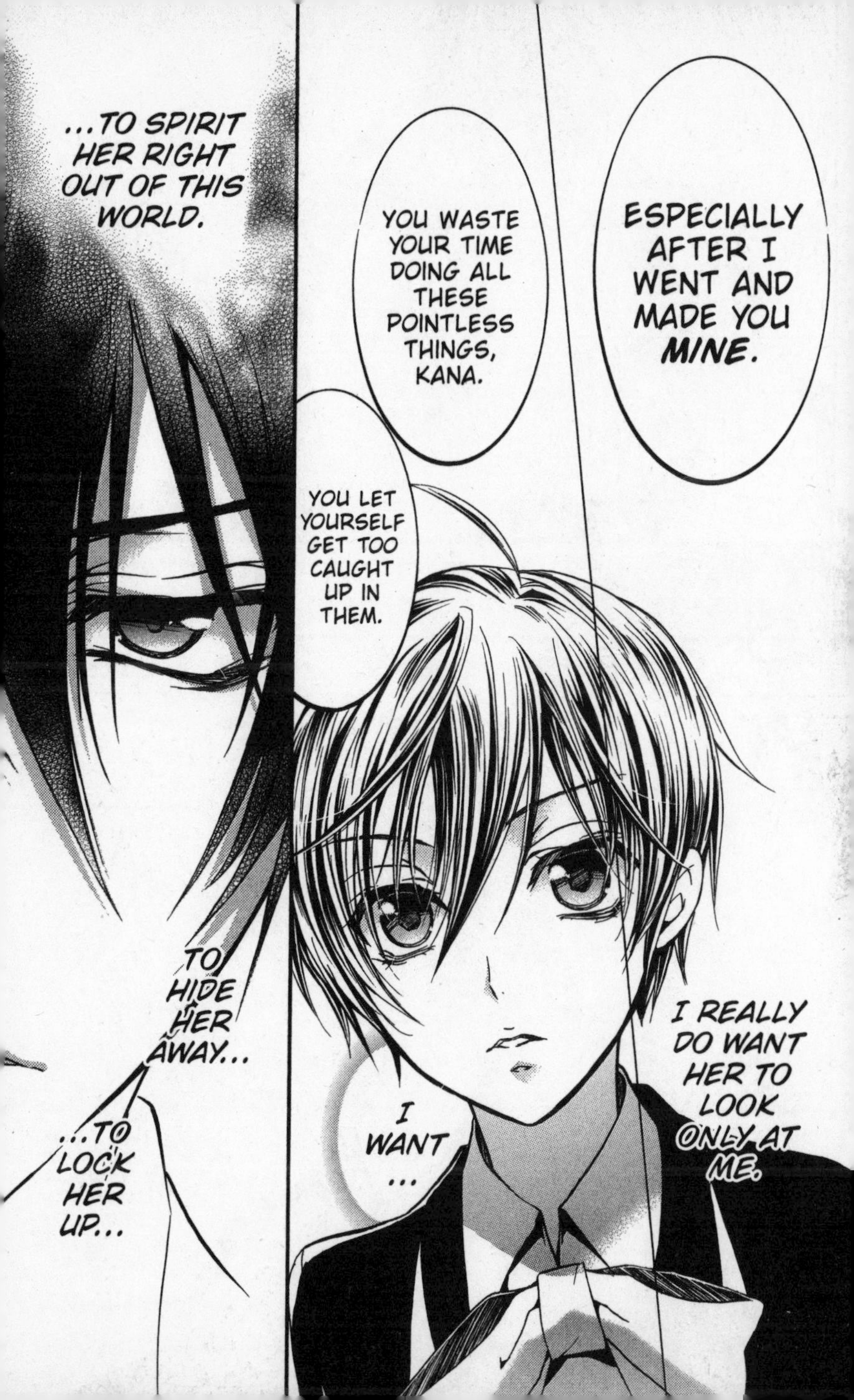
ESPECIALLY AFTER I WENT AND MADE YOU *MINE*.
YOU WASTE YOUR TIME DOING ALL THESE POINTLESS THINGS, KANA.
YOU LET YOURSELF GET TOO CAUGHT UP IN THEM.
I REALLY DO WANT HER TO LOOK ONLY AT ME.
I WANT ...
...TO SPIRIT HER RIGHT OUT OF THIS WORLD.
TO HIDE HER AWAY...
...TO LOCK HER UP...

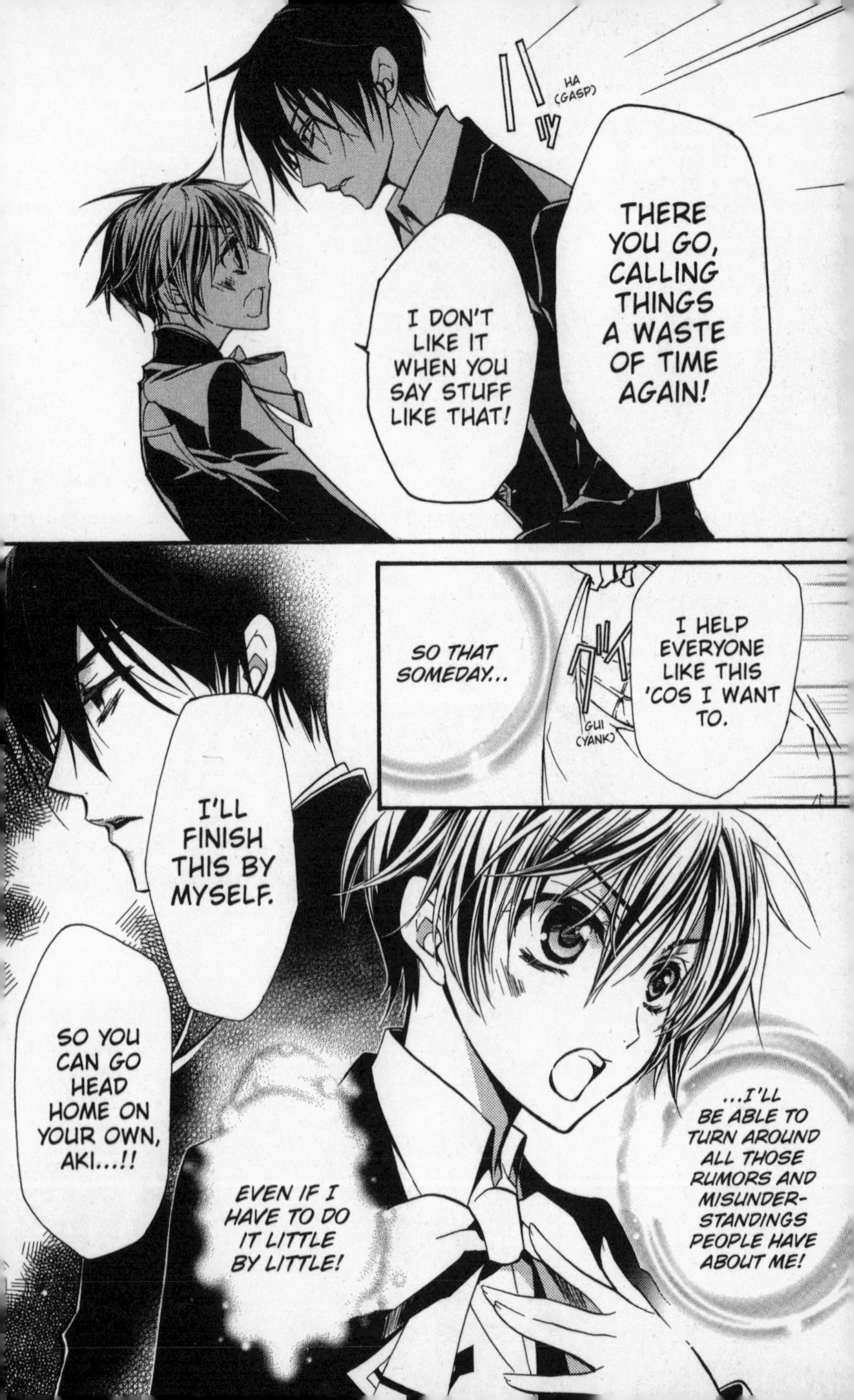
HA (GASP)
THERE YOU GO, CALLING THINGS A WASTE OF TIME AGAIN!
I DON'T LIKE IT WHEN YOU SAY STUFF LIKE THAT!
I HELP EVERYONE LIKE THIS 'COS I WANT TO.
GUI (YANK)
SO THAT SOMEDAY...
...I'LL BE ABLE TO TURN AROUND ALL THOSE RUMORS AND MISUNDER-STANDINGS PEOPLE HAVE ABOUT ME!
EVEN IF I HAVE TO DO IT LITTLE BY LITTLE!
I'LL FINISH THIS BY MYSELF.
SO YOU CAN GO HEAD HOME ON YOUR OWN, AKI...!!

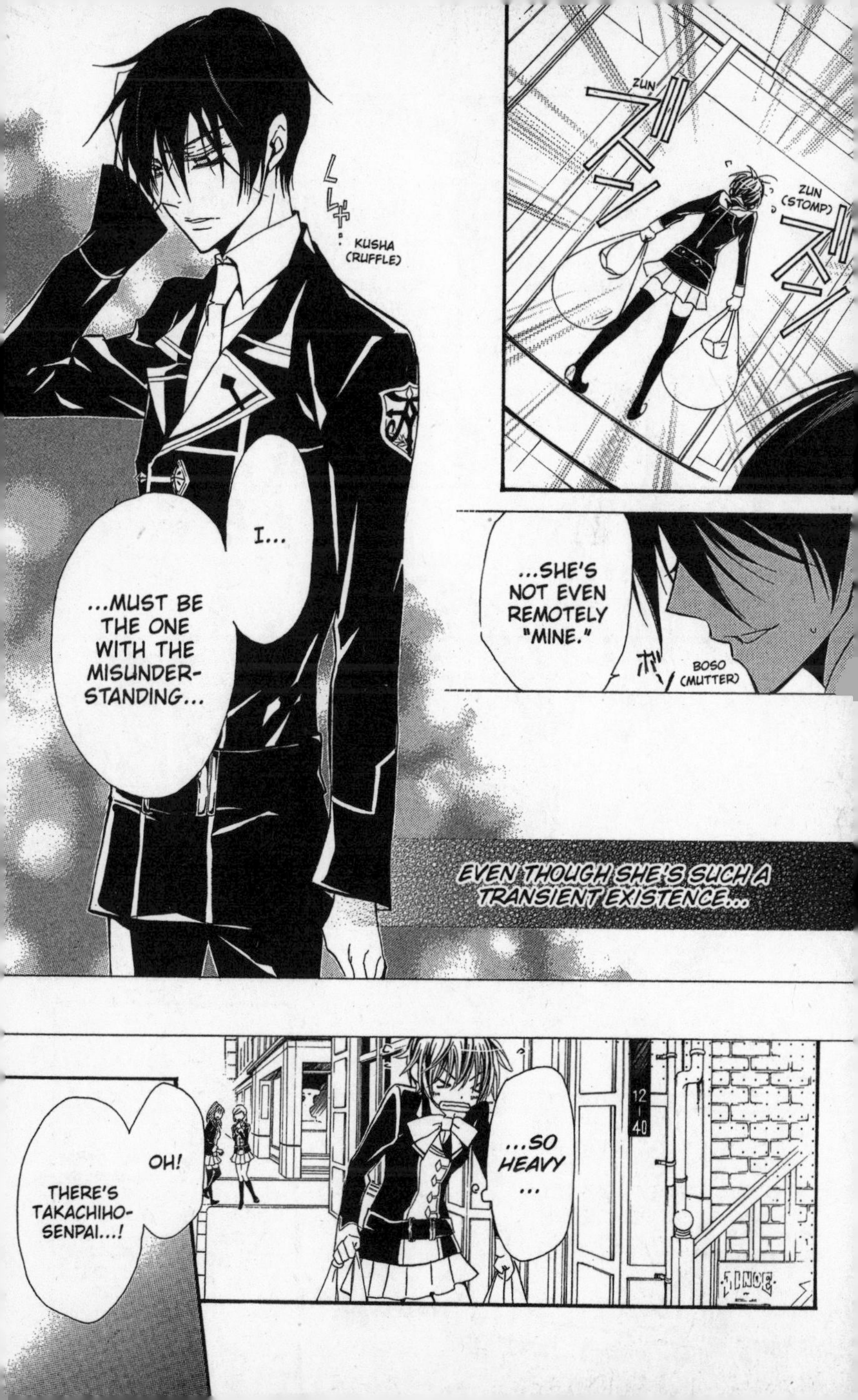
ZUN
ZUN (STOMP)
...SHE'S NOT EVEN REMOTELY "MINE."
BOSO (MUTTER)
KUSHA (RUFFLE)
I...
...MUST BE THE ONE WITH THE MISUNDERSTANDING...
EVEN THOUGH SHE'S SUCH A TRANSIENT EXISTENCE...
...SO HEAVY ...
OH!
THERE'S TAKACHIHO-SENPAI...!

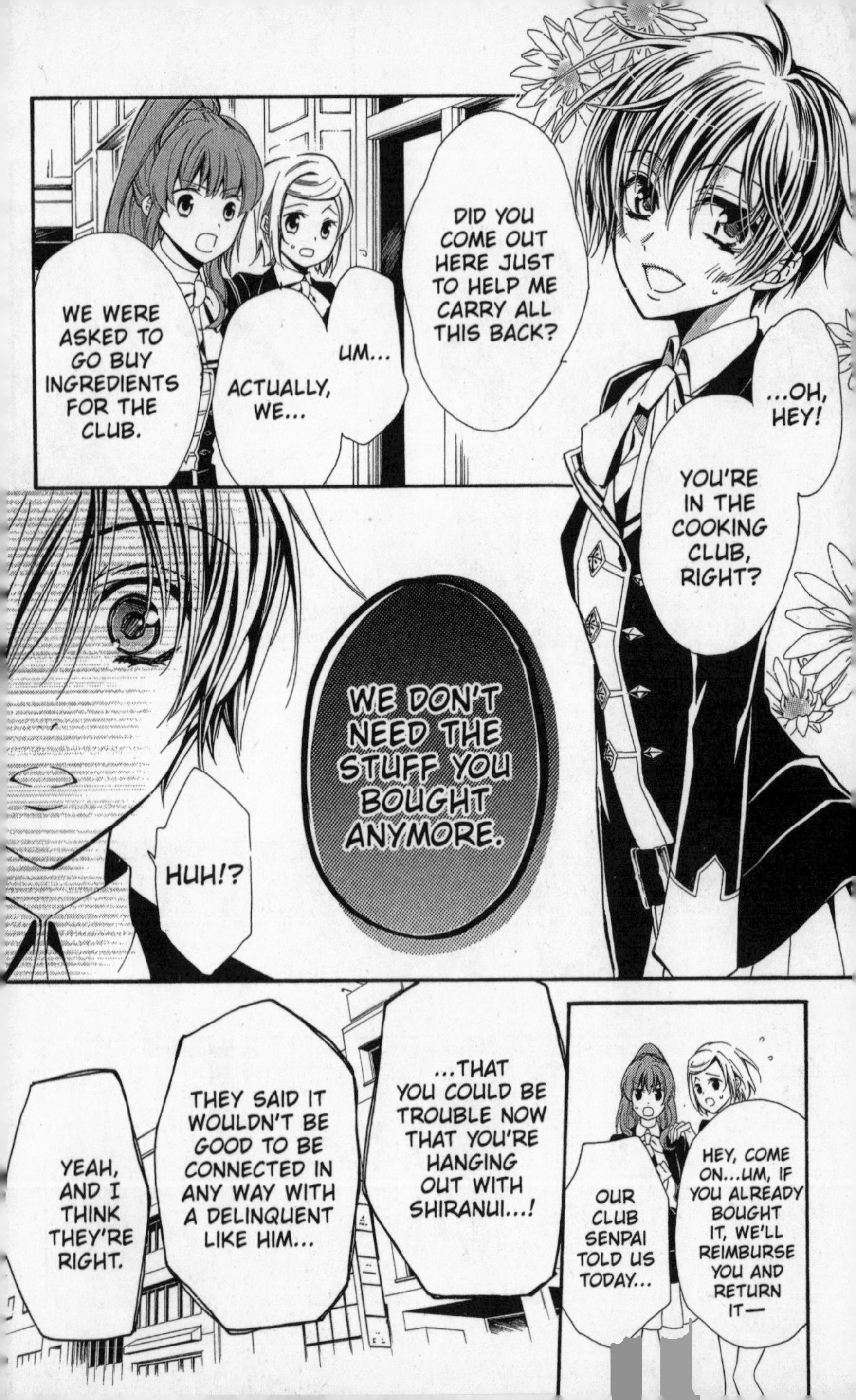
...OH, HEY!
YOU'RE IN THE COOKING CLUB, RIGHT?
DID YOU COME OUT HERE JUST TO HELP ME CARRY ALL THIS BACK?
UM...
ACTUALLY, WE...
WE WERE ASKED TO GO BUY INGREDIENTS FOR THE CLUB.
WE DON'T NEED THE STUFF YOU BOUGHT ANYMORE.
HUH!?
HEY, COME ON...UM, IF YOU ALREADY BOUGHT IT, WE'LL REIMBURSE YOU AND RETURN IT—
OUR CLUB SENPAI TOLD US TODAY...
...THAT YOU COULD BE TROUBLE NOW THAT YOU'RE HANGING OUT WITH SHIRANUI...!
THEY SAID IT WOULDN'T BE GOOD TO BE CONNECTED IN ANY WAY WITH A DELINQUENT LIKE HIM...
YEAH, AND I THINK THEY'RE RIGHT.

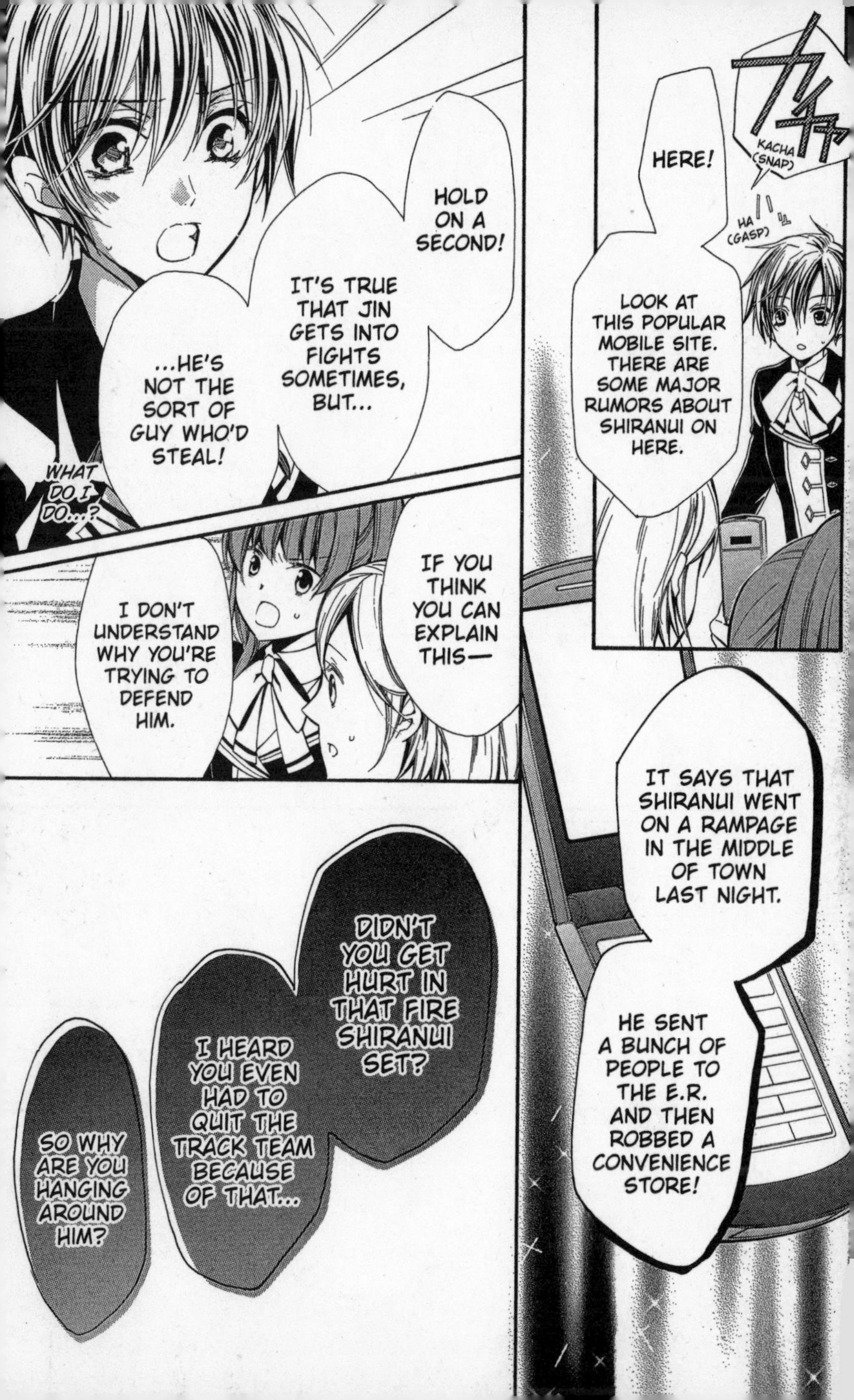
KACHA (SNAP)
HERE!
HA (GASP)
LOOK AT THIS POPULAR MOBILE SITE. THERE ARE SOME MAJOR RUMORS ABOUT SHIRANUI ON HERE.
IT SAYS THAT SHIRANUI WENT ON A RAMPAGE IN THE MIDDLE OF TOWN LAST NIGHT.
HE SENT A BUNCH OF PEOPLE TO THE E.R. AND THEN ROBBED A CONVENIENCE STORE!
HOLD ON A SECOND!
IT'S TRUE THAT JIN GETS INTO FIGHTS SOMETIMES, BUT...
...HE'S NOT THE SORT OF GUY WHO'D STEAL!
WHAT DO I DO...?
IF YOU THINK YOU CAN EXPLAIN THIS—
I DON'T UNDERSTAND WHY YOU'RE TRYING TO DEFEND HIM.
DIDN'T YOU GET HURT IN THAT FIRE SHIRANUI SET?
I HEARD YOU EVEN HAD TO QUIT THE TRACK TEAM BECAUSE OF THAT...
SO WHY ARE YOU HANGING AROUND HIM?

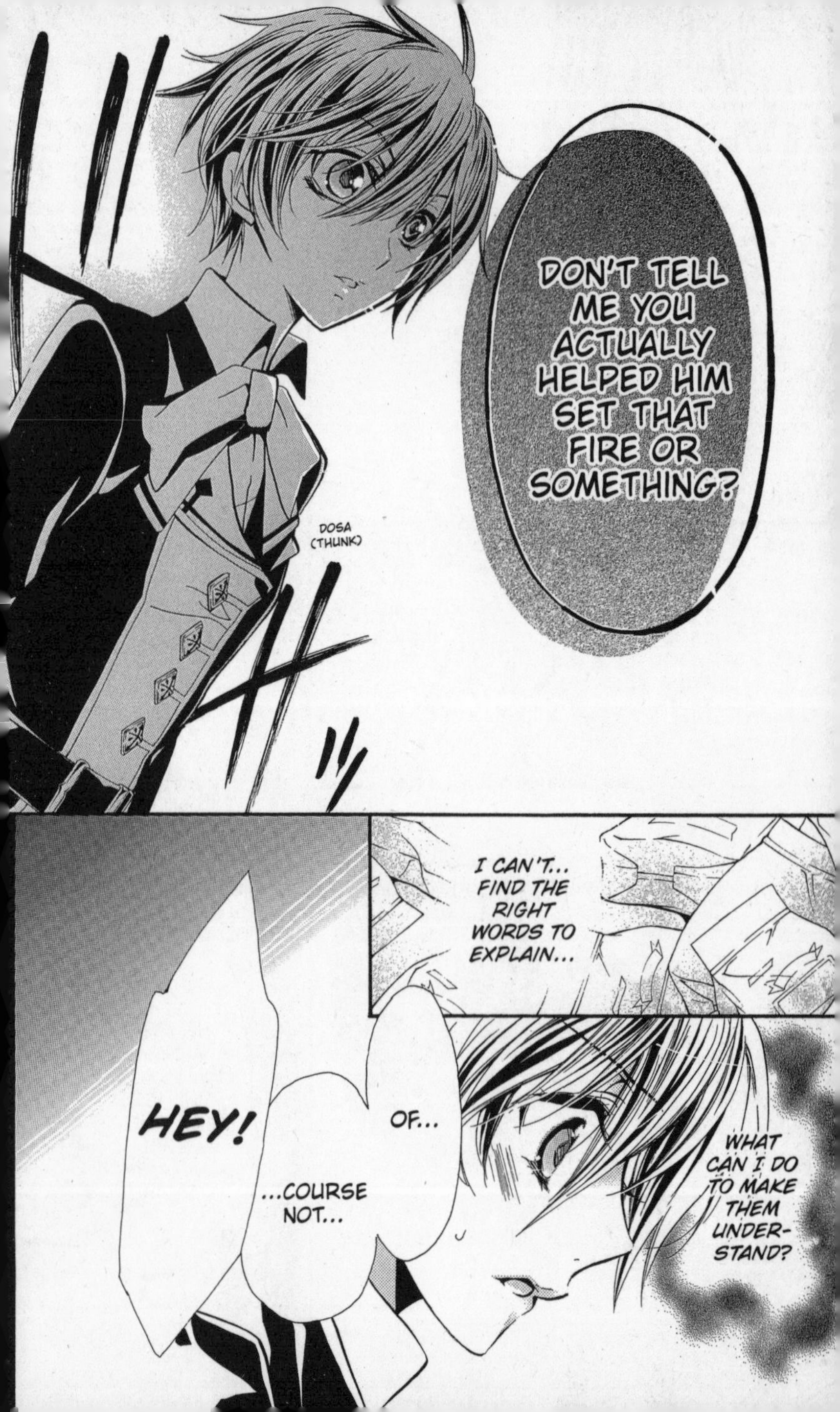
DON'T TELL ME YOU ACTUALLY HELPED HIM SET THAT FIRE OR SOMETHING?
DOSA (THUNK)
I CAN'T... FIND THE RIGHT WORDS TO EXPLAIN...
WHAT CAN I DO TO MAKE THEM UNDER-STAND?
OF...
...COURSE NOT...
HEY!

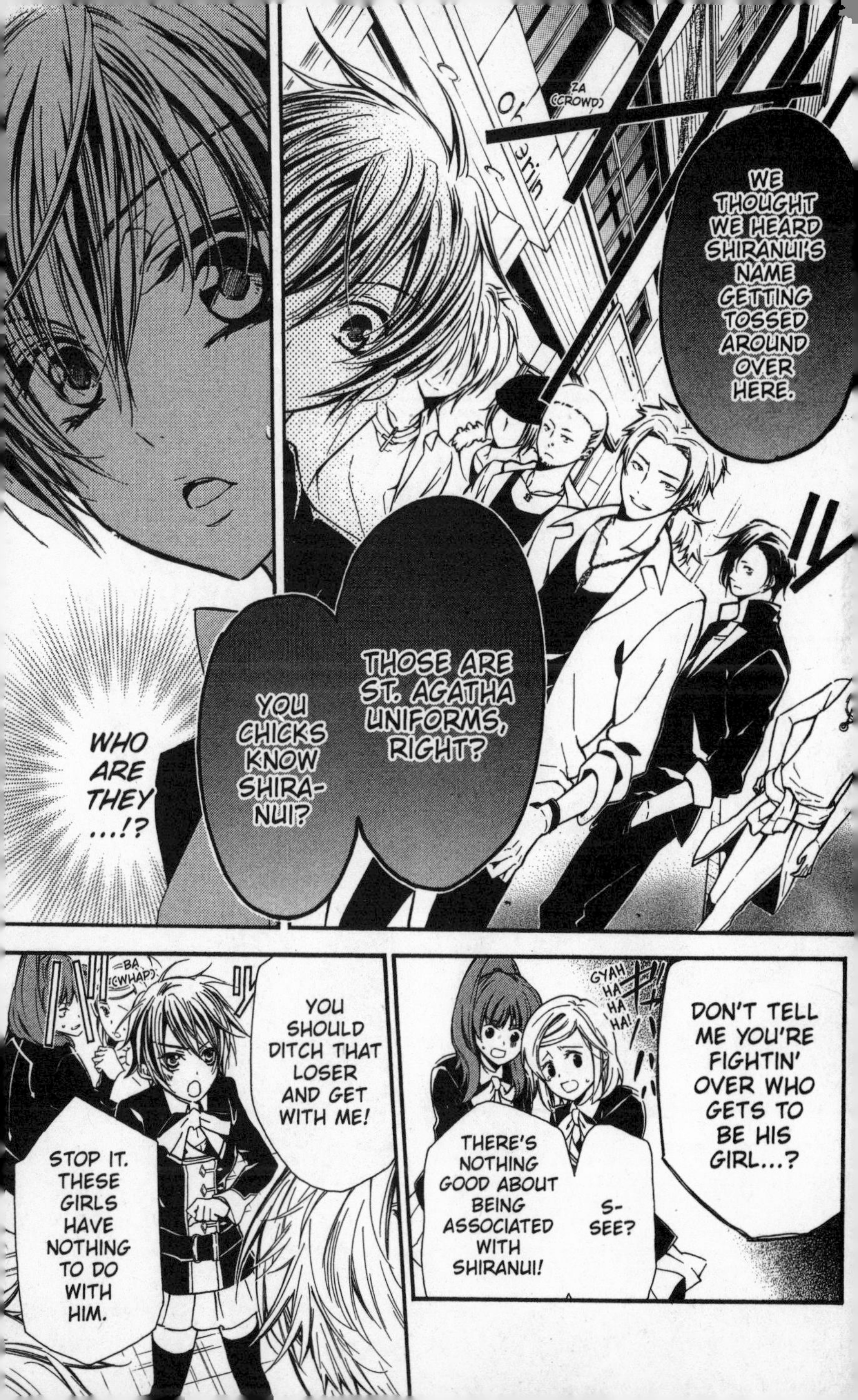
ZA (CROWD)
WE THOUGHT WE HEARD SHIRANUI'S NAME GETTING TOSSED AROUND OVER HERE.
THOSE ARE ST. AGATHA UNIFORMS, RIGHT?
YOU CHICKS KNOW SHIRA-NUI?
WHO ARE THEY ...!?
GYAH HA HA HA!
DON'T TELL ME YOU'RE FIGHTIN' OVER WHO GETS TO BE HIS GIRL...?
S-SEE?
THERE'S NOTHING GOOD ABOUT BEING ASSOCIATED WITH SHIRANUI!
BA (WHAP)
YOU SHOULD DITCH THAT LOSER AND GET WITH ME!
STOP IT. THESE GIRLS HAVE NOTHING TO DO WITH HIM.

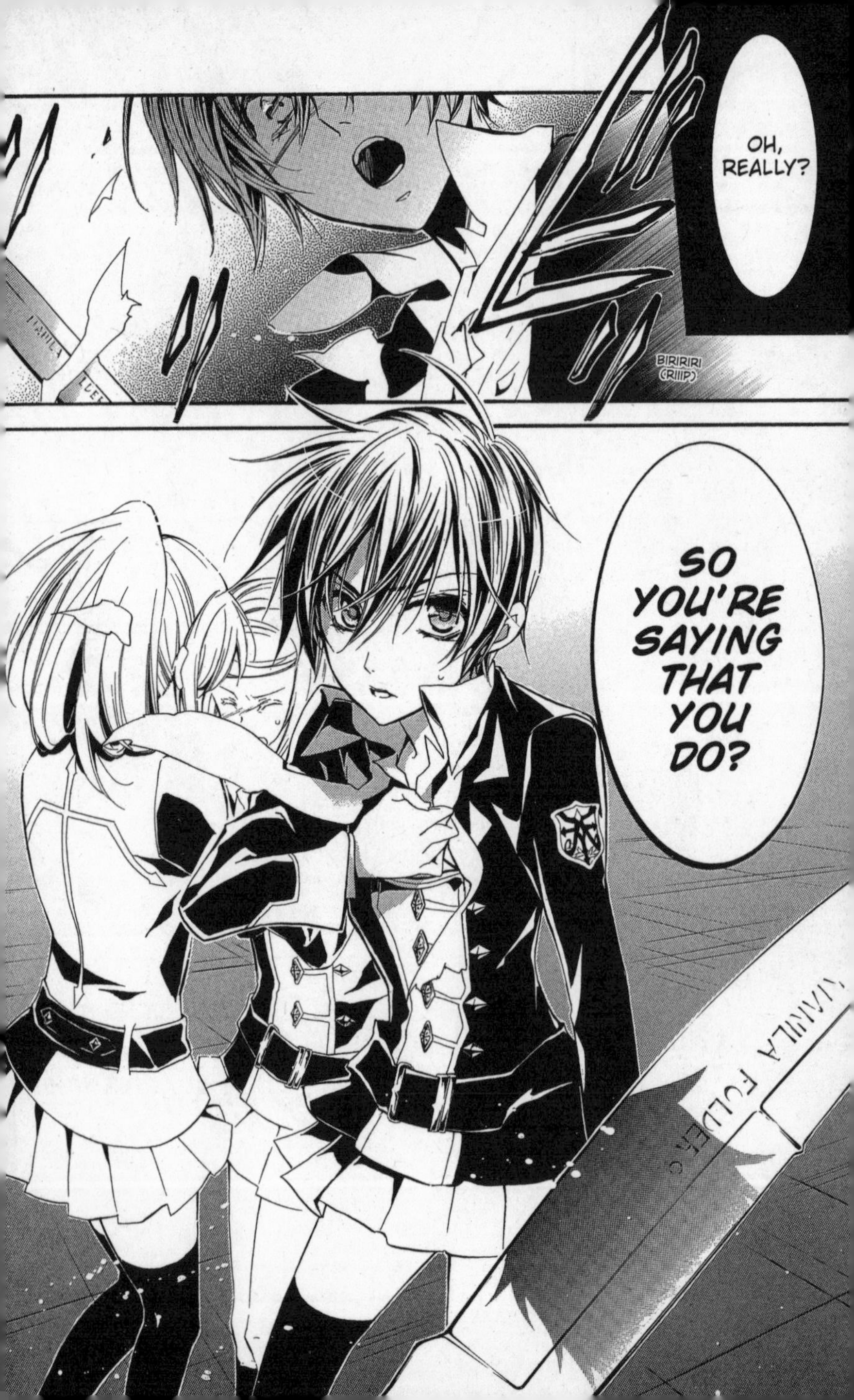
OH, REALLY?
BIRIRIRI (RIIIP)
SO YOU'RE SAYING THAT YOU DO?

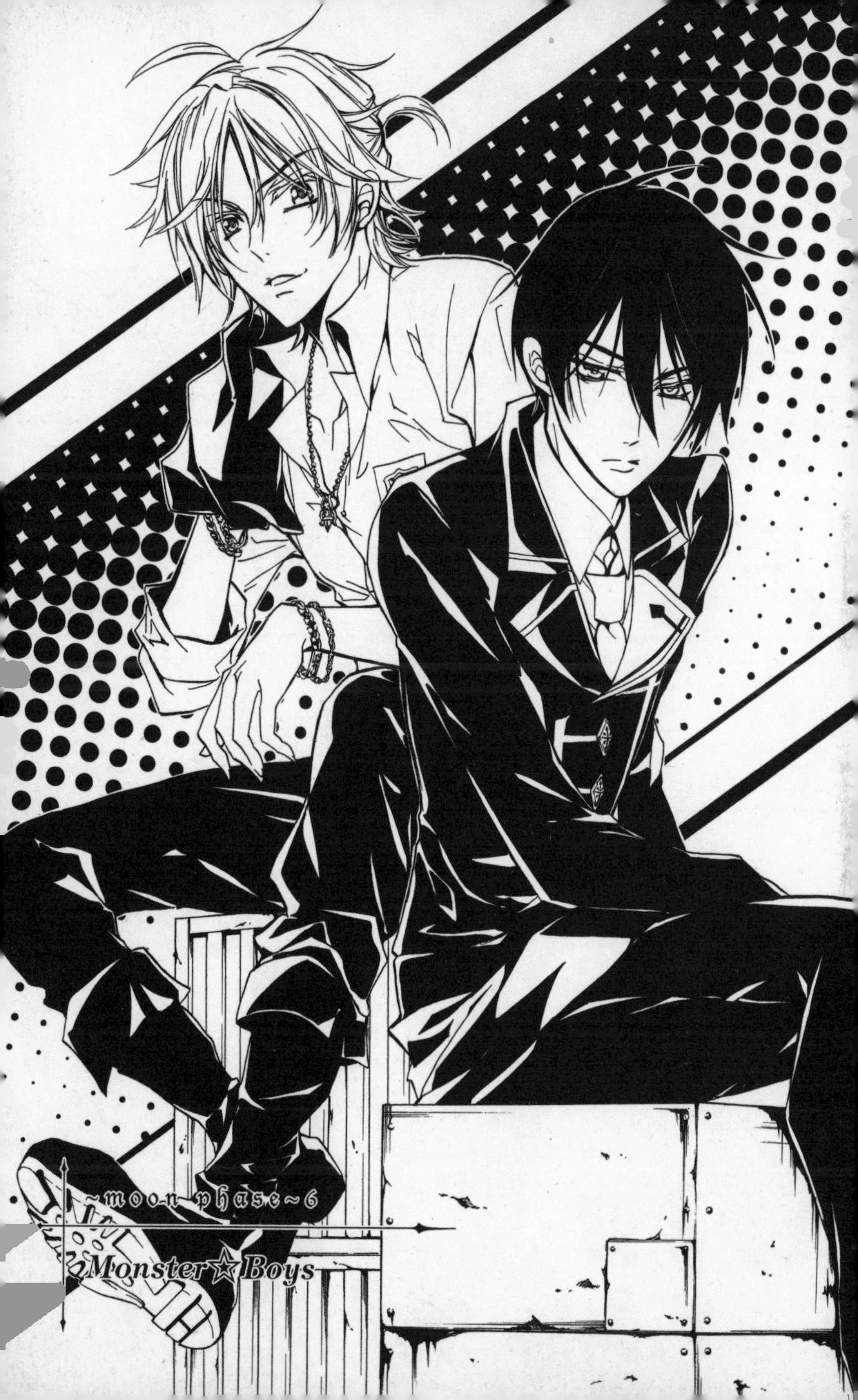
~moon phase~6
Monster☆Boys

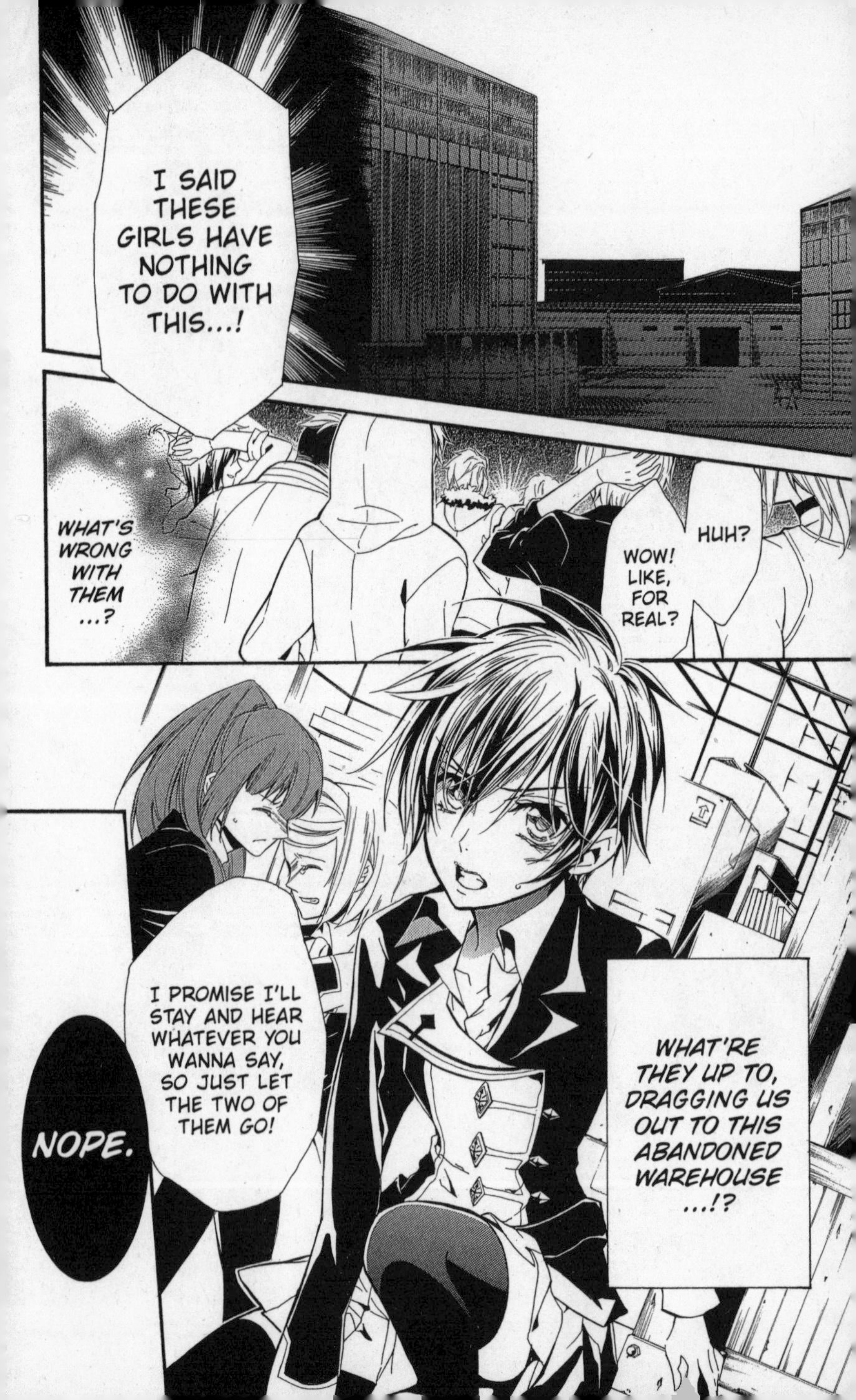
I SAID THESE GIRLS HAVE NOTHING TO DO WITH THIS...!
HUH?
WOW! LIKE, FOR REAL?
WHAT'S WRONG WITH THEM ...?
WHAT'RE THEY UP TO, DRAGGING US OUT TO THIS ABANDONED WAREHOUSE ...!?
I PROMISE I'LL STAY AND HEAR WHATEVER YOU WANNA SAY, SO JUST LET THE TWO OF THEM GO!
NOPE.

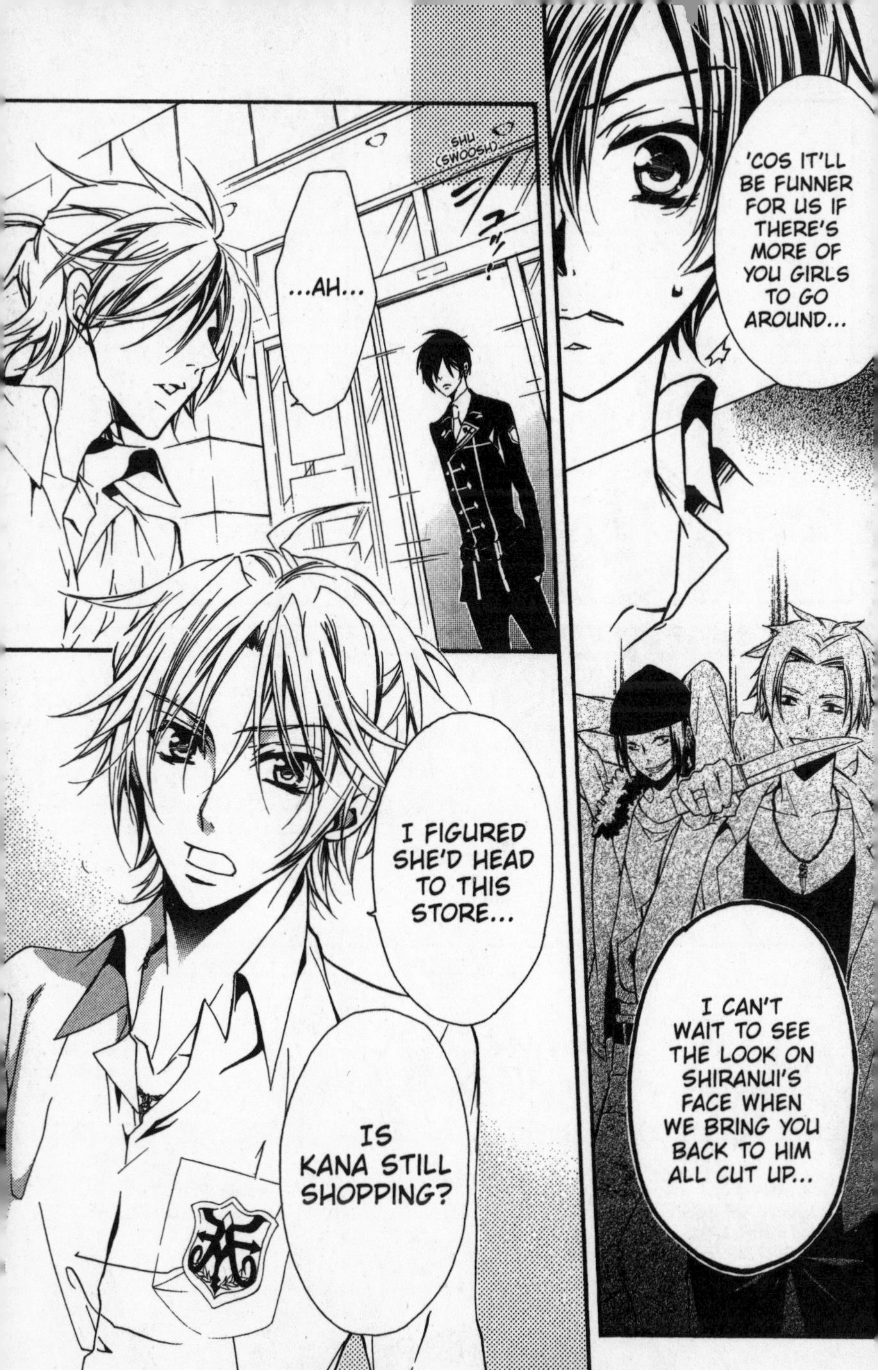
'COS IT'LL BE FUNNER FOR US IF THERE'S MORE OF YOU GIRLS TO GO AROUND...
I CAN'T WAIT TO SEE THE LOOK ON SHIRANUI'S FACE WHEN WE BRING YOU BACK TO HIM ALL CUT UP...
SHU (SWOOSH)
...AH...
I FIGURED SHE'D HEAD TO THIS STORE...
IS KANA STILL SHOPPING?

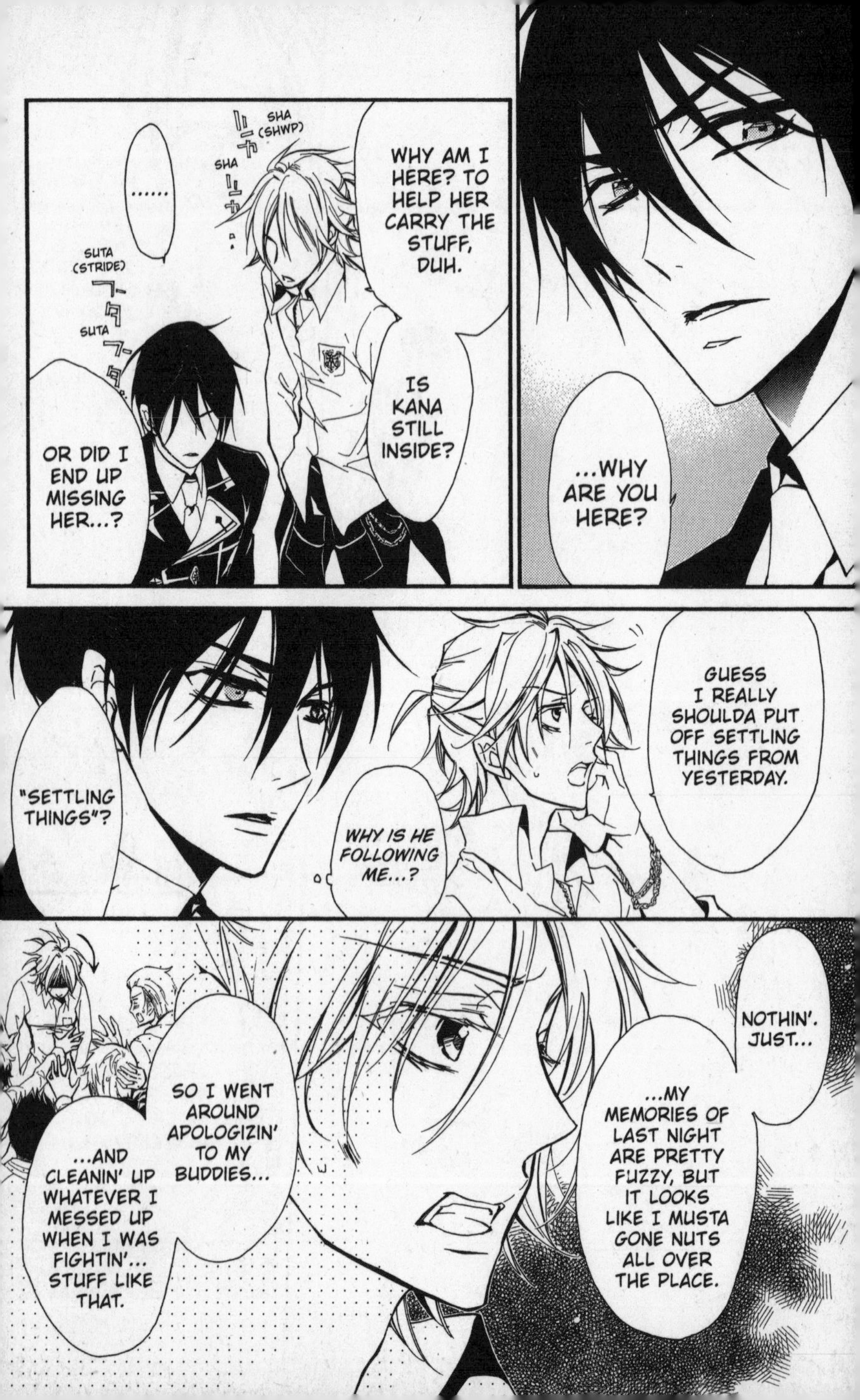
...WHY ARE YOU HERE?
WHY AM I HERE? TO HELP HER CARRY THE STUFF, DUH.
SHA (SHWP)
SHA
......
IS KANA STILL INSIDE?
SUTA (STRIDE)
SUTA
OR DID I END UP MISSING HER...?
GUESS I REALLY SHOULDA PUT OFF SETTLING THINGS FROM YESTERDAY.
WHY IS HE FOLLOWING ME...?
"SETTLING THINGS"?
NOTHIN'. JUST...
...MY MEMORIES OF LAST NIGHT ARE PRETTY FUZZY, BUT IT LOOKS LIKE I MUSTA GONE NUTS ALL OVER THE PLACE.
SO I WENT AROUND APOLOGIZIN' TO MY BUDDIES...
...AND CLEANIN' UP WHATEVER I MESSED UP WHEN I WAS FIGHTIN'... STUFF LIKE THAT.

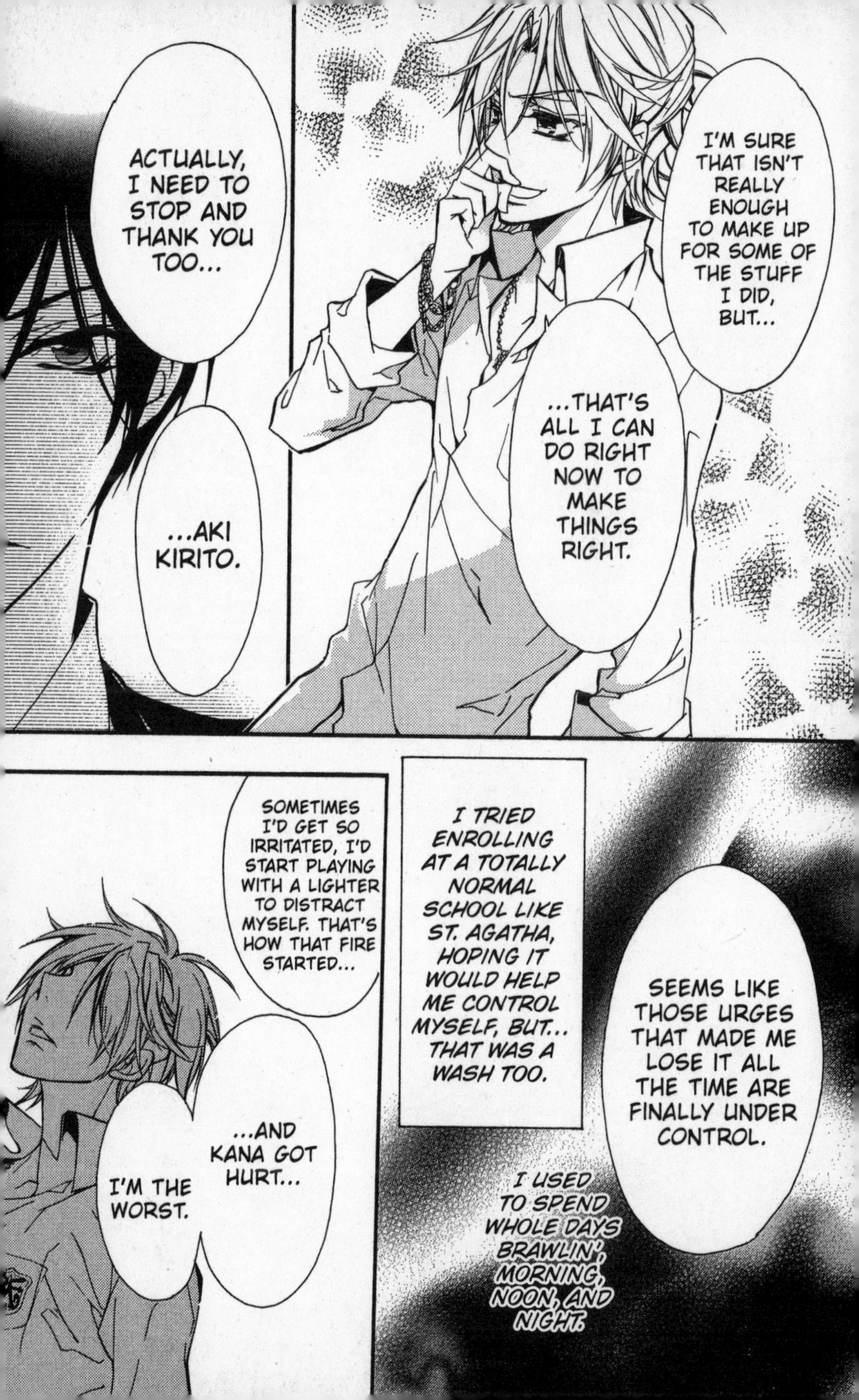
I'M SURE THAT ISN'T REALLY ENOUGH TO MAKE UP FOR SOME OF THE STUFF I DID, BUT...
...THAT'S ALL I CAN DO RIGHT NOW TO MAKE THINGS RIGHT.
ACTUALLY, I NEED TO STOP AND THANK YOU TOO...
...AKI KIRITO.
SEEMS LIKE THOSE URGES THAT MADE ME LOSE IT ALL THE TIME ARE FINALLY UNDER CONTROL.
I USED TO SPEND WHOLE DAYS BRAWLIN', MORNING, NOON, AND NIGHT.
I TRIED ENROLLING AT A TOTALLY NORMAL SCHOOL LIKE ST. AGATHA, HOPING IT WOULD HELP ME CONTROL MYSELF, BUT... THAT WAS A WASH TOO.
SOMETIMES I'D GET SO IRRITATED, I'D START PLAYING WITH A LIGHTER TO DISTRACT MYSELF. THAT'S HOW THAT FIRE STARTED...
...AND KANA GOT HURT...
I'M THE WORST.

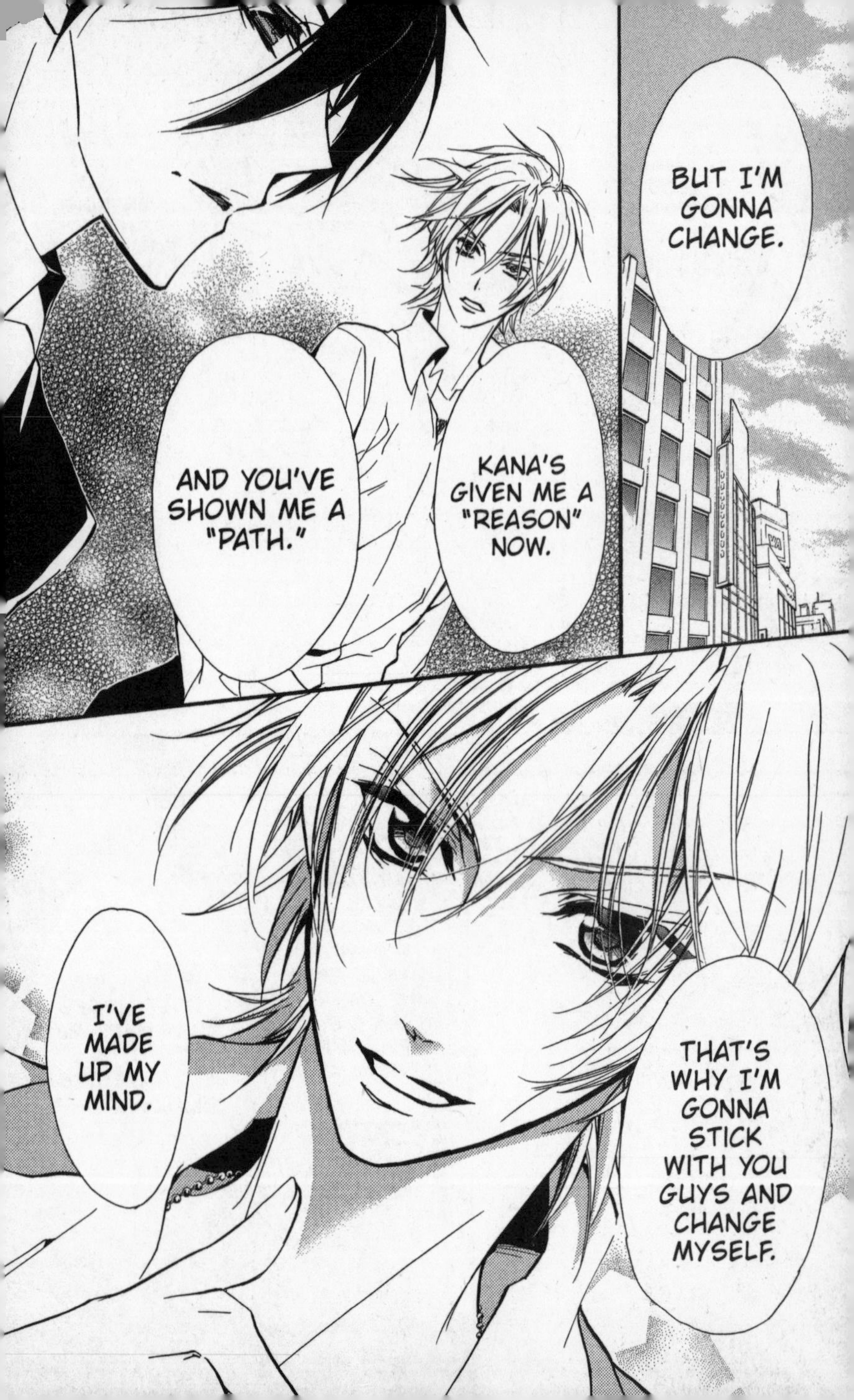
BUT I'M GONNA CHANGE.
KANA'S GIVEN ME A "REASON" NOW.
AND YOU'VE SHOWN ME A "PATH."
I'VE MADE UP MY MIND.
THAT'S WHY I'M GONNA STICK WITH YOU GUYS AND CHANGE MYSELF.

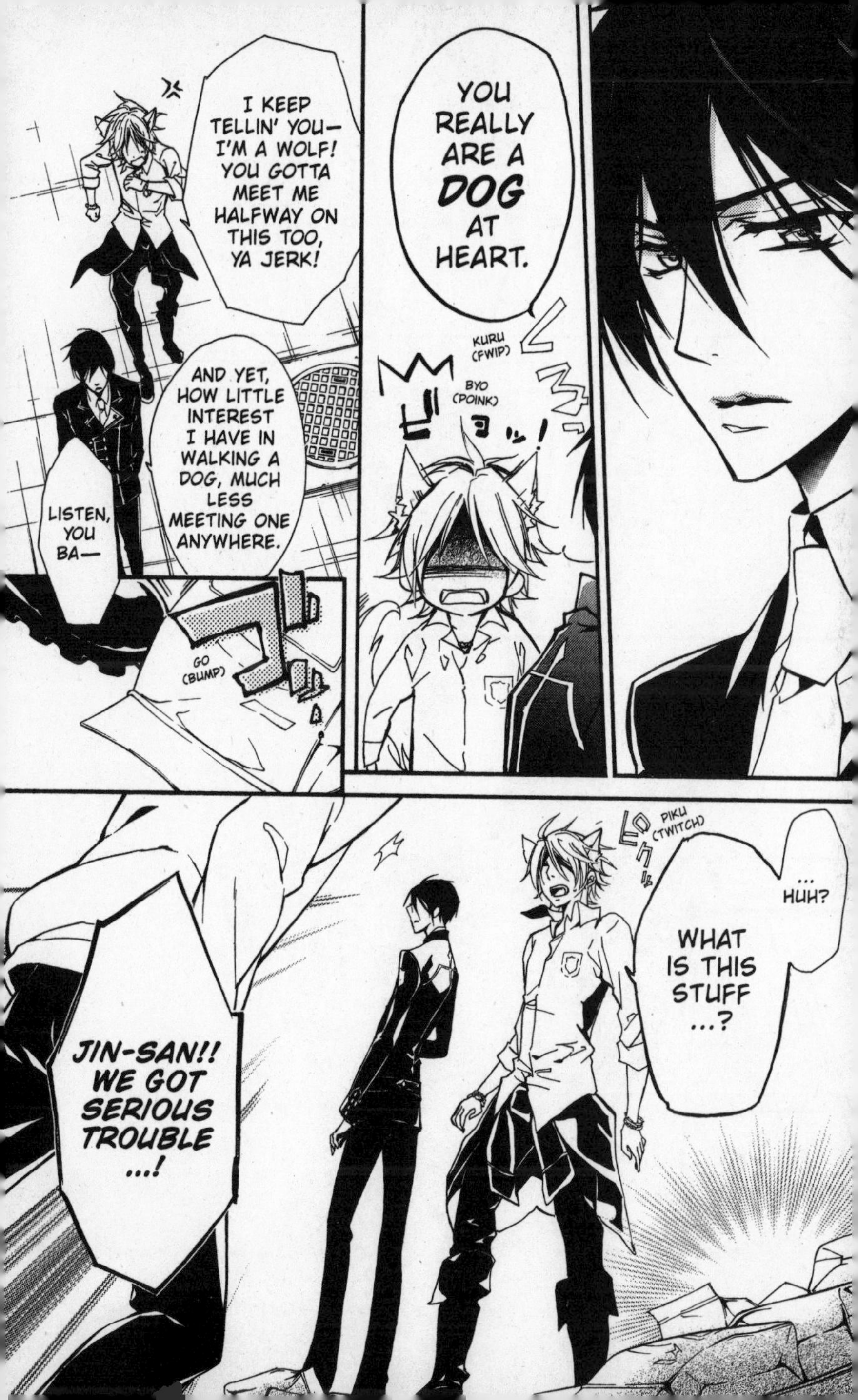
YOU REALLY ARE A DOG AT HEART.
KURU (FWIP)
BYO (POINK)
I KEEP TELLIN' YOU— I'M A WOLF! YOU GOTTA MEET ME HALFWAY ON THIS TOO, YA JERK!
AND YET, HOW LITTLE INTEREST I HAVE IN WALKING A DOG, MUCH LESS MEETING ONE ANYWHERE.
LISTEN, YOU BA—
GO (BUMP)
PIKU (TWITCH)
... HUH?
WHAT IS THIS STUFF ...?
JIN-SAN!! WE GOT SERIOUS TROUBLE ...!

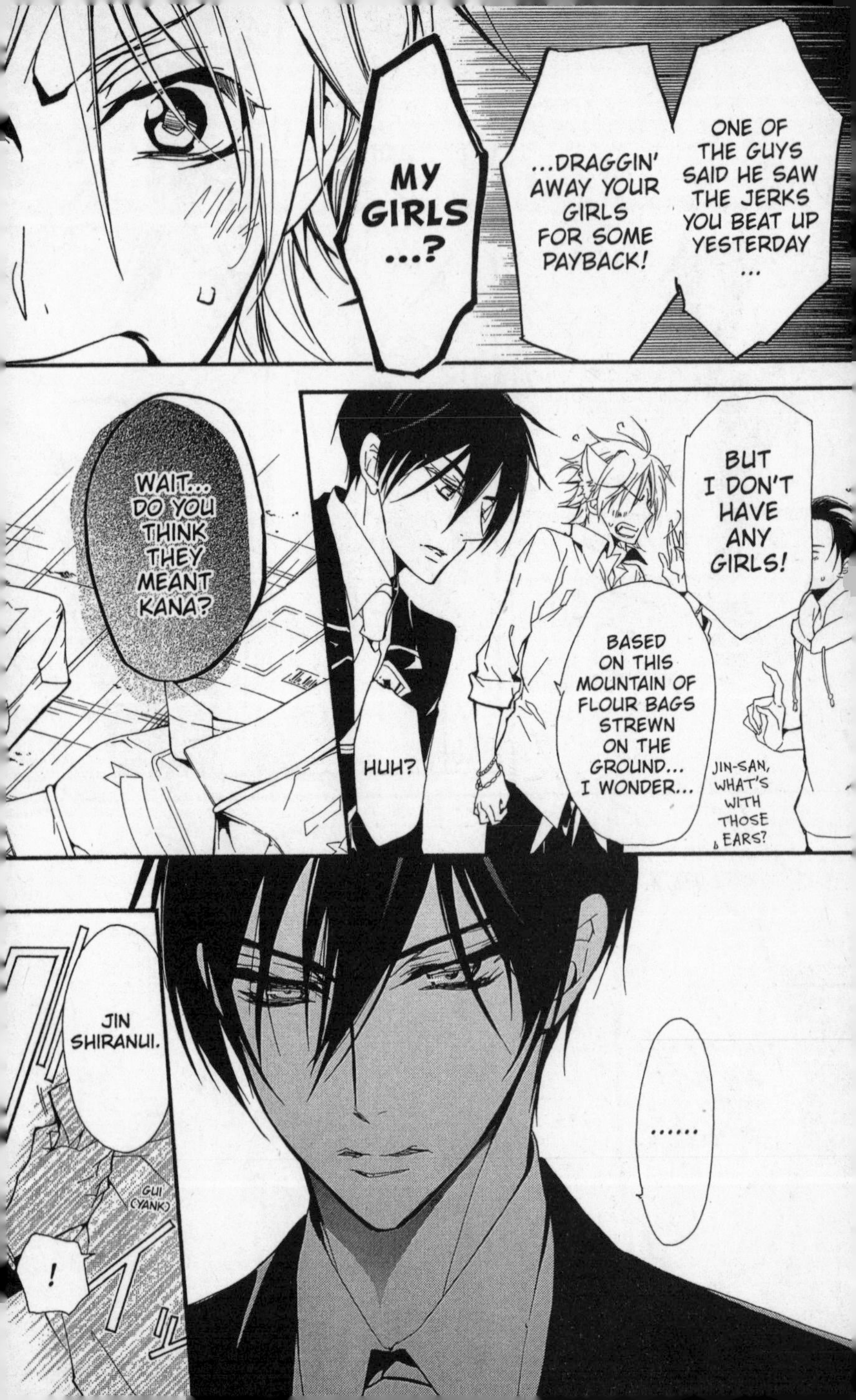
ONE OF THE GUYS SAID HE SAW THE JERKS YOU BEAT UP YESTERDAY...
...DRAGGIN' AWAY YOUR GIRLS FOR SOME PAYBACK!
MY GIRLS...?
BUT I DON'T HAVE ANY GIRLS!
JIN-SAN, WHAT'S WITH THOSE EARS?
BASED ON THIS MOUNTAIN OF FLOUR BAGS STREWN ON THE GROUND... I WONDER...
HUH?
WAIT... DO YOU THINK THEY MEANT KANA?
......
JIN SHIRANUI.
GUI (YANK)
!

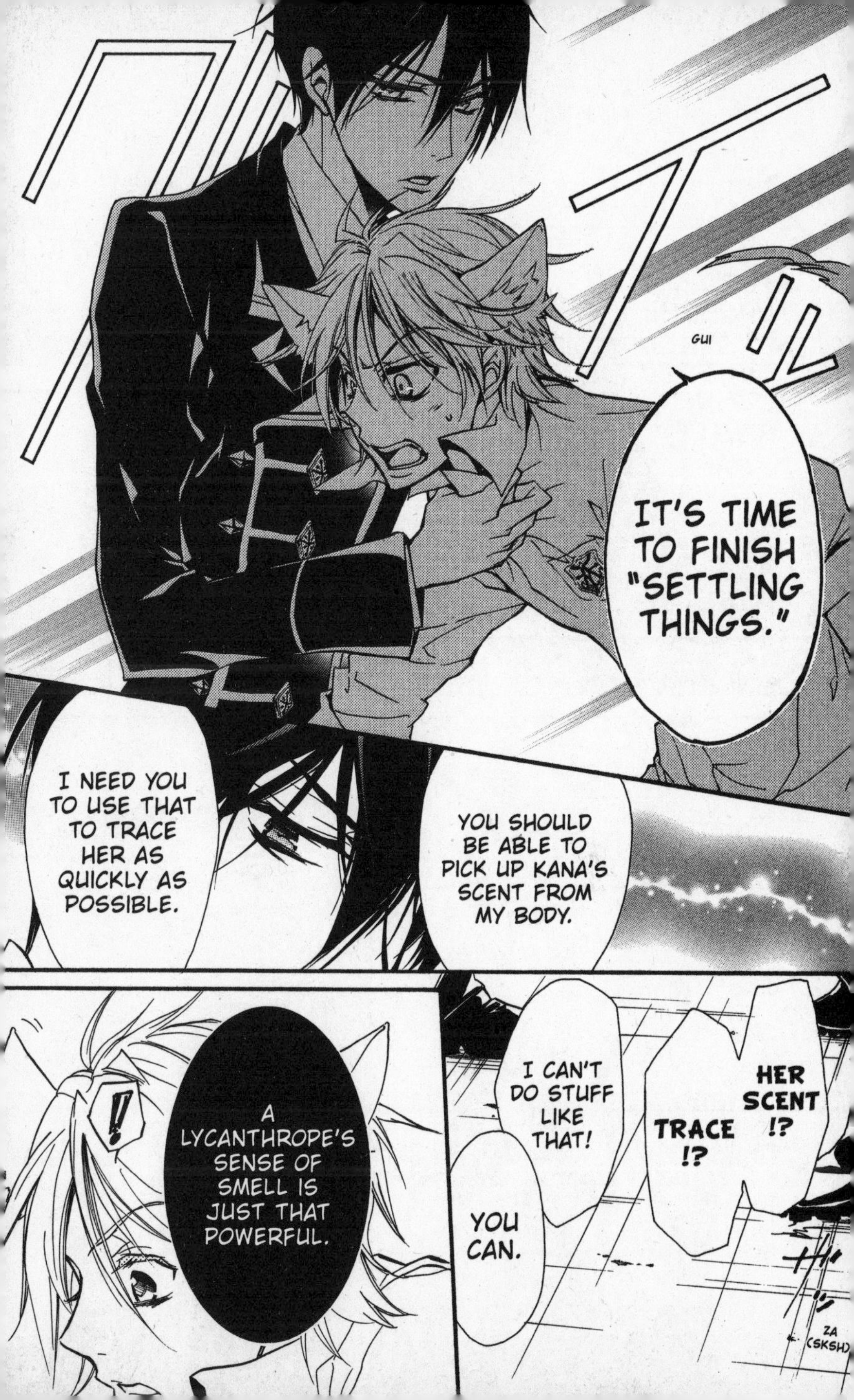
GUI
IT'S TIME TO FINISH "SETTLING THINGS."
YOU SHOULD BE ABLE TO PICK UP KANA'S SCENT FROM MY BODY.
I NEED YOU TO USE THAT TO TRACE HER AS QUICKLY AS POSSIBLE.
HER SCENT !?
TRACE !?
I CAN'T DO STUFF LIKE THAT!
YOU CAN.
ZA (SKSH)
A LYCANTHROPE'S SENSE OF SMELL IS JUST THAT POWERFUL.

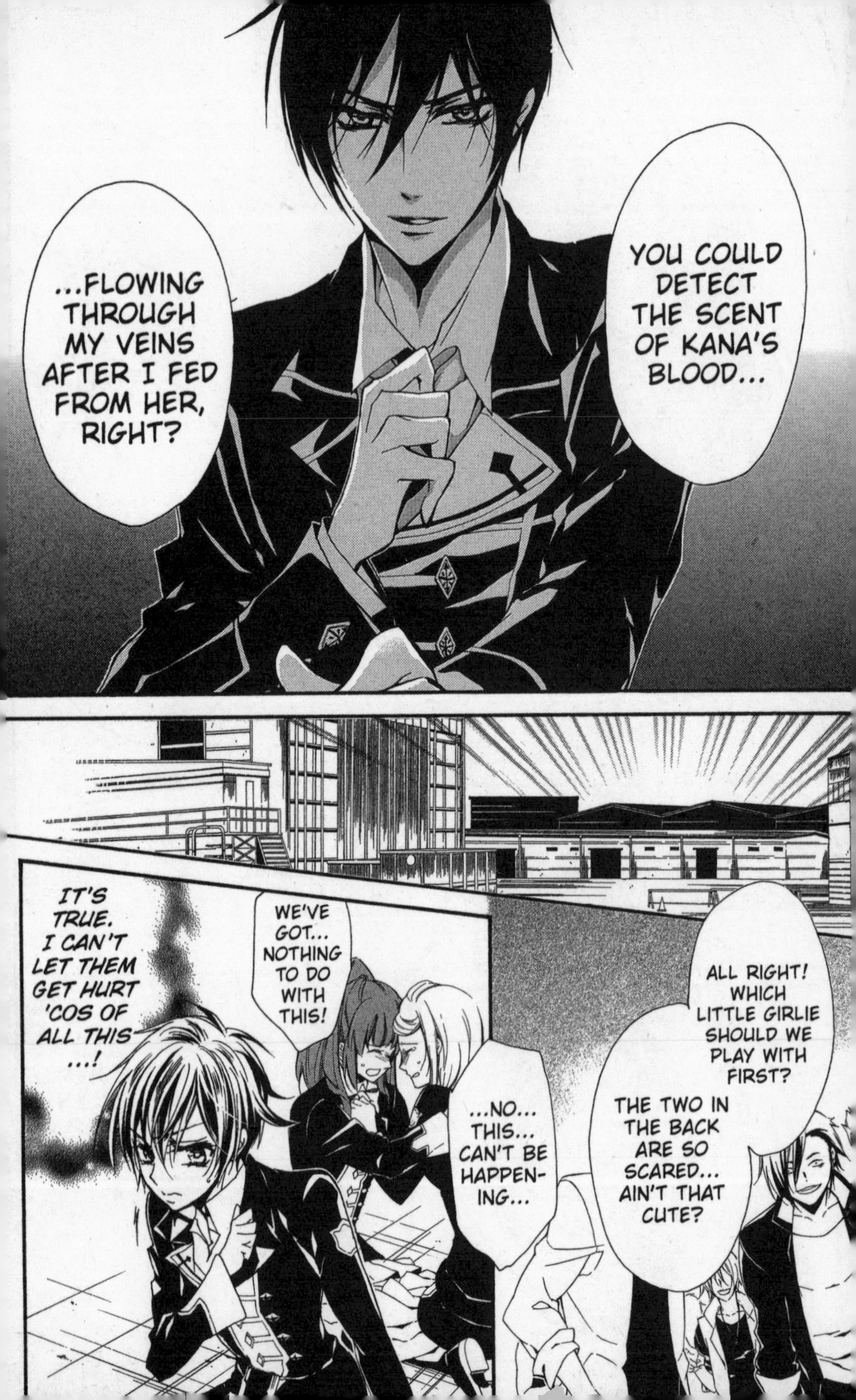
YOU COULD DETECT THE SCENT OF KANA'S BLOOD...
...FLOWING THROUGH MY VEINS AFTER I FED FROM HER, RIGHT?
ALL RIGHT! WHICH LITTLE GIRLIE SHOULD WE PLAY WITH FIRST?
THE TWO IN THE BACK ARE SO SCARED... AIN'T THAT CUTE?
...NO... THIS... CAN'T BE HAPPEN-ING...
WE'VE GOT... NOTHING TO DO WITH THIS!
IT'S TRUE. I CAN'T LET THEM GET HURT 'COS OF ALL THIS ...!

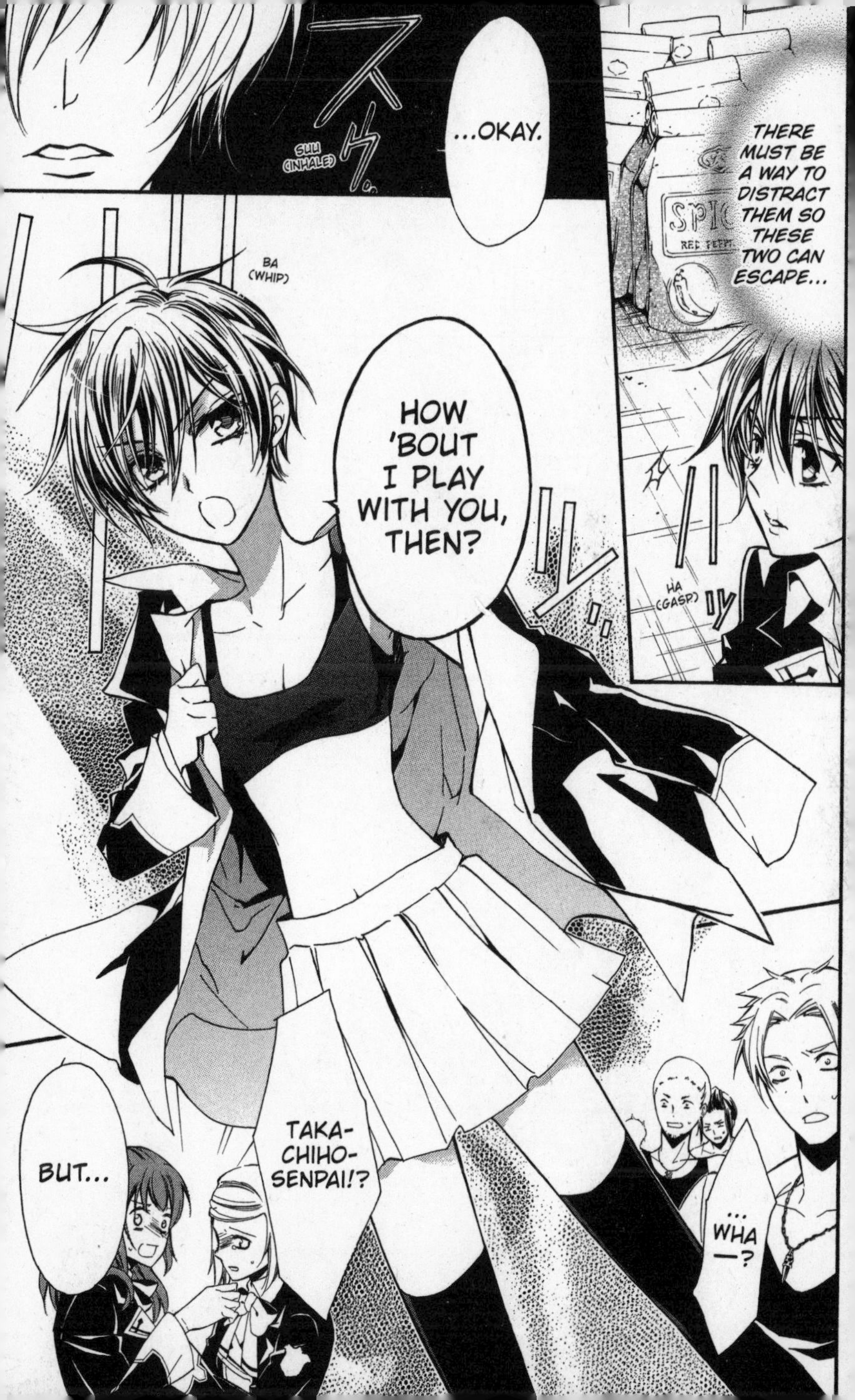
THERE MUST BE A WAY TO DISTRACT THEM SO THESE TWO CAN ESCAPE...
HA (GASP)
...OKAY.
SUU (INHALE)
BA (WHIP)
HOW 'BOUT I PLAY WITH YOU, THEN?
...WHA—?
TAKA-CHIHO-SENPAI!?
BUT...

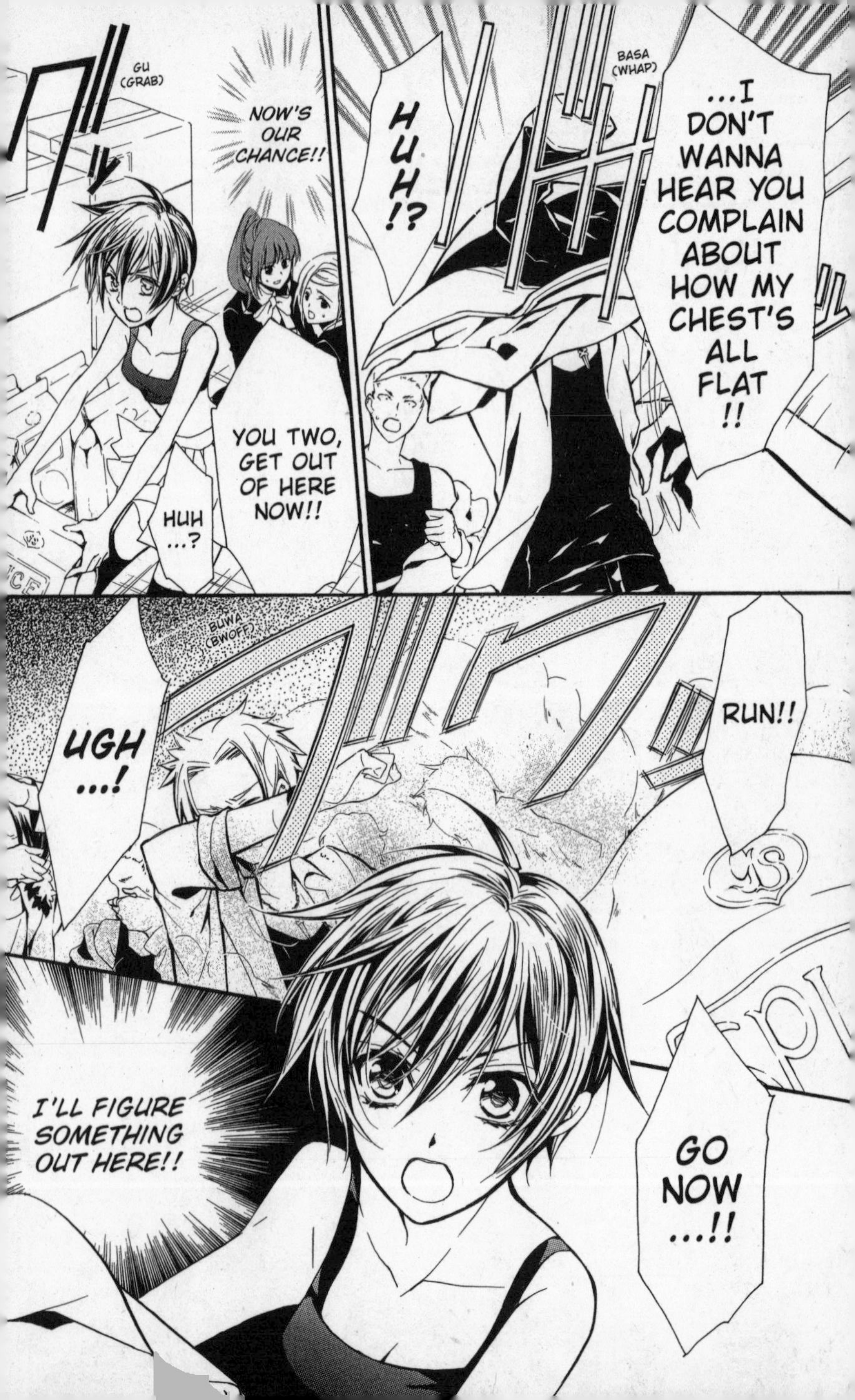
BASA (WHAP)
...I DON'T WANNA HEAR YOU COMPLAIN ABOUT HOW MY CHEST'S ALL FLAT!!
HUH!?
GU (GRAB)
NOW'S OUR CHANCE!!
YOU TWO, GET OUT OF HERE NOW!!
HUH...?
RUN!!
BUWA (BWOFF)
UGH...!
GO NOW...!!
I'LL FIGURE SOMETHING OUT HERE!!

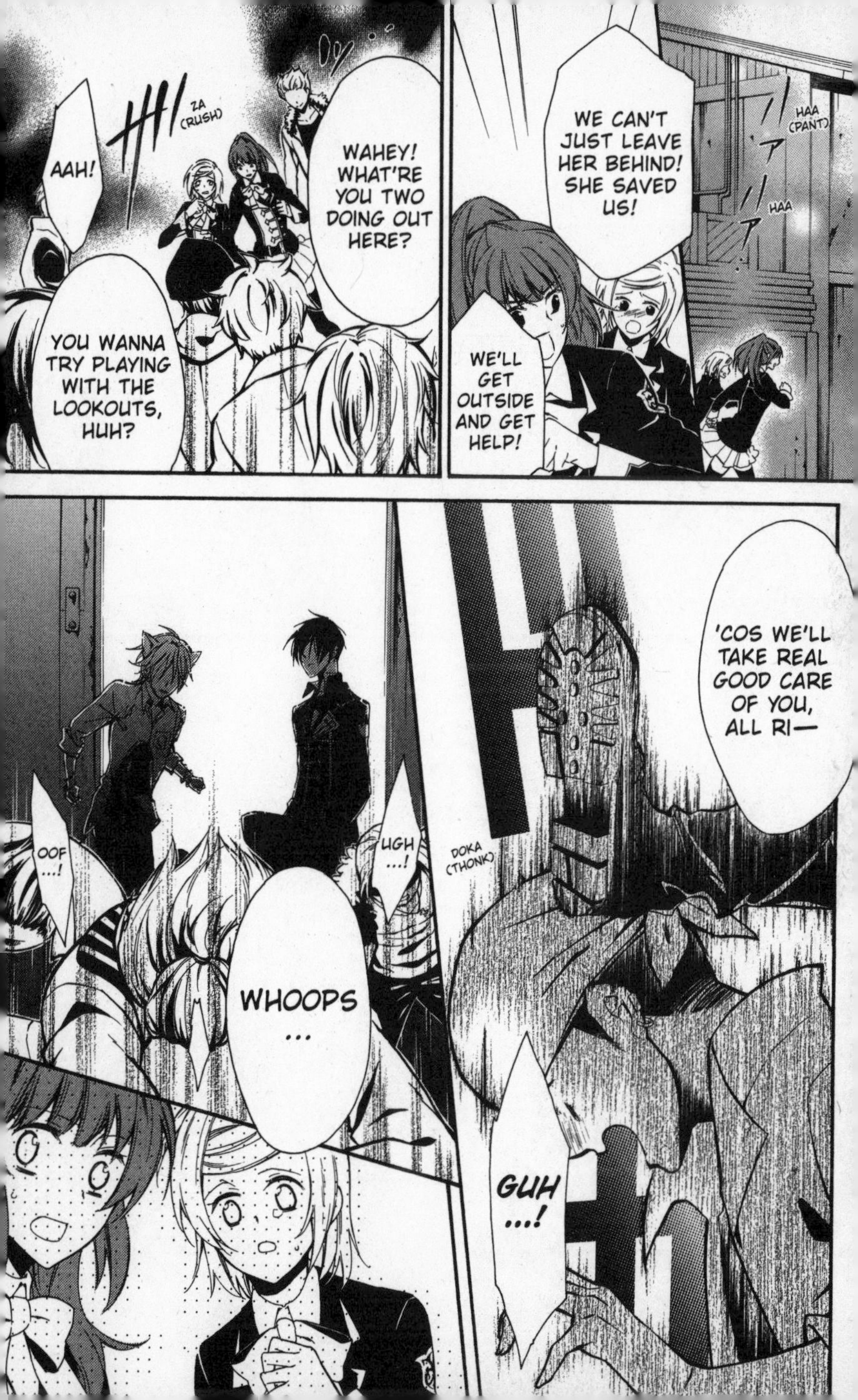
WE CAN'T JUST LEAVE HER BEHIND! SHE SAVED US!
HAA (PANT)
HAA
WE'LL GET OUTSIDE AND GET HELP!
WAHEY! WHAT'RE YOU TWO DOING OUT HERE?
ZA (RUSH)
AAH!
YOU WANNA TRY PLAYING WITH THE LOOKOUTS, HUH?
'COS WE'LL TAKE REAL GOOD CARE OF YOU, ALL RI—
DOKA (THONK)
GUH ...!
UGH ...!
OOF ...!
WHOOPS ...

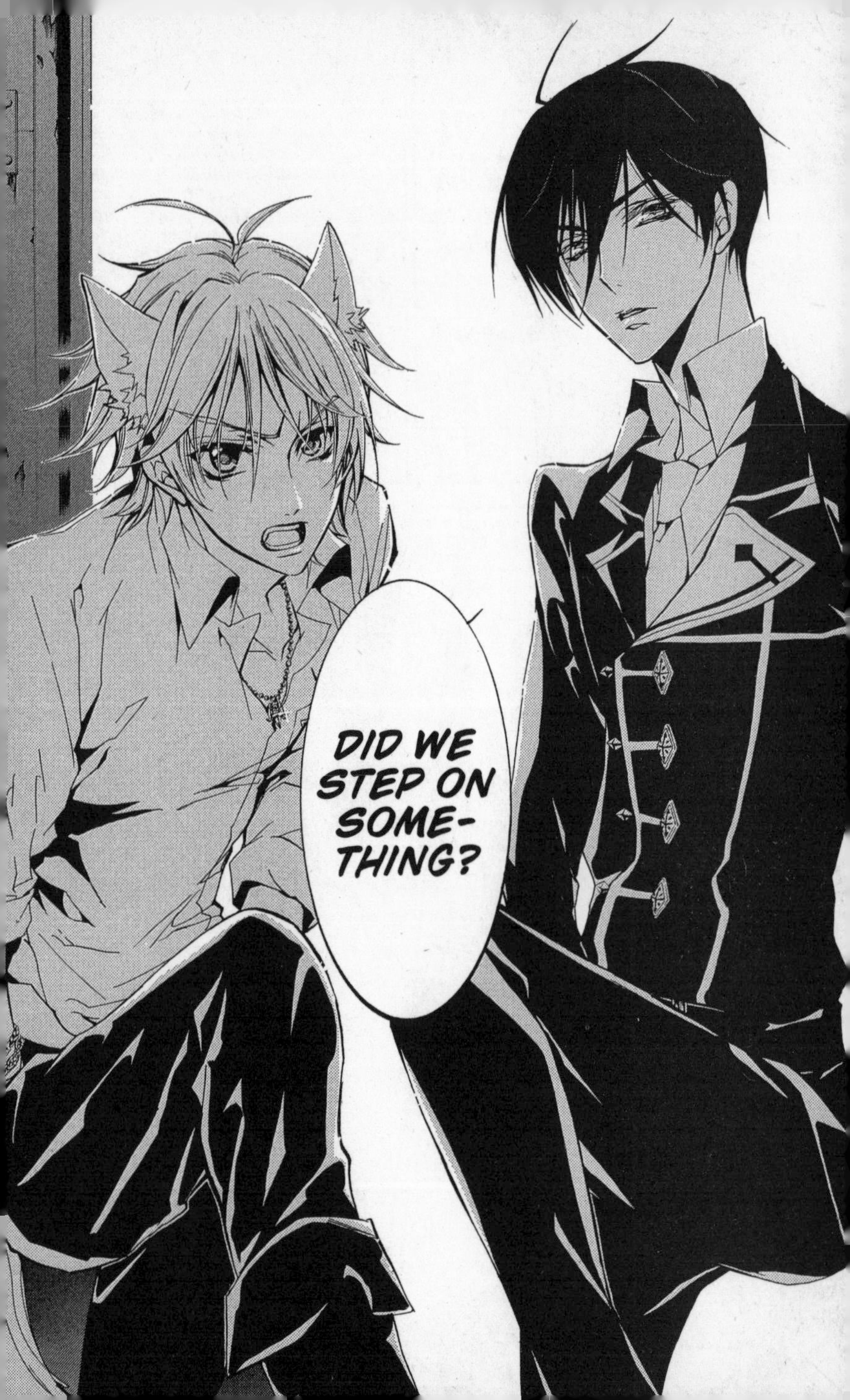
DID WE STEP ON SOME-THING?

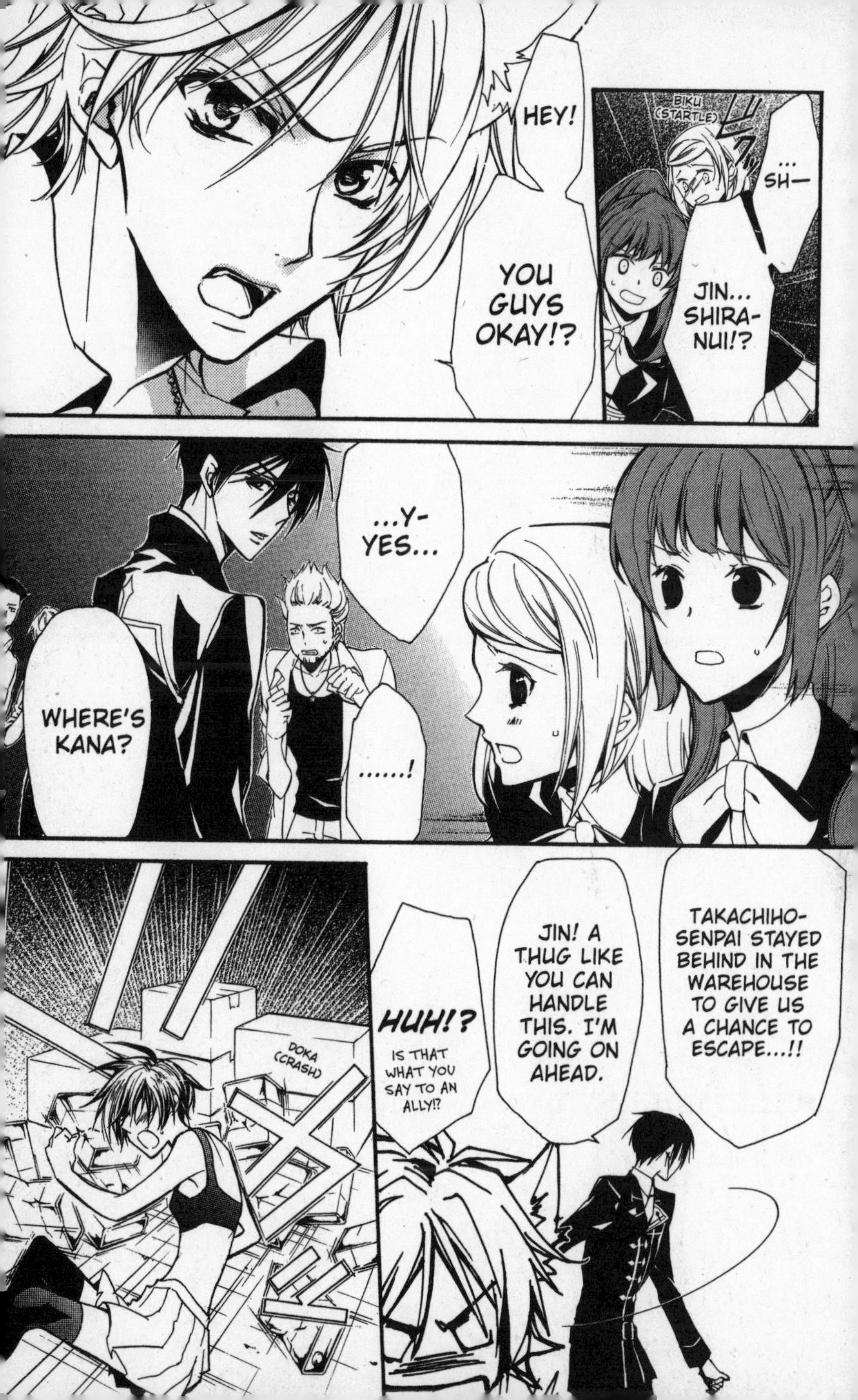
BIKU (STARTLE)
...SH—
JIN... SHIRA-NUI!?
HEY!
YOU GUYS OKAY!?
...Y- YES...
......!
WHERE'S KANA?
TAKACHIHO-SENPAI STAYED BEHIND IN THE WAREHOUSE TO GIVE US A CHANCE TO ESCAPE...!!
JIN! A THUG LIKE YOU CAN HANDLE THIS. I'M GOING ON AHEAD.
HUH!?
IS THAT WHAT YOU SAY TO AN ALLY!?
DOKA (CRASH)

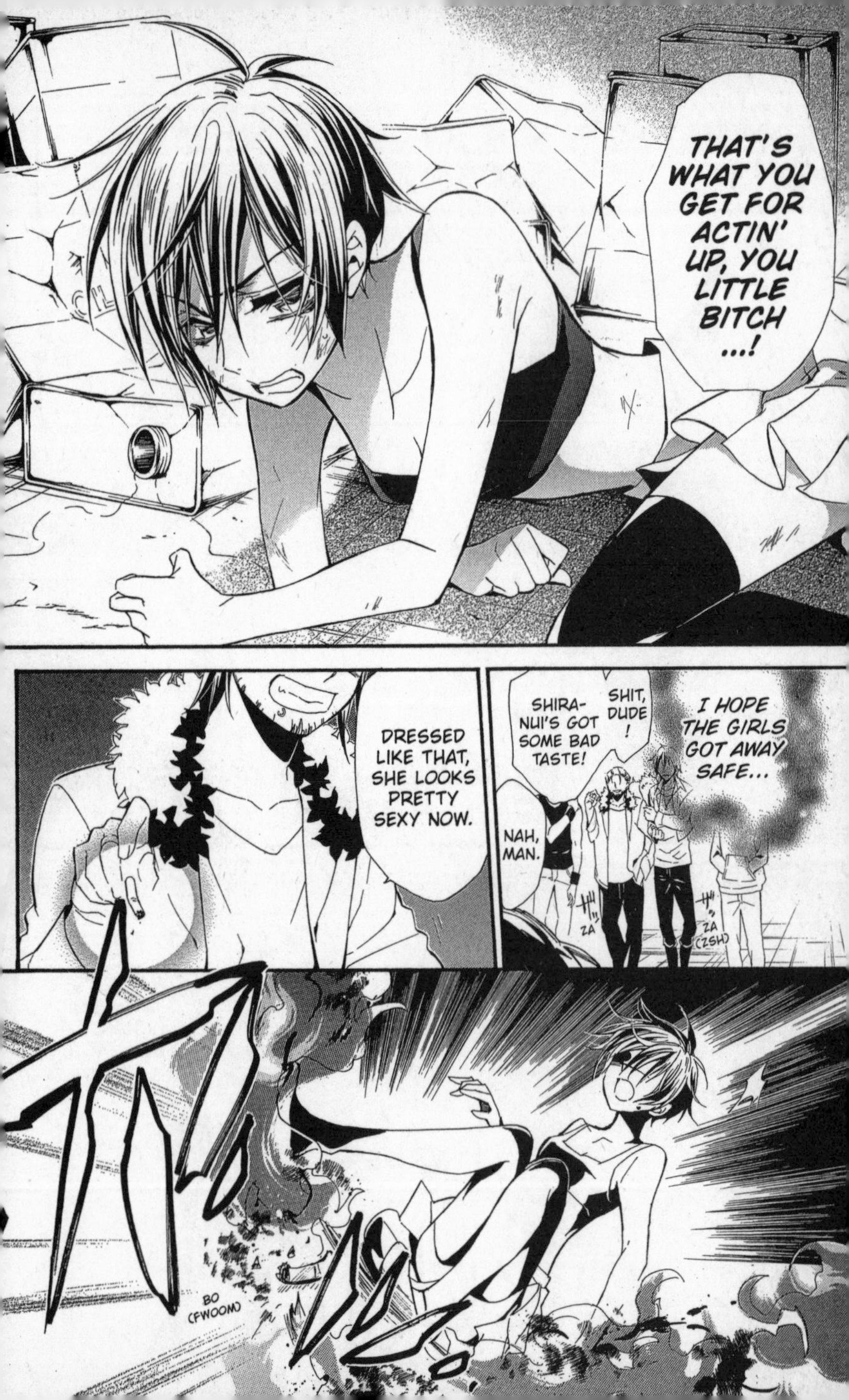
THAT'S WHAT YOU GET FOR ACTIN' UP, YOU LITTLE BITCH ...!
I HOPE THE GIRLS GOT AWAY SAFE...
SHIT, DUDE!
SHIRA-NUI'S GOT SOME BAD TASTE!
NAH, MAN.
ZA (ZSH)
ZA
DRESSED LIKE THAT, SHE LOOKS PRETTY SEXY NOW.
BO (FWOOM)

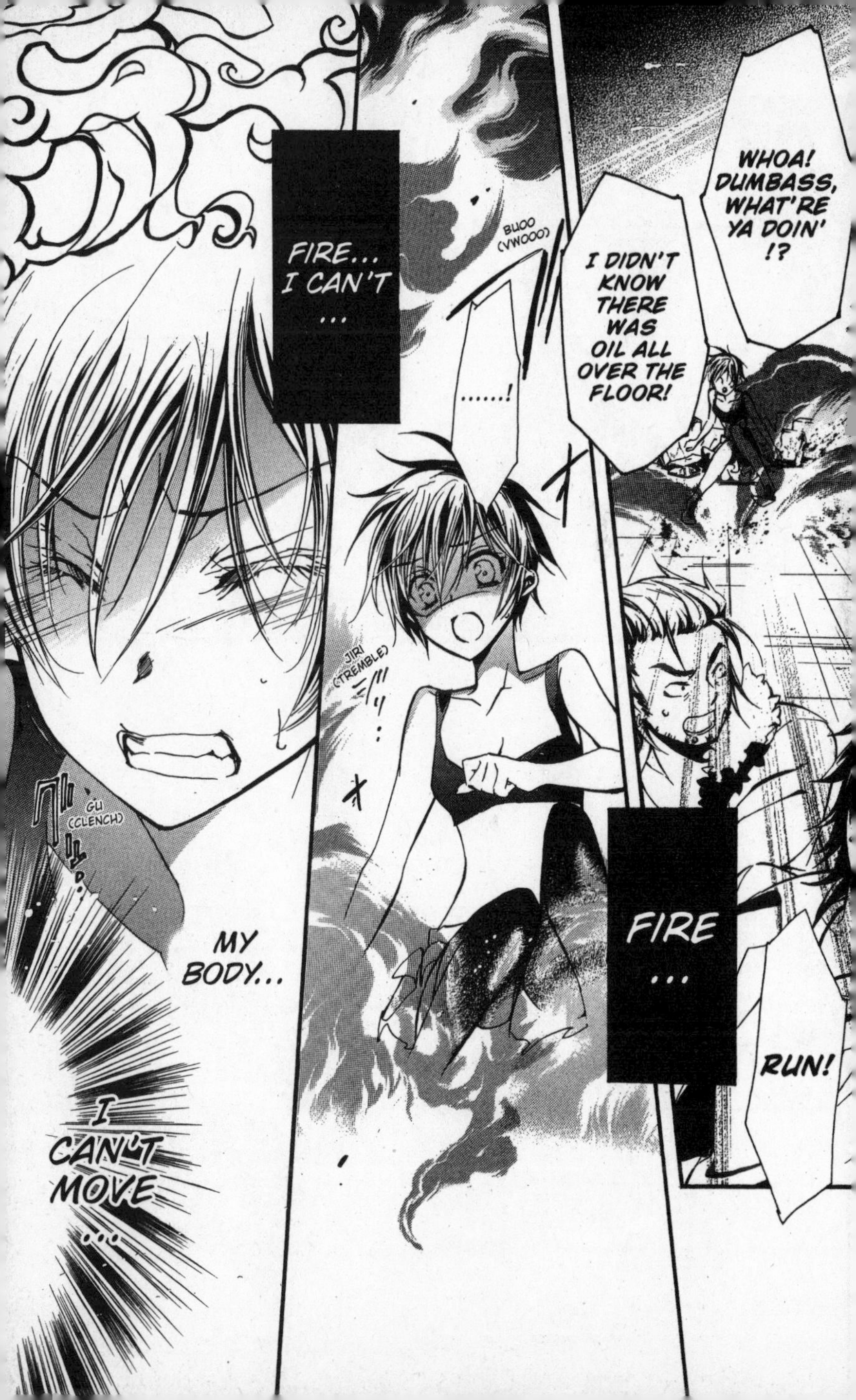
WHOA! DUMBASS, WHAT'RE YA DOIN'!?
I DIDN'T KNOW THERE WAS OIL ALL OVER THE FLOOR!
RUN!
FIRE...
BUOO (VWOOO)
......!
JIRI (TREMBLE)
FIRE... I CAN'T ...
GU (CLENCH)
MY BODY...
I CAN'T MOVE ...

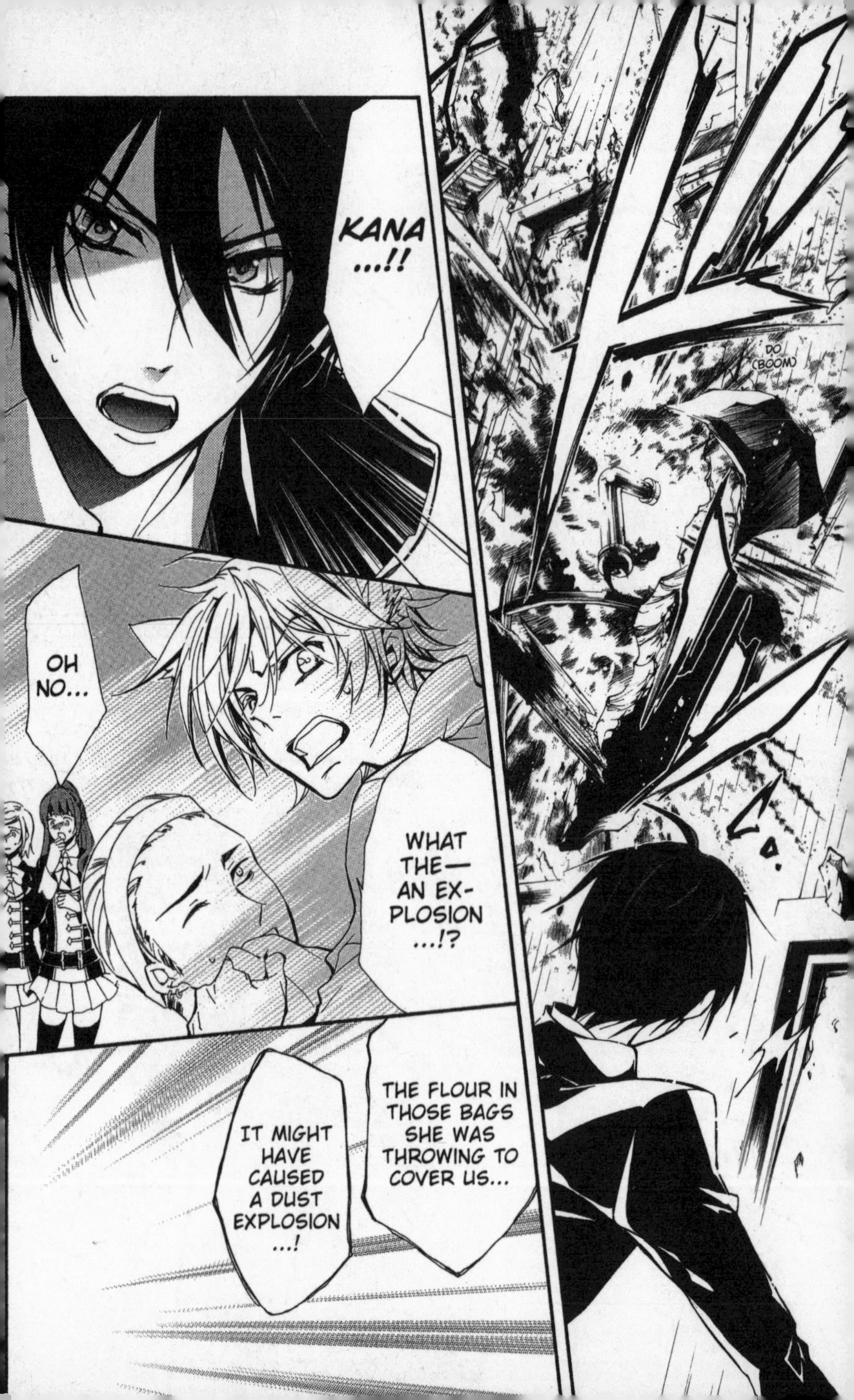
DO
(BOOM)
KANA ...!!
WHAT THE— AN EX-PLOSION ...!?
OH NO...
THE FLOUR IN THOSE BAGS SHE WAS THROWING TO COVER US...
IT MIGHT HAVE CAUSED A DUST EXPLOSION ...!

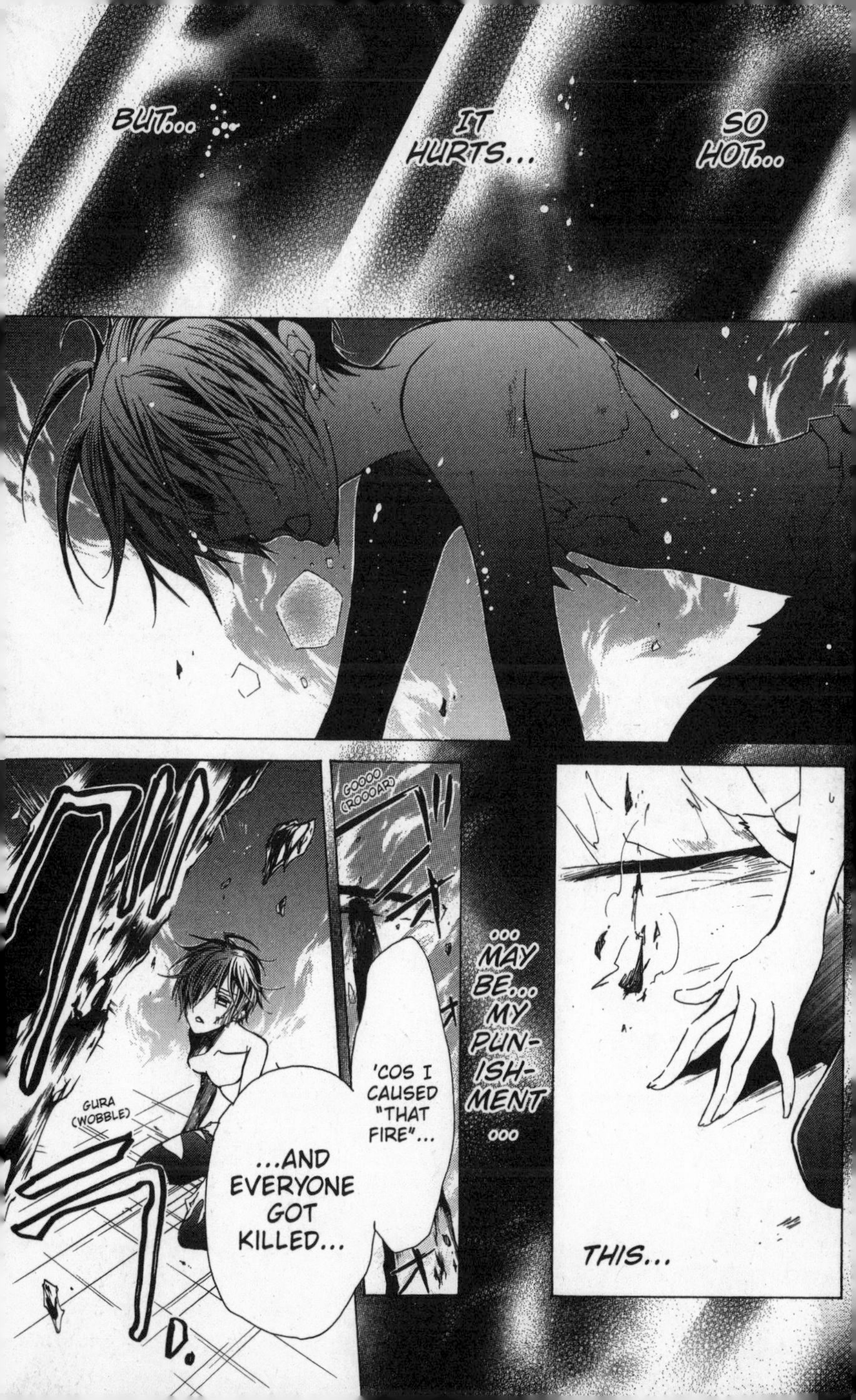
SO HOT...
IT HURTS...
BUT...
THIS...
...MAYBE... MY PUNISHMENT...
GOOOO (ROOOAR)
'COS I CAUSED "THAT FIRE"...
...AND EVERYONE GOT KILLED...
GURA (WOBBLE)

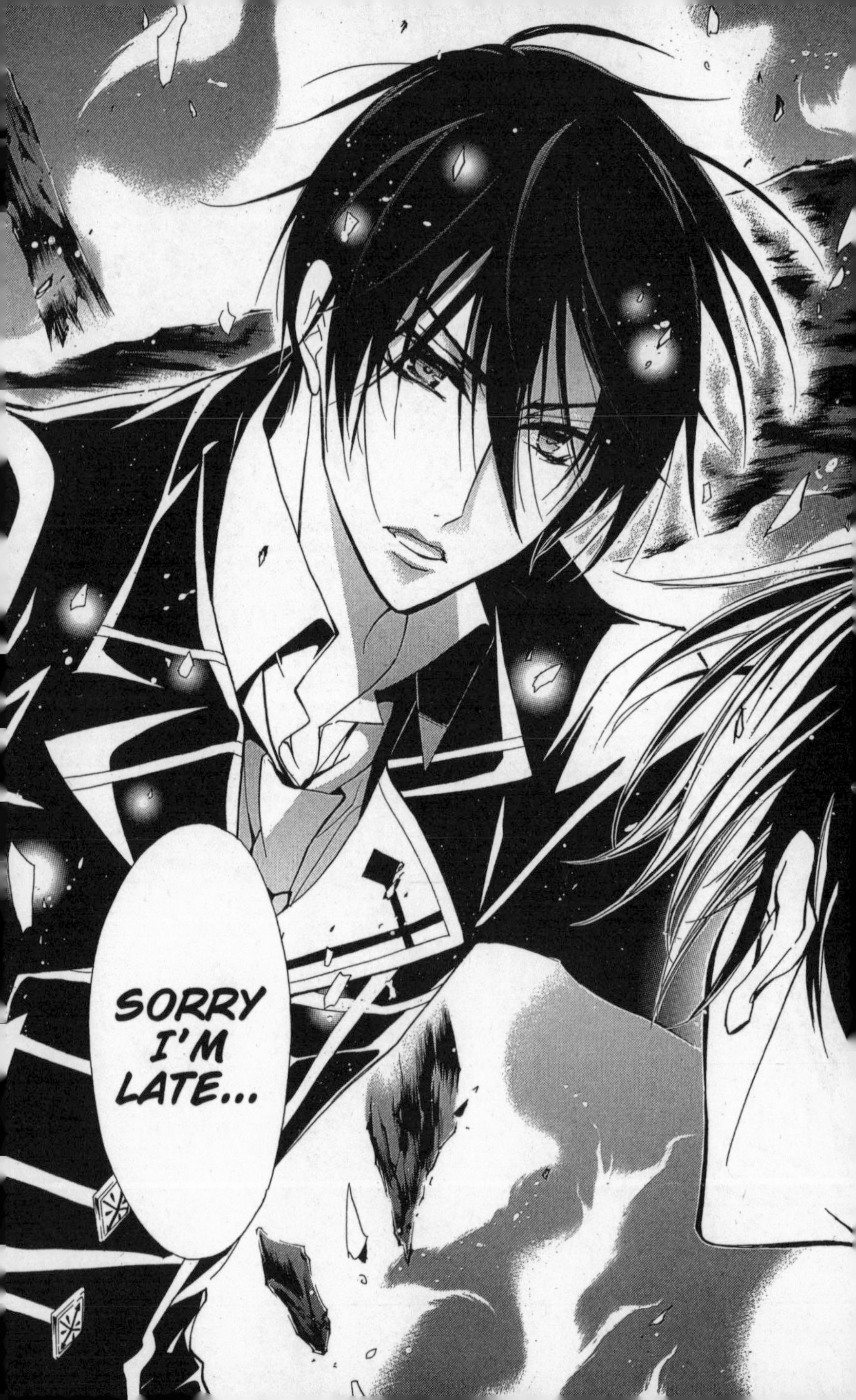
SORRY I'M LATE...

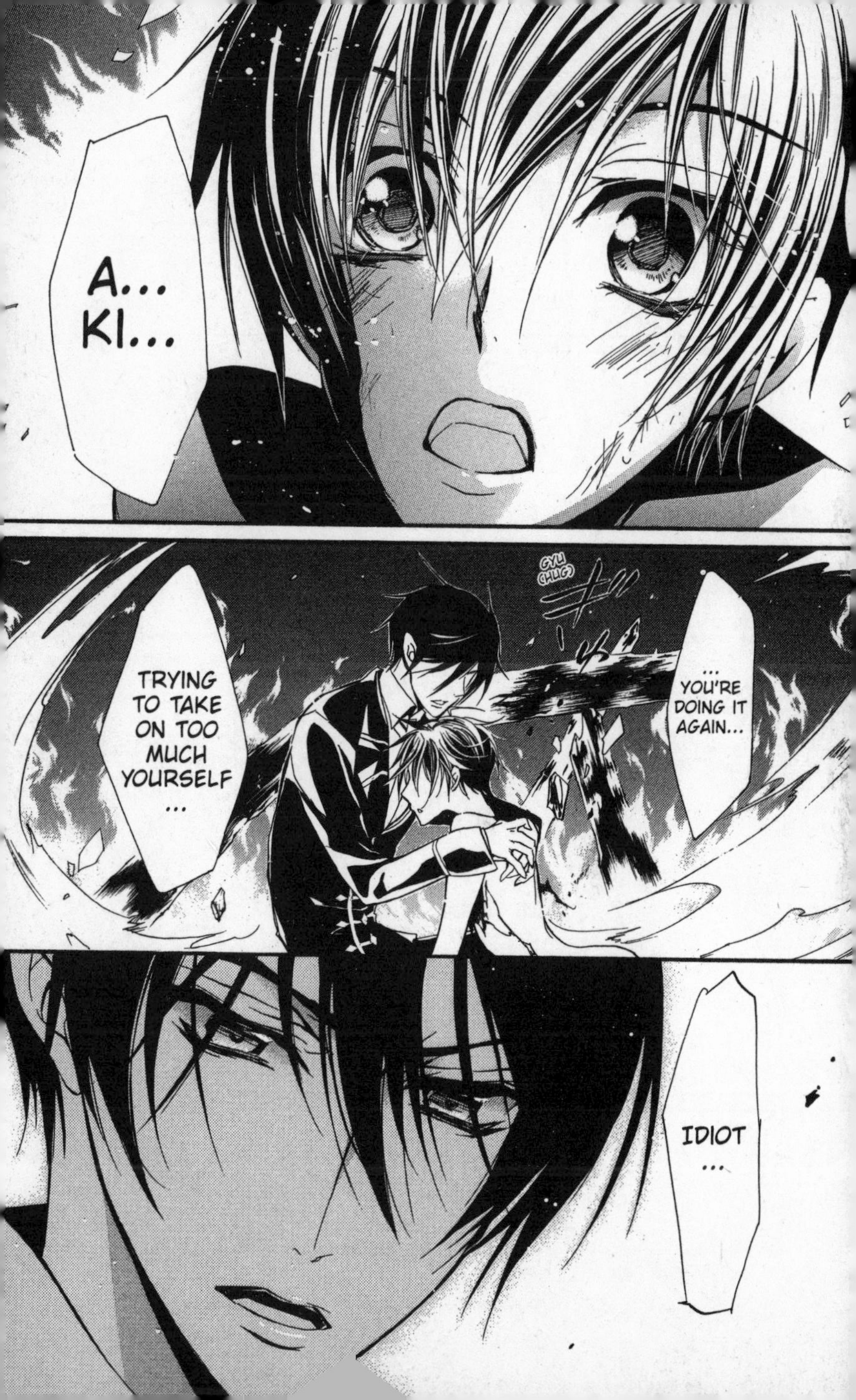
A... KI...
... YOU'RE DOING IT AGAIN...
GYU (HUG)
TRYING TO TAKE ON TOO MUCH YOURSELF ...
IDIOT ...

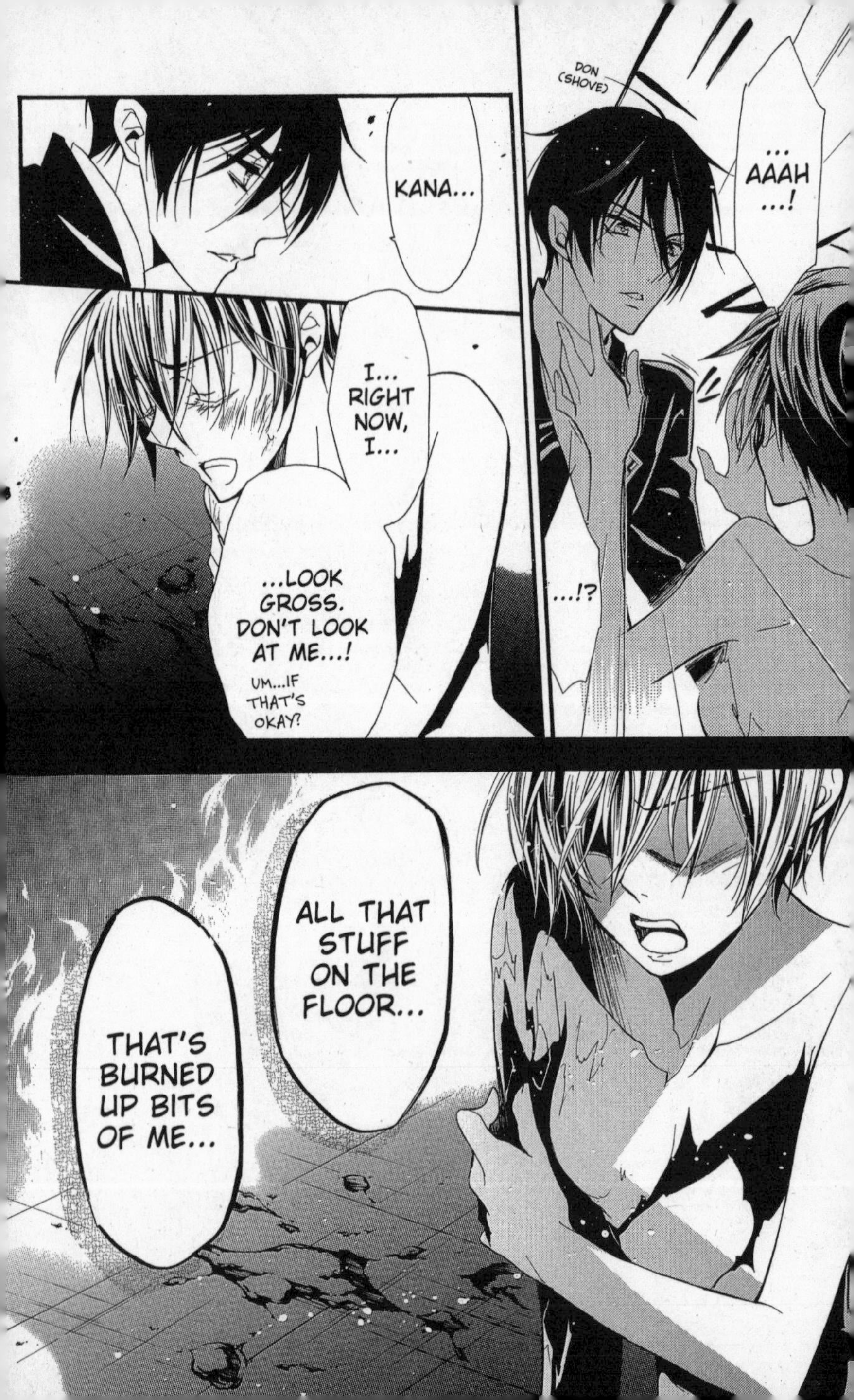
DON (SHOVE)
...AAAH...!
...!?
KANA...
I... RIGHT NOW, I...
...LOOK GROSS. DON'T LOOK AT ME...!
UM...IF THAT'S OKAY?
ALL THAT STUFF ON THE FLOOR...
THAT'S BURNED UP BITS OF ME...

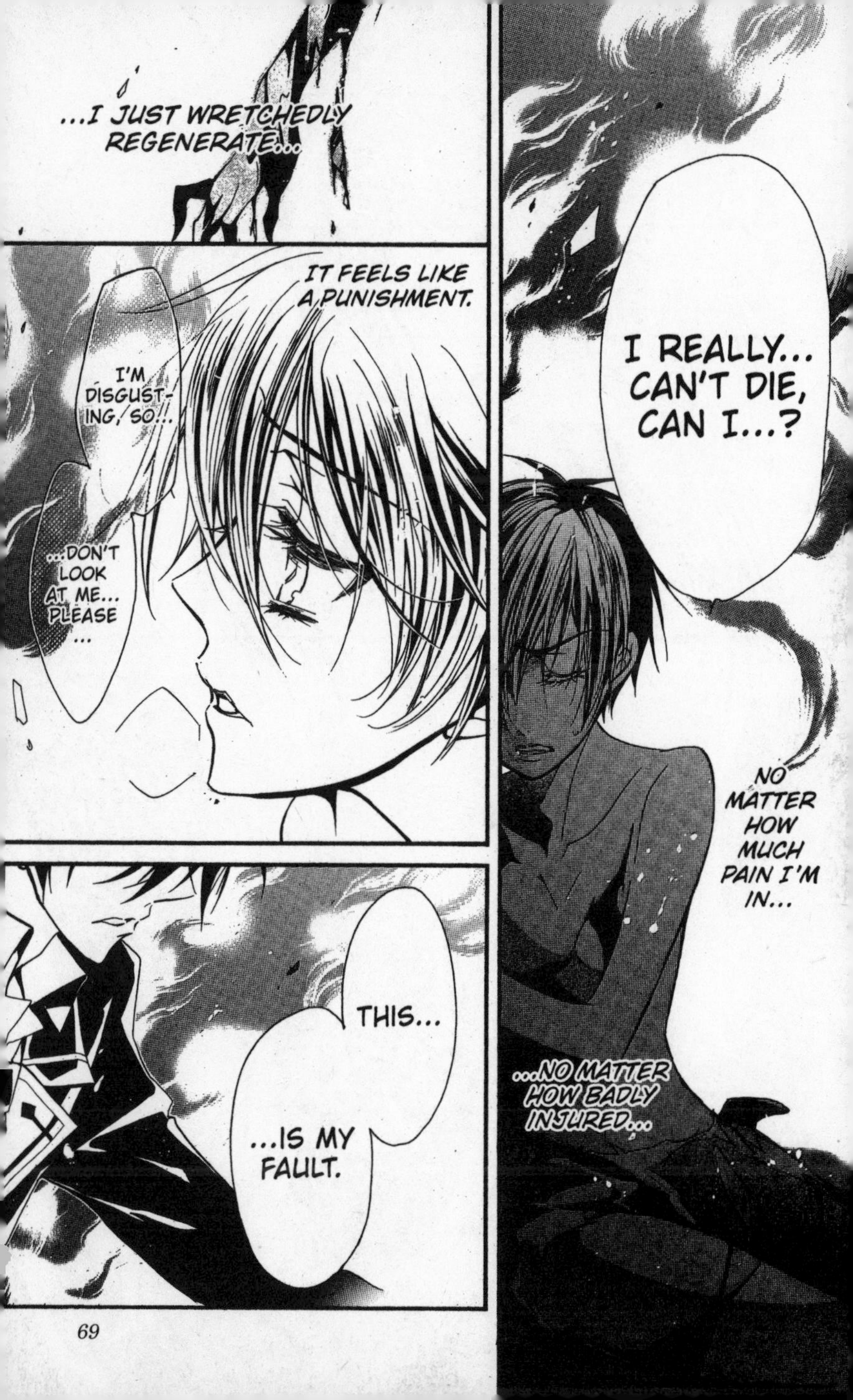
I REALLY... CAN'T DIE, CAN I...?
NO MATTER HOW MUCH PAIN I'M IN...
...NO MATTER HOW BADLY INJURED...
...I JUST WRETCHEDLY REGENERATE...
IT FEELS LIKE A PUNISHMENT.
I'M DISGUSTING, SO...
...DON'T LOOK AT ME... PLEASE...
THIS...
...IS MY FAULT.

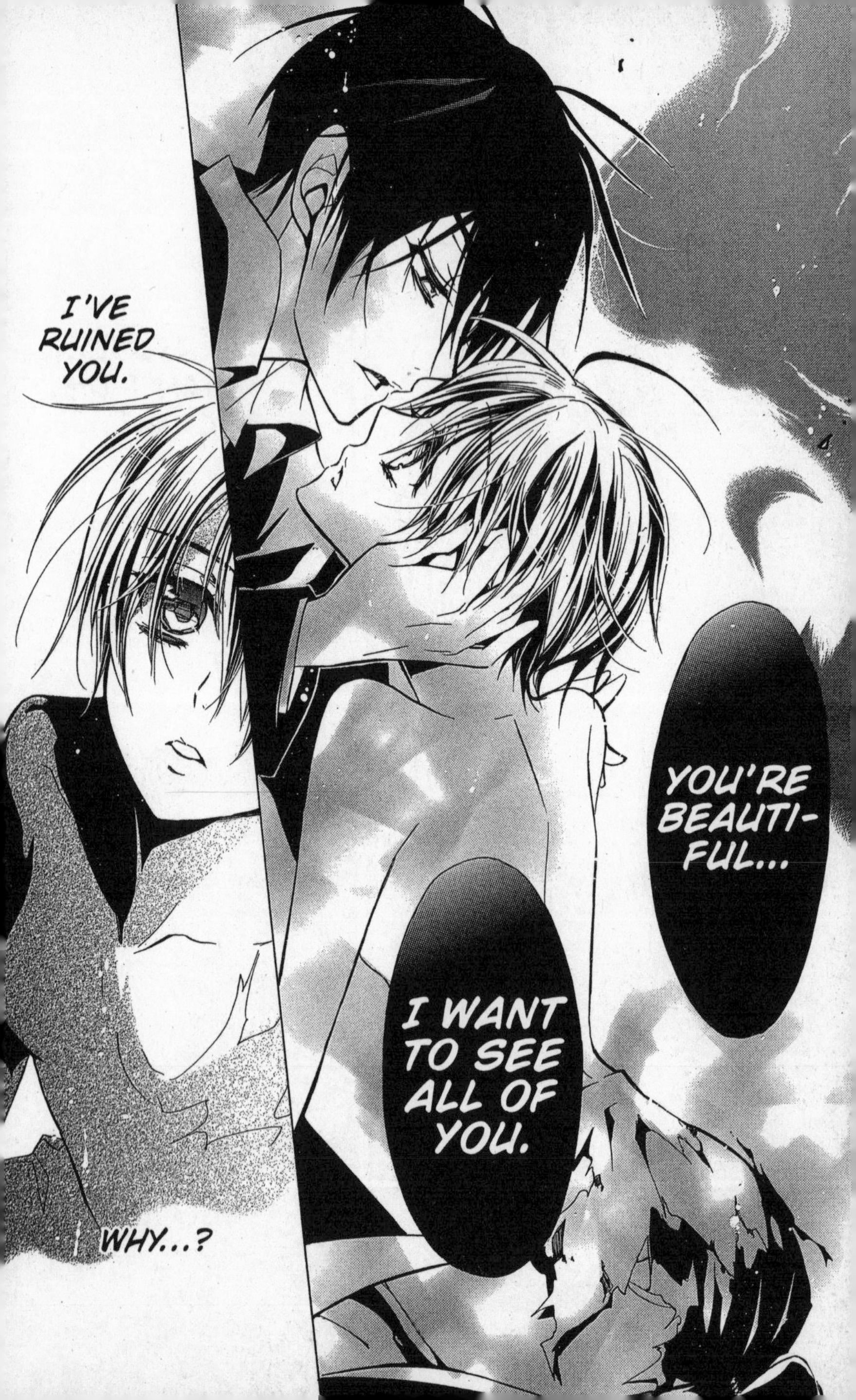
YOU'RE BEAUTI-FUL...
I WANT TO SEE ALL OF YOU.
I'VE RUINED YOU.
WHY...?

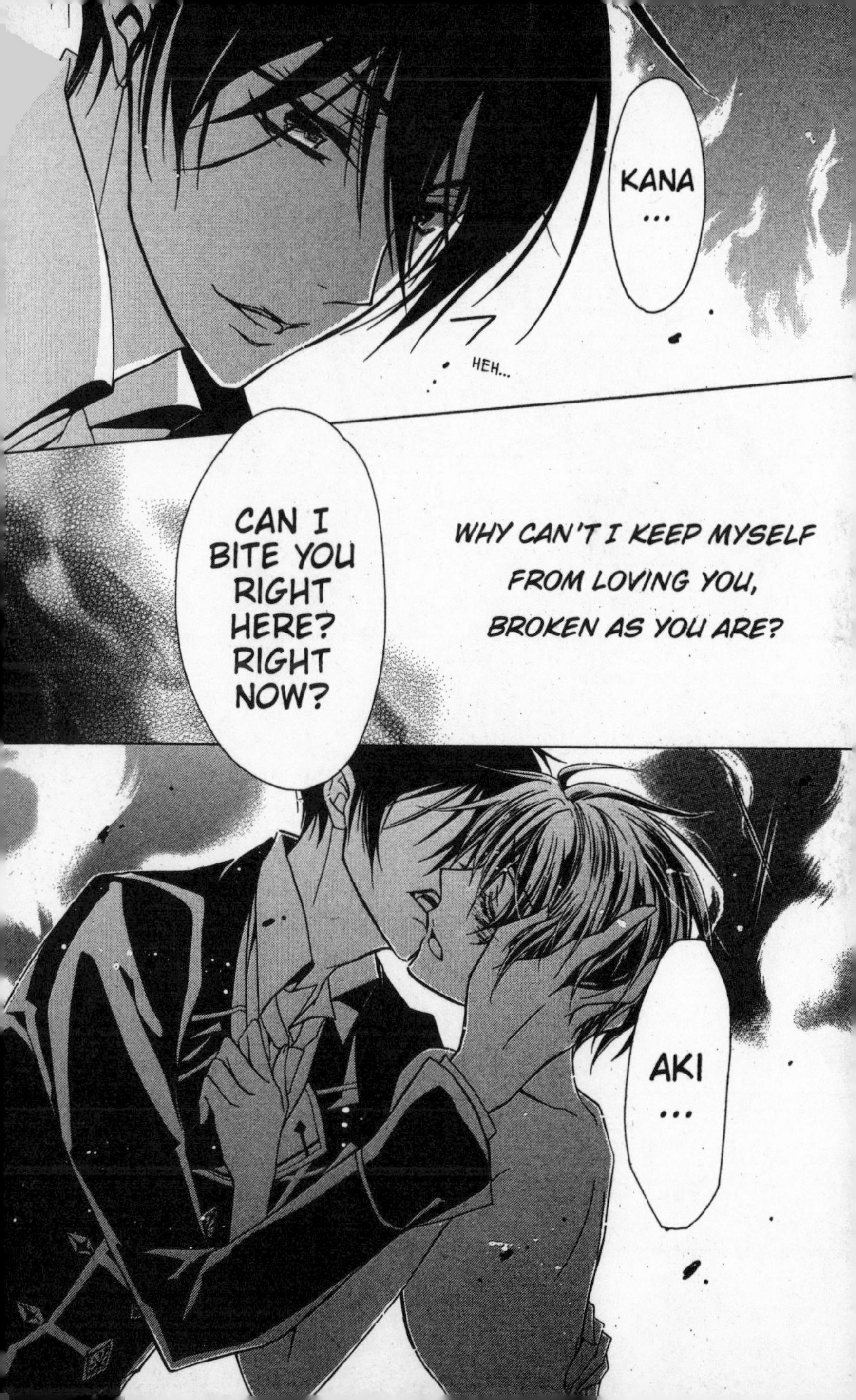
KANA ...
HEH...
WHY CAN'T I KEEP MYSELF FROM LOVING YOU, BROKEN AS YOU ARE?
CAN I BITE YOU RIGHT HERE? RIGHT NOW?
AKI ...

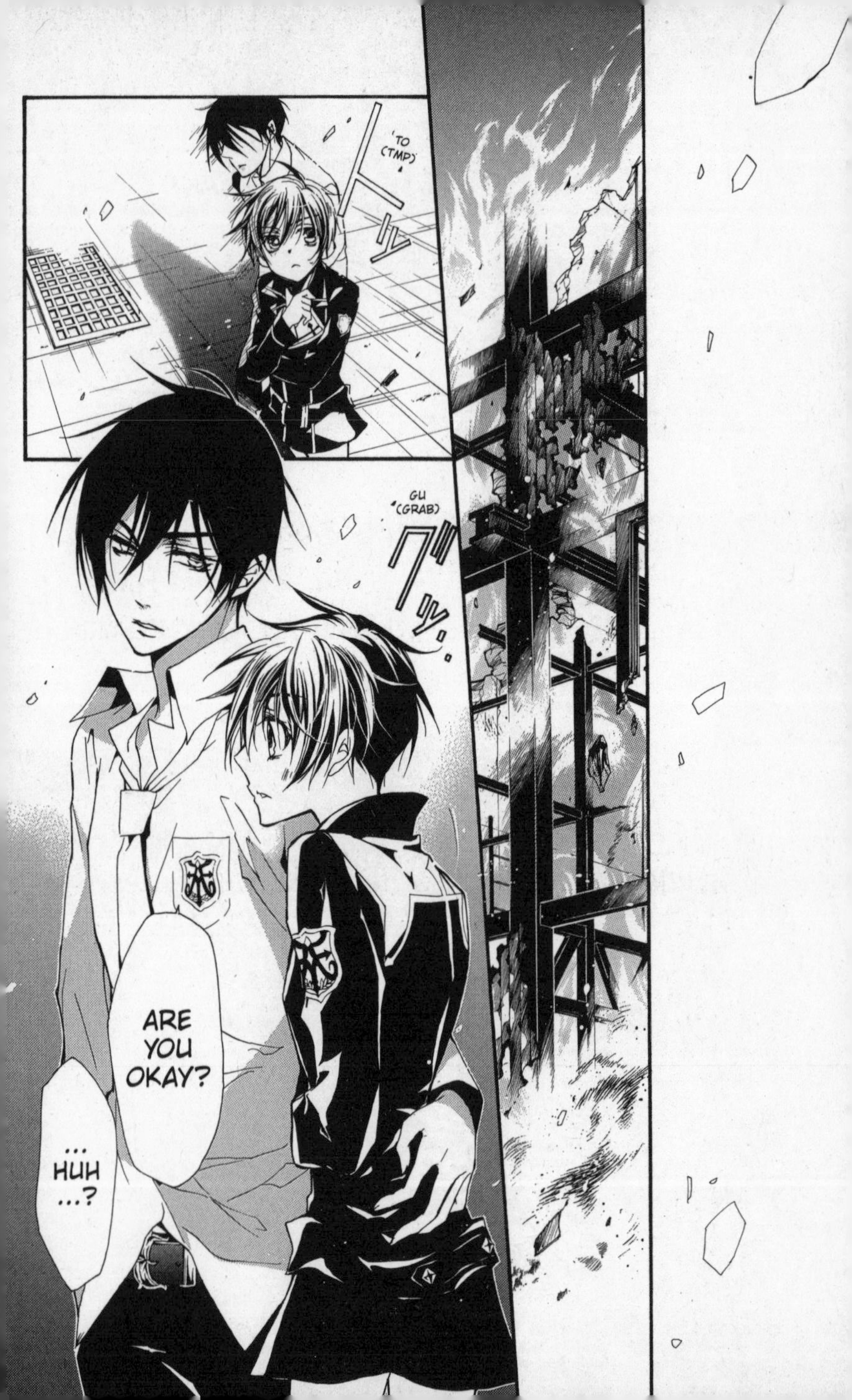
TO (TMP)
トッ
GU (GRAB)
グッ
ARE YOU OKAY?
...HUH ...?

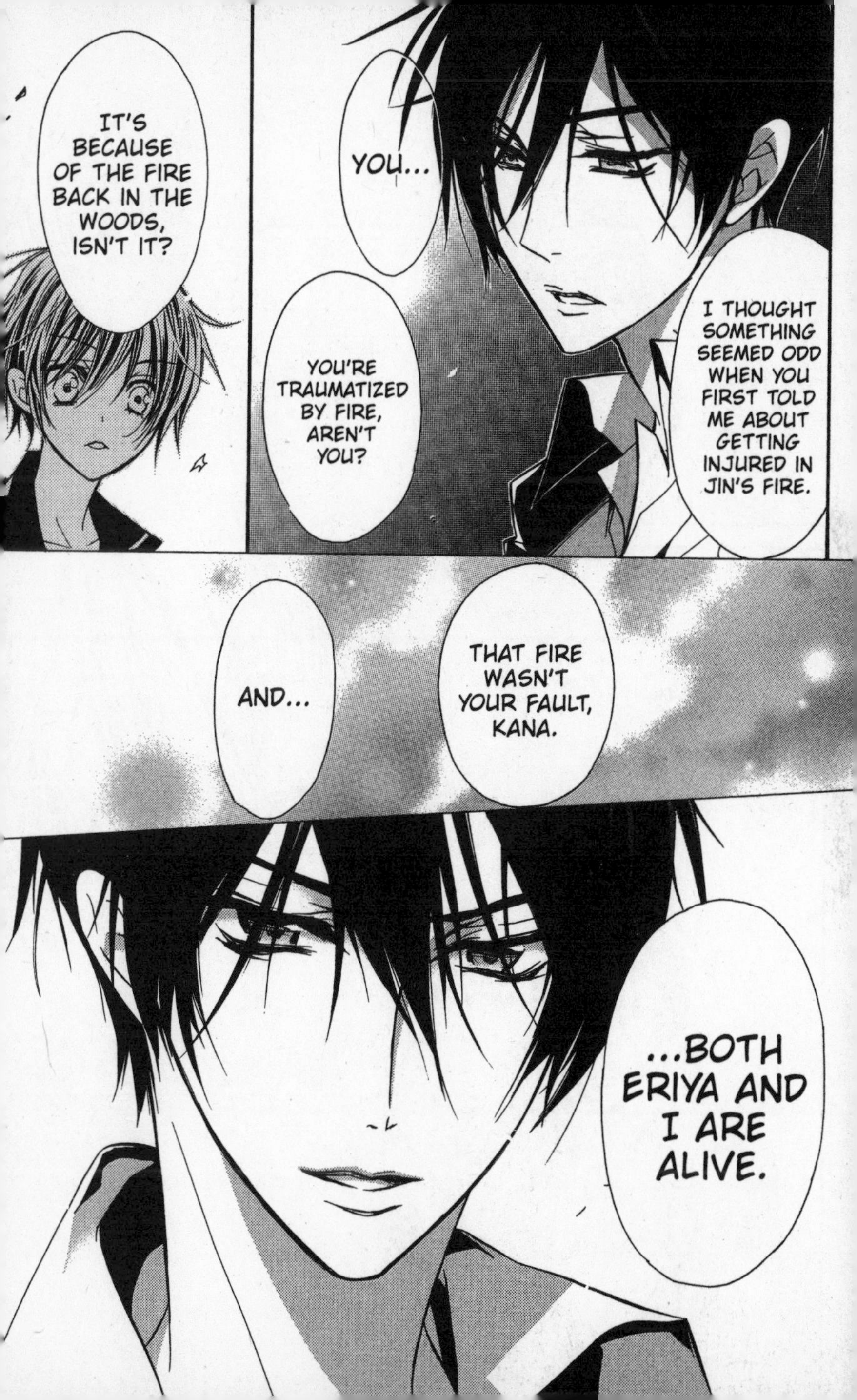
I THOUGHT SOMETHING SEEMED ODD WHEN YOU FIRST TOLD ME ABOUT GETTING INJURED IN JIN'S FIRE.
YOU...
YOU'RE TRAUMATIZED BY FIRE, AREN'T YOU?
IT'S BECAUSE OF THE FIRE BACK IN THE WOODS, ISN'T IT?
THAT FIRE WASN'T YOUR FAULT, KANA.
AND...
...BOTH ERIYA AND I ARE ALIVE.

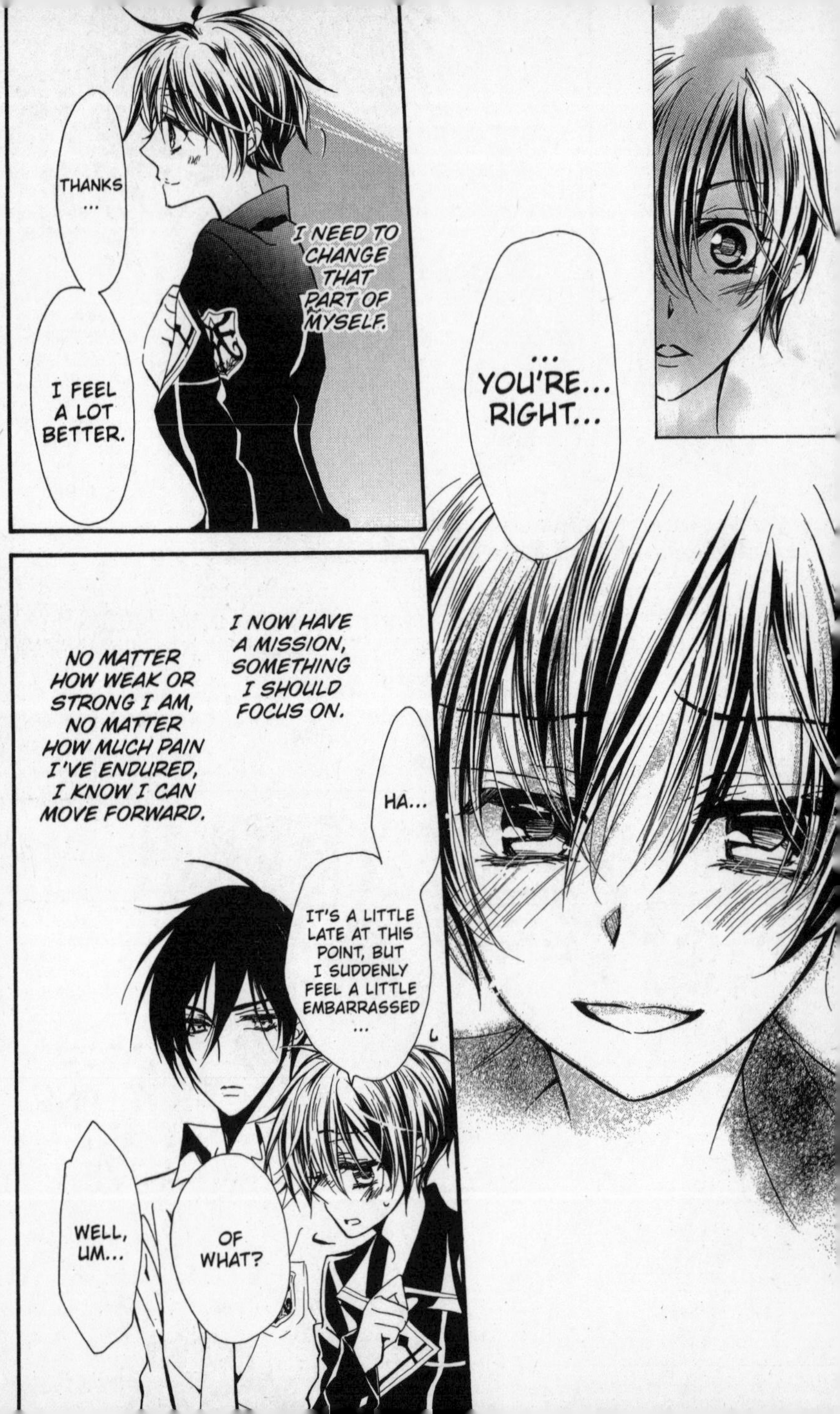

... YOU'RE... RIGHT...
THANKS ...
I FEEL A LOT BETTER.
I NEED TO CHANGE THAT PART OF MYSELF.
I NOW HAVE A MISSION, SOMETHING I SHOULD FOCUS ON.
NO MATTER HOW WEAK OR STRONG I AM, NO MATTER HOW MUCH PAIN I'VE ENDURED, I KNOW I CAN MOVE FORWARD.
HA...
IT'S A LITTLE LATE AT THIS POINT, BUT I SUDDENLY FEEL A LITTLE EMBARRASSED ...
OF WHAT?
WELL, UM...

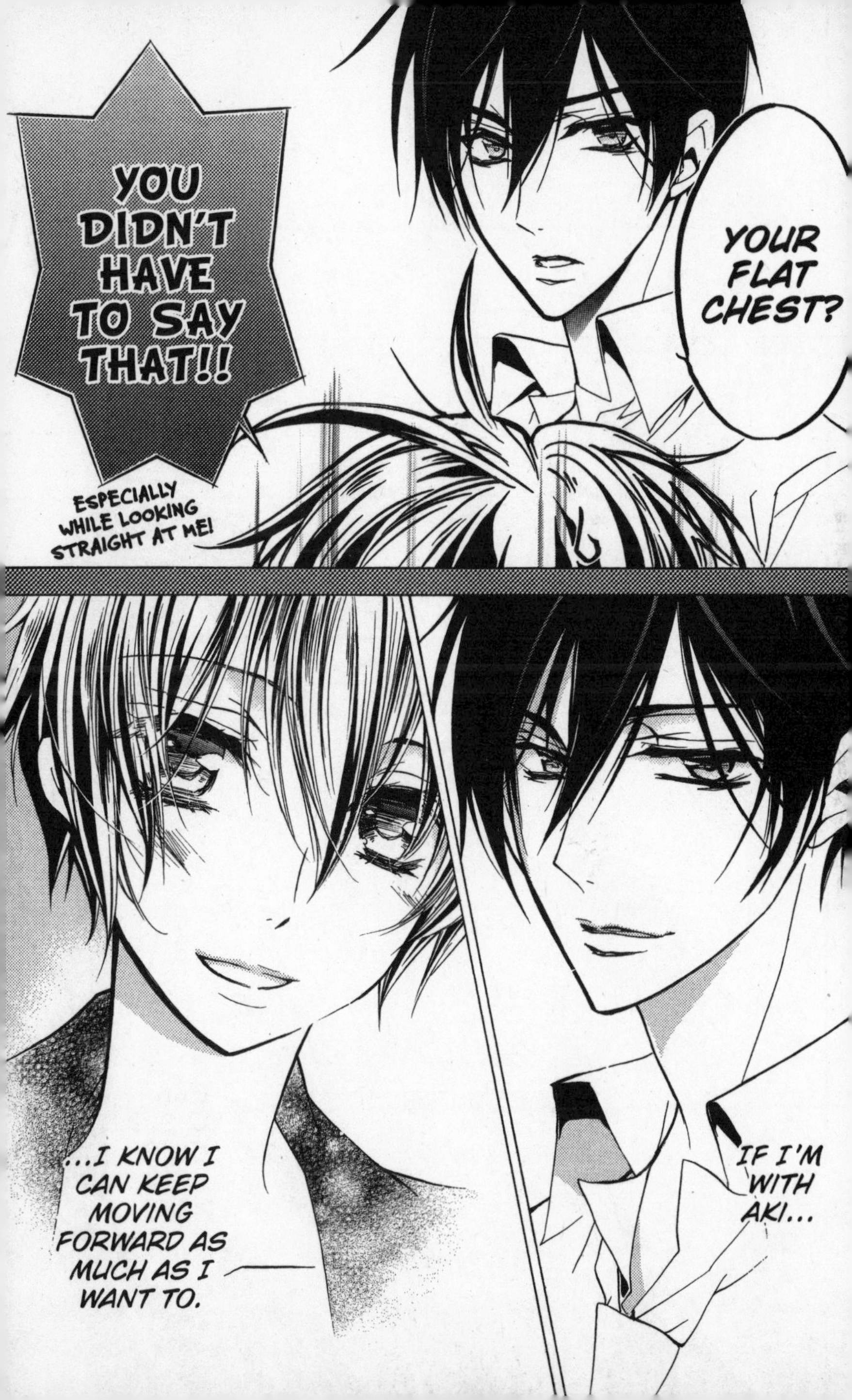
YOUR FLAT CHEST?
YOU DIDN'T HAVE TO SAY THAT!!
ESPECIALLY WHILE LOOKING STRAIGHT AT ME!
IF I'M WITH AKI...
...I KNOW I CAN KEEP MOVING FORWARD AS MUCH AS I WANT TO.

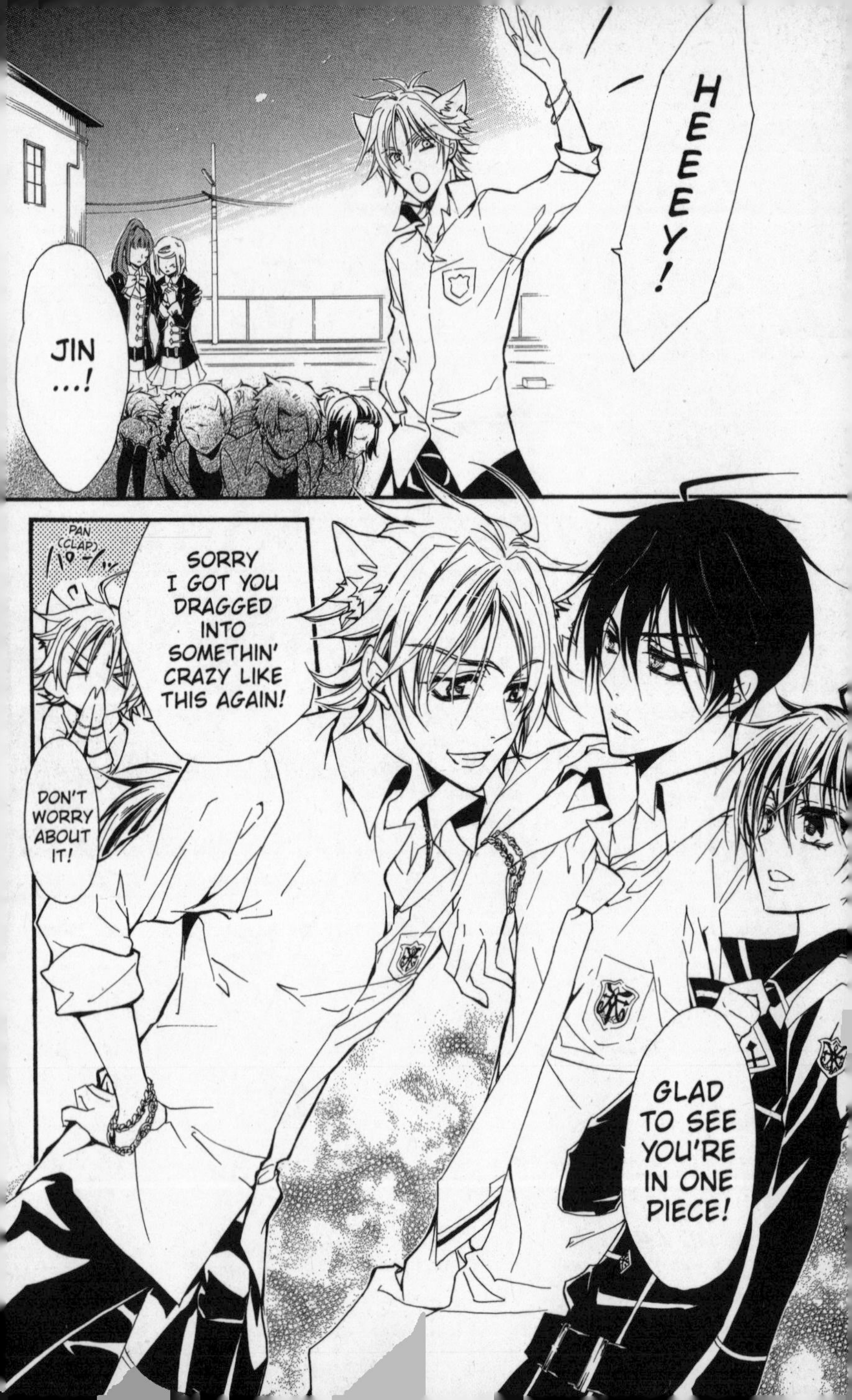
HEEEY!
JIN ...!
PAN (CLAP)
SORRY I GOT YOU DRAGGED INTO SOMETHIN' CRAZY LIKE THIS AGAIN!
DON'T WORRY ABOUT IT!
GLAD TO SEE YOU'RE IN ONE PIECE!

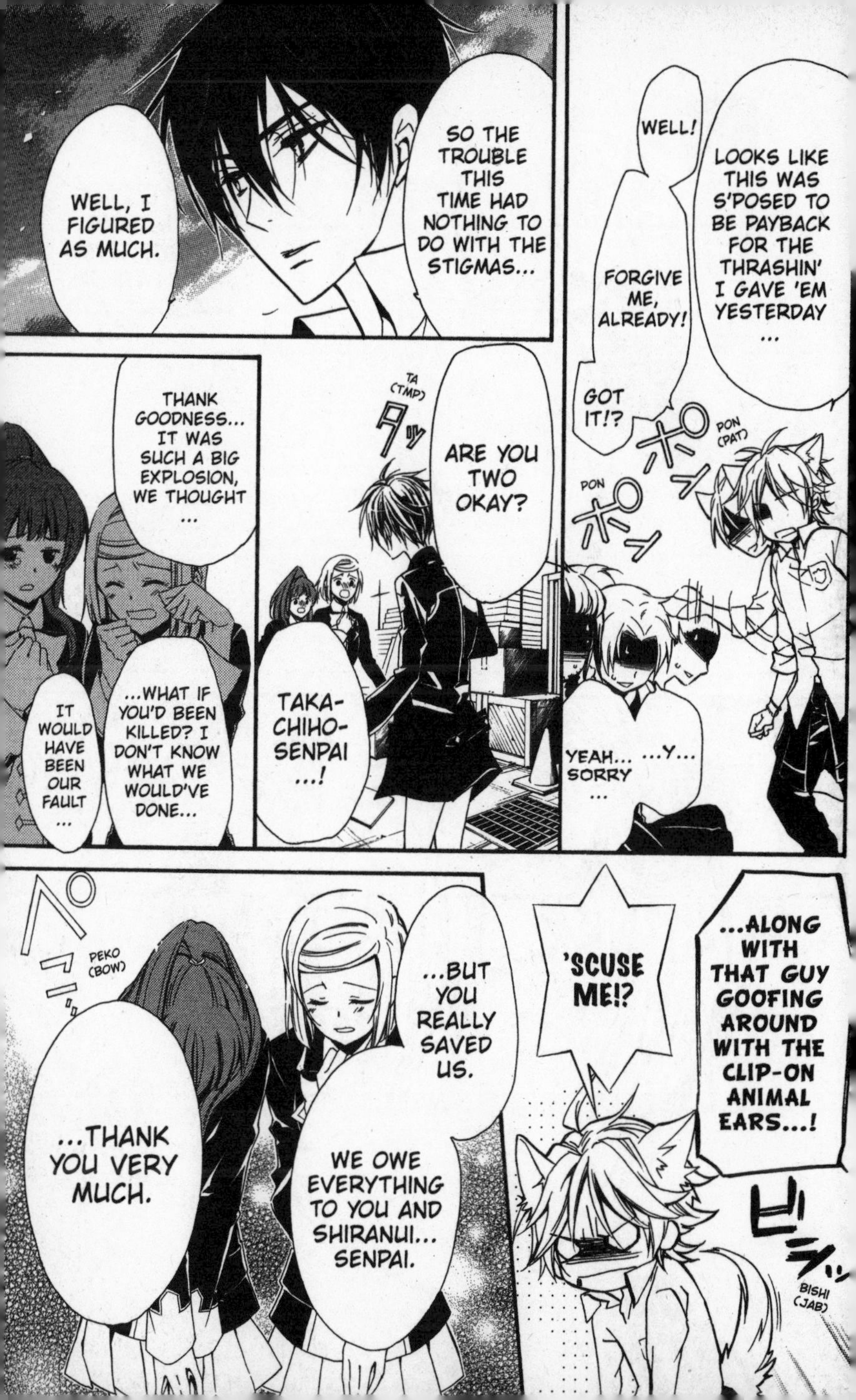
LOOKS LIKE THIS WAS S'POSED TO BE PAYBACK FOR THE THRASHIN' I GAVE 'EM YESTERDAY...
WELL! FORGIVE ME, ALREADY! GOT IT!?
PON (PAT)
PON
SO THE TROUBLE THIS TIME HAD NOTHING TO DO WITH THE STIGMAS...
WELL, I FIGURED AS MUCH.
...Y...
YEAH... SORRY...
TA (TMP)
ARE YOU TWO OKAY?
TAKA-CHIHO-SENPAI...!
THANK GOODNESS... IT WAS SUCH A BIG EXPLOSION, WE THOUGHT...
...WHAT IF YOU'D BEEN KILLED? I DON'T KNOW WHAT WE WOULD'VE DONE...
IT WOULD HAVE BEEN OUR FAULT...
...ALONG WITH THAT GUY GOOFING AROUND WITH THE CLIP-ON ANIMAL EARS...!
'SCUSE ME!?
BISHI (JAB)
...BUT YOU REALLY SAVED US.
WE OWE EVERYTHING TO YOU AND SHIRANUI... SENPAI.
PEKO (BOW)
...THANK YOU VERY MUCH.

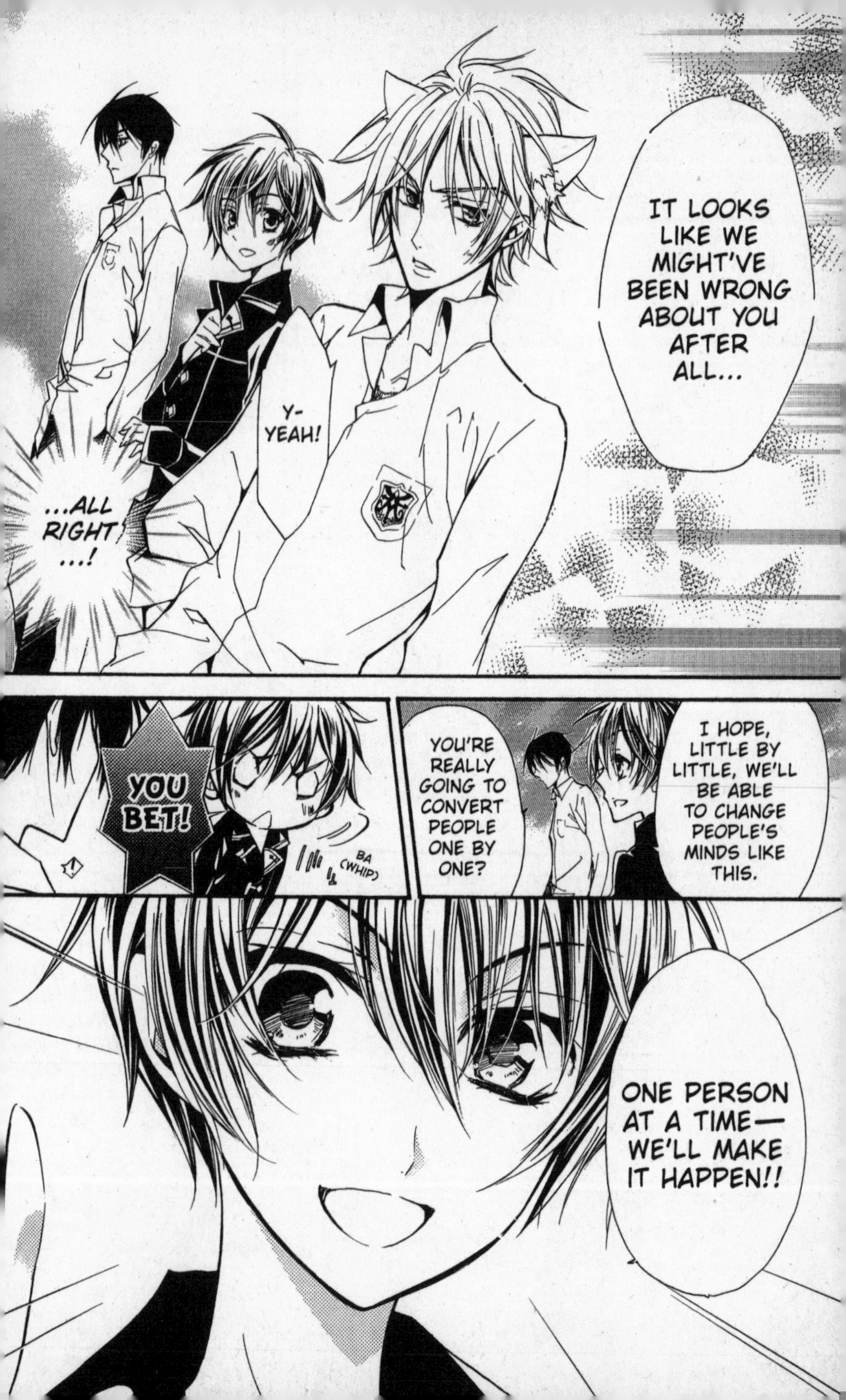
IT LOOKS LIKE WE MIGHT'VE BEEN WRONG ABOUT YOU AFTER ALL...
Y-YEAH!
...ALL RIGHT ...!
I HOPE, LITTLE BY LITTLE, WE'LL BE ABLE TO CHANGE PEOPLE'S MINDS LIKE THIS.
YOU'RE REALLY GOING TO CONVERT PEOPLE ONE BY ONE?
YOU BET!
BA (WHIP)
ONE PERSON AT A TIME—WE'LL MAKE IT HAPPEN!!

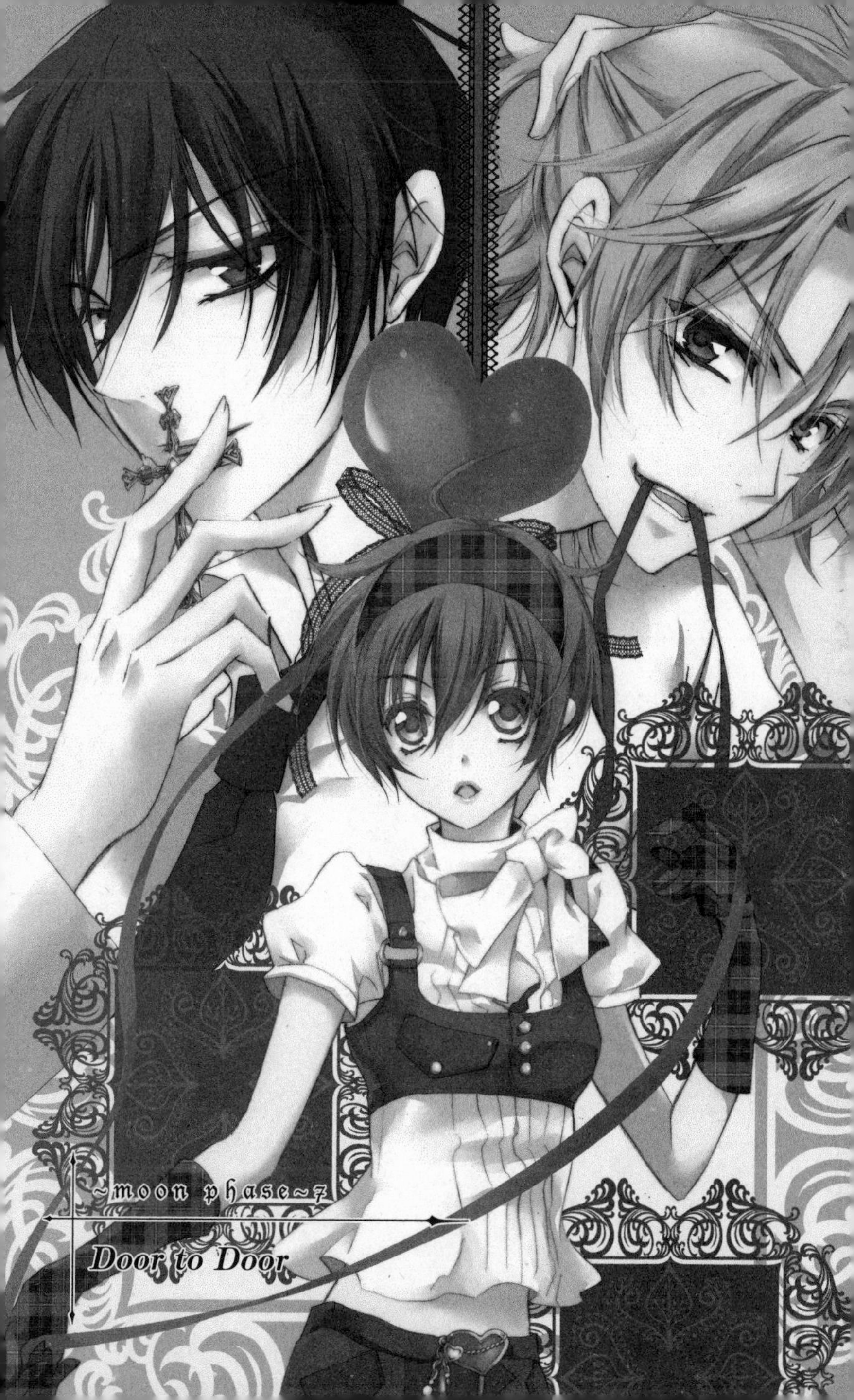
~moon phase~7
Door to Door

He's my only vampire
Aya Shouoto

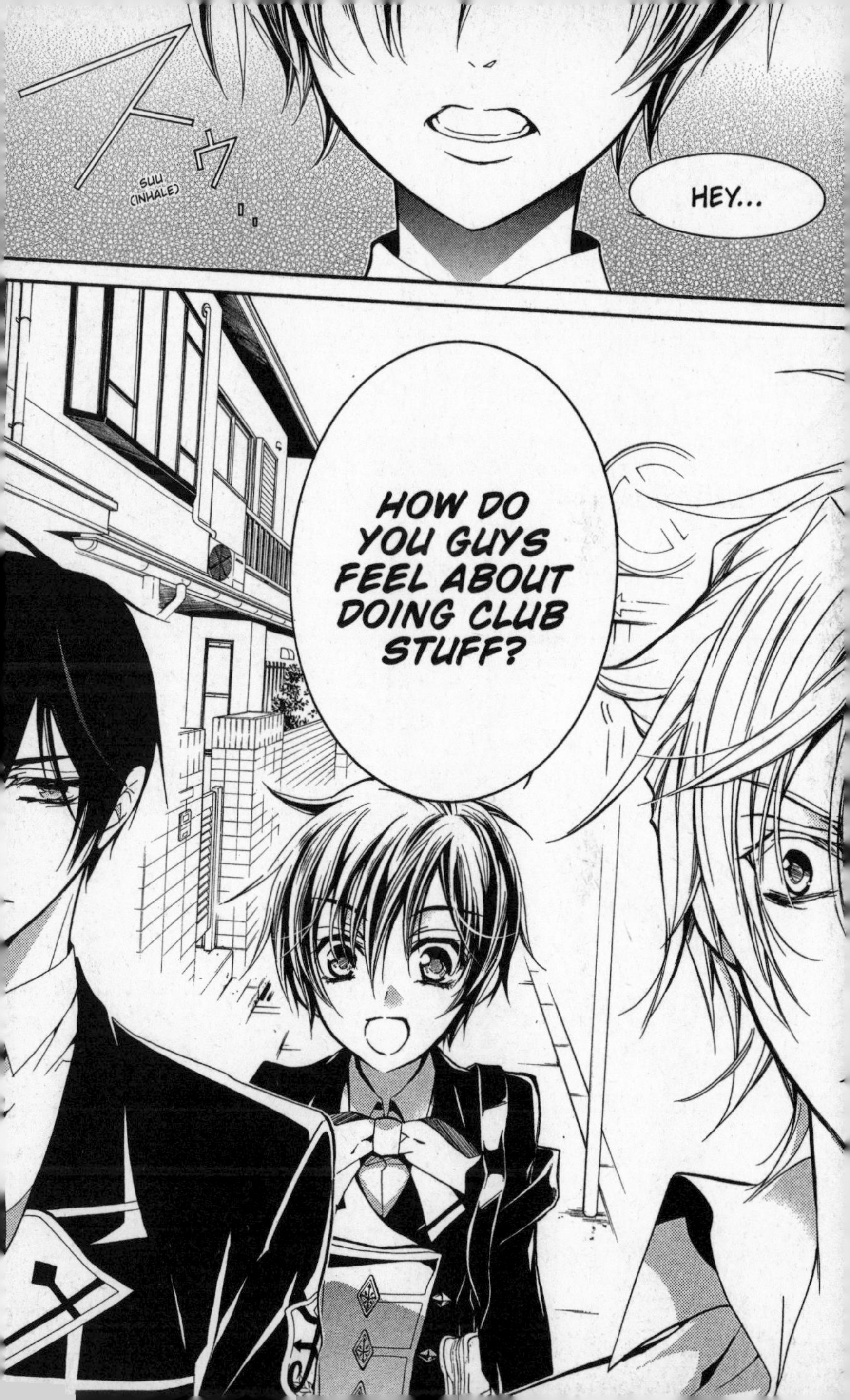
SUU (INHALE)
HEY...
HOW DO YOU GUYS FEEL ABOUT DOING CLUB STUFF?

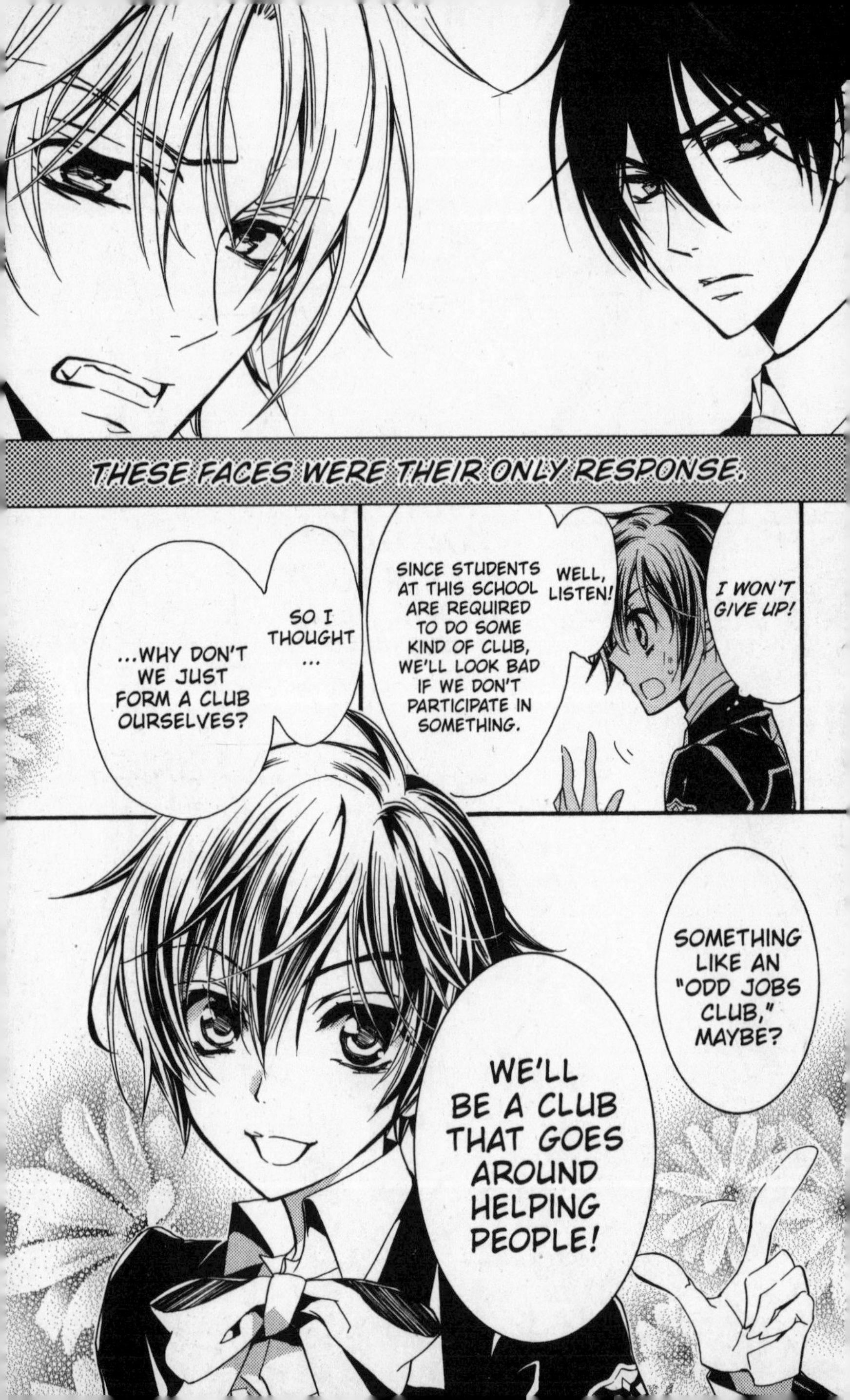
THESE FACES WERE THEIR ONLY RESPONSE.
I WON'T GIVE UP!
WELL, LISTEN!
SINCE STUDENTS AT THIS SCHOOL ARE REQUIRED TO DO SOME KIND OF CLUB, WE'LL LOOK BAD IF WE DON'T PARTICIPATE IN SOMETHING.
SO I THOUGHT...
...WHY DON'T WE JUST FORM A CLUB OURSELVES?
SOMETHING LIKE AN "ODD JOBS CLUB," MAYBE?
WE'LL BE A CLUB THAT GOES AROUND HELPING PEOPLE!

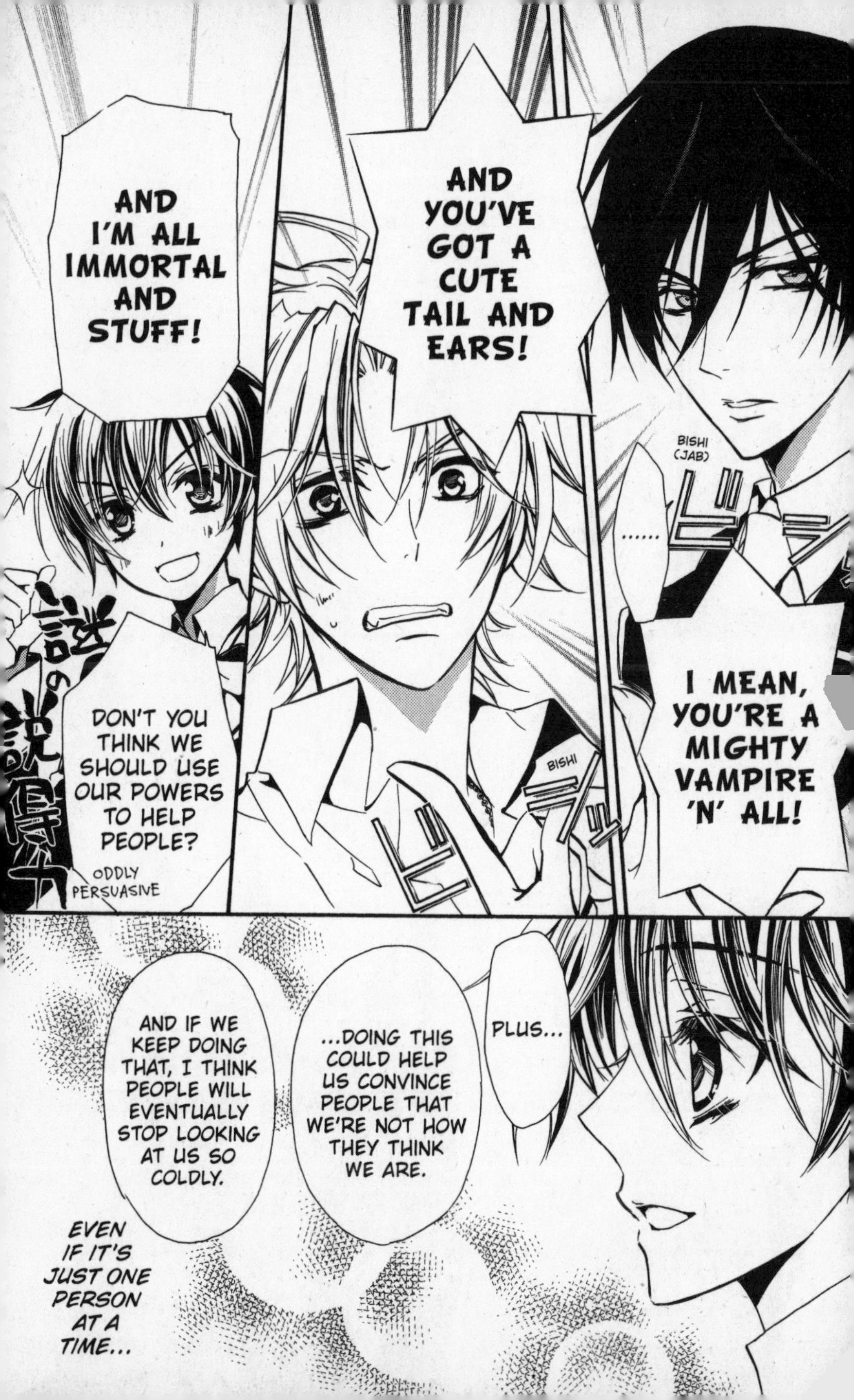
......
BISHI (JAB)
I MEAN, YOU'RE A MIGHTY VAMPIRE 'N' ALL!
AND YOU'VE GOT A CUTE TAIL AND EARS!
BISHI
AND I'M ALL IMMORTAL AND STUFF!
DON'T YOU THINK WE SHOULD USE OUR POWERS TO HELP PEOPLE?
謎の説得力
ODDLY PERSUASIVE
PLUS...
...DOING THIS COULD HELP US CONVINCE PEOPLE THAT WE'RE NOT HOW THEY THINK WE ARE.
AND IF WE KEEP DOING THAT, I THINK PEOPLE WILL EVENTUALLY STOP LOOKING AT US SO COLDLY.
EVEN IF IT'S JUST ONE PERSON AT A TIME...

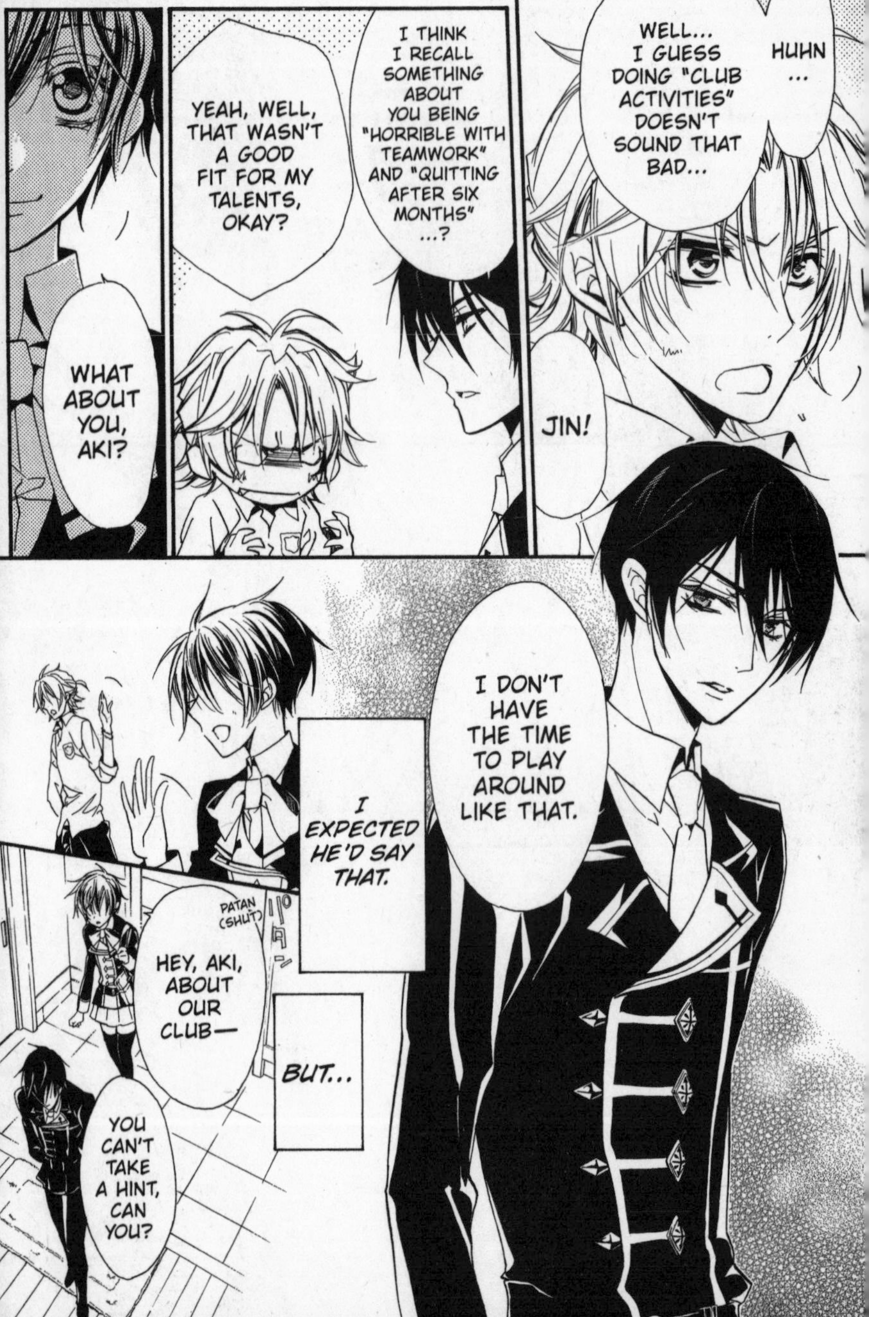
HUHN ...
WELL... I GUESS DOING "CLUB ACTIVITIES" DOESN'T SOUND THAT BAD...
JIN!
I THINK I RECALL SOMETHING ABOUT YOU BEING "HORRIBLE WITH TEAMWORK" AND "QUITTING AFTER SIX MONTHS" ...?
YEAH, WELL, THAT WASN'T A GOOD FIT FOR MY TALENTS, OKAY?
WHAT ABOUT YOU, AKI?
I DON'T HAVE THE TIME TO PLAY AROUND LIKE THAT.
I EXPECTED HE'D SAY THAT.
BUT...
PATAN (SHUT)
HEY, AKI, ABOUT OUR CLUB—
YOU CAN'T TAKE A HINT, CAN YOU?

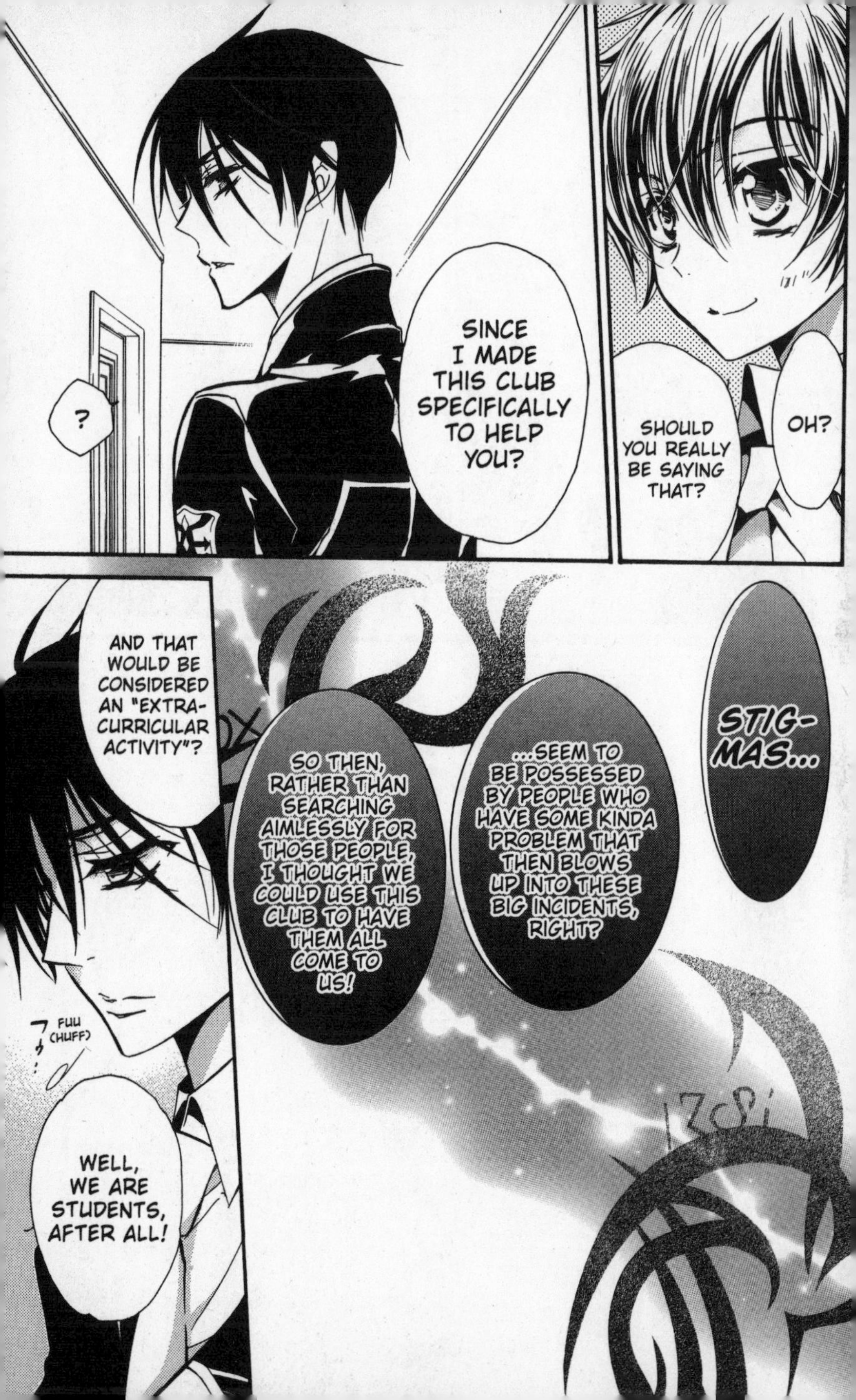
OH?
SHOULD YOU REALLY BE SAYING THAT?
SINCE I MADE THIS CLUB SPECIFICALLY TO HELP YOU?
?
STIG-MAS...
...SEEM TO BE POSSESSED BY PEOPLE WHO HAVE SOME KINDA PROBLEM THAT THEN BLOWS UP INTO THESE BIG INCIDENTS, RIGHT?
SO THEN, RATHER THAN SEARCHING AIMLESSLY FOR THOSE PEOPLE, I THOUGHT WE COULD USE THIS CLUB TO HAVE THEM ALL COME TO US!
AND THAT WOULD BE CONSIDERED AN "EXTRA-CURRICULAR ACTIVITY"?
FUU (HUFF)
WELL, WE ARE STUDENTS, AFTER ALL!

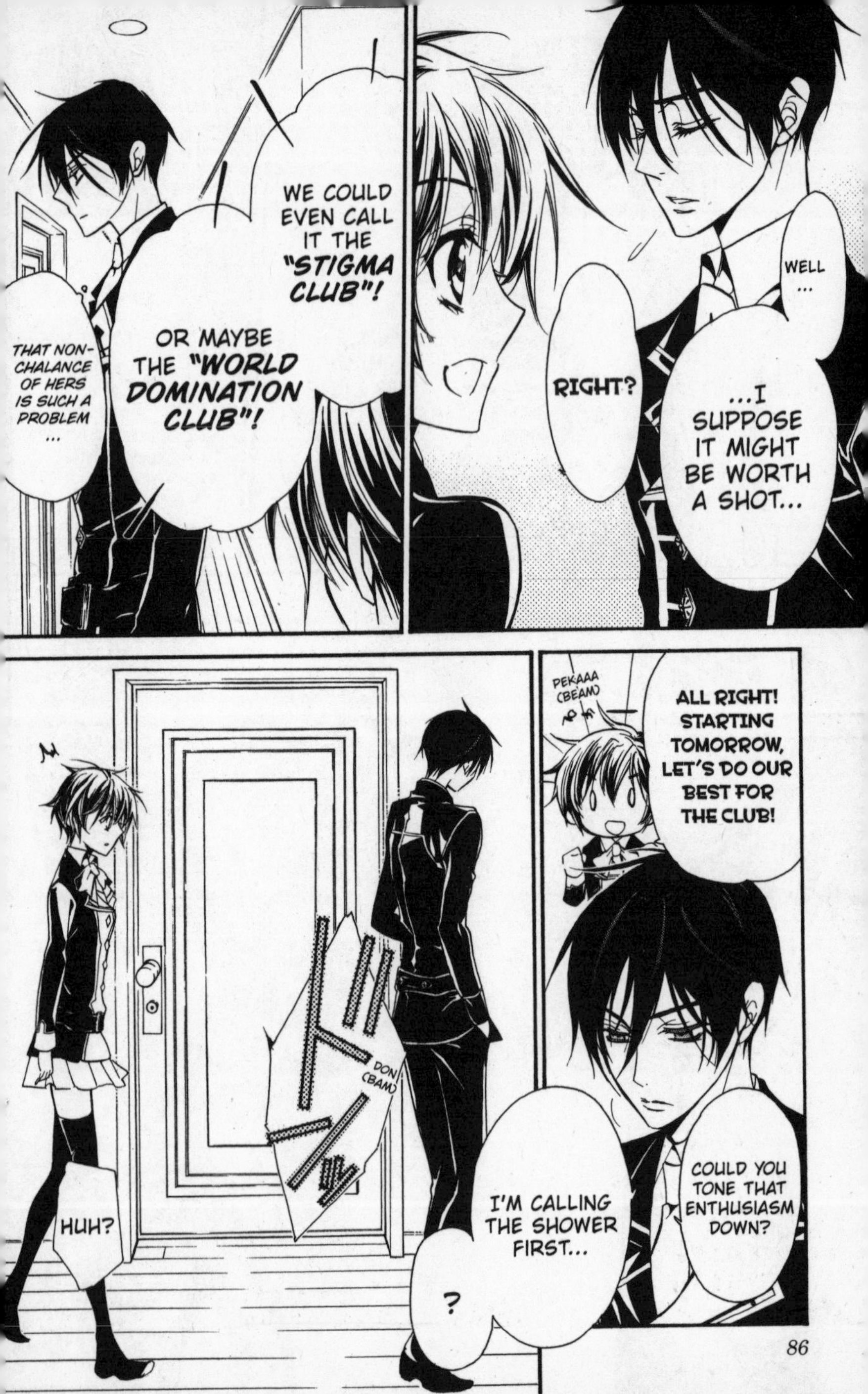

WELL ...
RIGHT?
...I SUPPOSE IT MIGHT BE WORTH A SHOT...
WE COULD EVEN CALL IT THE "STIGMA CLUB"!
OR MAYBE THE "WORLD DOMINATION CLUB"!
THAT NON-CHALANCE OF HERS IS SUCH A PROBLEM ...
PEKAAA (BEAM)
ALL RIGHT! STARTING TOMORROW, LET'S DO OUR BEST FOR THE CLUB!
COULD YOU TONE THAT ENTHUSIASM DOWN?
I'M CALLING THE SHOWER FIRST...
?
DON (BAM)
HUH?

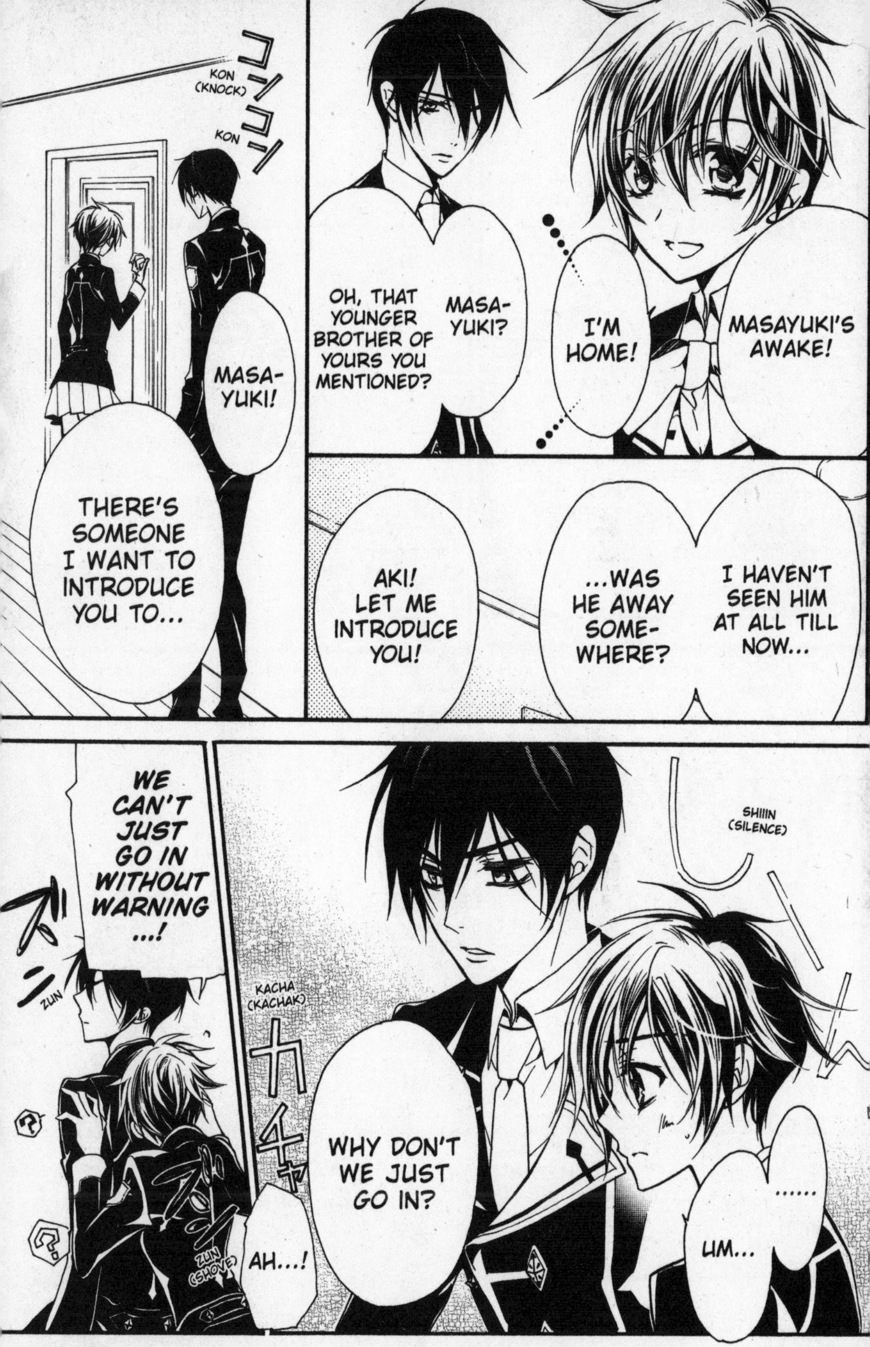
MASAYUKI'S AWAKE!
...I'M HOME!...
MASA-YUKI?
OH, THAT YOUNGER BROTHER OF YOURS YOU MENTIONED?
I HAVEN'T SEEN HIM AT ALL TILL NOW...
...WAS HE AWAY SOME-WHERE?
AKI! LET ME INTRODUCE YOU!
KON (KNOCK)
KON
MASA-YUKI!
THERE'S SOMEONE I WANT TO INTRODUCE YOU TO...
SHIIIN (SILENCE)
......
UM...
WHY DON'T WE JUST GO IN?
KACHA (KACHAK)
WE CAN'T JUST GO IN WITHOUT WARNING...!
ZUN
ZUN (SHOVE)
AH...!

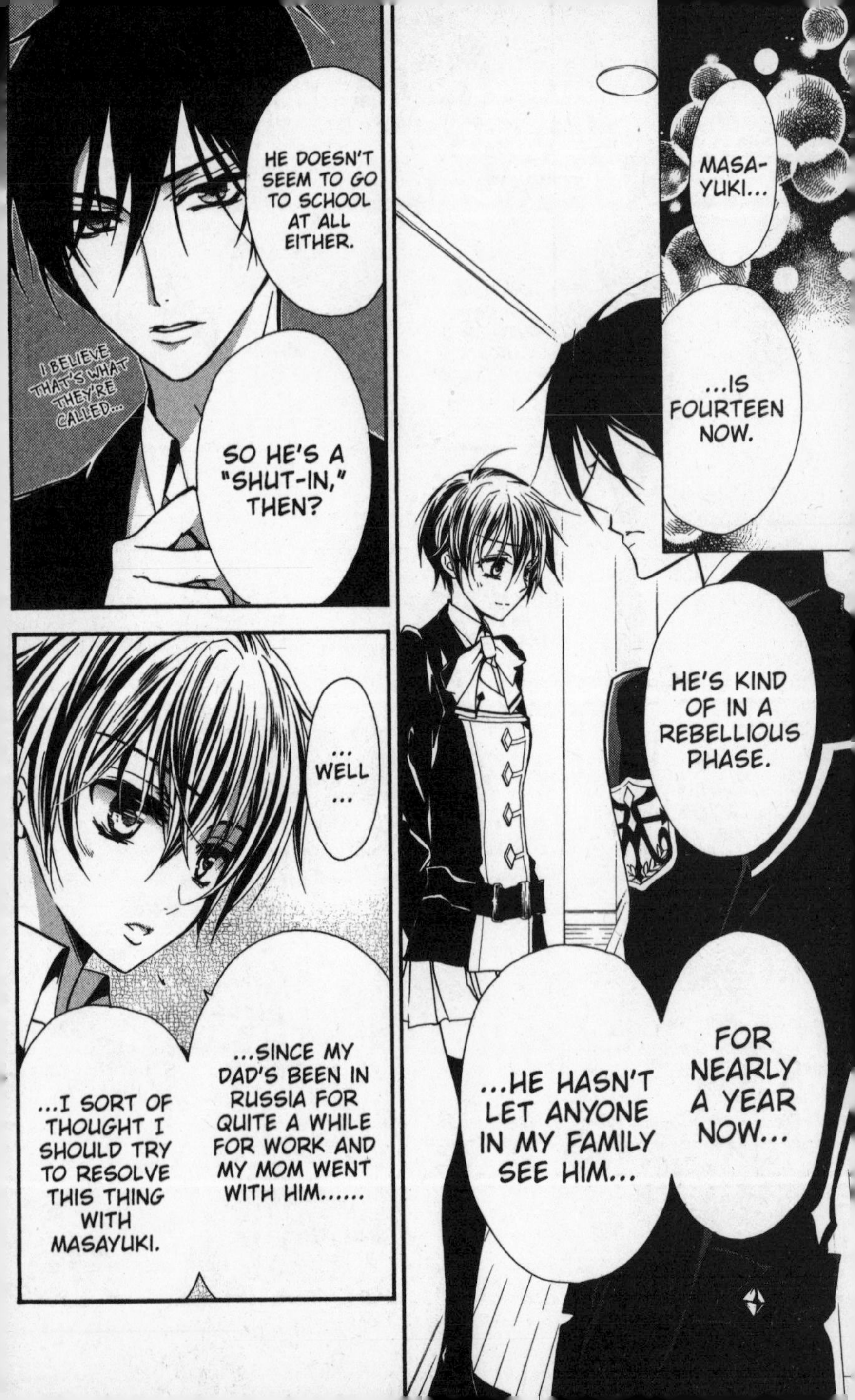
MASA-YUKI...
...IS FOURTEEN NOW.
HE'S KIND OF IN A REBELLIOUS PHASE.
FOR NEARLY A YEAR NOW...
...HE HASN'T LET ANYONE IN MY FAMILY SEE HIM...
HE DOESN'T SEEM TO GO TO SCHOOL AT ALL EITHER.
SO HE'S A "SHUT-IN," THEN?
I BELIEVE THAT'S WHAT THEY'RE CALLED...
...WELL...
...SINCE MY DAD'S BEEN IN RUSSIA FOR QUITE A WHILE FOR WORK AND MY MOM WENT WITH HIM......
...I SORT OF THOUGHT I SHOULD TRY TO RESOLVE THIS THING WITH MASAYUKI.

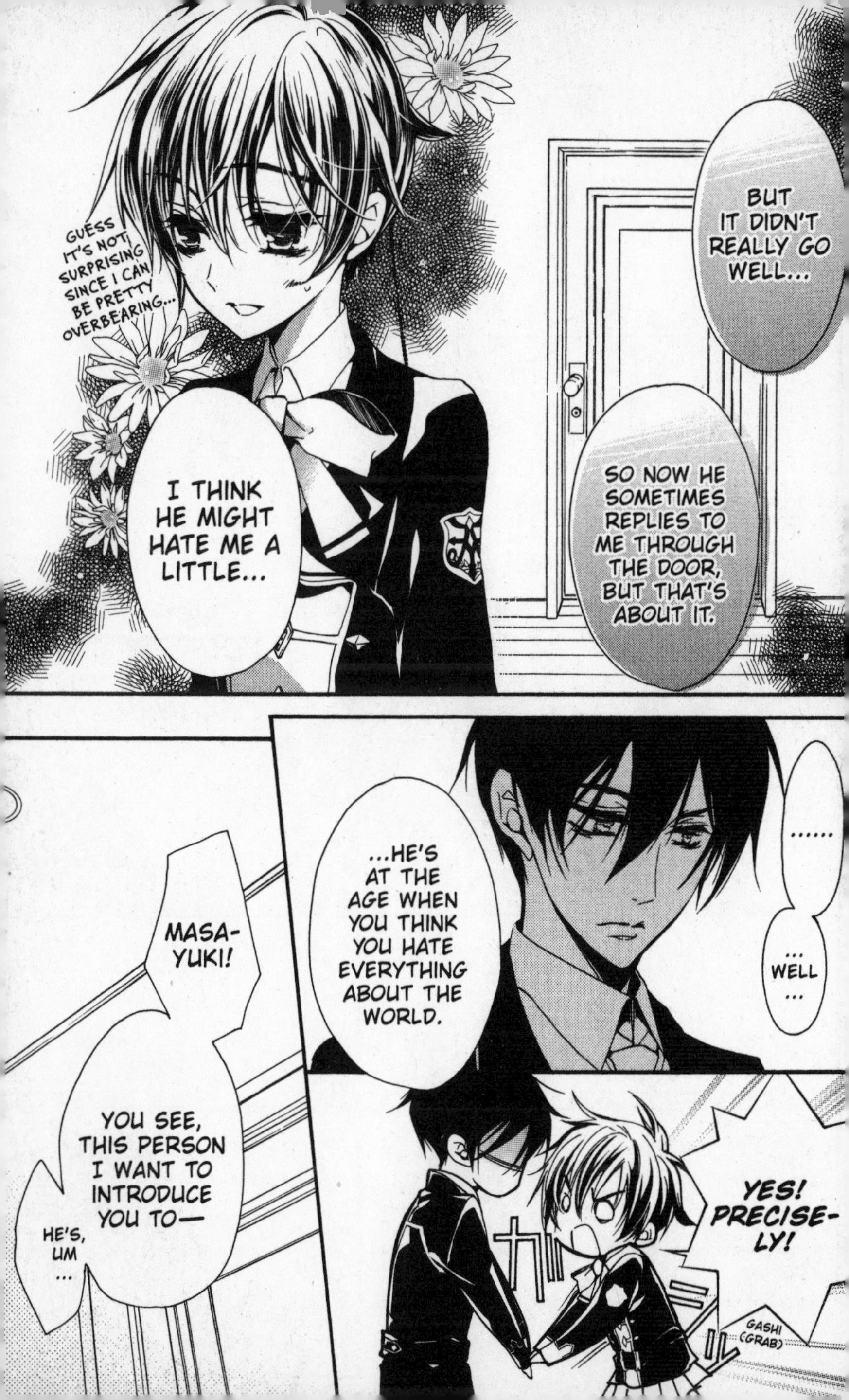
BUT IT DIDN'T REALLY GO WELL...
SO NOW HE SOMETIMES REPLIES TO ME THROUGH THE DOOR, BUT THAT'S ABOUT IT.
I THINK HE MIGHT HATE ME A LITTLE...
GUESS IT'S NOT SURPRISING SINCE I CAN BE PRETTY OVERBEARING...
......
...WELL...
...HE'S AT THE AGE WHEN YOU THINK YOU HATE EVERYTHING ABOUT THE WORLD.
YES! PRECISE-LY!
GASHI (GRAB)
MASA-YUKI!
YOU SEE, THIS PERSON I WANT TO INTRODUCE YOU TO—
HE'S, UM...

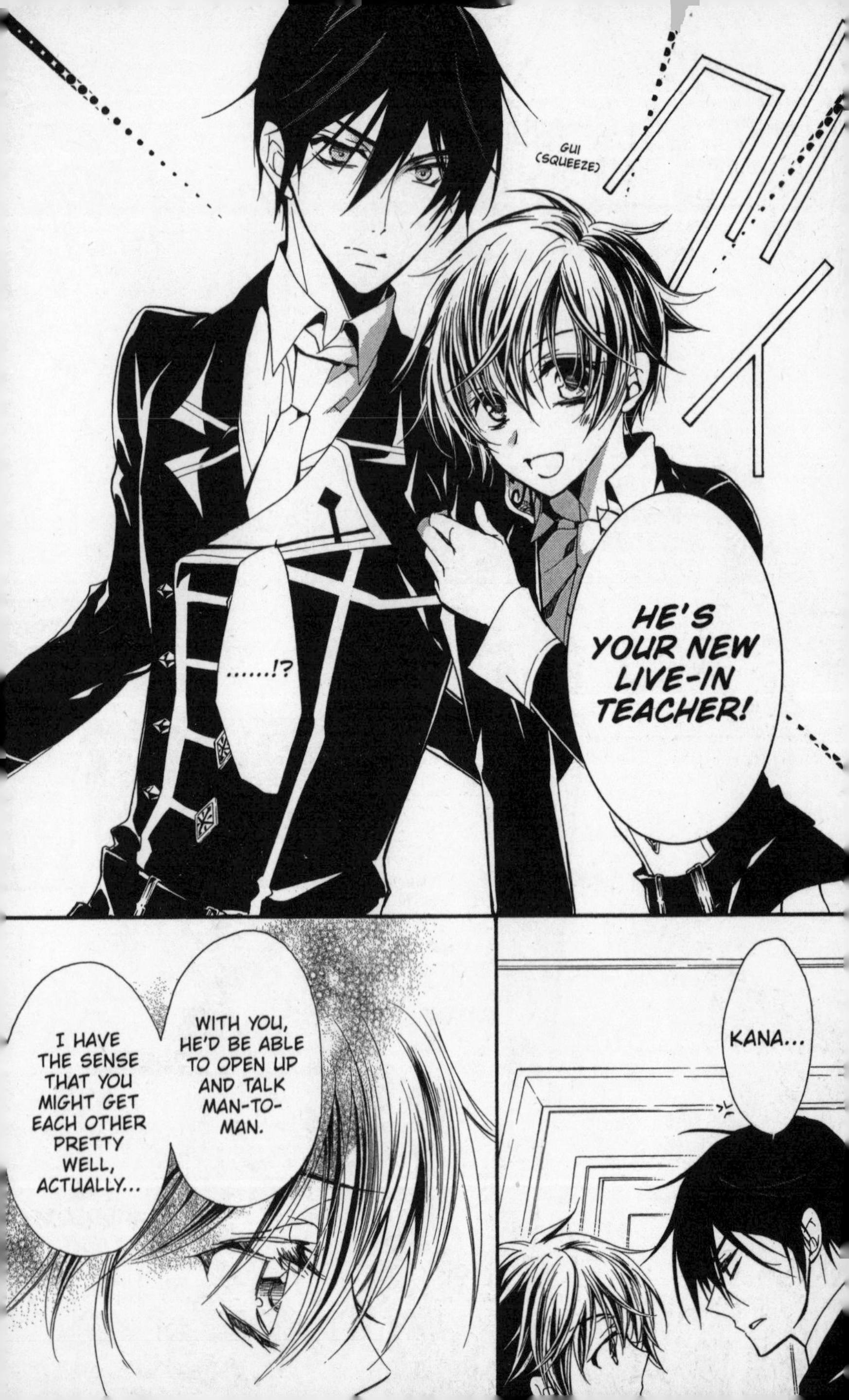
GUI (SQUEEZE)
HE'S YOUR NEW LIVE-IN TEACHER!
......!?
KANA...
WITH YOU, HE'D BE ABLE TO OPEN UP AND TALK MAN-TO-MAN.
I HAVE THE SENSE THAT YOU MIGHT GET EACH OTHER PRETTY WELL, ACTUALLY...

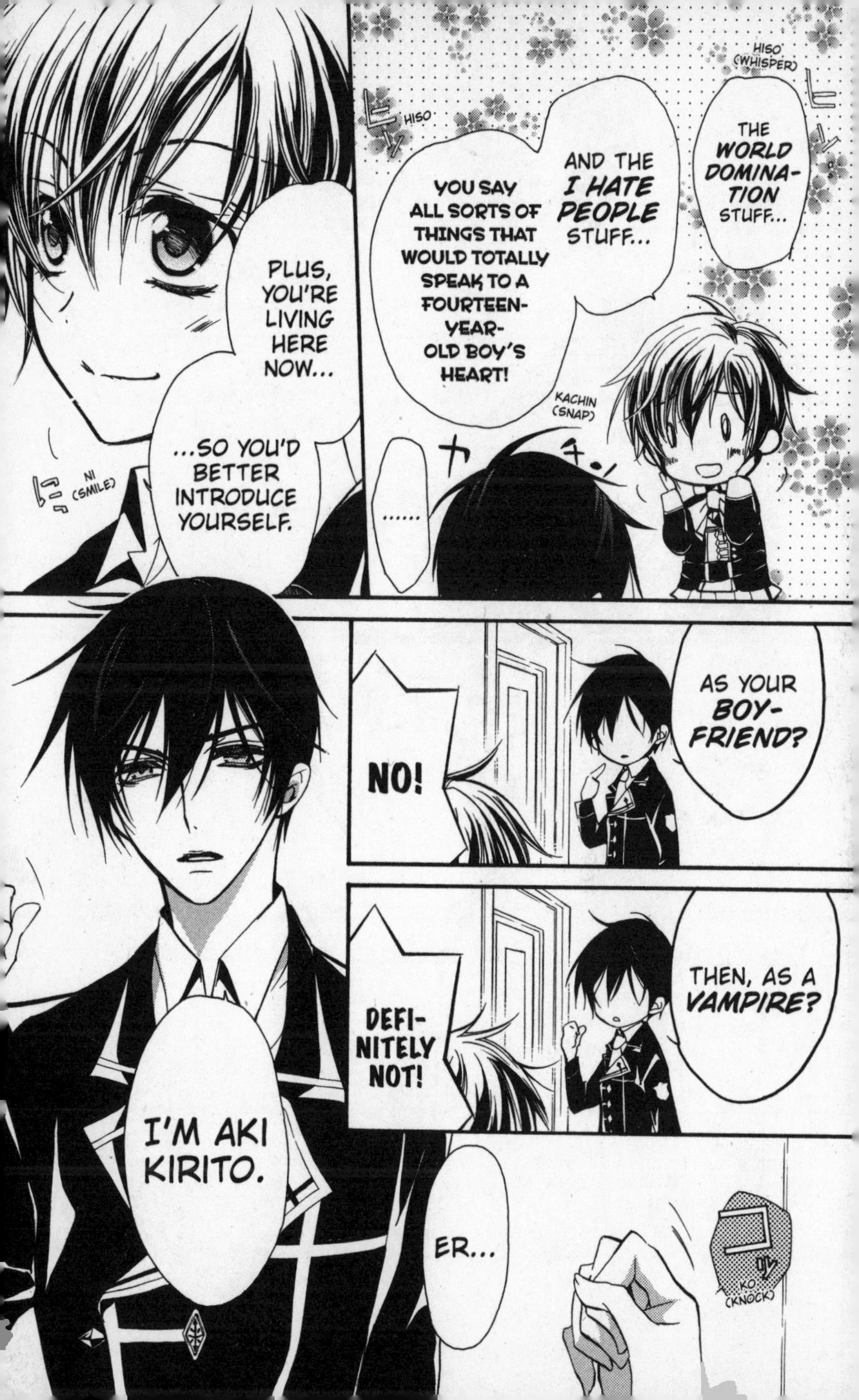
HISO (WHISPER)
THE WORLD DOMINATION STUFF...
HISO
AND THE I HATE PEOPLE STUFF...
YOU SAY ALL SORTS OF THINGS THAT WOULD TOTALLY SPEAK TO A FOURTEEN-YEAR-OLD BOY'S HEART!
KACHIN (SNAP)
......
PLUS, YOU'RE LIVING HERE NOW...
...SO YOU'D BETTER INTRODUCE YOURSELF.
NI (SMILE)
AS YOUR BOY-FRIEND?
NO!
THEN, AS A VAMPIRE?
DEFI-NITELY NOT!
KO (KNOCK)
ER...
I'M AKI KIRITO.

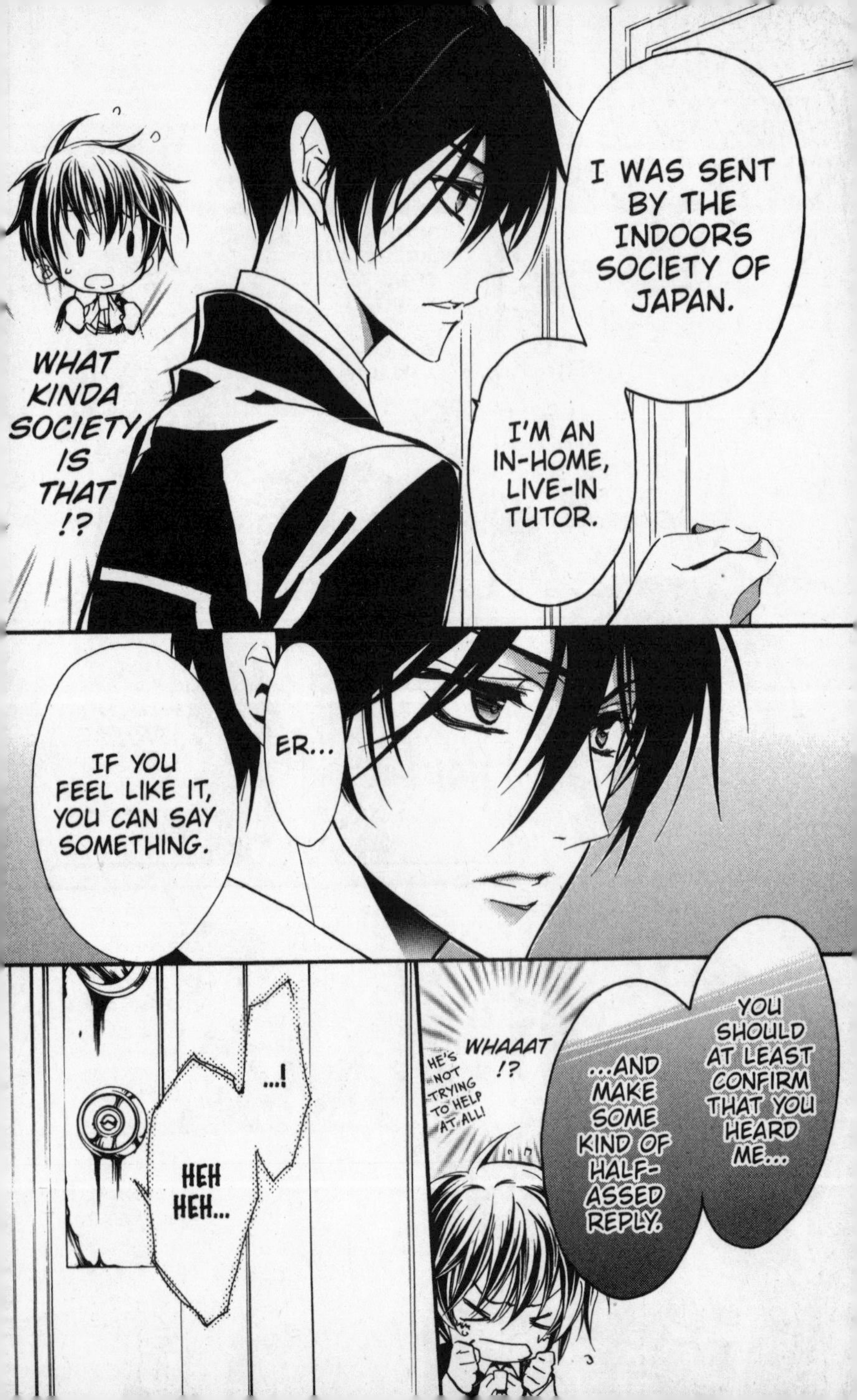
I WAS SENT BY THE INDOORS SOCIETY OF JAPAN.
I'M AN IN-HOME, LIVE-IN TUTOR.
WHAT KINDA SOCIETY IS THAT!?
ER...
IF YOU FEEL LIKE IT, YOU CAN SAY SOMETHING.
YOU SHOULD AT LEAST CONFIRM THAT YOU HEARD ME...
...AND MAKE SOME KIND OF HALF-ASSED REPLY.
WHAAAT!?
HE'S NOT TRYING TO HELP AT ALL!
...!
HEH HEH...

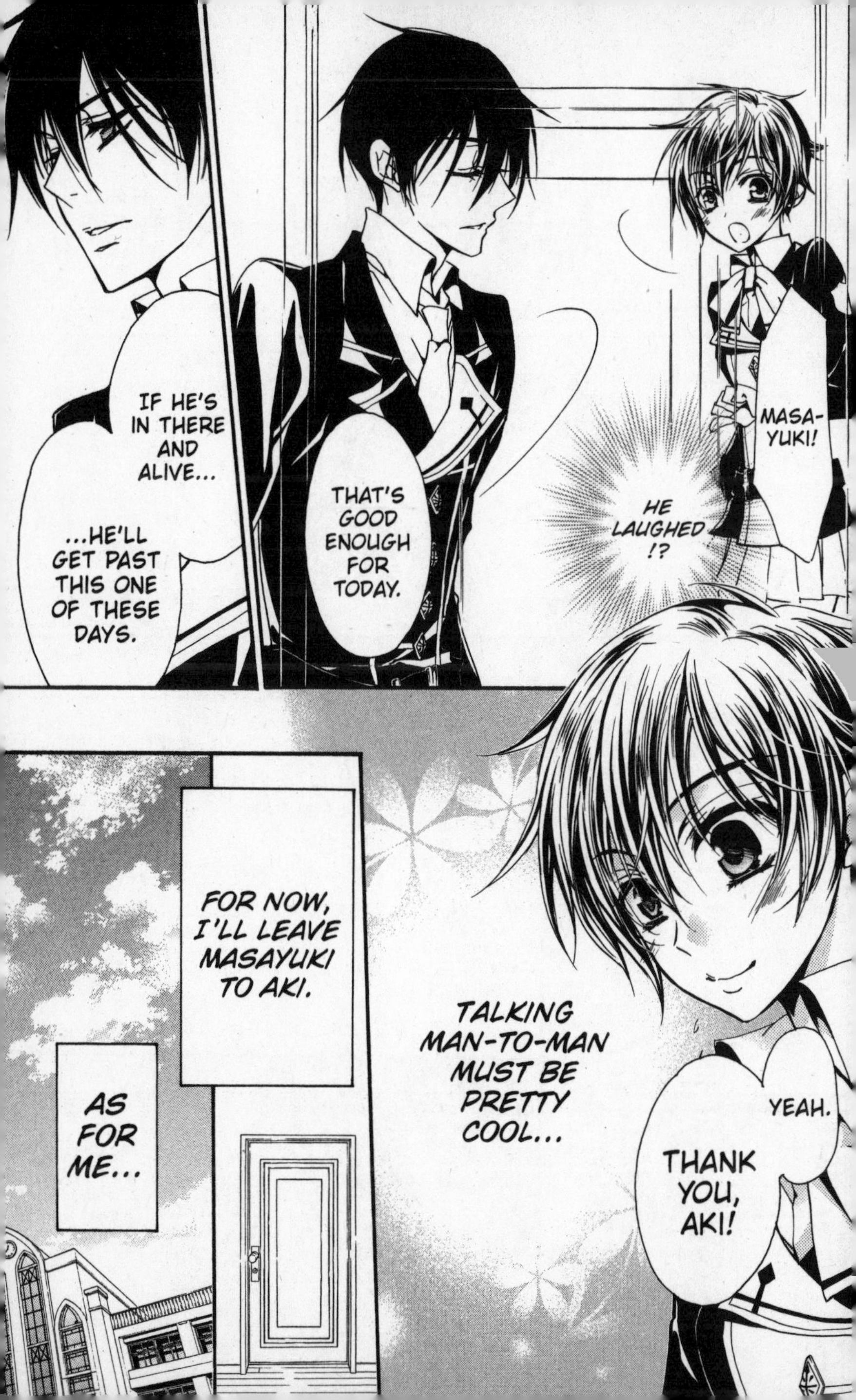
MASA-YUKI!
HE LAUGHED!?
THAT'S GOOD ENOUGH FOR TODAY.
IF HE'S IN THERE AND ALIVE...
...HE'LL GET PAST THIS ONE OF THESE DAYS.
YEAH.
THANK YOU, AKI!
TALKING MAN-TO-MAN MUST BE PRETTY COOL...
FOR NOW, I'LL LEAVE MASAYUKI TO AKI.
AS FOR ME...

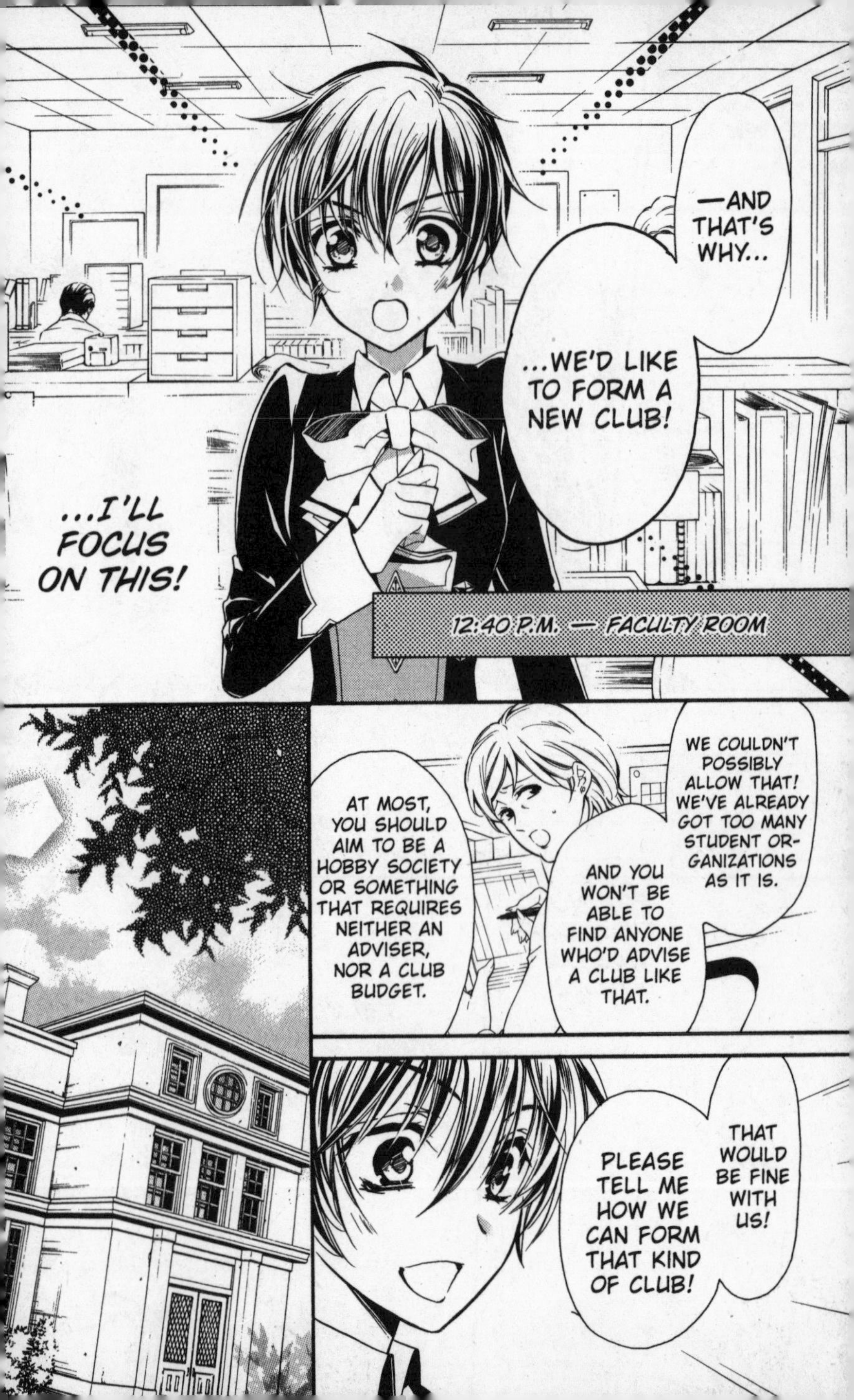
—AND THAT'S WHY...
...WE'D LIKE TO FORM A NEW CLUB!
...I'LL FOCUS ON THIS!
12:40 P.M. — FACULTY ROOM
WE COULDN'T POSSIBLY ALLOW THAT! WE'VE ALREADY GOT TOO MANY STUDENT OR-GANIZATIONS AS IT IS.
AND YOU WON'T BE ABLE TO FIND ANYONE WHO'D ADVISE A CLUB LIKE THAT.
AT MOST, YOU SHOULD AIM TO BE A HOBBY SOCIETY OR SOMETHING THAT REQUIRES NEITHER AN ADVISER, NOR A CLUB BUDGET.
THAT WOULD BE FINE WITH US!
PLEASE TELL ME HOW WE CAN FORM THAT KIND OF CLUB!

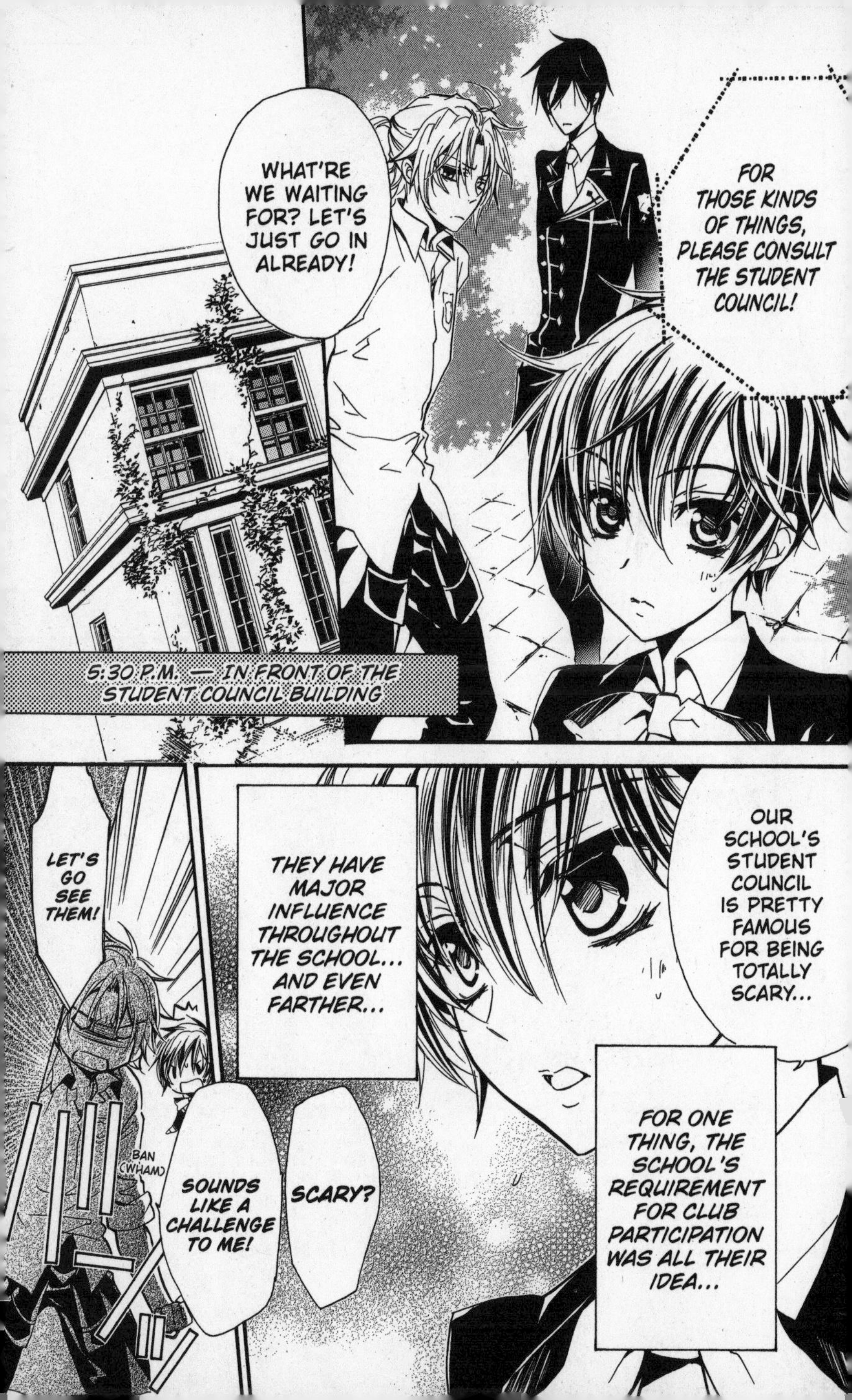
FOR THOSE KINDS OF THINGS, PLEASE CONSULT THE STUDENT COUNCIL!
WHAT'RE WE WAITING FOR? LET'S JUST GO IN ALREADY!
5:30 P.M. — IN FRONT OF THE STUDENT COUNCIL BUILDING
OUR SCHOOL'S STUDENT COUNCIL IS PRETTY FAMOUS FOR BEING TOTALLY SCARY...
THEY HAVE MAJOR INFLUENCE THROUGHOUT THE SCHOOL... AND EVEN FARTHER...
FOR ONE THING, THE SCHOOL'S REQUIREMENT FOR CLUB PARTICIPATION WAS ALL THEIR IDEA...
SCARY?
SOUNDS LIKE A CHALLENGE TO ME!
LET'S GO SEE THEM!
BAN (WHAM)

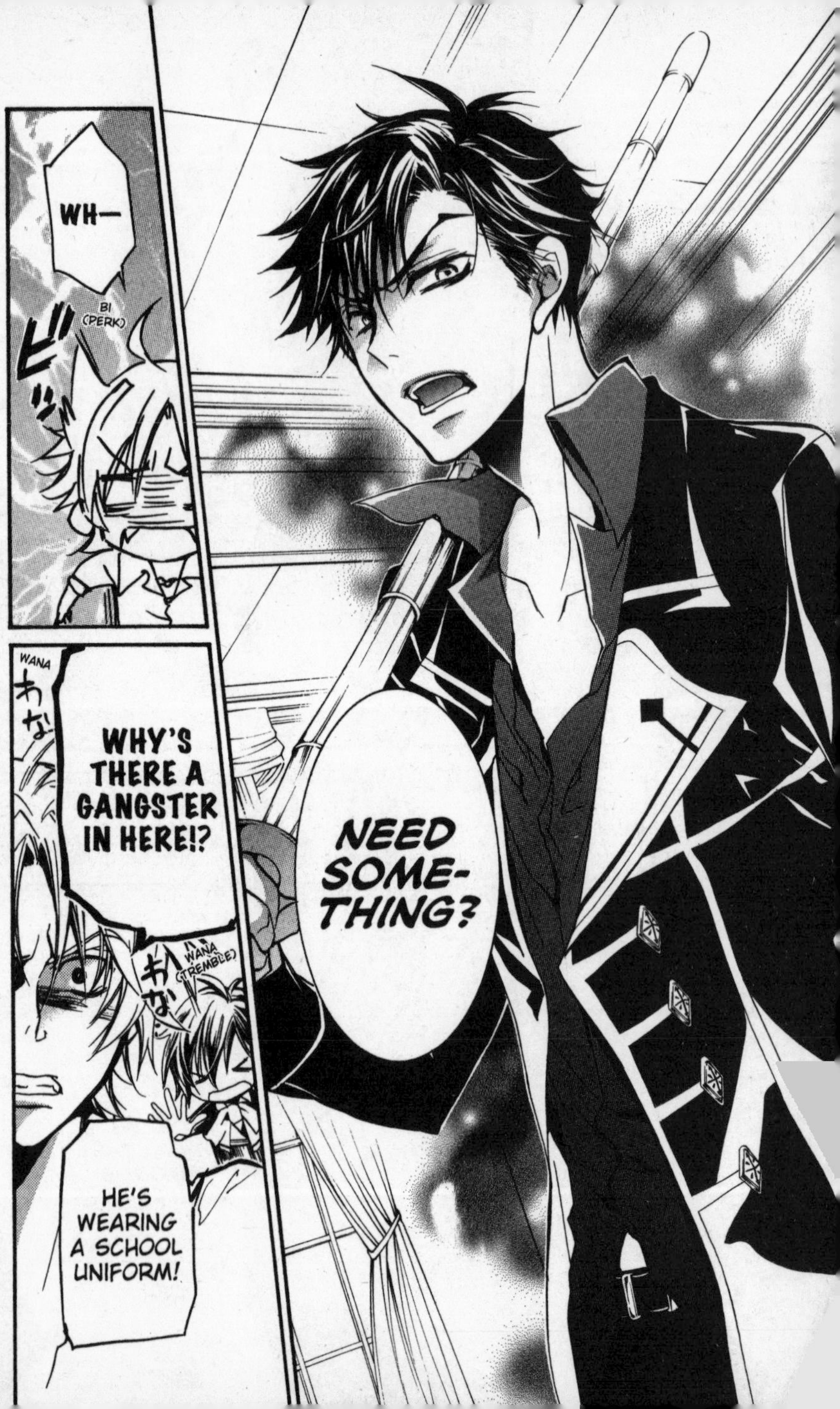
NEED SOME-THING?
WH—
BI (PERK)
WANA
WHY'S THERE A GANGSTER IN HERE!?
WANA (TREMBLE)
HE'S WEARING A SCHOOL UNIFORM!

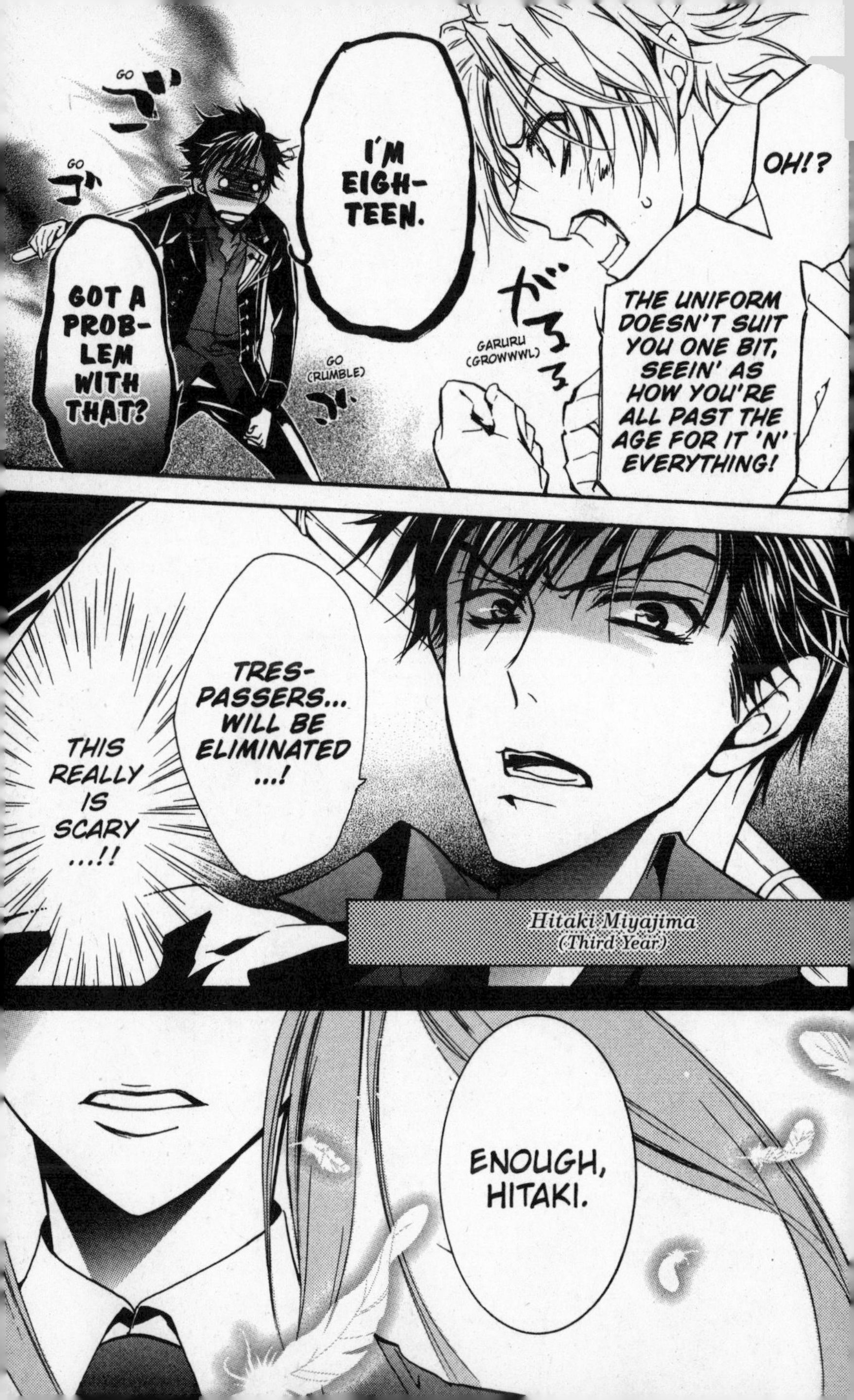
OH!?
THE UNIFORM DOESN'T SUIT YOU ONE BIT, SEEIN' AS HOW YOU'RE ALL PAST THE AGE FOR IT 'N' EVERYTHING!
GARURU (GROWWWL)
I'M EIGHTEEN.
GO
GO
GOT A PROBLEM WITH THAT?
GO (RUMBLE)
Hitaki Miyajima (Third Year)
TRESPASSERS... WILL BE ELIMINATED ...!
THIS REALLY IS SCARY ...!!
ENOUGH, HITAKI.

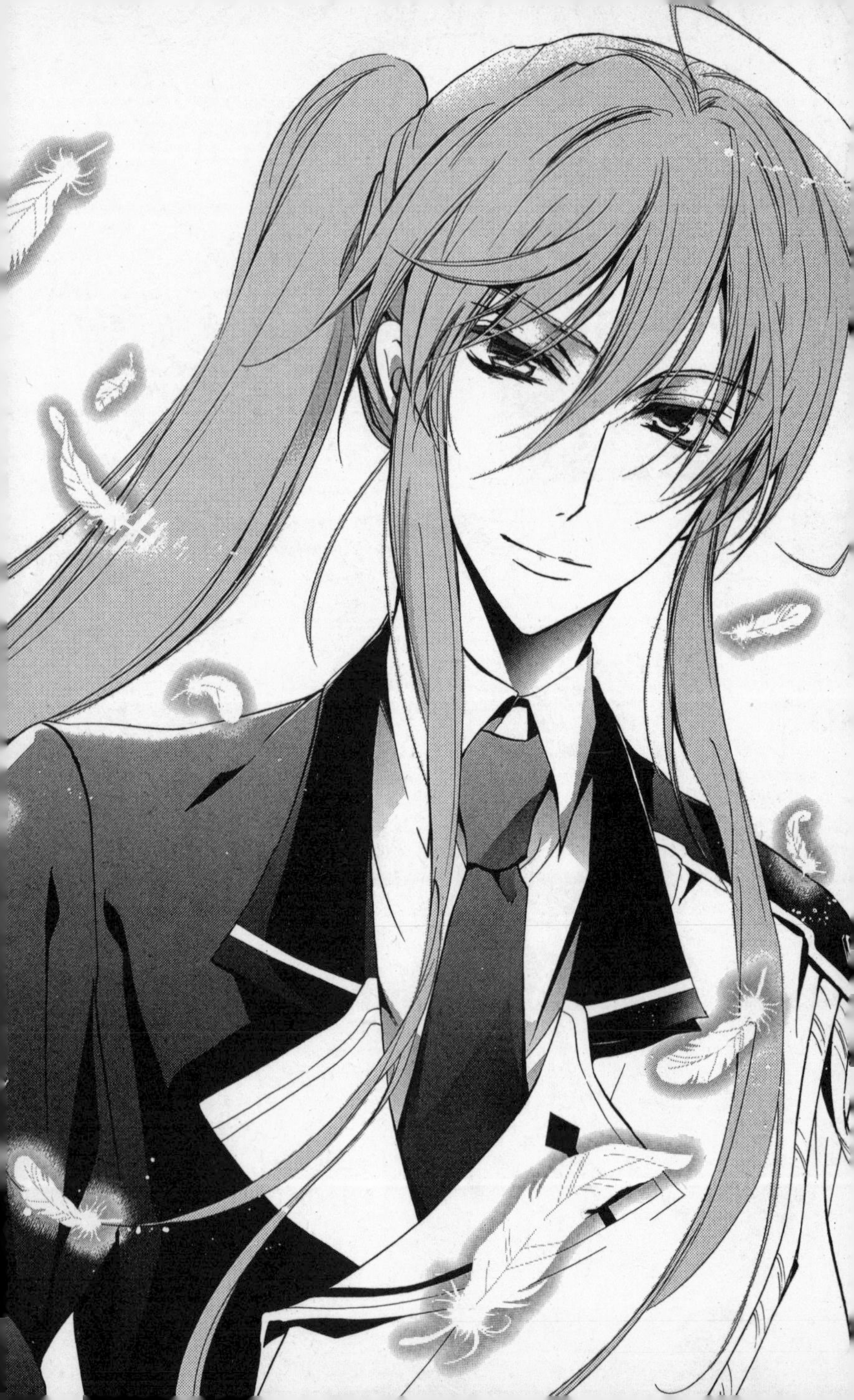

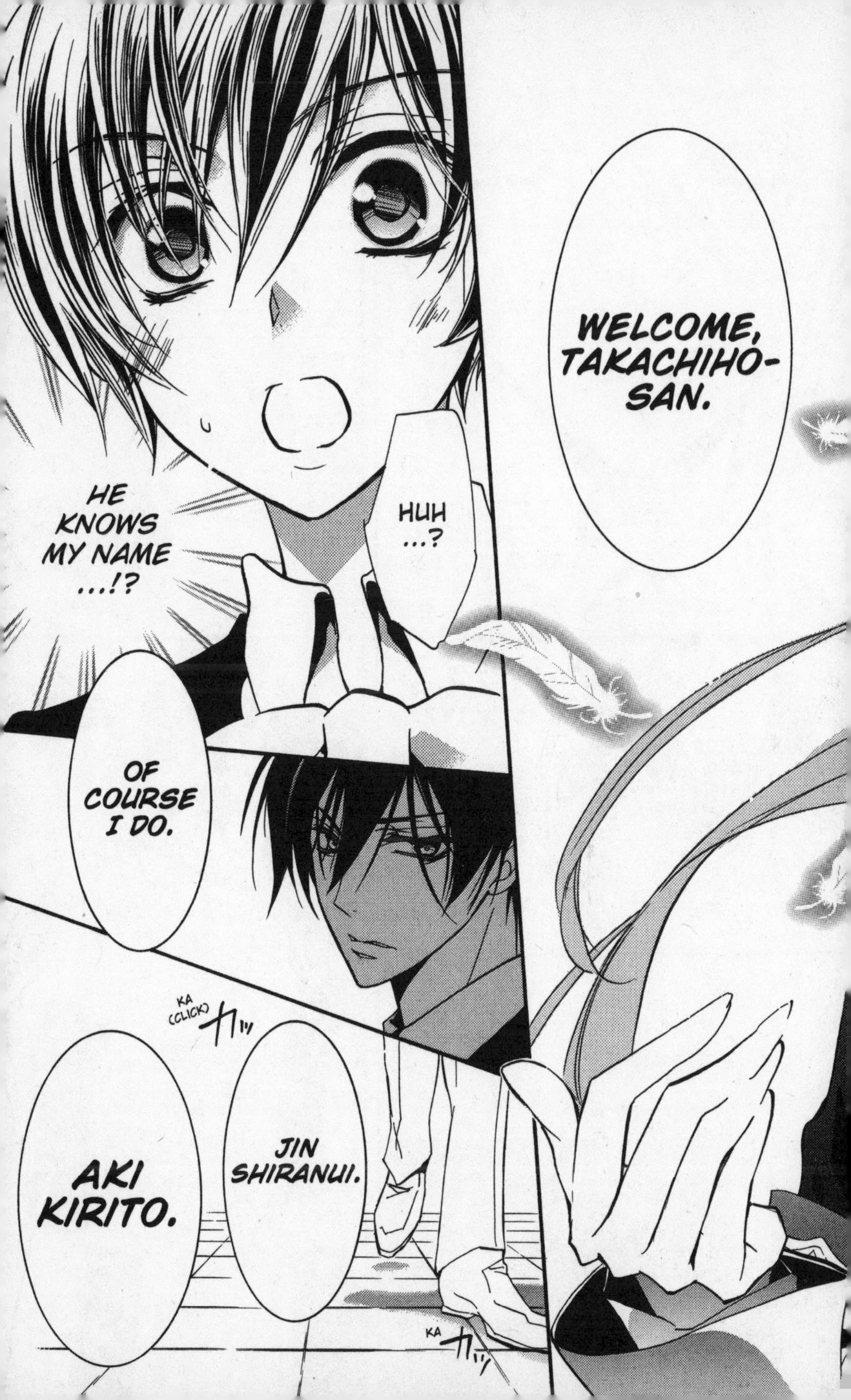
WELCOME, TAKACHIHO-SAN.
HUH ...?
HE KNOWS MY NAME ...!?
OF COURSE I DO.
KA
KA (CLICK)
JIN SHIRANUI.
AKI KIRITO.

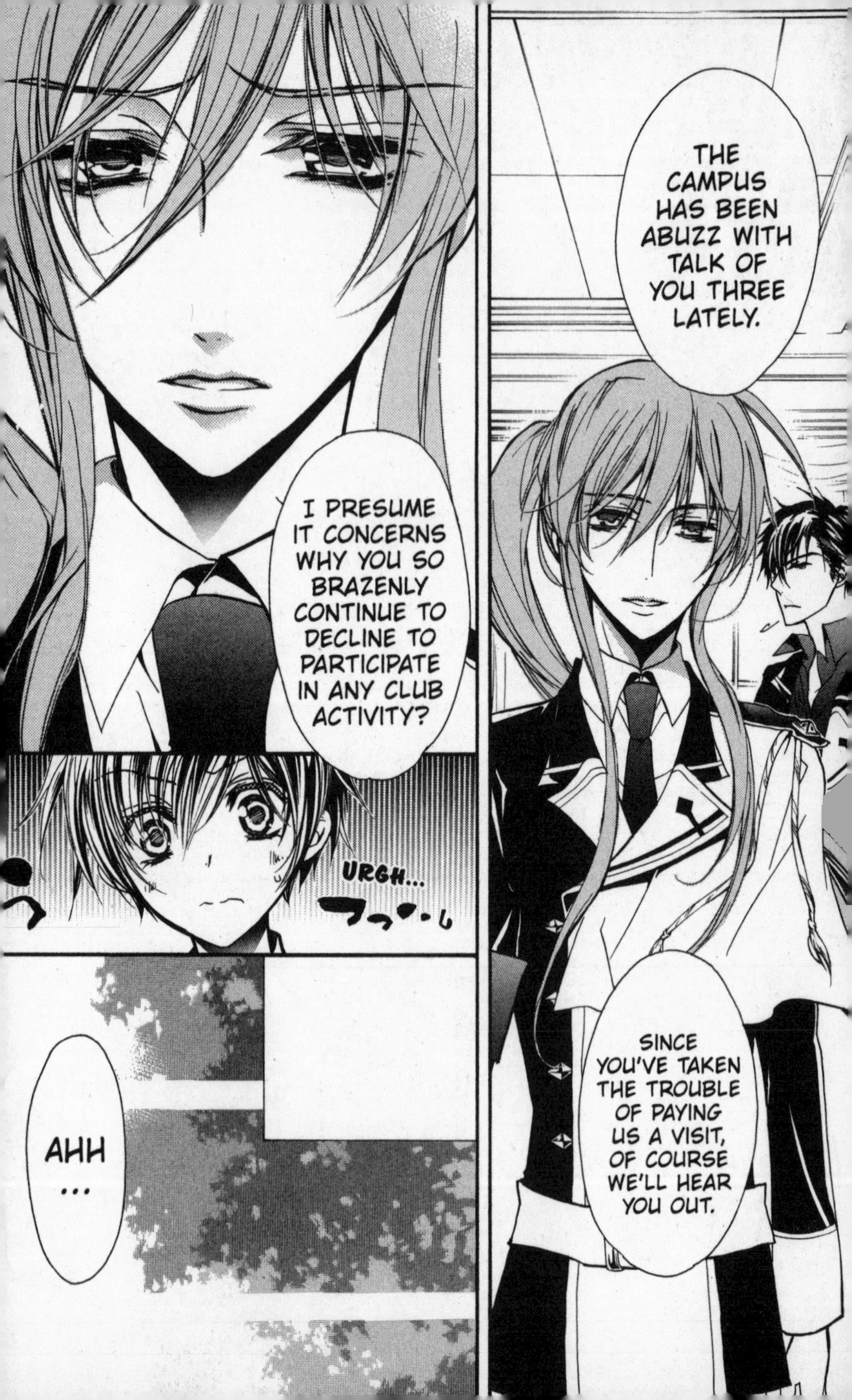
THE CAMPUS HAS BEEN ABUZZ WITH TALK OF YOU THREE LATELY.
SINCE YOU'VE TAKEN THE TROUBLE OF PAYING US A VISIT, OF COURSE WE'LL HEAR YOU OUT.
I PRESUME IT CONCERNS WHY YOU SO BRAZENLY CONTINUE TO DECLINE TO PARTICIPATE IN ANY CLUB ACTIVITY?
URGH...
AHH ...

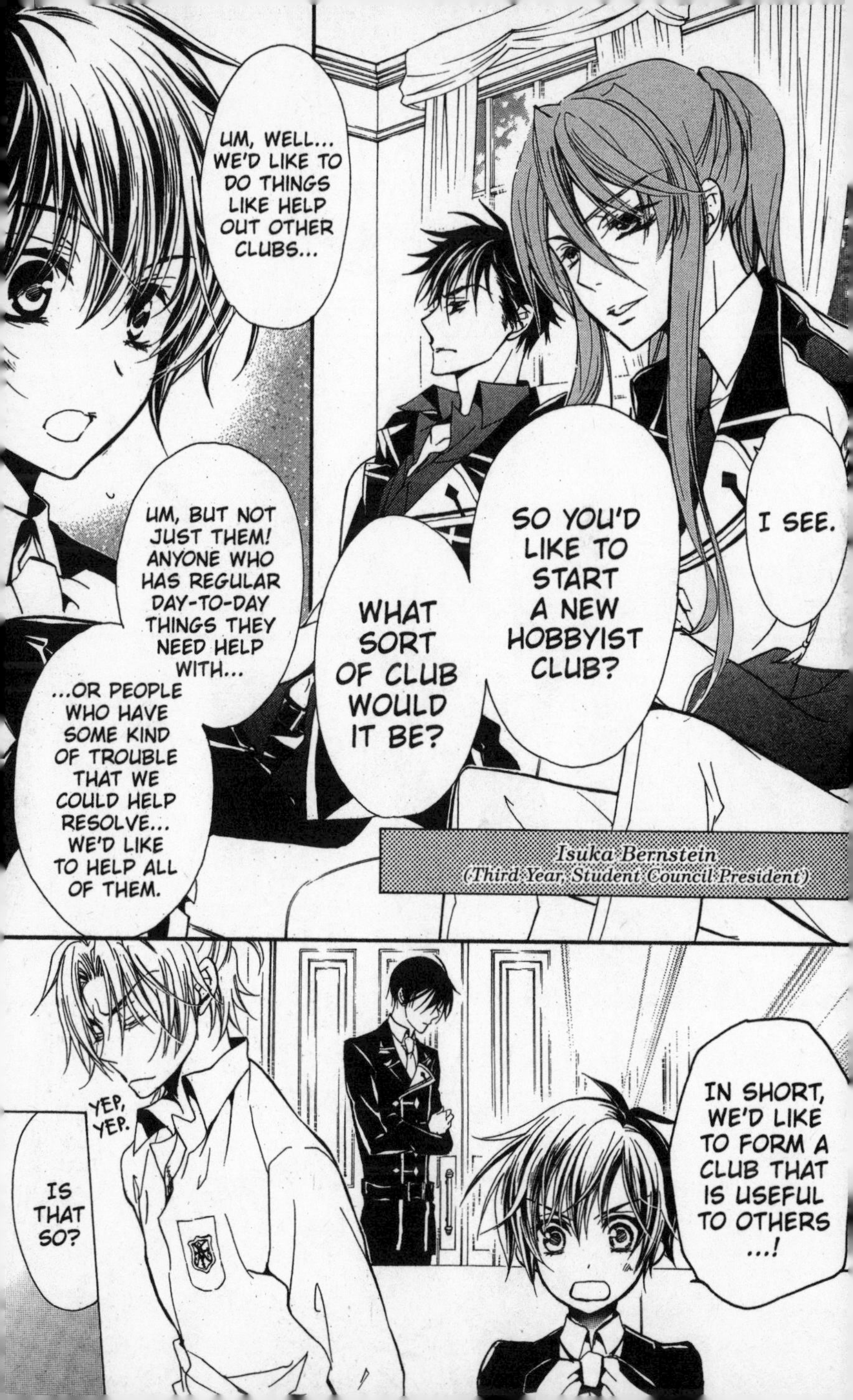
I SEE.
SO YOU'D LIKE TO START A NEW HOBBYIST CLUB?
WHAT SORT OF CLUB WOULD IT BE?
UM, WELL... WE'D LIKE TO DO THINGS LIKE HELP OUT OTHER CLUBS...
UM, BUT NOT JUST THEM! ANYONE WHO HAS REGULAR DAY-TO-DAY THINGS THEY NEED HELP WITH...
...OR PEOPLE WHO HAVE SOME KIND OF TROUBLE THAT WE COULD HELP RESOLVE... WE'D LIKE TO HELP ALL OF THEM.
Isuka Bernstein
(Third Year, Student Council President)
IN SHORT, WE'D LIKE TO FORM A CLUB THAT IS USEFUL TO OTHERS ...!
YEP, YEP.
IS THAT SO?

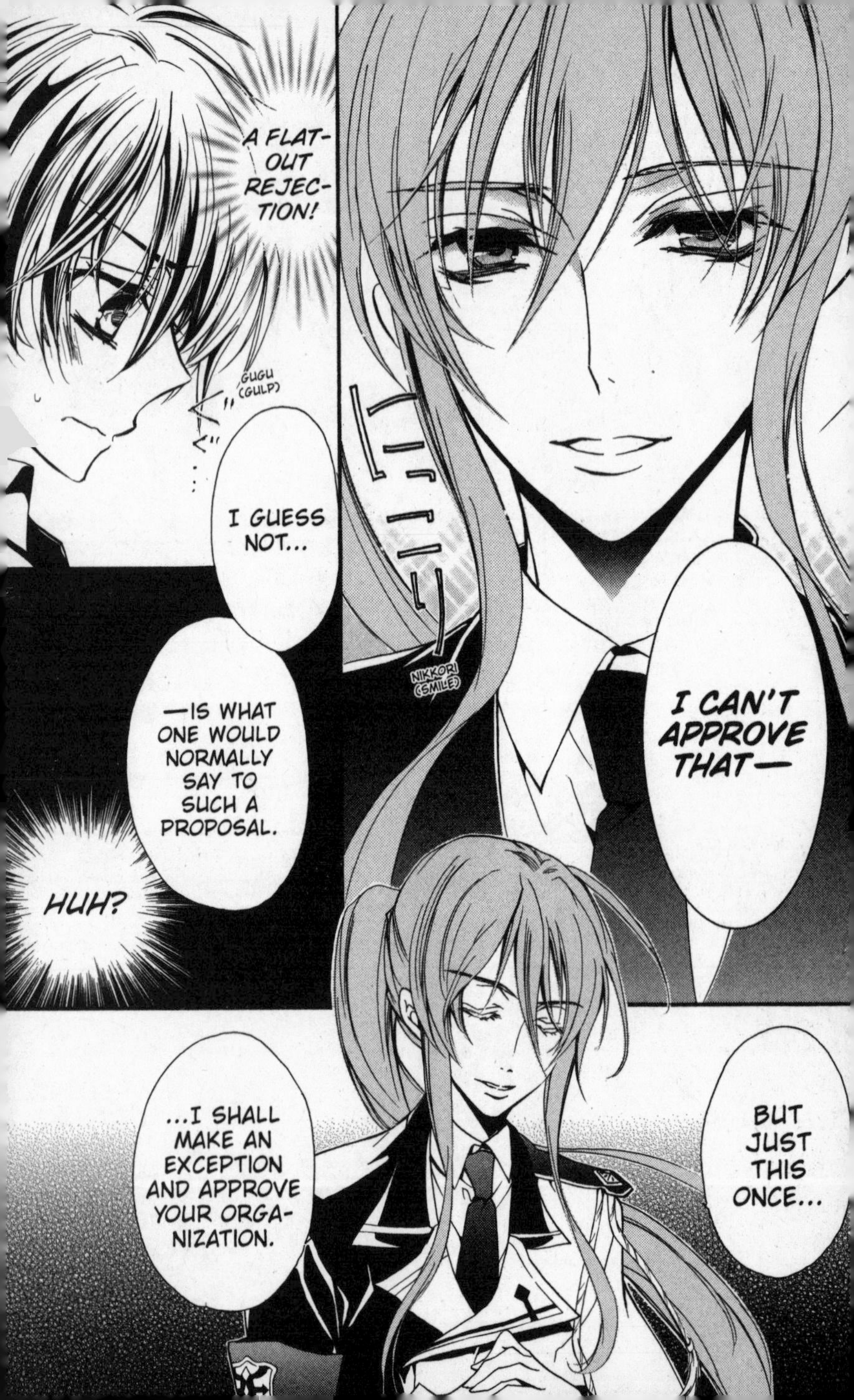
NIKKORI (SMILE)
I CAN'T APPROVE THAT—
A FLAT-OUT REJECTION!
GUGU (GULP)
I GUESS NOT...
—IS WHAT ONE WOULD NORMALLY SAY TO SUCH A PROPOSAL.
HUH?
BUT JUST THIS ONCE...
...I SHALL MAKE AN EXCEPTION AND APPROVE YOUR ORGANIZATION.

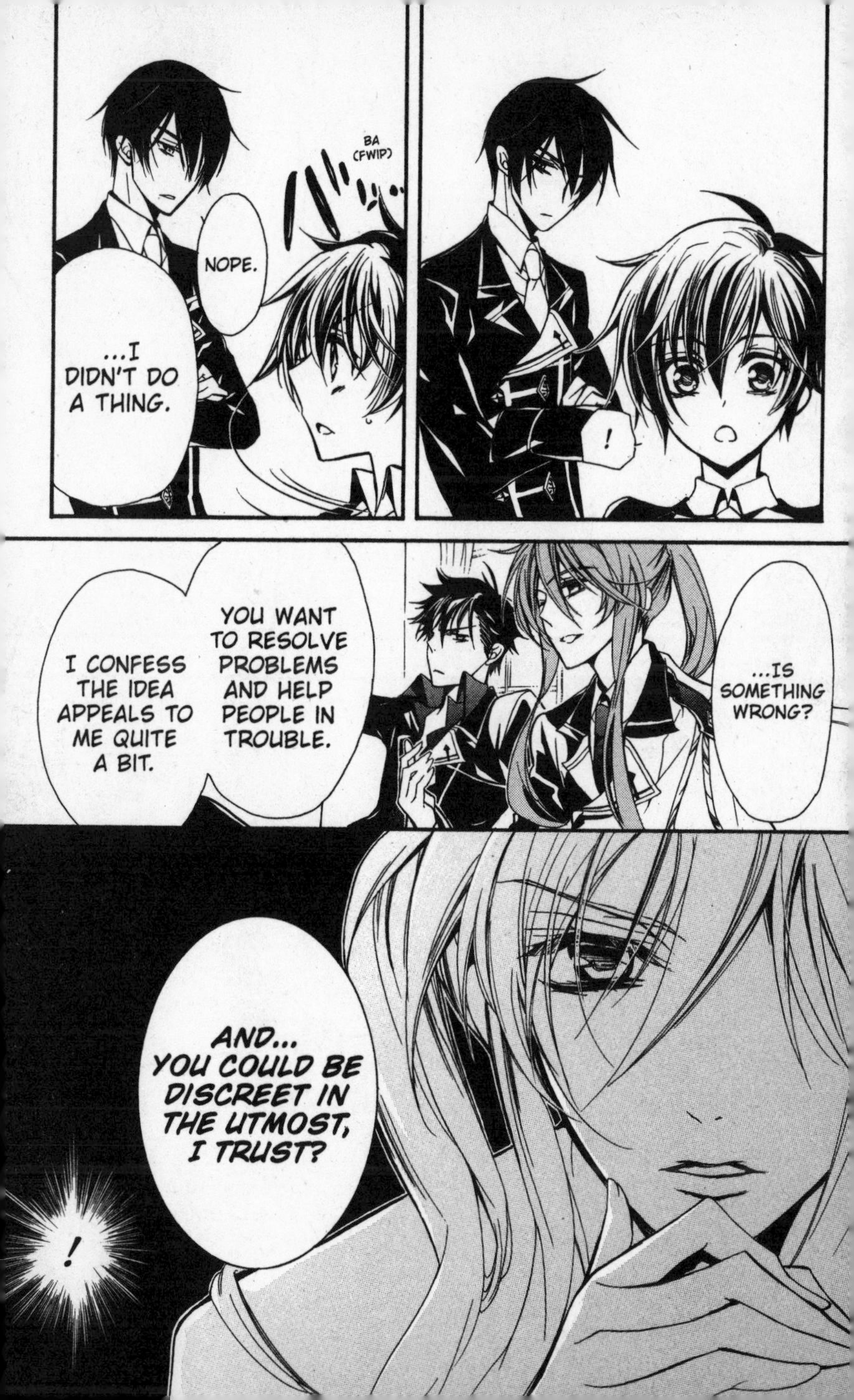
!
BA (FWIP)
NOPE.
...I DIDN'T DO A THING.
...IS SOMETHING WRONG?
YOU WANT TO RESOLVE PROBLEMS AND HELP PEOPLE IN TROUBLE.
I CONFESS THE IDEA APPEALS TO ME QUITE A BIT.
AND... YOU COULD BE DISCREET IN THE UTMOST, I TRUST?
!

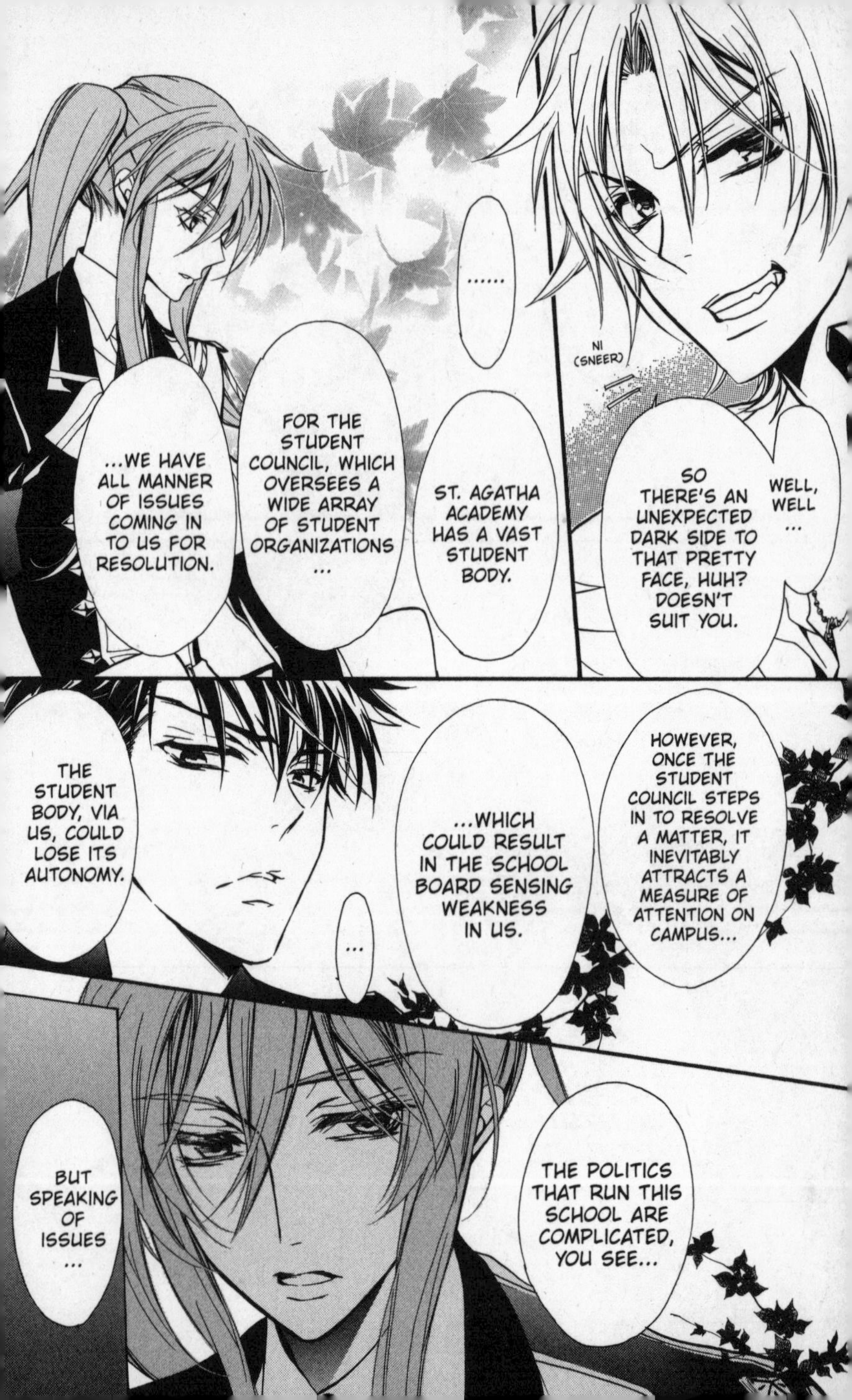

NI (SNEER)
WELL, WELL ...
SO THERE'S AN UNEXPECTED DARK SIDE TO THAT PRETTY FACE, HUH? DOESN'T SUIT YOU.
......
ST. AGATHA ACADEMY HAS A VAST STUDENT BODY.
FOR THE STUDENT COUNCIL, WHICH OVERSEES A WIDE ARRAY OF STUDENT ORGANIZATIONS ...
...WE HAVE ALL MANNER OF ISSUES COMING IN TO US FOR RESOLUTION.
HOWEVER, ONCE THE STUDENT COUNCIL STEPS IN TO RESOLVE A MATTER, IT INEVITABLY ATTRACTS A MEASURE OF ATTENTION ON CAMPUS...
...WHICH COULD RESULT IN THE SCHOOL BOARD SENSING WEAKNESS IN US.
...
THE STUDENT BODY, VIA US, COULD LOSE ITS AUTONOMY.
THE POLITICS THAT RUN THIS SCHOOL ARE COMPLICATED, YOU SEE...
BUT SPEAKING OF ISSUES ...

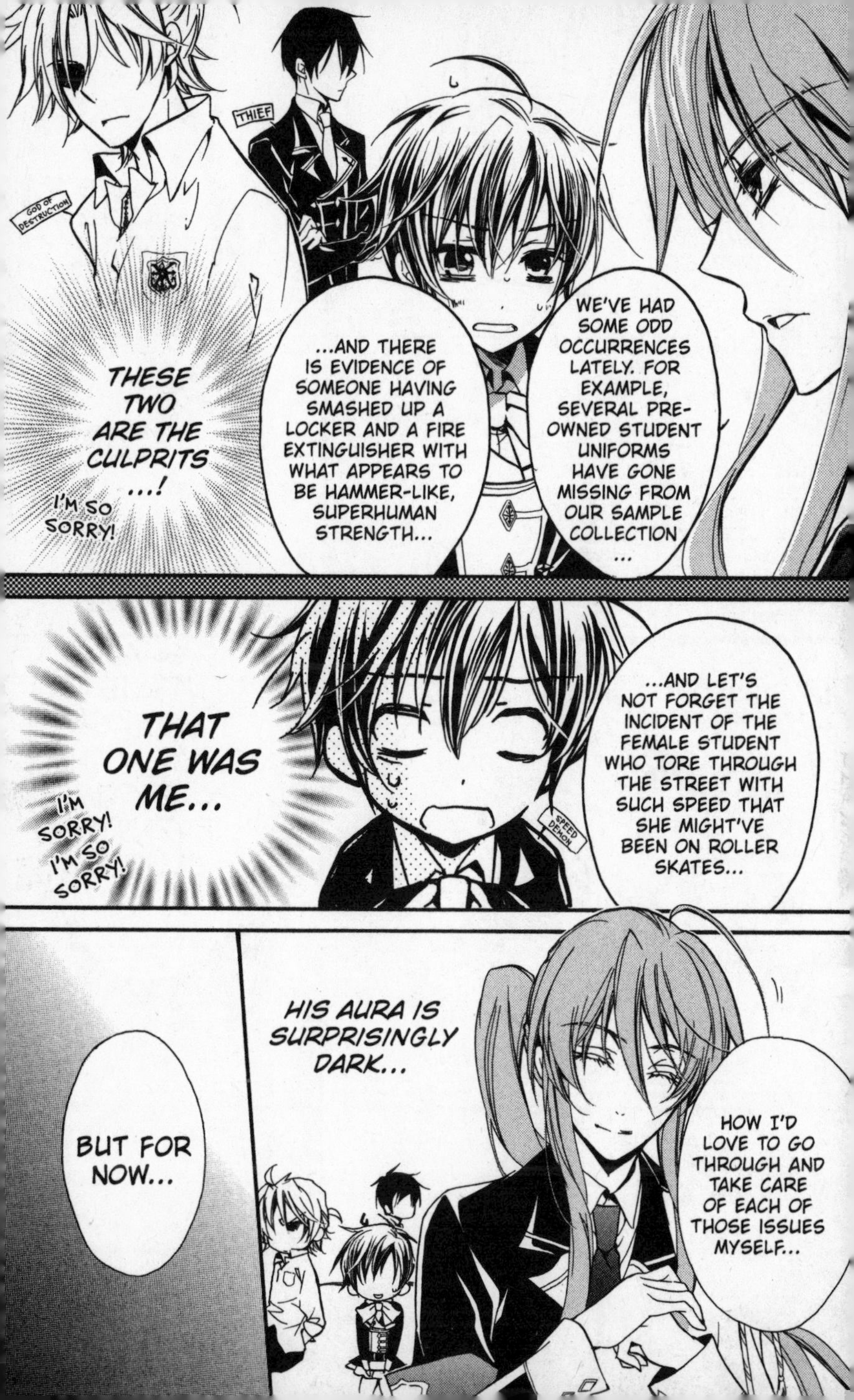
WE'VE HAD SOME ODD OCCURRENCES LATELY. FOR EXAMPLE, SEVERAL PRE-OWNED STUDENT UNIFORMS HAVE GONE MISSING FROM OUR SAMPLE COLLECTION ...
...AND THERE IS EVIDENCE OF SOMEONE HAVING SMASHED UP A LOCKER AND A FIRE EXTINGUISHER WITH WHAT APPEARS TO BE HAMMER-LIKE, SUPERHUMAN STRENGTH...
THIEF
GOD OF DESTRUCTION
THESE TWO ARE THE CULPRITS ...!
I'M SO SORRY!
...AND LET'S NOT FORGET THE INCIDENT OF THE FEMALE STUDENT WHO TORE THROUGH THE STREET WITH SUCH SPEED THAT SHE MIGHT'VE BEEN ON ROLLER SKATES...
SPEED DEMON
THAT ONE WAS ME...
I'M SORRY! I'M SO SORRY!
HOW I'D LOVE TO GO THROUGH AND TAKE CARE OF EACH OF THOSE ISSUES MYSELF...
HIS AURA IS SURPRISINGLY DARK...
BUT FOR NOW...

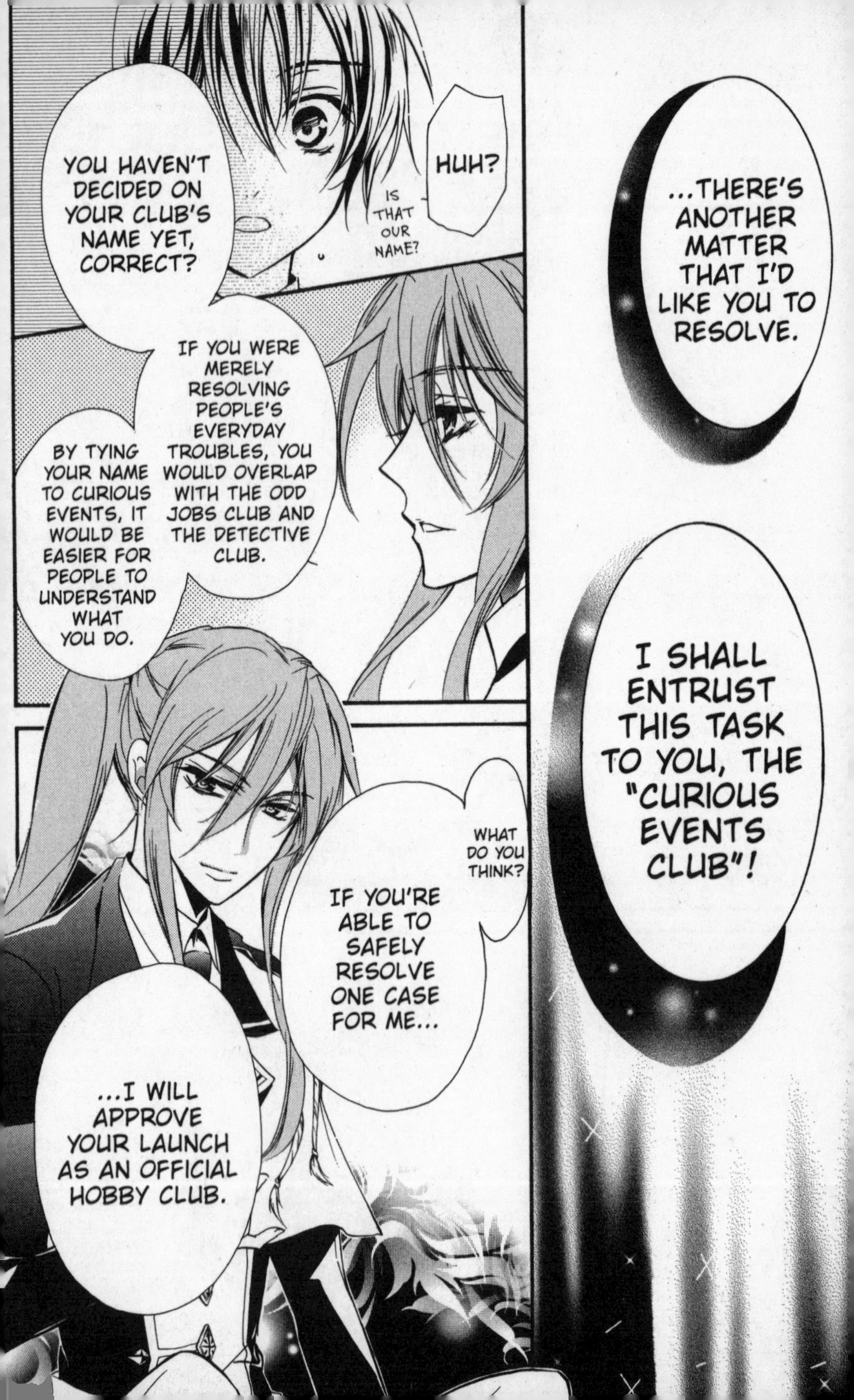
...THERE'S ANOTHER MATTER THAT I'D LIKE YOU TO RESOLVE.
I SHALL ENTRUST THIS TASK TO YOU, THE "CURIOUS EVENTS CLUB"!
YOU HAVEN'T DECIDED ON YOUR CLUB'S NAME YET, CORRECT?
HUH?
IS THAT OUR NAME?
IF YOU WERE MERELY RESOLVING PEOPLE'S EVERYDAY TROUBLES, YOU WOULD OVERLAP WITH THE ODD JOBS CLUB AND THE DETECTIVE CLUB.
BY TYING YOUR NAME TO CURIOUS EVENTS, IT WOULD BE EASIER FOR PEOPLE TO UNDERSTAND WHAT YOU DO.
WHAT DO YOU THINK?
IF YOU'RE ABLE TO SAFELY RESOLVE ONE CASE FOR ME...
...I WILL APPROVE YOUR LAUNCH AS AN OFFICIAL HOBBY CLUB.

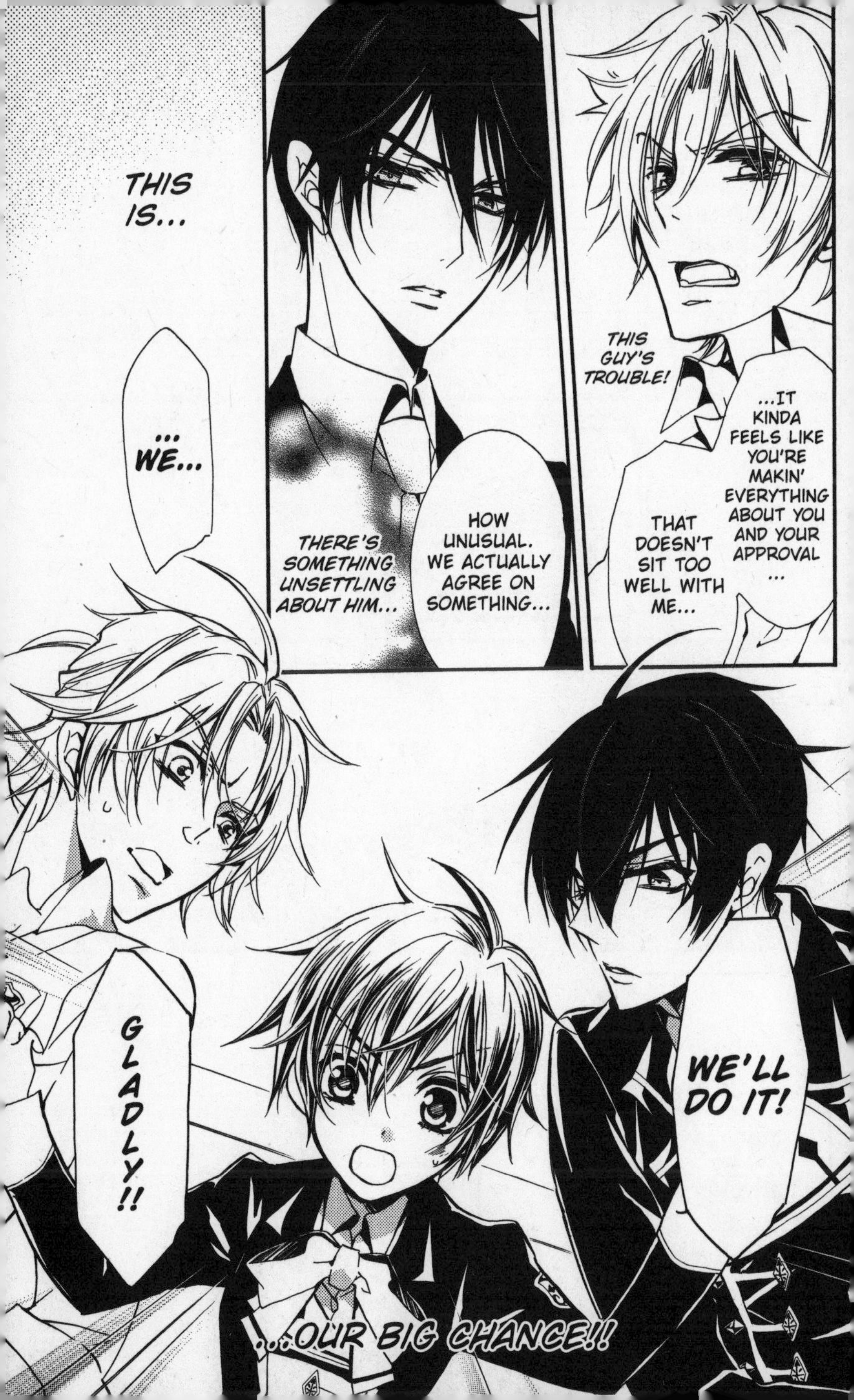
THIS GUY'S TROUBLE!
...IT KINDA FEELS LIKE YOU'RE MAKIN' EVERYTHING ABOUT YOU AND YOUR APPROVAL ...
THAT DOESN'T SIT TOO WELL WITH ME...
HOW UNUSUAL. WE ACTUALLY AGREE ON SOMETHING...
THERE'S SOMETHING UNSETTLING ABOUT HIM...
THIS IS...
... WE...
WE'LL DO IT!
GLADLY!!
...OUR BIG CHANCE!!

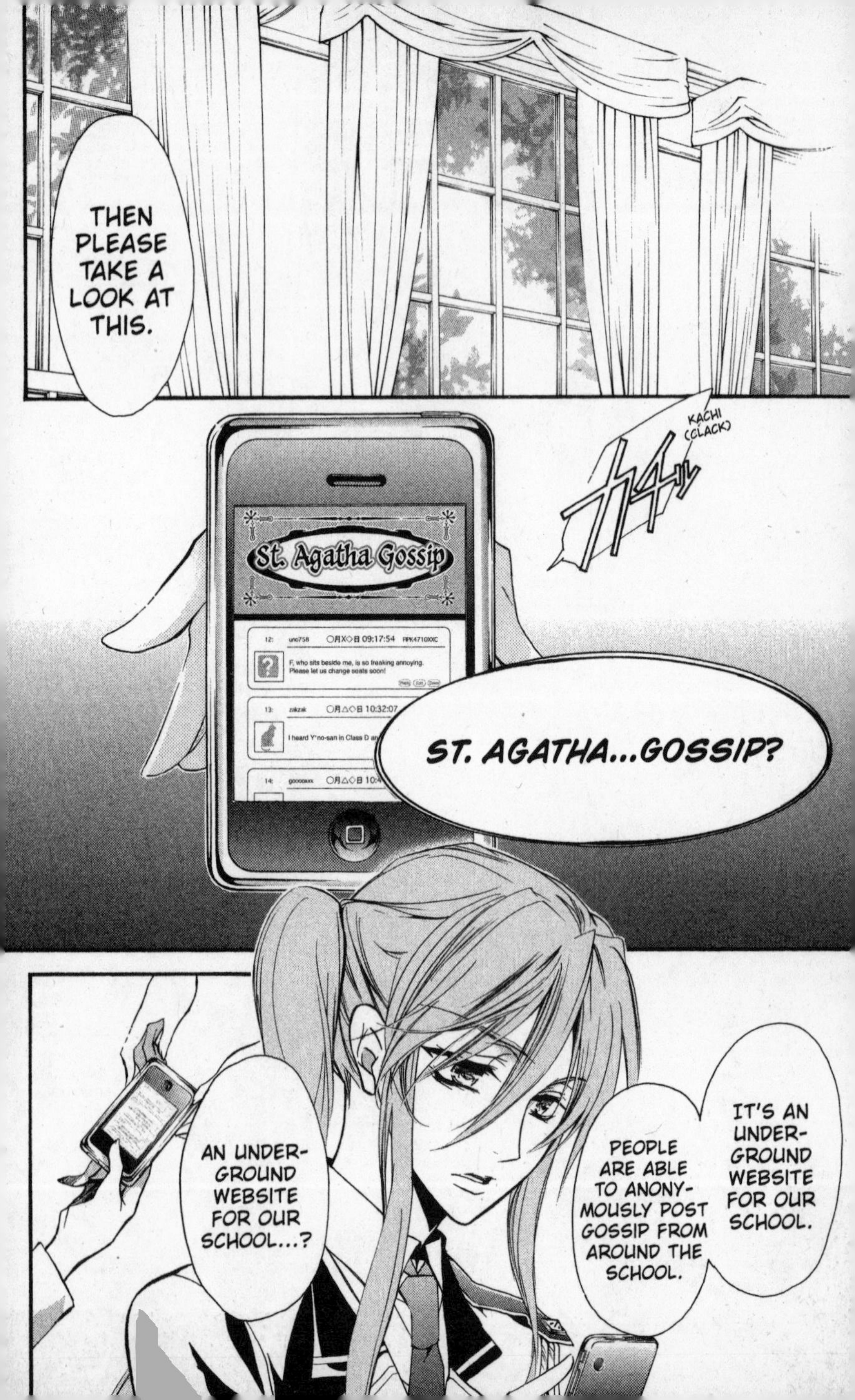
THEN PLEASE TAKE A LOOK AT THIS.
KACHI (CLACK)
St. Agatha Gossip
F, who sits beside me, is so freaking annoying. Please let us change seats soon!
ST. AGATHA...GOSSIP?
IT'S AN UNDER-GROUND WEBSITE FOR OUR SCHOOL.
PEOPLE ARE ABLE TO ANONY-MOUSLY POST GOSSIP FROM AROUND THE SCHOOL.
AN UNDER-GROUND WEBSITE FOR OUR SCHOOL...?

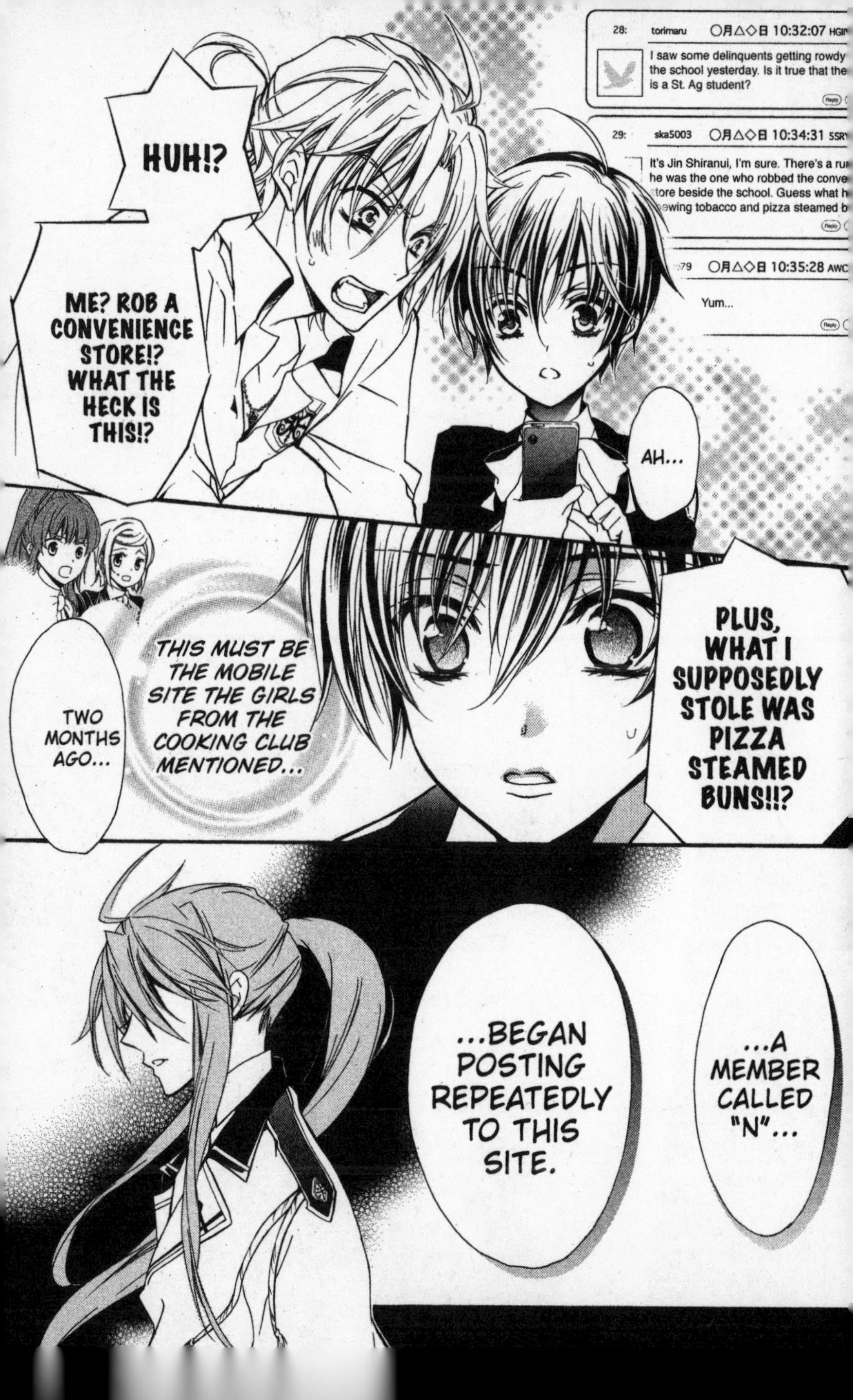

28: torimaru ○月△◇日 10:32:07
I saw some delinquents getting rowdy the school yesterday. Is it true that the is a St. Ag student?
Reply
29: ska5003 ○月△◇日 10:34:31
It's Jin Shiranui, I'm sure. There's a ru he was the one who robbed the conv tore beside the school. Guess what h ewing tobacco and pizza steamed b
Reply
○月△◇日 10:35:28
Yum...
Reply
AH...
HUH!?
ME? ROB A CONVENIENCE STORE!? WHAT THE HECK IS THIS!?
PLUS, WHAT I SUPPOSEDLY STOLE WAS PIZZA STEAMED BUNS!!?
THIS MUST BE THE MOBILE SITE THE GIRLS FROM THE COOKING CLUB MENTIONED...
TWO MONTHS AGO...
...A MEMBER CALLED "N"...
...BEGAN POSTING REPEATEDLY TO THIS SITE.

THE NUMBER OF PEOPLE SEEKING ADVICE FROM "N," AS THOUGH HE WERE A FORTUNE-TELLER, GREATLY INCREASED.

HIS ACCURATE PREDICTIONS CONTINUED TO INCREASE IN NUMBER AS WELL.

THEN, ONE DAY...

THE NUMBER OF POSTS N HAS MADE OUTSTRIPS ANYONE ELSE'S BY FAR.

REGARDLESS OF THE TRUTH OF THE RUMORS HE'S POSTED, HIS POSTS WERE NOTICEABLE FOR THEIR RANDOMNESS AND UNIQUE BREVITY, WHICH MADE HIM SOUND MYSTERIOUS.

EVENTUALLY, HE CAME TO BE CALLED "PROPHET N," A CHARISMATIC FIGURE ON THE MESSAGE BOARD.

06 : "N"   ×月○×日 08:45:16   4ZLQWD0OXX
S from Class A has been mulling over something lately.
(Reply)

The transfer st
hopeful that h

se who are

(Reply) (Edit) (Delete)

37 : "N"   □月△○日 21:54:23   4ZLQWD00XX
The Biology teacher's hair is a toupee.

81 : "N

24 : "N"   ◇月△□
Three volumes of Jap

:03:14   4Z WD0OXX   "N"
tally angry.
(Reply) (Edit) (Dele

17:38:01 4ZLQWD0OXX
g?
Is our s   us to begin with, but...
It was never that
(Reply) (Edit) (Delete)

Of all the things I've dropped, the shiny things tend to get found first.

□月○◇日
endeavor to stop dat

39 : "N"   ○月×日
All the bullying
work

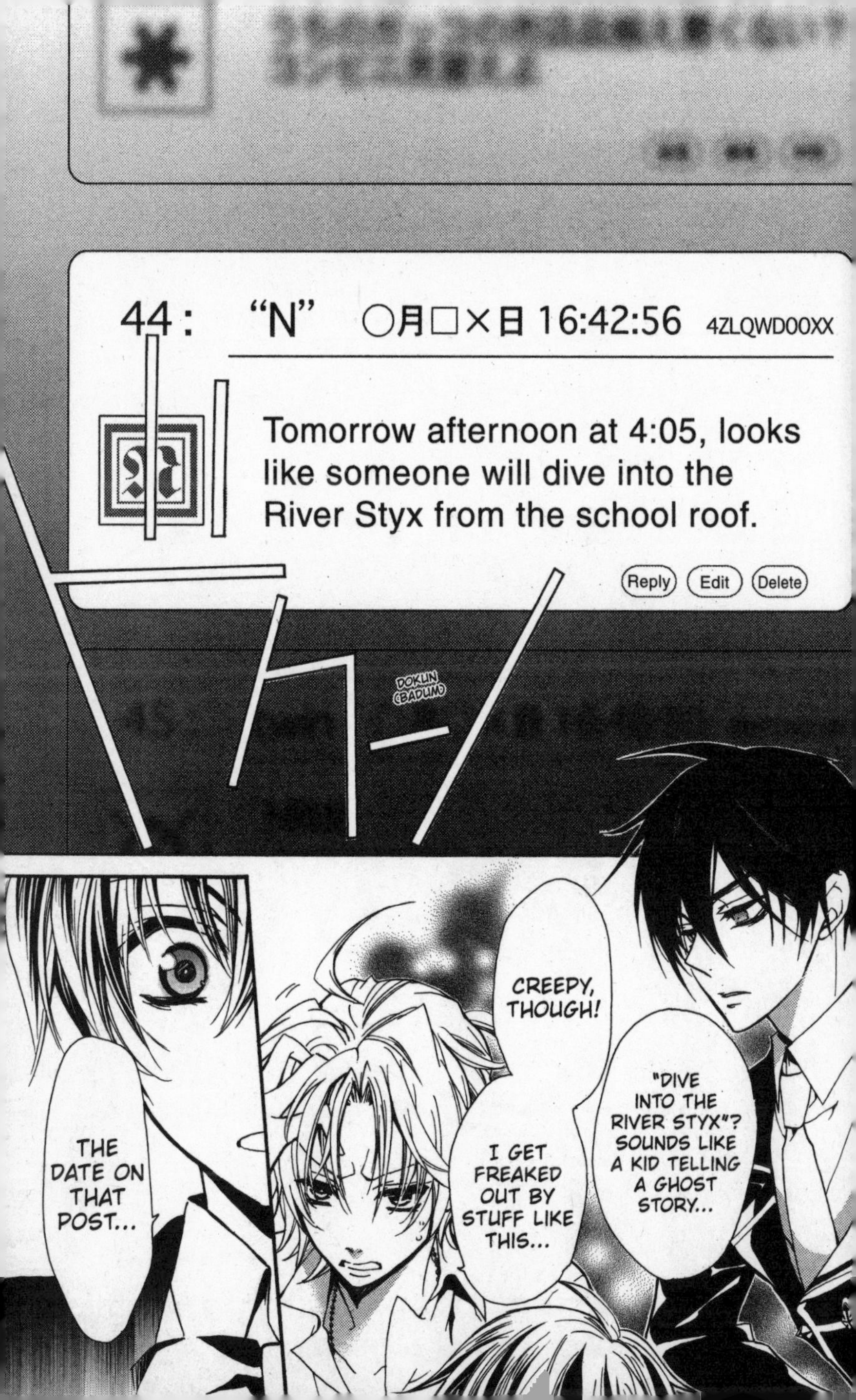
44: "N" ○月□×日 16:42:56 4ZLQWDOOXX
Tomorrow afternoon at 4:05, looks like someone will dive into the River Styx from the school roof.
Reply
Edit
Delete
DOKUN (BADUM)
"DIVE INTO THE RIVER STYX"? SOUNDS LIKE A KID TELLING A GHOST STORY...
CREEPY, THOUGH!
I GET FREAKED OUT BY STUFF LIKE THIS...
THE DATE ON THAT POST...

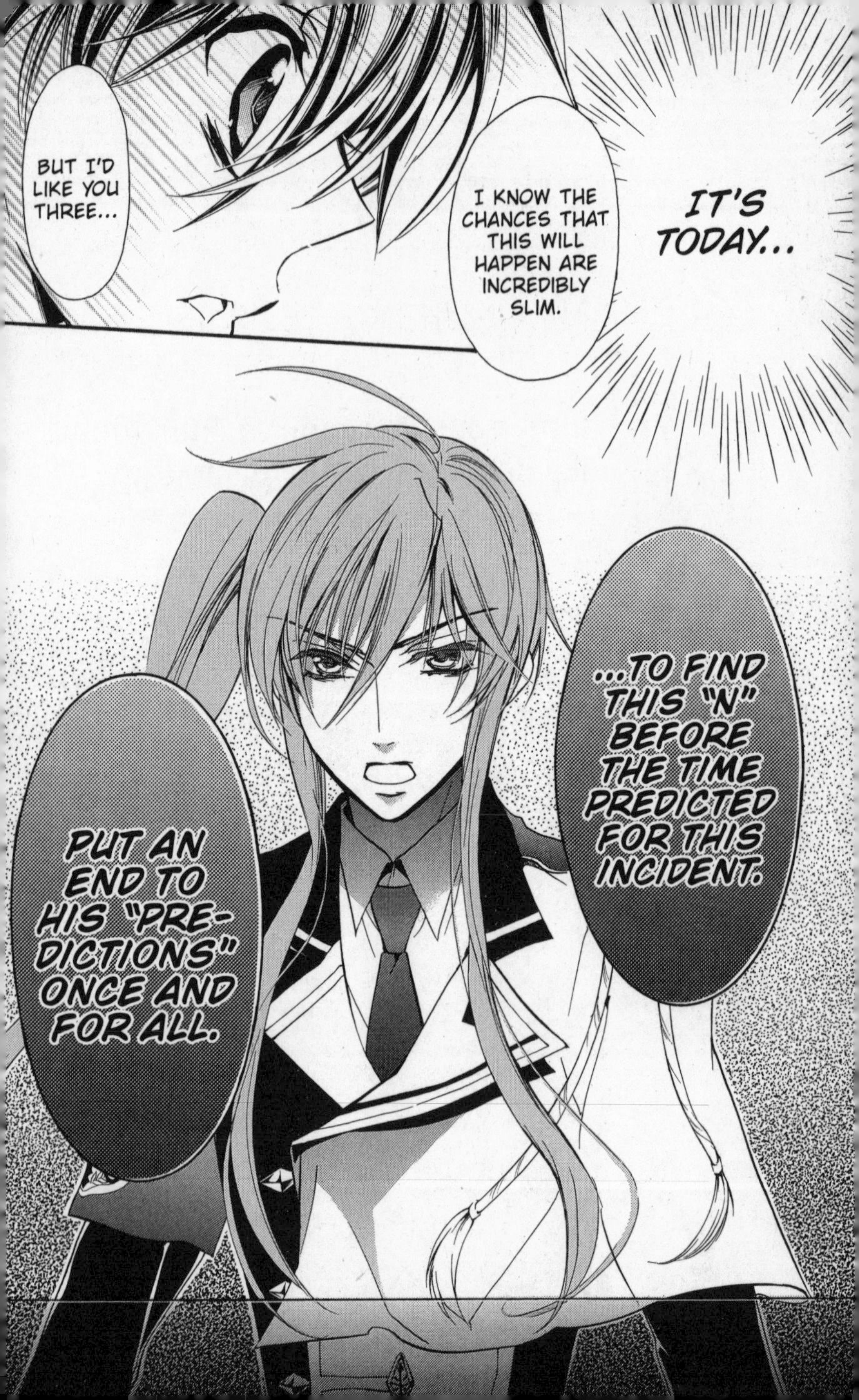
IT'S TODAY...
I KNOW THE CHANCES THAT THIS WILL HAPPEN ARE INCREDIBLY SLIM.
BUT I'D LIKE YOU THREE...
...TO FIND THIS "N" BEFORE THE TIME PREDICTED FOR THIS INCIDENT.
PUT AN END TO HIS "PRE-DICTIONS" ONCE AND FOR ALL.

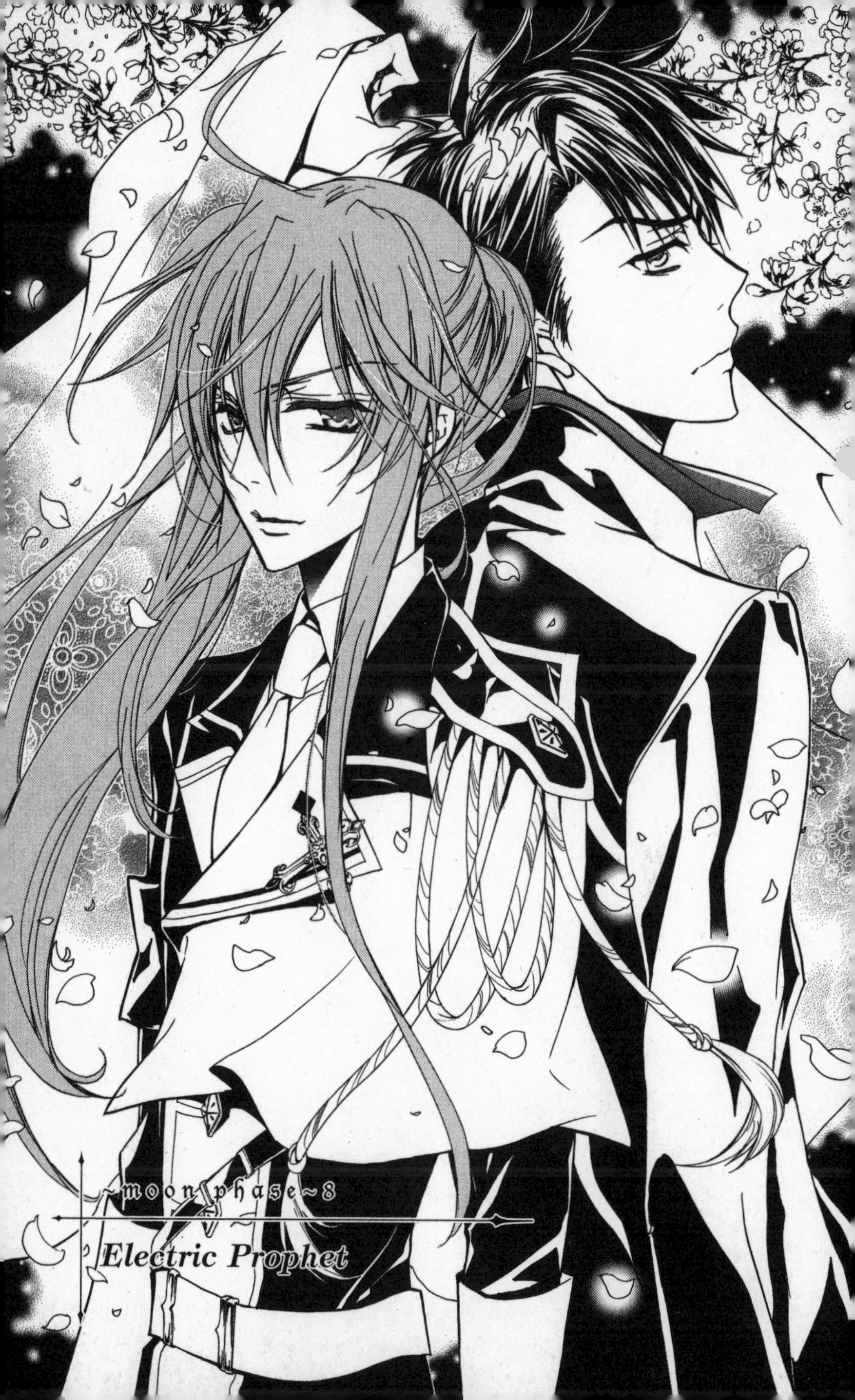
~moon phase~8
Electric Prophet

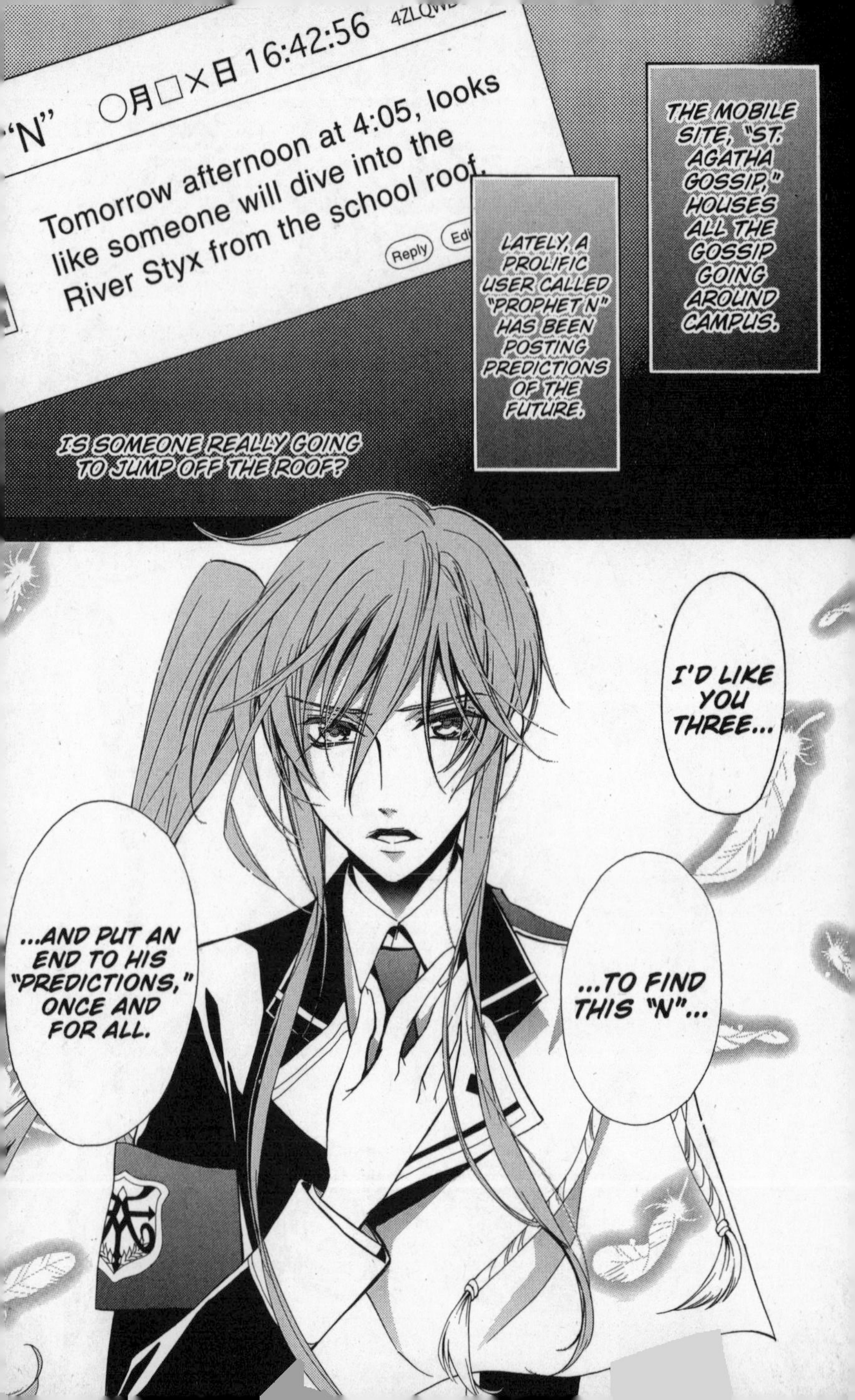
THE MOBILE SITE, "ST. AGATHA GOSSIP," HOUSES ALL THE GOSSIP GOING AROUND CAMPUS.
LATELY, A PROLIFIC USER CALLED "PROPHET N" HAS BEEN POSTING PREDICTIONS OF THE FUTURE.
“N” ○月□×日 16:42:56
Tomorrow afternoon at 4:05, looks like someone will dive into the River Styx from the school roof.
Reply
IS SOMEONE REALLY GOING TO JUMP OFF THE ROOF?
I'D LIKE YOU THREE...
...TO FIND THIS "N"...
...AND PUT AN END TO HIS "PREDICTIONS," ONCE AND FOR ALL.

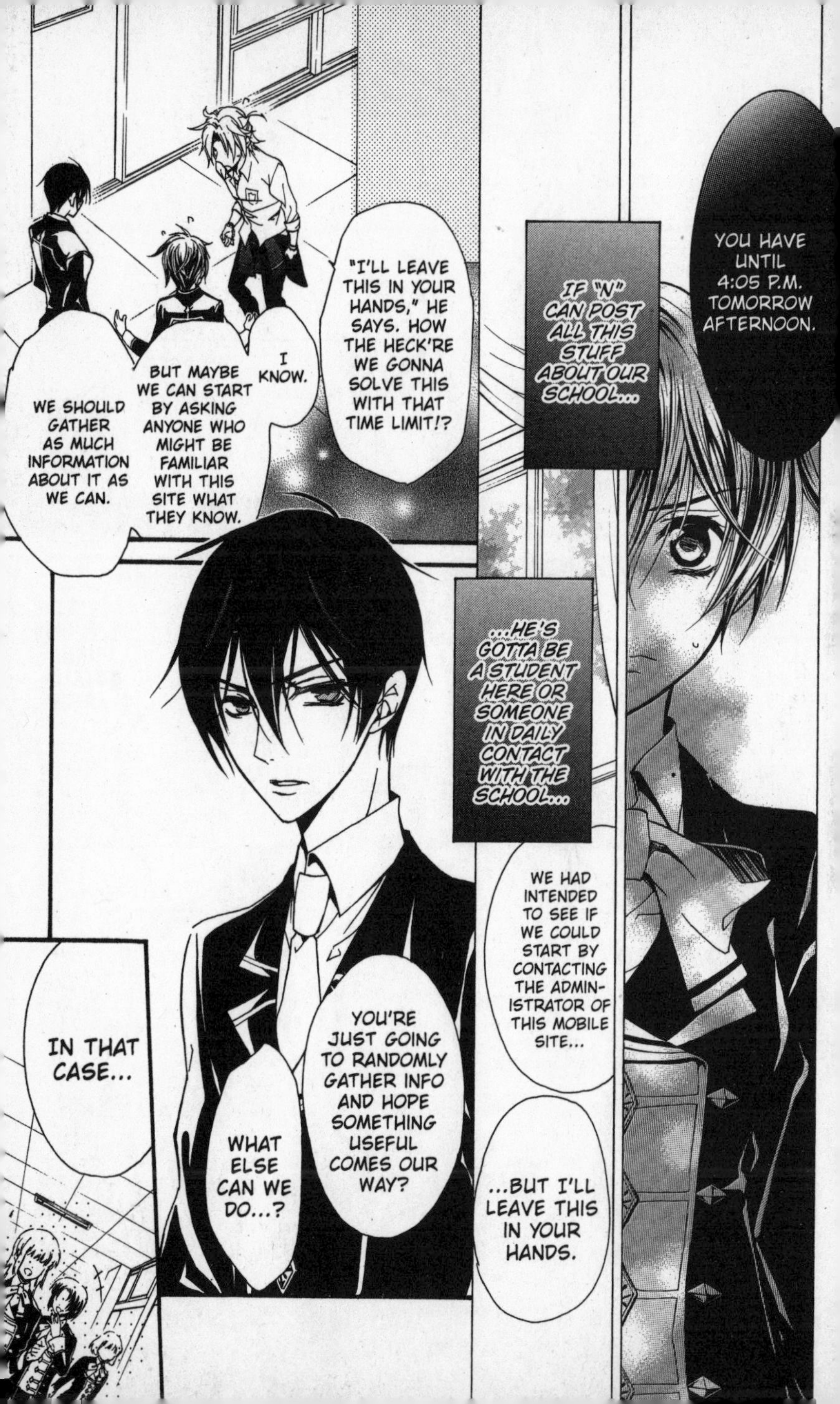
YOU HAVE UNTIL 4:05 P.M. TOMORROW AFTERNOON.
IF "N" CAN POST ALL THIS STUFF ABOUT OUR SCHOOL...
...HE'S GOTTA BE A STUDENT HERE OR SOMEONE IN DAILY CONTACT WITH THE SCHOOL...
WE HAD INTENDED TO SEE IF WE COULD START BY CONTACTING THE ADMIN-ISTRATOR OF THIS MOBILE SITE...
...BUT I'LL LEAVE THIS IN YOUR HANDS.
"I'LL LEAVE THIS IN YOUR HANDS," HE SAYS. HOW THE HECK'RE WE GONNA SOLVE THIS WITH THAT TIME LIMIT!?
I KNOW.
BUT MAYBE WE CAN START BY ASKING ANYONE WHO MIGHT BE FAMILIAR WITH THIS SITE WHAT THEY KNOW.
WE SHOULD GATHER AS MUCH INFORMATION ABOUT IT AS WE CAN.
YOU'RE JUST GOING TO RANDOMLY GATHER INFO AND HOPE SOMETHING USEFUL COMES OUR WAY?
WHAT ELSE CAN WE DO...?
IN THAT CASE...

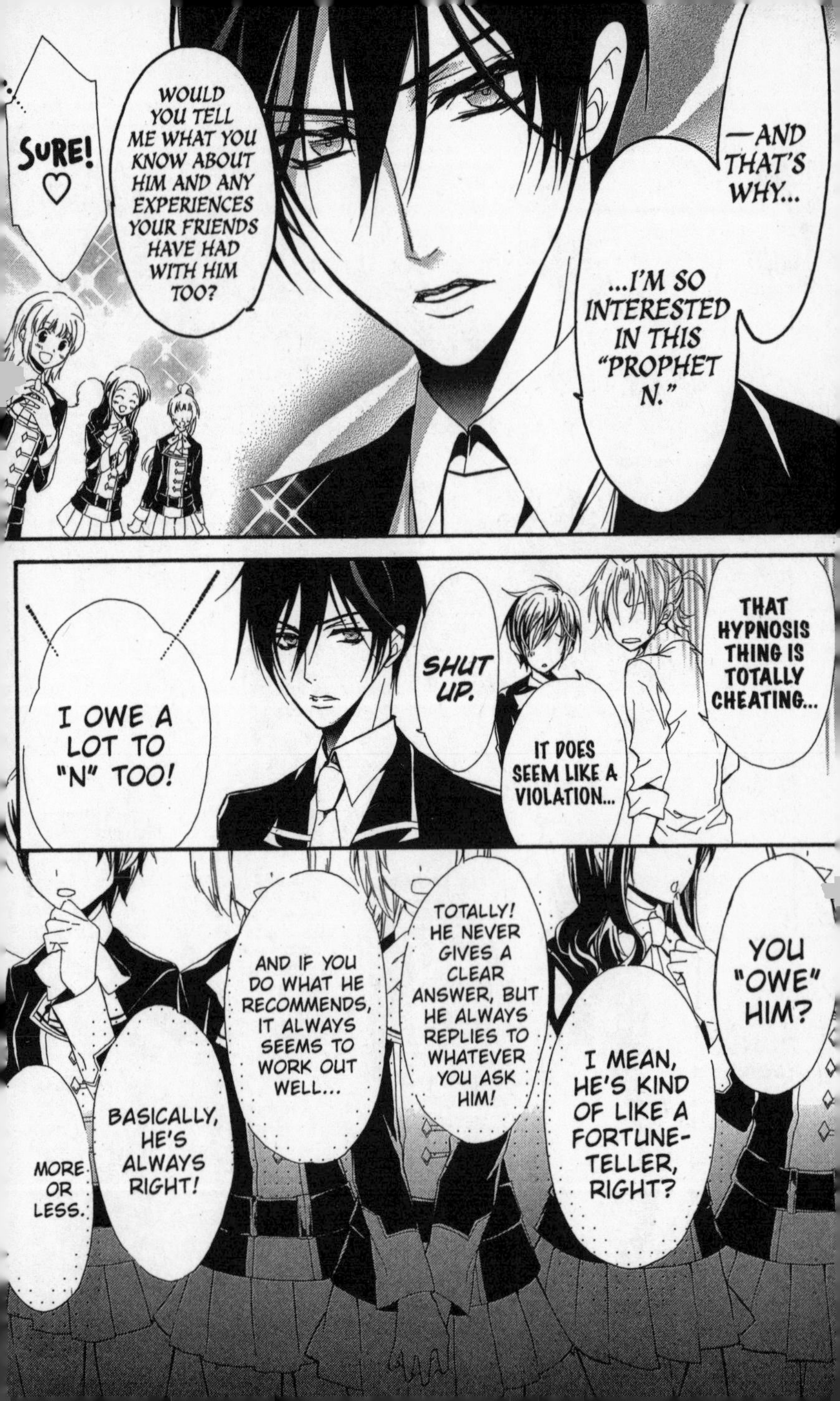
—AND THAT'S WHY...
...I'M SO INTERESTED IN THIS "PROPHET N."
WOULD YOU TELL ME WHAT YOU KNOW ABOUT HIM AND ANY EXPERIENCES YOUR FRIENDS HAVE HAD WITH HIM TOO?
SURE! ♡
THAT HYPNOSIS THING IS TOTALLY CHEATING...
IT DOES SEEM LIKE A VIOLATION...
SHUT UP.
I OWE A LOT TO "N" TOO!
YOU "OWE" HIM?
I MEAN, HE'S KIND OF LIKE A FORTUNE-TELLER, RIGHT?
TOTALLY! HE NEVER GIVES A CLEAR ANSWER, BUT HE ALWAYS REPLIES TO WHATEVER YOU ASK HIM!
AND IF YOU DO WHAT HE RECOMMENDS, IT ALWAYS SEEMS TO WORK OUT WELL...
BASICALLY, HE'S ALWAYS RIGHT!
MORE OR LESS.

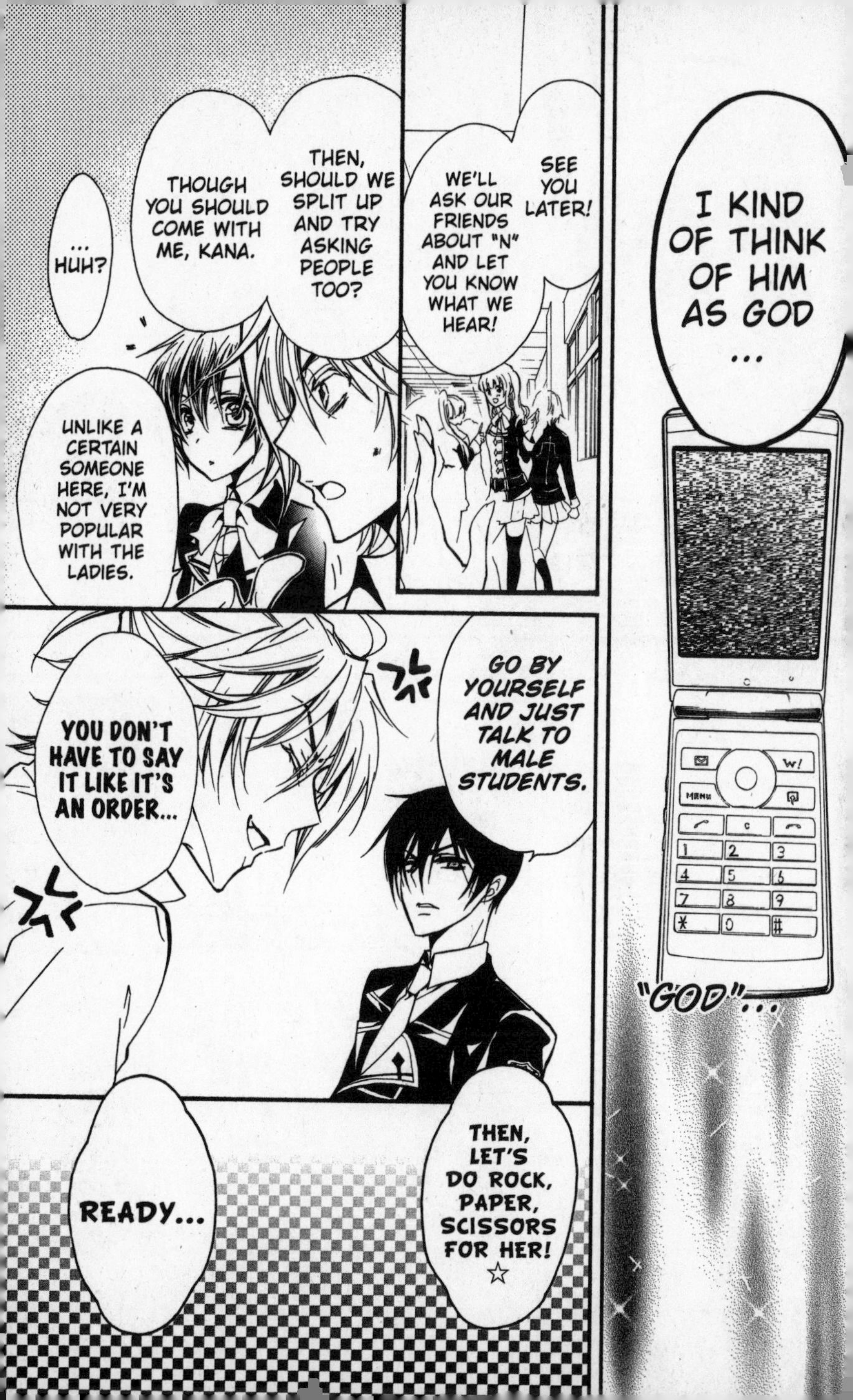
I KIND OF THINK OF HIM AS GOD ...
"GOD"...
SEE YOU LATER!
WE'LL ASK OUR FRIENDS ABOUT "N" AND LET YOU KNOW WHAT WE HEAR!
THEN, SHOULD WE SPLIT UP AND TRY ASKING PEOPLE TOO?
THOUGH YOU SHOULD COME WITH ME, KANA.
... HUH?
UNLIKE A CERTAIN SOMEONE HERE, I'M NOT VERY POPULAR WITH THE LADIES.
GO BY YOURSELF AND JUST TALK TO MALE STUDENTS.
YOU DON'T HAVE TO SAY IT LIKE IT'S AN ORDER...
THEN, LET'S DO ROCK, PAPER, SCISSORS FOR HER! ☆
READY...

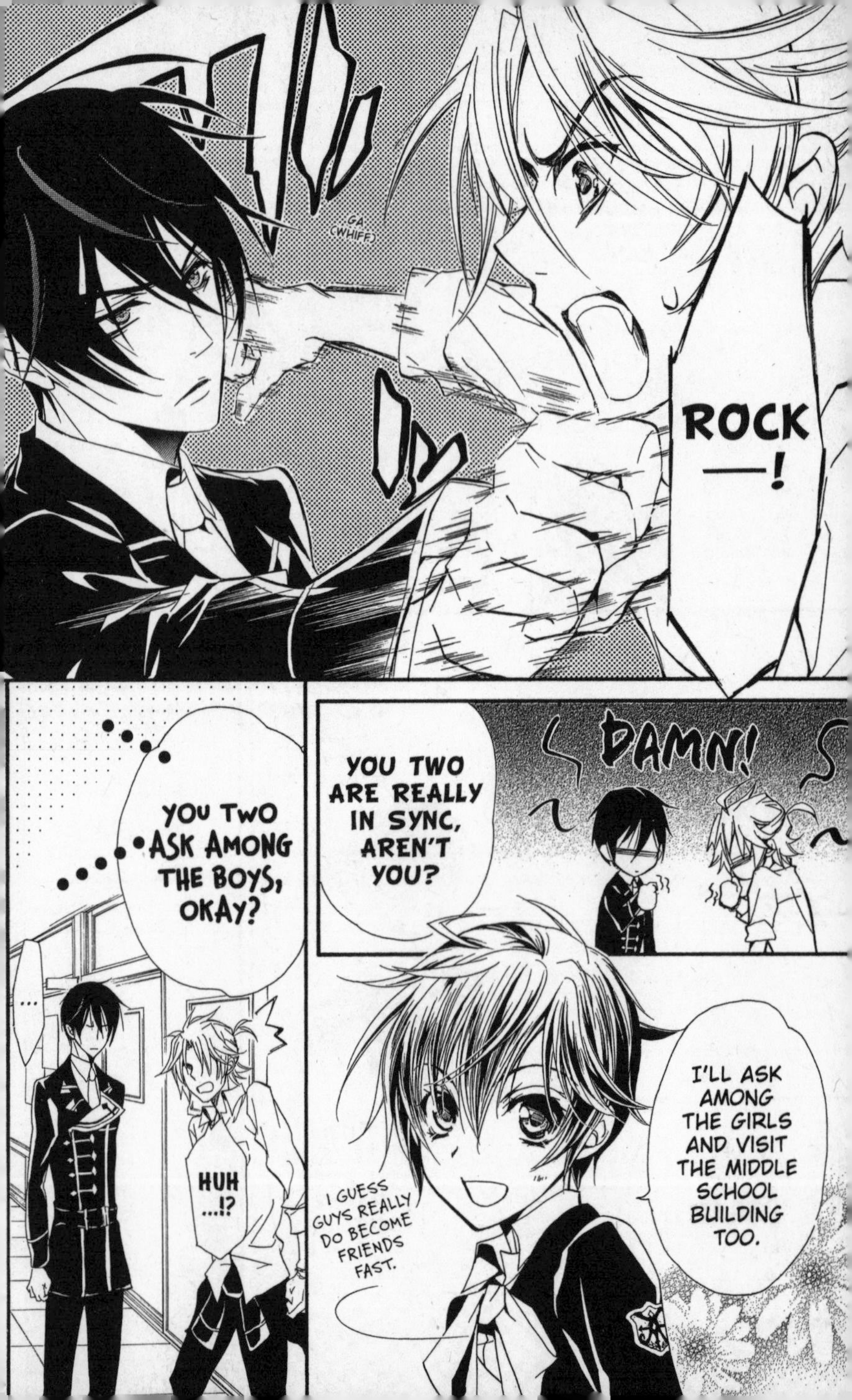
ROCK —!
GA (WHIFF)
DAMN!
YOU TWO ARE REALLY IN SYNC, AREN'T YOU?
I'LL ASK AMONG THE GIRLS AND VISIT THE MIDDLE SCHOOL BUILDING TOO.
I GUESS GUYS REALLY DO BECOME FRIENDS FAST.
YOU TWO ASK AMONG THE BOYS, OKAY?
HUH ...!?
...

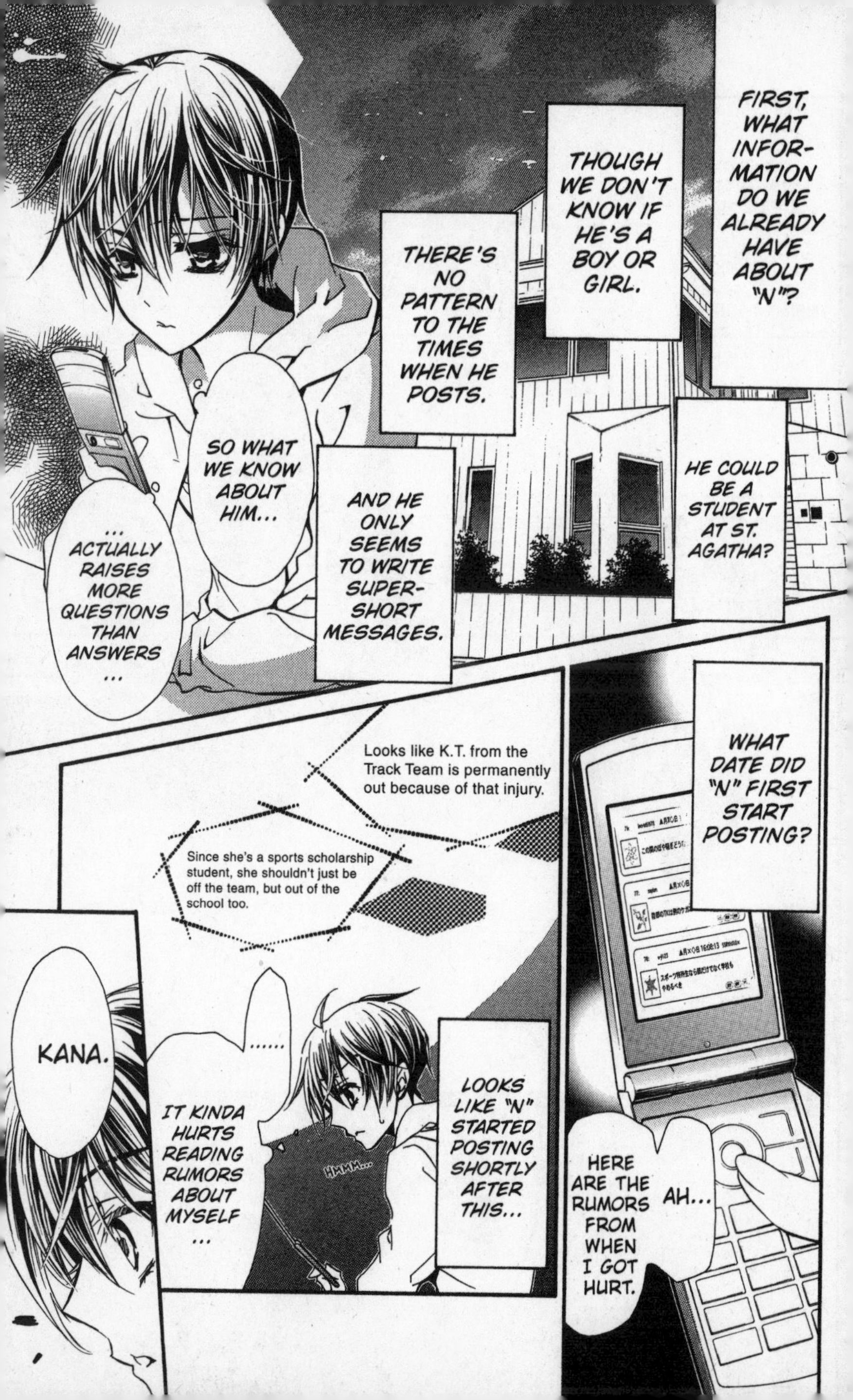
FIRST, WHAT INFORMATION DO WE ALREADY HAVE ABOUT "N"?
THOUGH WE DON'T KNOW IF HE'S A BOY OR GIRL.
HE COULD BE A STUDENT AT ST. AGATHA?
THERE'S NO PATTERN TO THE TIMES WHEN HE POSTS.
AND HE ONLY SEEMS TO WRITE SUPER-SHORT MESSAGES.
SO WHAT WE KNOW ABOUT HIM...
...ACTUALLY RAISES MORE QUESTIONS THAN ANSWERS...
WHAT DATE DID "N" FIRST START POSTING?
AH...
HERE ARE THE RUMORS FROM WHEN I GOT HURT.
Looks like K.T. from the Track Team is permanently out because of that injury.
Since she's a sports scholarship student, she shouldn't just be off the team, but out of the school too.
LOOKS LIKE "N" STARTED POSTING SHORTLY AFTER THIS...
HMMM...
......
IT KINDA HURTS READING RUMORS ABOUT MYSELF...
KANA.

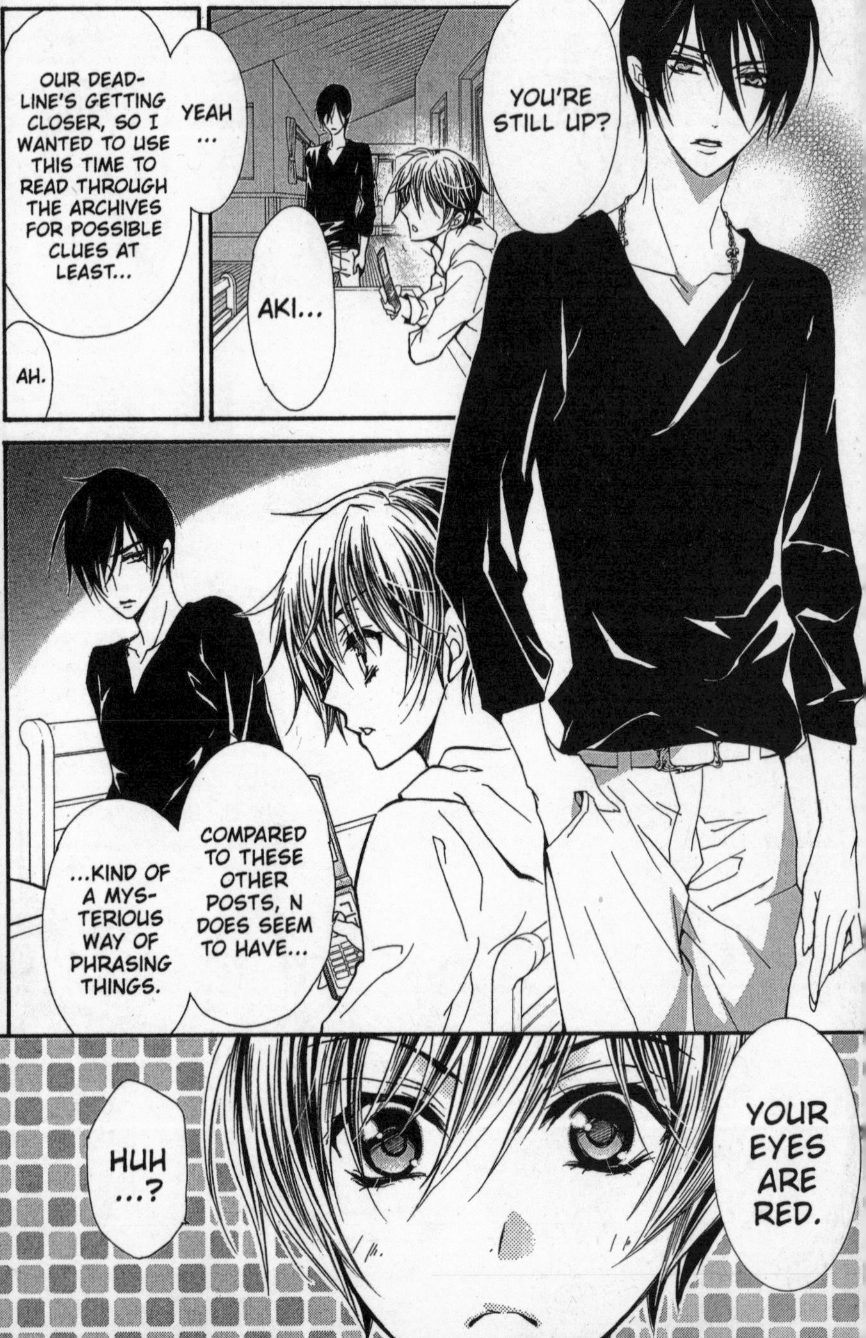
YOU'RE STILL UP?
AKI...
YEAH ...
OUR DEAD-LINE'S GETTING CLOSER, SO I WANTED TO USE THIS TIME TO READ THROUGH THE ARCHIVES FOR POSSIBLE CLUES AT LEAST...
AH.
COMPARED TO THESE OTHER POSTS, N DOES SEEM TO HAVE...
...KIND OF A MYS-TERIOUS WAY OF PHRASING THINGS.
YOUR EYES ARE RED.
HUH ...?

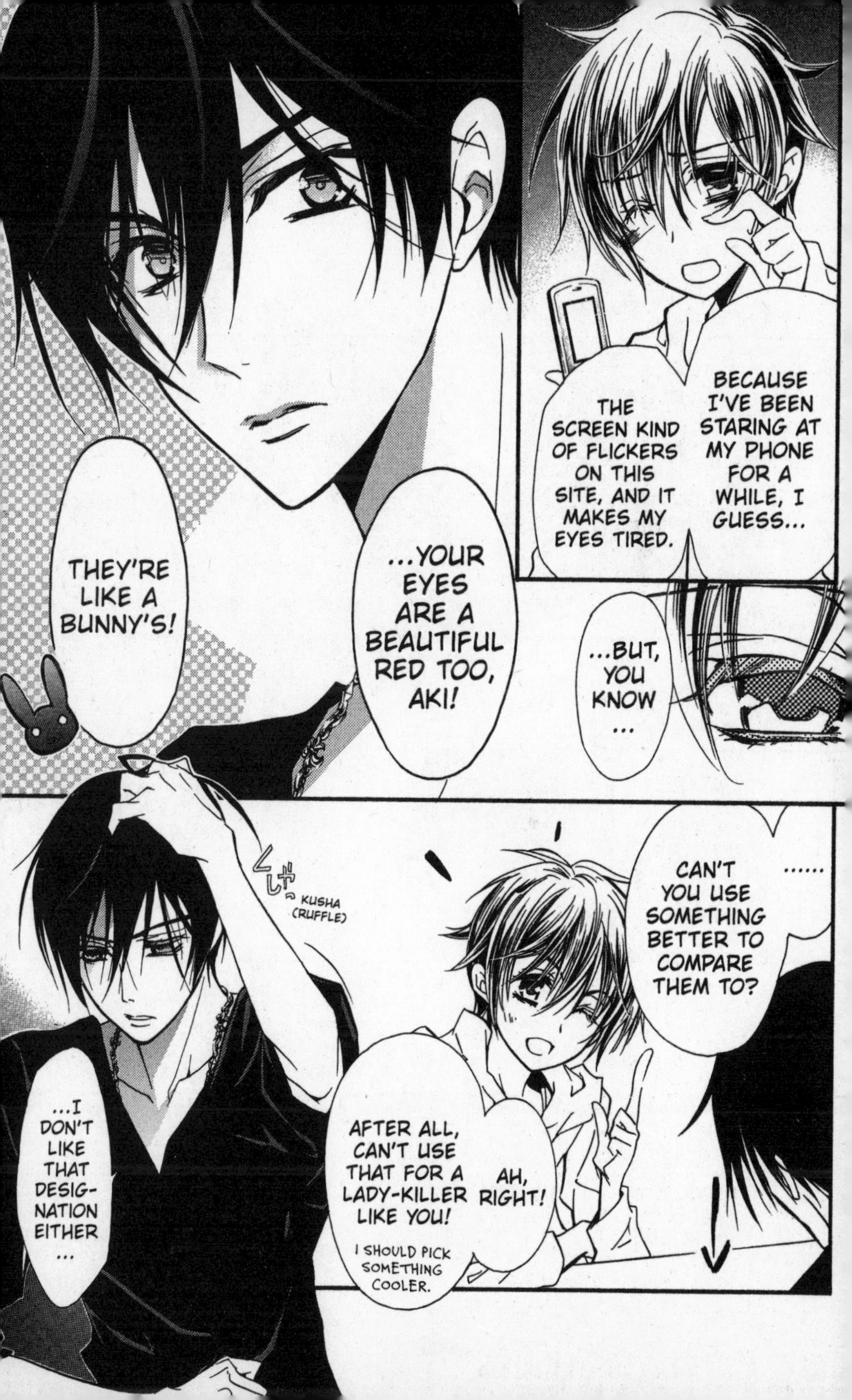
BECAUSE I'VE BEEN STARING AT MY PHONE FOR A WHILE, I GUESS...
THE SCREEN KIND OF FLICKERS ON THIS SITE, AND IT MAKES MY EYES TIRED.
...BUT, YOU KNOW ...
...YOUR EYES ARE A BEAUTIFUL RED TOO, AKI!
THEY'RE LIKE A BUNNY'S!
......
CAN'T YOU USE SOMETHING BETTER TO COMPARE THEM TO?
AH, RIGHT!
AFTER ALL, CAN'T USE THAT FOR A LADY-KILLER LIKE YOU!
I SHOULD PICK SOMETHING COOLER.
KUSHA (RUFFLE)
...I DON'T LIKE THAT DESIGNATION EITHER ...

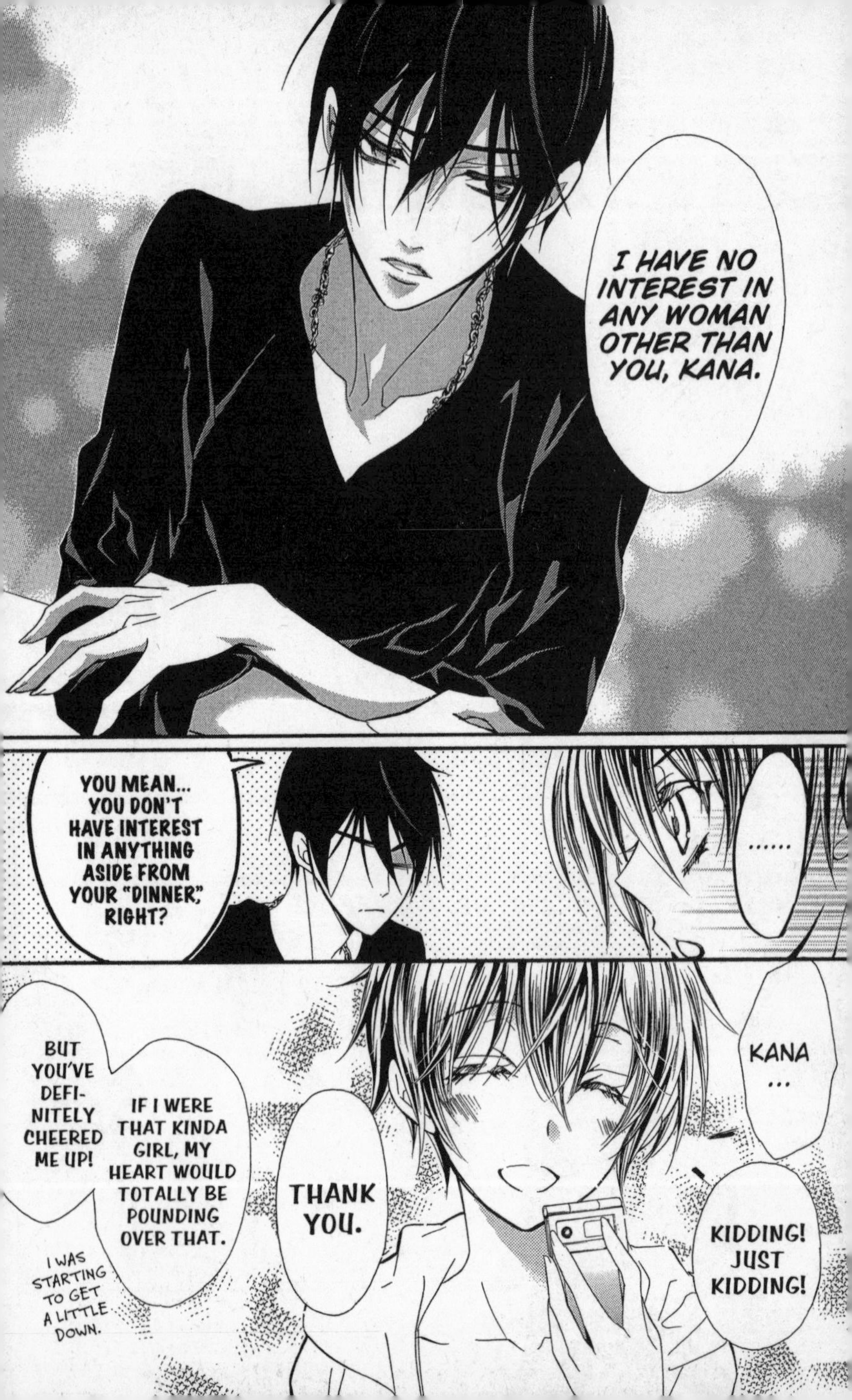
I HAVE NO INTEREST IN ANY WOMAN OTHER THAN YOU, KANA.
......
YOU MEAN... YOU DON'T HAVE INTEREST IN ANYTHING ASIDE FROM YOUR "DINNER," RIGHT?
KANA...
KIDDING! JUST KIDDING!
THANK YOU.
IF I WERE THAT KINDA GIRL, MY HEART WOULD TOTALLY BE POUNDING OVER THAT.
BUT YOU'VE DEFI- NITELY CHEERED ME UP!
I WAS STARTING TO GET A LITTLE DOWN.

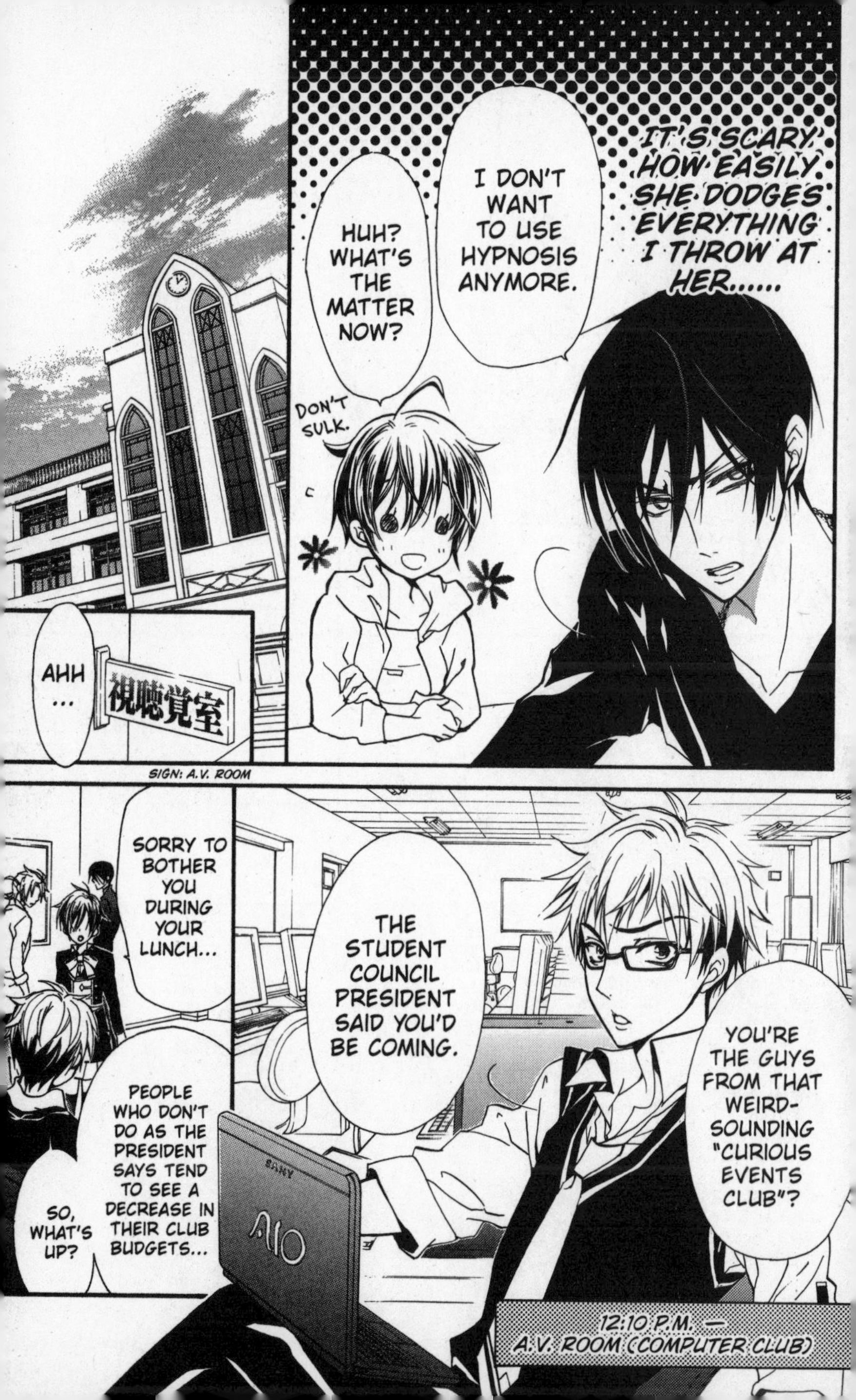
IT'S SCARY HOW EASILY SHE DODGES EVERYTHING I THROW AT HER......
I DON'T WANT TO USE HYPNOSIS ANYMORE.
HUH? WHAT'S THE MATTER NOW?
DON'T SULK.
AHH ...
視聴覚室
SIGN: A.V. ROOM
12:10 P.M. — A.V. ROOM (COMPUTER CLUB)
YOU'RE THE GUYS FROM THAT WEIRD-SOUNDING "CURIOUS EVENTS CLUB"?
THE STUDENT COUNCIL PRESIDENT SAID YOU'D BE COMING.
PEOPLE WHO DON'T DO AS THE PRESIDENT SAYS TEND TO SEE A DECREASE IN THEIR CLUB BUDGETS...
SO, WHAT'S UP?
SORRY TO BOTHER YOU DURING YOUR LUNCH...

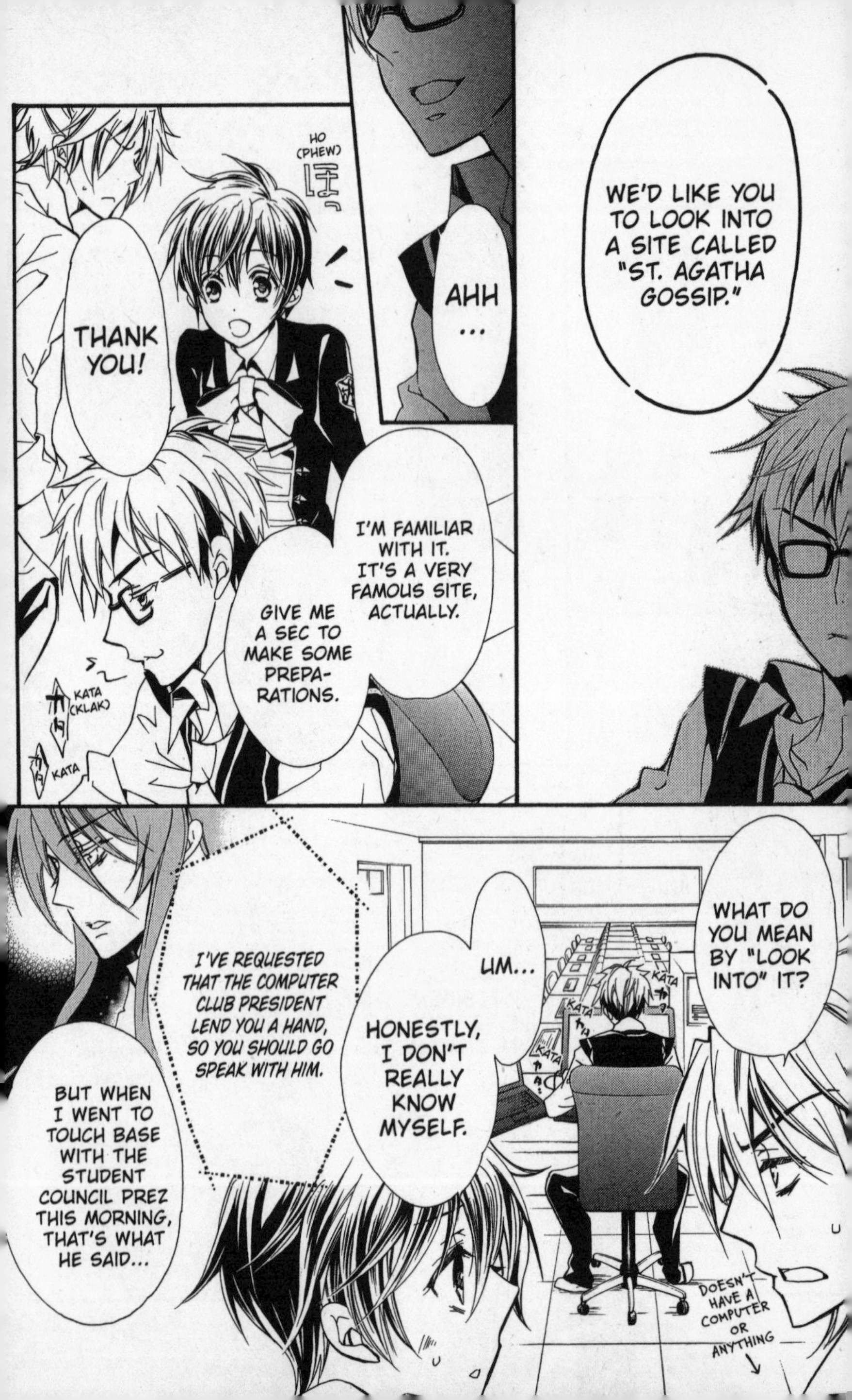
WE'D LIKE YOU TO LOOK INTO A SITE CALLED "ST. AGATHA GOSSIP."
AHH ...
HO (PHEW)
ほっ
THANK YOU!
I'M FAMILIAR WITH IT. IT'S A VERY FAMOUS SITE, ACTUALLY.
GIVE ME A SEC TO MAKE SOME PREPA-RATIONS.
KATA (KLAK)
カタ
カタ
KATA
WHAT DO YOU MEAN BY "LOOK INTO" IT?
UM...
HONESTLY, I DON'T REALLY KNOW MYSELF.
KATA
KATA
KATA
I'VE REQUESTED THAT THE COMPUTER CLUB PRESIDENT LEND YOU A HAND, SO YOU SHOULD GO SPEAK WITH HIM.
BUT WHEN I WENT TO TOUCH BASE WITH THE STUDENT COUNCIL PREZ THIS MORNING, THAT'S WHAT HE SAID...
DOESN'T HAVE A COMPUTER OR ANYTHING

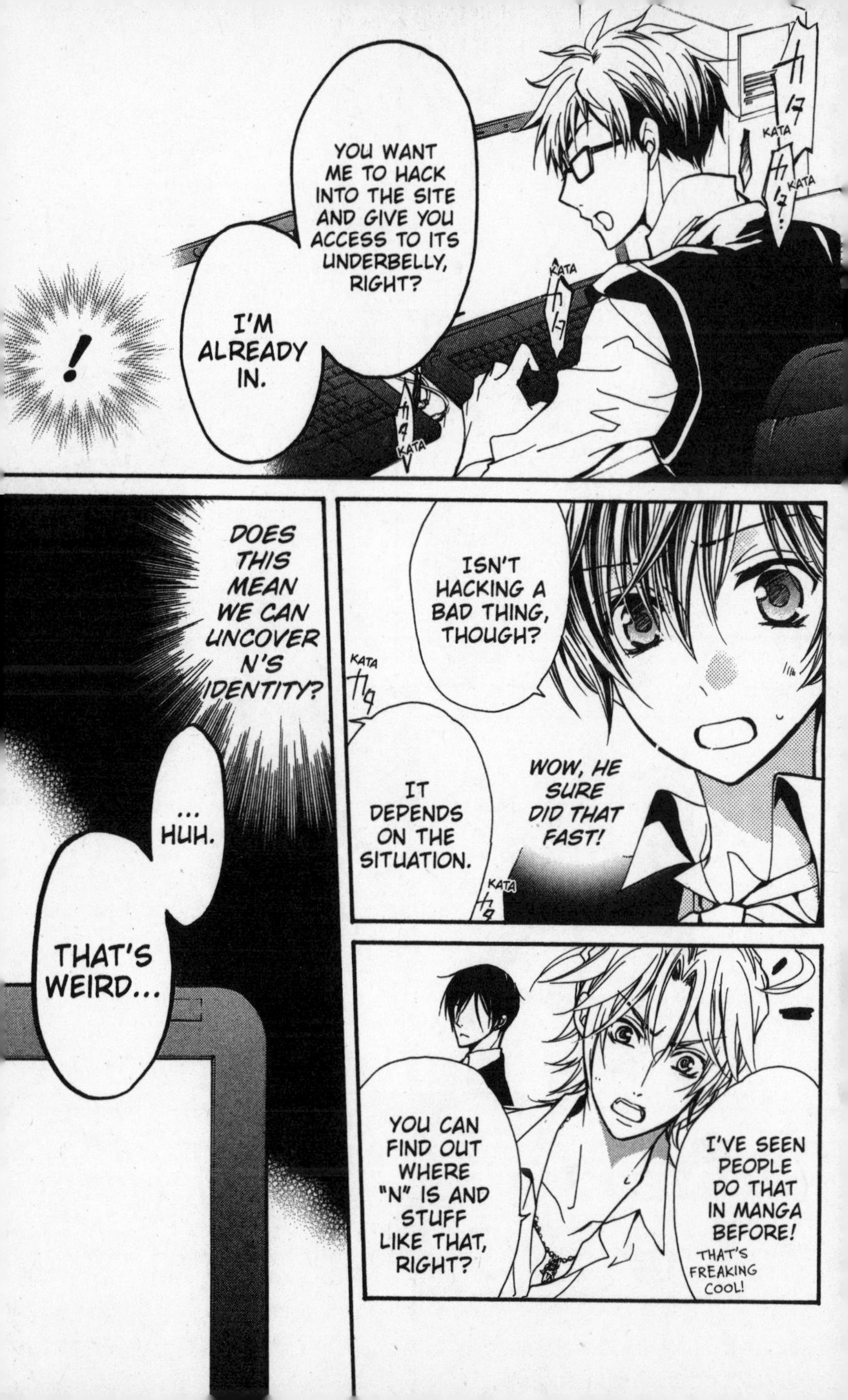
KATA
KATA
YOU WANT ME TO HACK INTO THE SITE AND GIVE YOU ACCESS TO ITS UNDERBELLY, RIGHT?
KATA
I'M ALREADY IN.
KATA
!
ISN'T HACKING A BAD THING, THOUGH?
WOW, HE SURE DID THAT FAST!
KATA
IT DEPENDS ON THE SITUATION.
KATA
I'VE SEEN PEOPLE DO THAT IN MANGA BEFORE!
THAT'S FREAKING COOL!
YOU CAN FIND OUT WHERE "N" IS AND STUFF LIKE THAT, RIGHT?
DOES THIS MEAN WE CAN UNCOVER N'S IDENTITY?
... HUH.
THAT'S WEIRD...

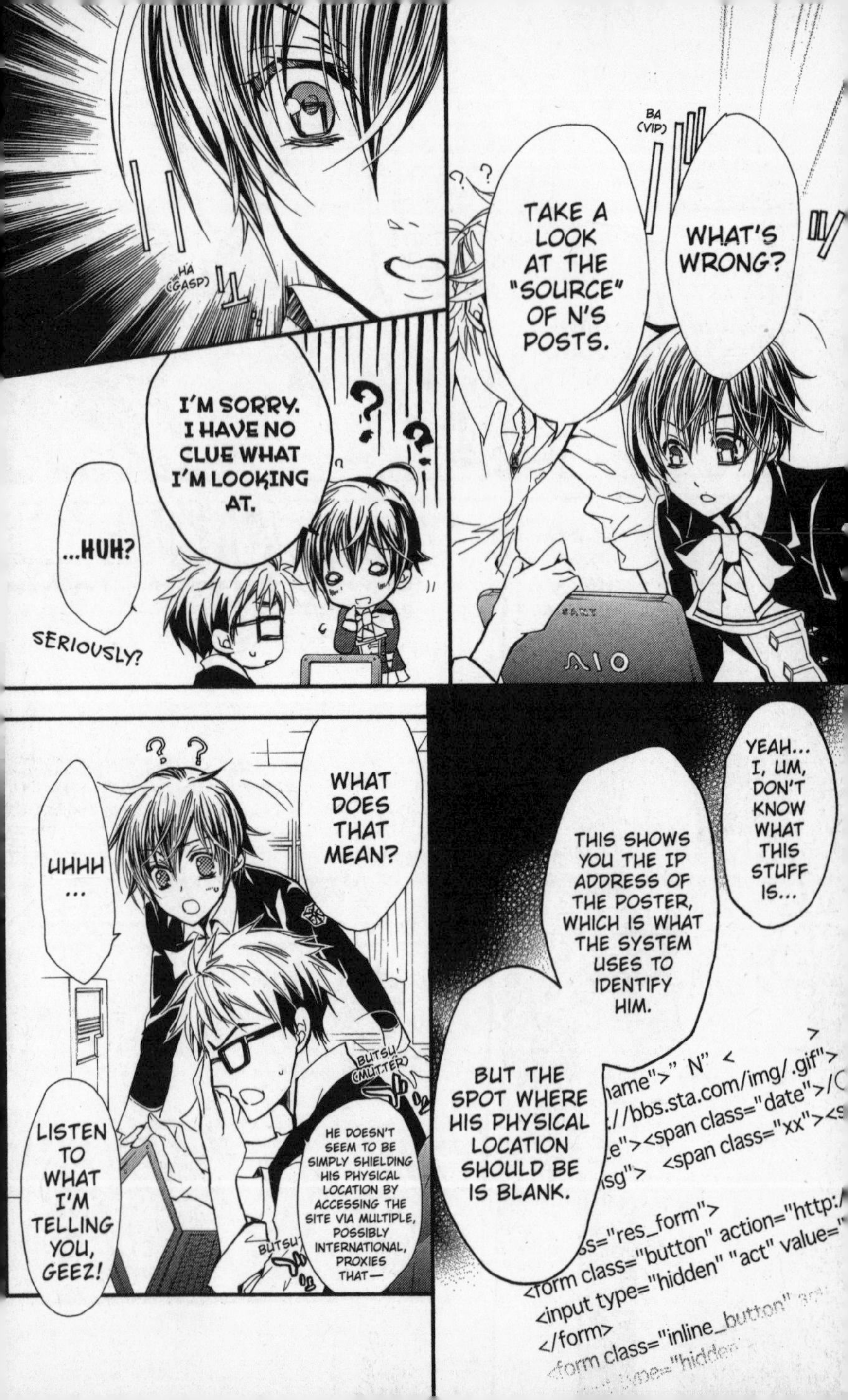
BA (VIP)
WHAT'S WRONG?
TAKE A LOOK AT THE "SOURCE" OF N'S POSTS.
HA (GASP)
I'M SORRY. I HAVE NO CLUE WHAT I'M LOOKING AT.
...HUH?
SERIOUSLY?
YEAH... I, UM, DON'T KNOW WHAT THIS STUFF IS...
THIS SHOWS YOU THE IP ADDRESS OF THE POSTER, WHICH IS WHAT THE SYSTEM USES TO IDENTIFY HIM.
BUT THE SPOT WHERE HIS PHYSICAL LOCATION SHOULD BE IS BLANK.
name">" N" <
://bbs.sta.com/img/.gif">
e"><span class="date">
<span class="xx">
sg">
="res_form">
<form class="button" action="http:/
<input type="hidden" "act" value="
</form>
<form class="inline_button"
WHAT DOES THAT MEAN?
UHHH ...
BUTSU (MUTTER)
HE DOESN'T SEEM TO BE SIMPLY SHIELDING HIS PHYSICAL LOCATION BY ACCESSING THE SITE VIA MULTIPLE, POSSIBLY INTERNATIONAL, PROXIES THAT—
BUTSU
LISTEN TO WHAT I'M TELLING YOU, GEEZ!

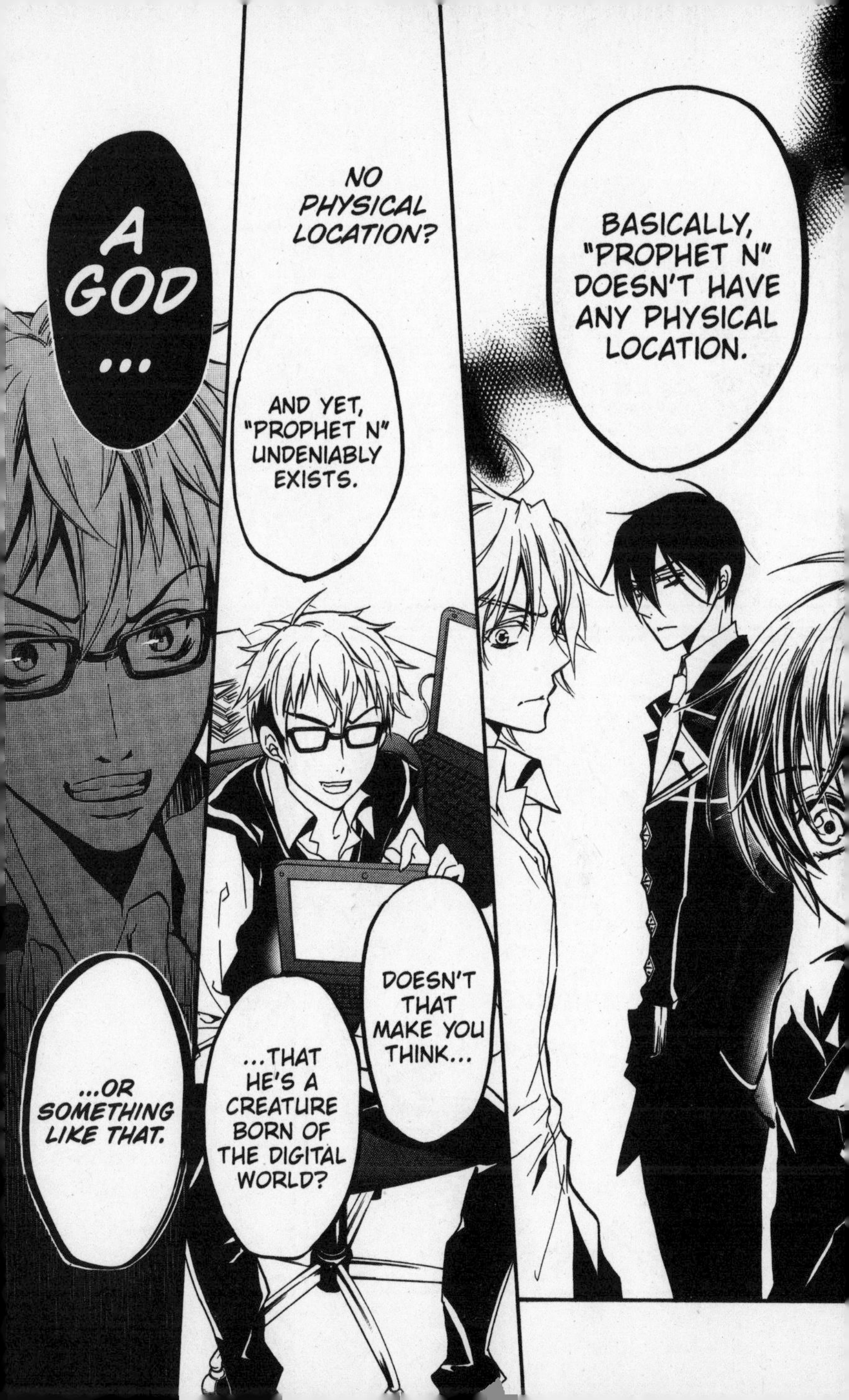
BASICALLY, "PROPHET N" DOESN'T HAVE ANY PHYSICAL LOCATION.
NO PHYSICAL LOCATION?
AND YET, "PROPHET N" UNDENIABLY EXISTS.
DOESN'T THAT MAKE YOU THINK...
...THAT HE'S A CREATURE BORN OF THE DIGITAL WORLD?
A GOD...
...OR SOMETHING LIKE THAT.

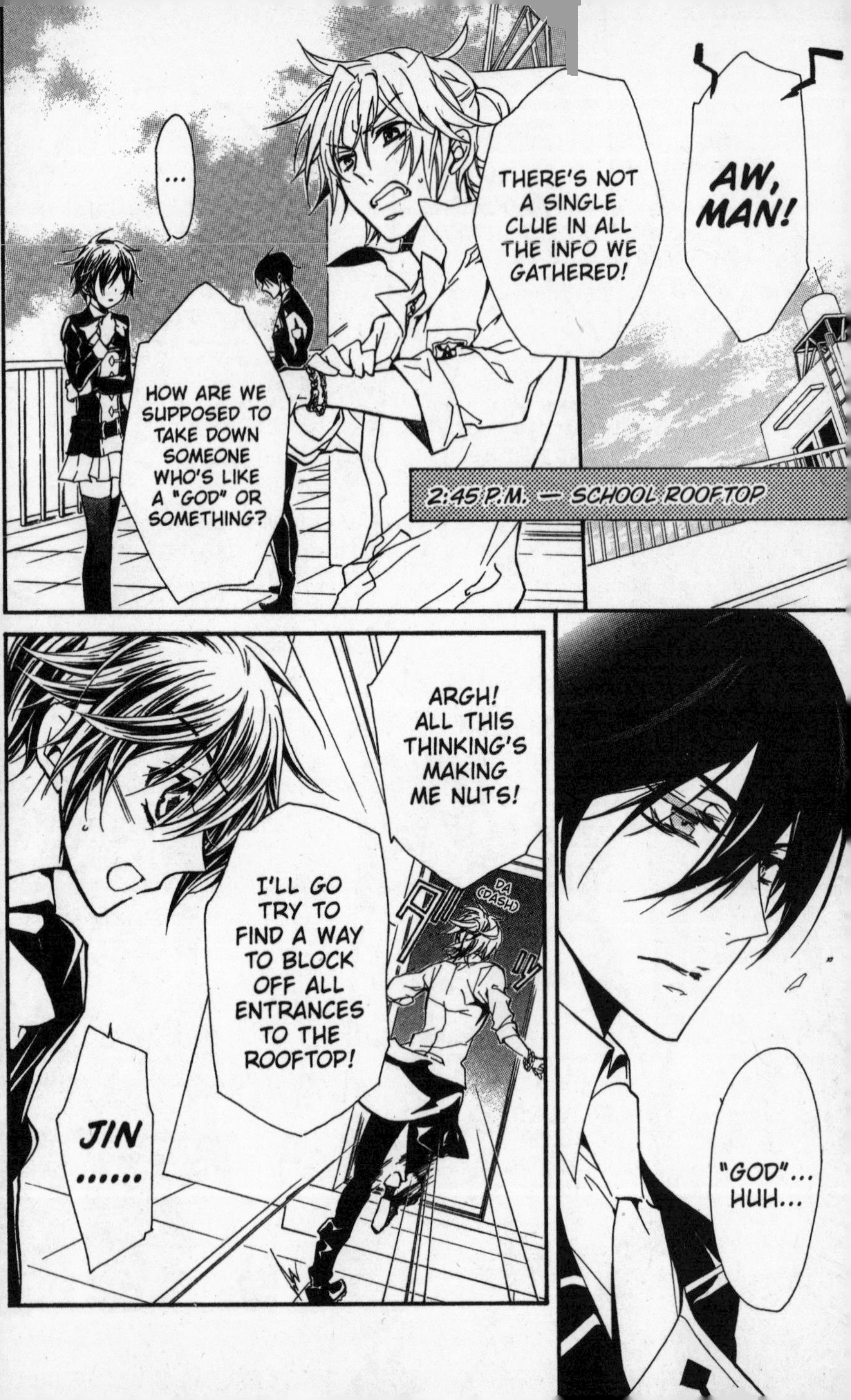
AW, MAN!
THERE'S NOT A SINGLE CLUE IN ALL THE INFO WE GATHERED!
...
HOW ARE WE SUPPOSED TO TAKE DOWN SOMEONE WHO'S LIKE A "GOD" OR SOMETHING?
2:45 P.M. — SCHOOL ROOFTOP
"GOD"... HUH...
ARGH! ALL THIS THINKING'S MAKING ME NUTS!
DA (DASH)
I'LL GO TRY TO FIND A WAY TO BLOCK OFF ALL ENTRANCES TO THE ROOFTOP!
JIN ......

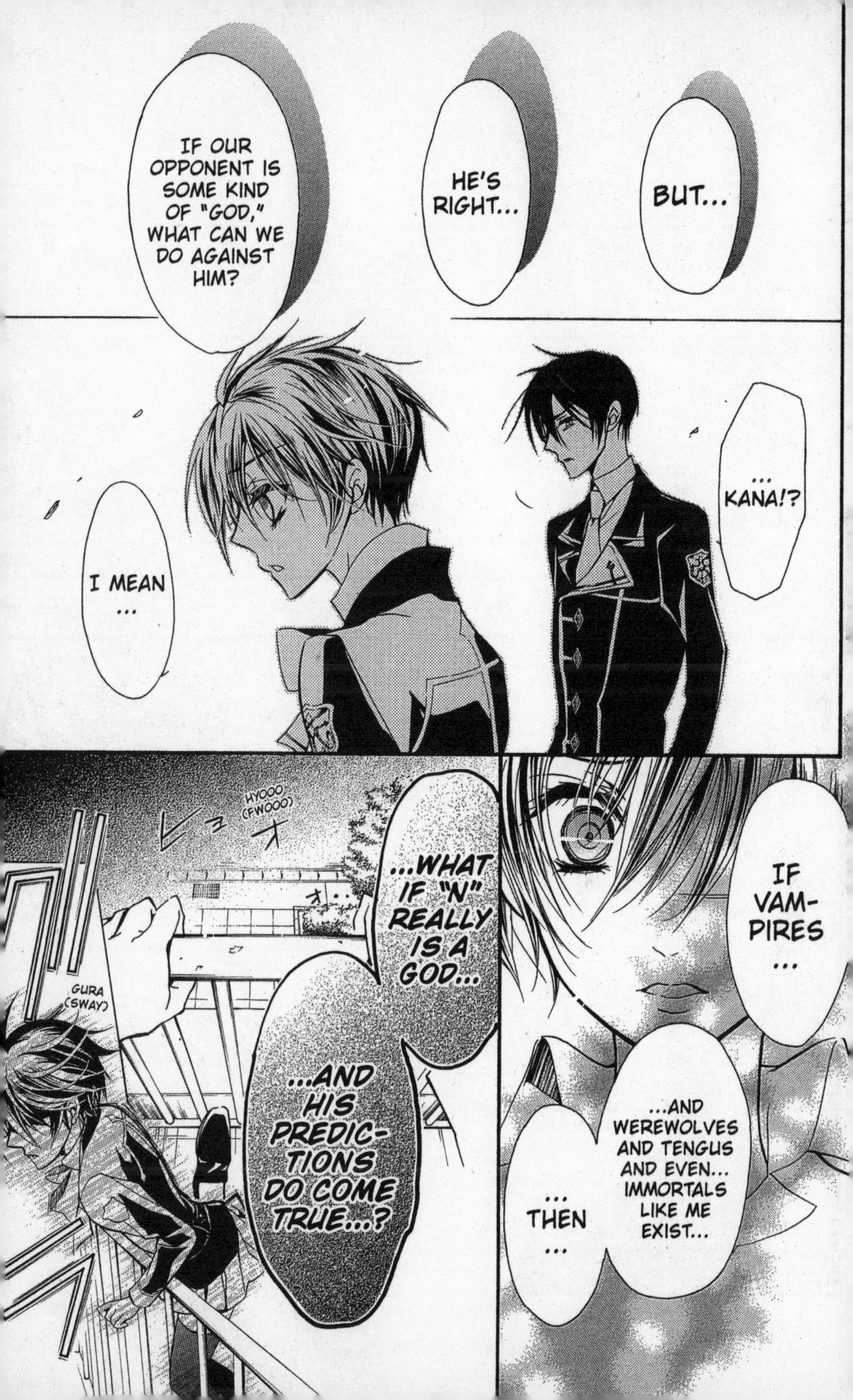
BUT...
HE'S RIGHT...
IF OUR OPPONENT IS SOME KIND OF "GOD," WHAT CAN WE DO AGAINST HIM?
...KANA!?
I MEAN...
IF VAMPIRES...
...AND WEREWOLVES AND TENGUS AND EVEN... IMMORTALS LIKE ME EXIST...
...THEN...
HYOOO (FWOOO)
...WHAT IF "N" REALLY IS A GOD...
...AND HIS PREDICTIONS DO COME TRUE...?
GURA (SWAY)

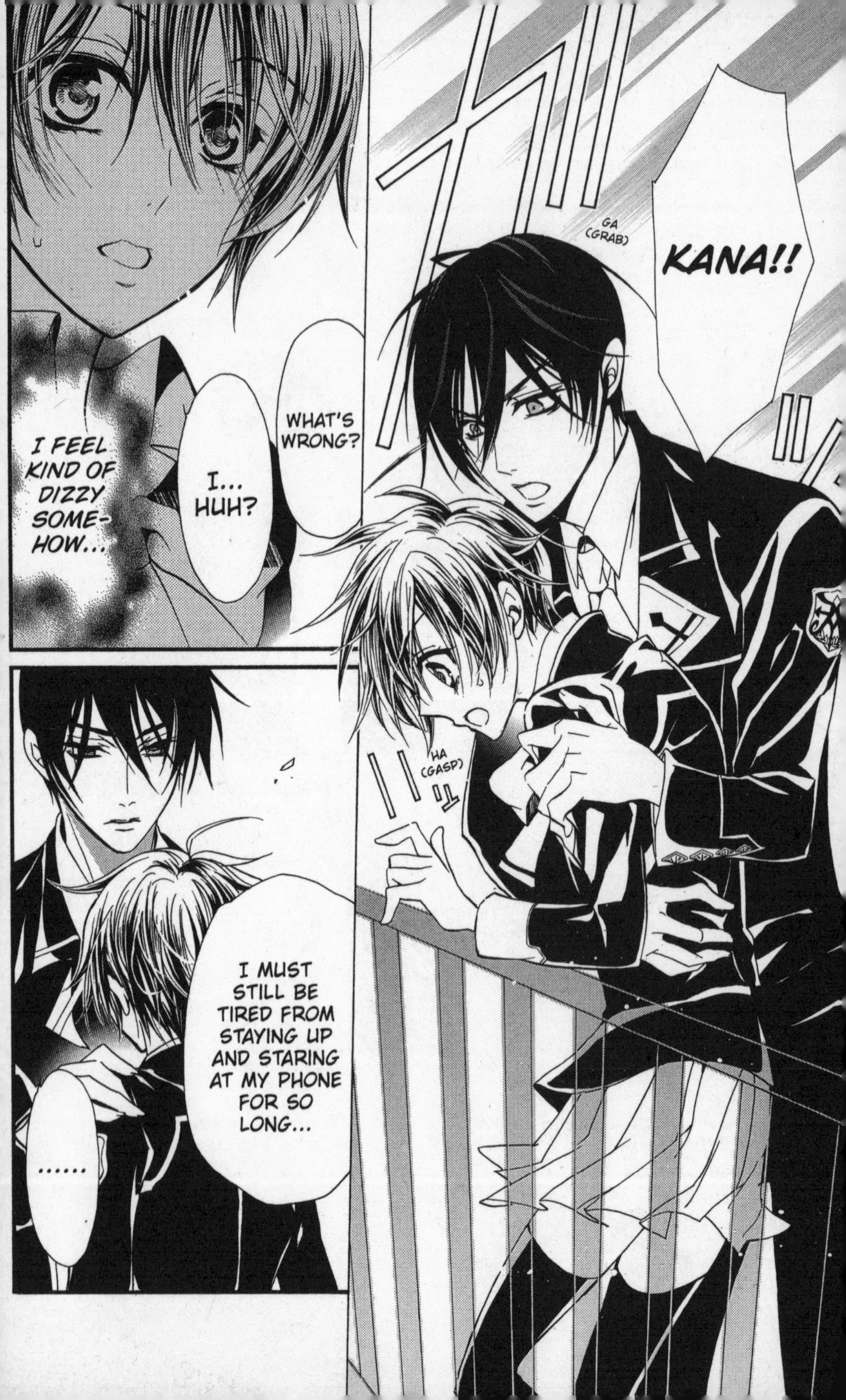
KANA!!
GA (GRAB)
HA (GASP)
WHAT'S WRONG?
I... HUH?
I FEEL KIND OF DIZZY SOME-HOW...
I MUST STILL BE TIRED FROM STAYING UP AND STARING AT MY PHONE FOR SO LONG...
......

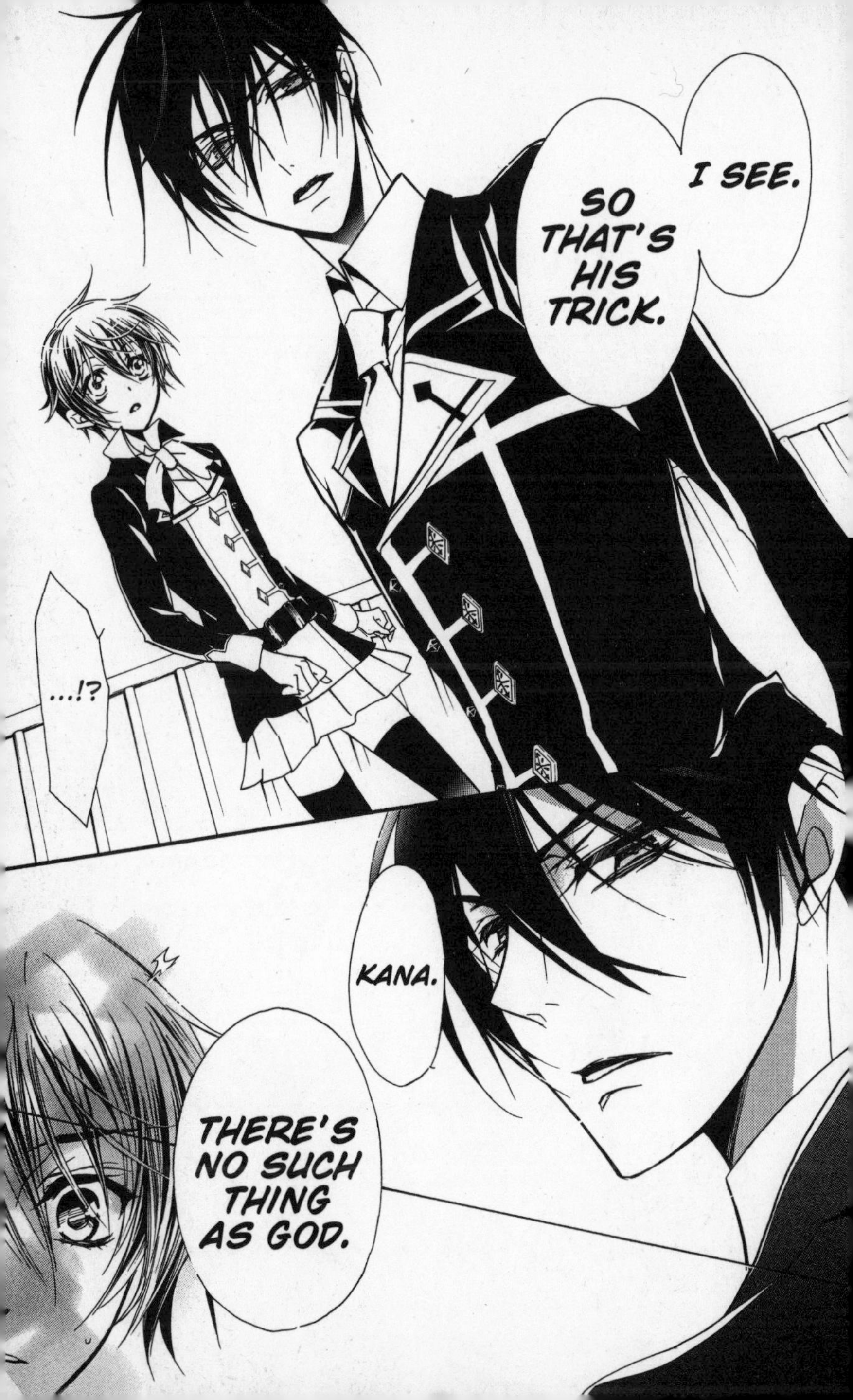
I SEE.
SO THAT'S HIS TRICK.
...!?
KANA.
THERE'S NO SUCH THING AS GOD.

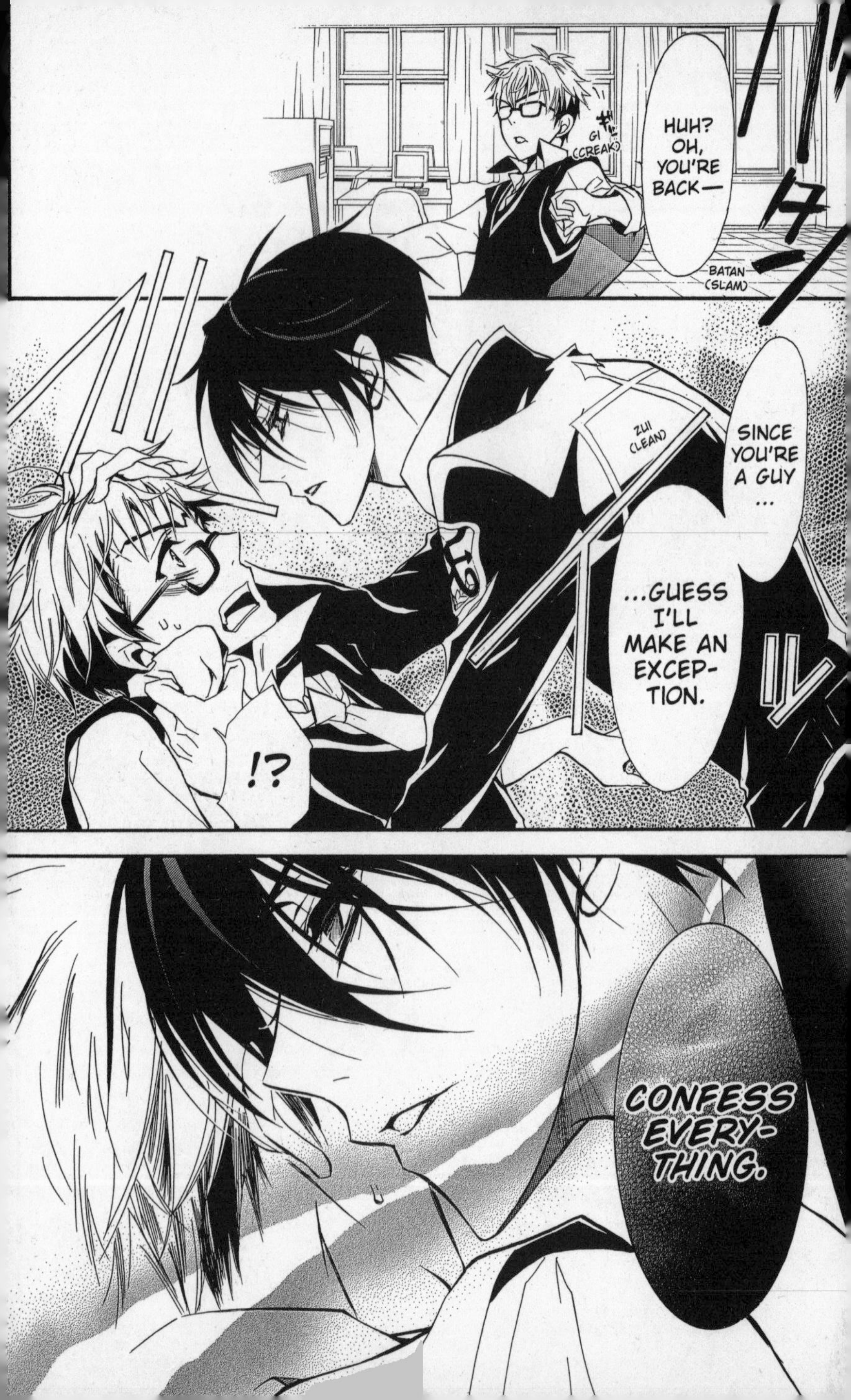
BATAN (SLAM)
HUH? OH, YOU'RE BACK—
GI (CREAK)
SINCE YOU'RE A GUY ...
...GUESS I'LL MAKE AN EXCEP-TION.
ZUI (LEAN)
!?
CONFESS EVERY-THING.

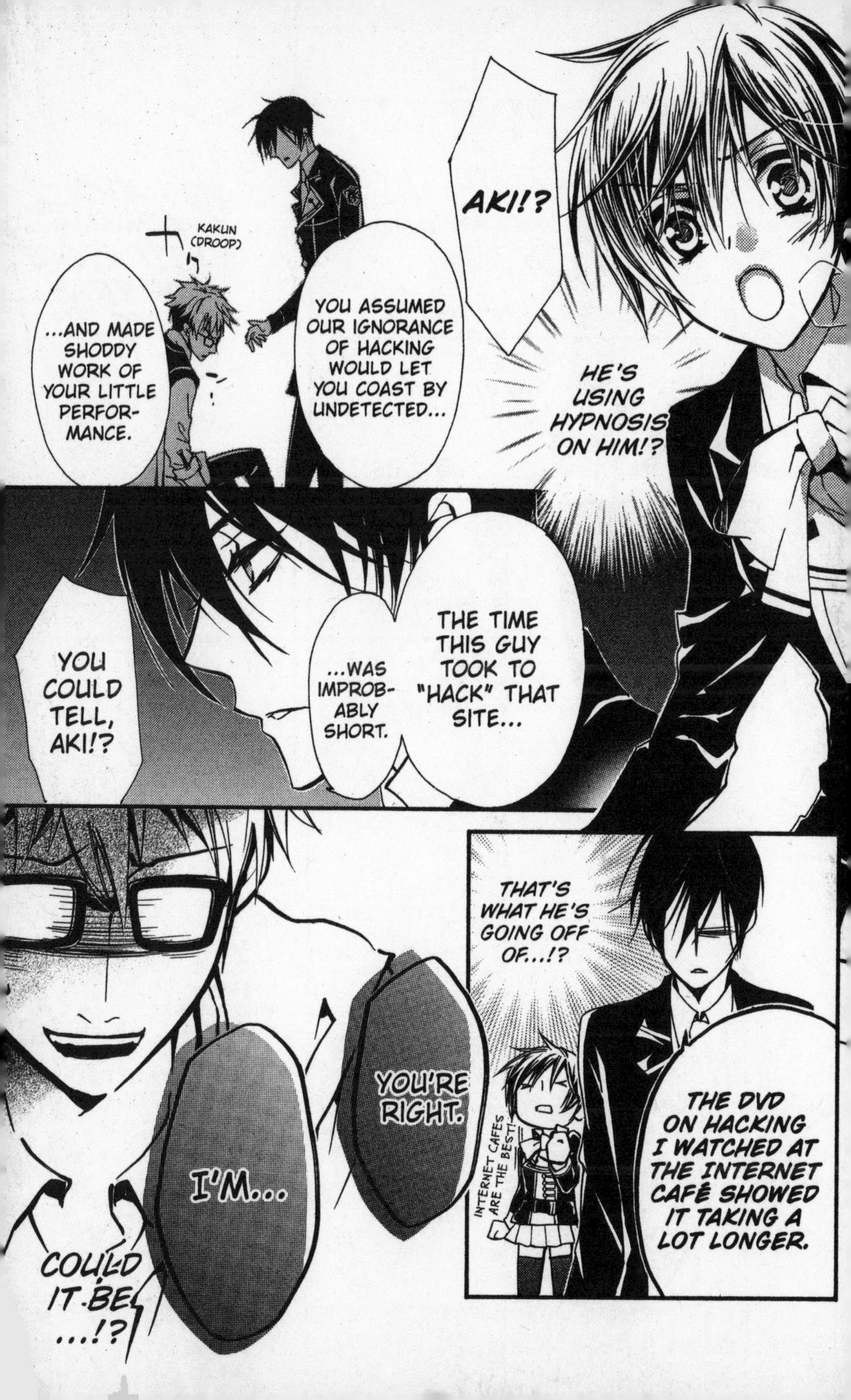
AKI!?
HE'S USING HYPNOSIS ON HIM!?
YOU ASSUMED OUR IGNORANCE OF HACKING WOULD LET YOU COAST BY UNDETECTED...
KAKUN (DROOP)
...AND MADE SHODDY WORK OF YOUR LITTLE PERFOR-MANCE.
THE TIME THIS GUY TOOK TO "HACK" THAT SITE...
...WAS IMPROB-ABLY SHORT.
YOU COULD TELL, AKI!?
THE DVD ON HACKING I WATCHED AT THE INTERNET CAFÉ SHOWED IT TAKING A LOT LONGER.
INTERNET CAFES ARE THE BEST!
THAT'S WHAT HE'S GOING OFF OF...!?
YOU'RE RIGHT.
I'M...
COULD IT BE ...!?

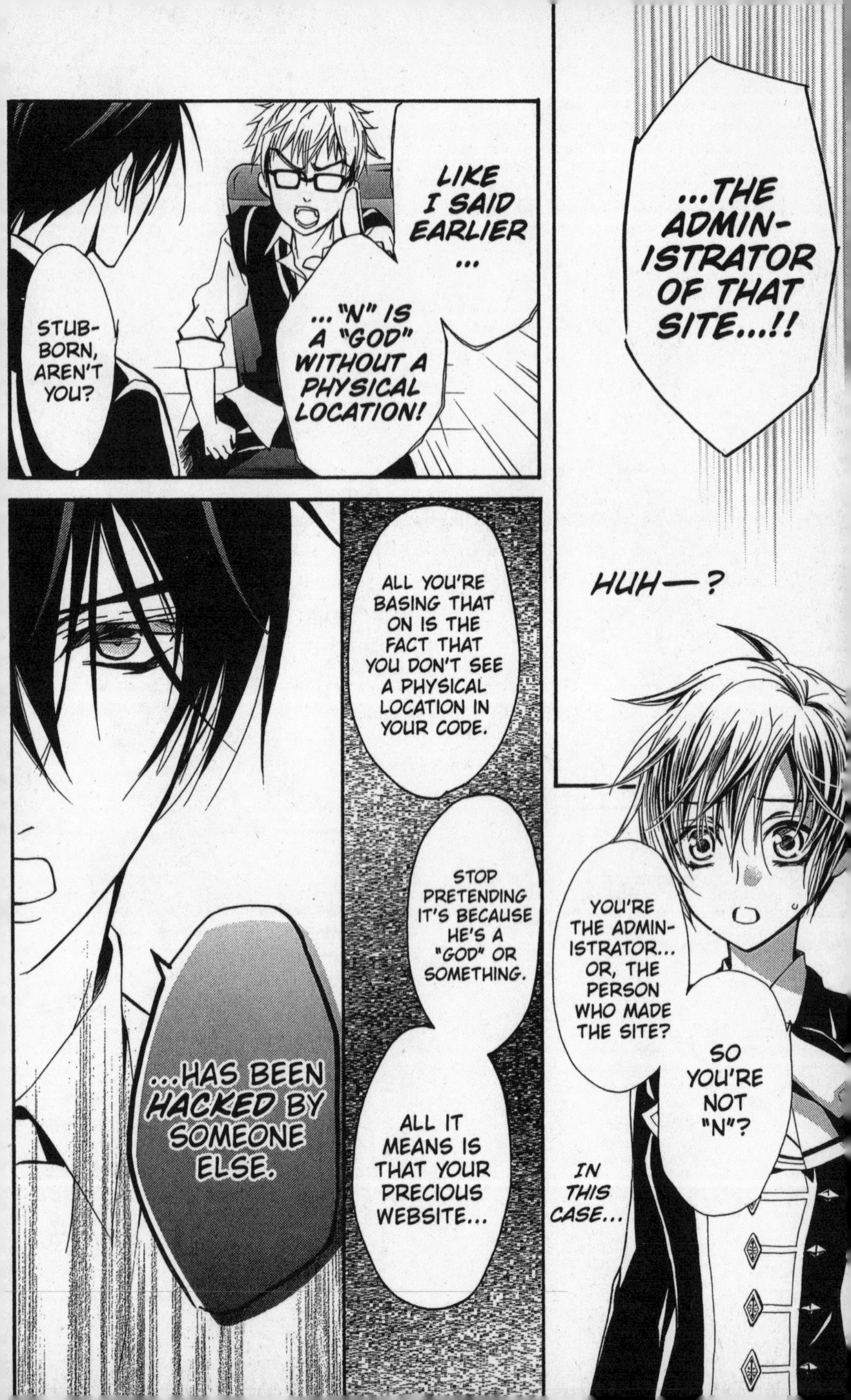
...THE ADMIN-ISTRATOR OF THAT SITE...!!
LIKE I SAID EARLIER ...
..."N" IS A "GOD" WITHOUT A PHYSICAL LOCATION!
STUB-BORN, AREN'T YOU?
HUH—?
YOU'RE THE ADMIN-ISTRATOR... OR, THE PERSON WHO MADE THE SITE?
SO YOU'RE NOT "N"?
IN THIS CASE...
ALL YOU'RE BASING THAT ON IS THE FACT THAT YOU DON'T SEE A PHYSICAL LOCATION IN YOUR CODE.
STOP PRETENDING IT'S BECAUSE HE'S A "GOD" OR SOMETHING.
ALL IT MEANS IS THAT YOUR PRECIOUS WEBSITE...
...HAS BEEN HACKED BY SOMEONE ELSE.

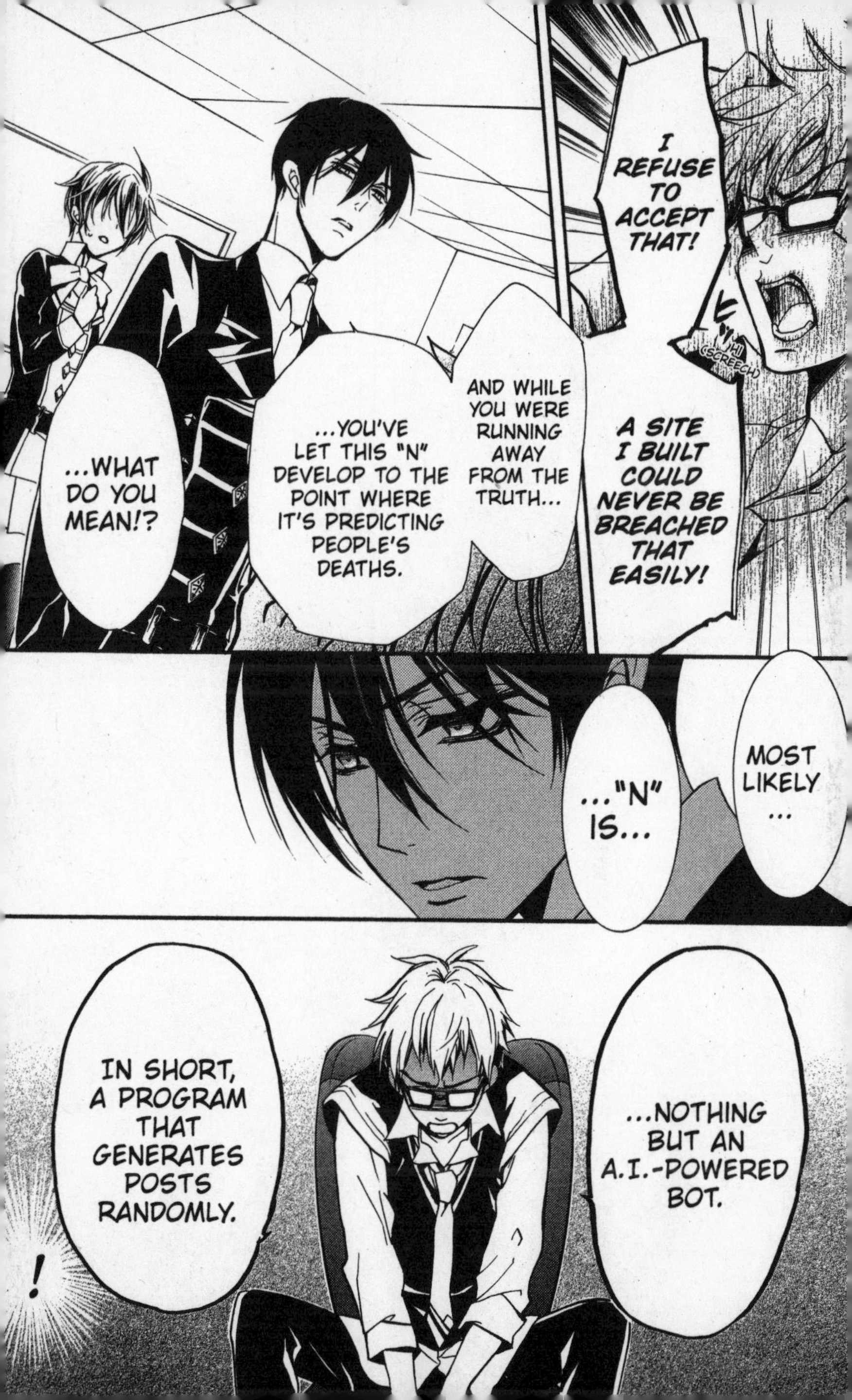

I REFUSE TO ACCEPT THAT!
HI (SCREECH)
A SITE I BUILT COULD NEVER BE BREACHED THAT EASILY!
AND WHILE YOU WERE RUNNING AWAY FROM THE TRUTH...
...YOU'VE LET THIS "N" DEVELOP TO THE POINT WHERE IT'S PREDICTING PEOPLE'S DEATHS.
...WHAT DO YOU MEAN!?
MOST LIKELY ...
..."N" IS...
...NOTHING BUT AN A.I.-POWERED BOT.
IN SHORT, A PROGRAM THAT GENERATES POSTS RANDOMLY.
!

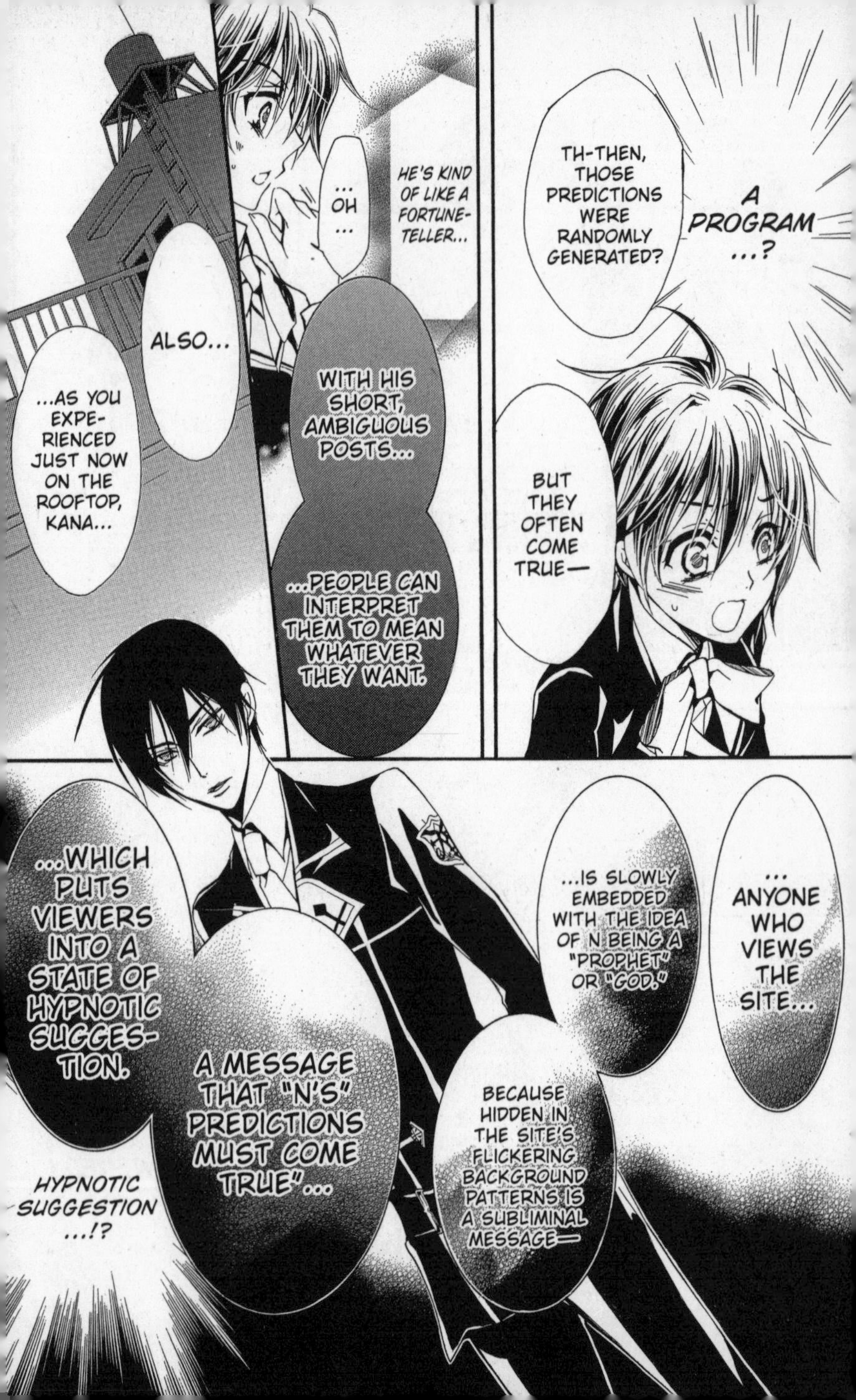
A PROGRAM ...?
TH-THEN, THOSE PREDICTIONS WERE RANDOMLY GENERATED?
BUT THEY OFTEN COME TRUE—
HE'S KIND OF LIKE A FORTUNE-TELLER...
...OH...
WITH HIS SHORT, AMBIGUOUS POSTS...
...PEOPLE CAN INTERPRET THEM TO MEAN WHATEVER THEY WANT.
ALSO...
...AS YOU EXPERIENCED JUST NOW ON THE ROOFTOP, KANA...
...ANYONE WHO VIEWS THE SITE...
...IS SLOWLY EMBEDDED WITH THE IDEA OF N BEING A "PROPHET" OR "GOD."
BECAUSE HIDDEN IN THE SITE'S FLICKERING BACKGROUND PATTERNS IS A SUBLIMINAL MESSAGE—
A MESSAGE THAT "N'S" PREDICTIONS MUST COME TRUE"...
...WHICH PUTS VIEWERS INTO A STATE OF HYPNOTIC SUGGESTION.
HYPNOTIC SUGGESTION ...!?

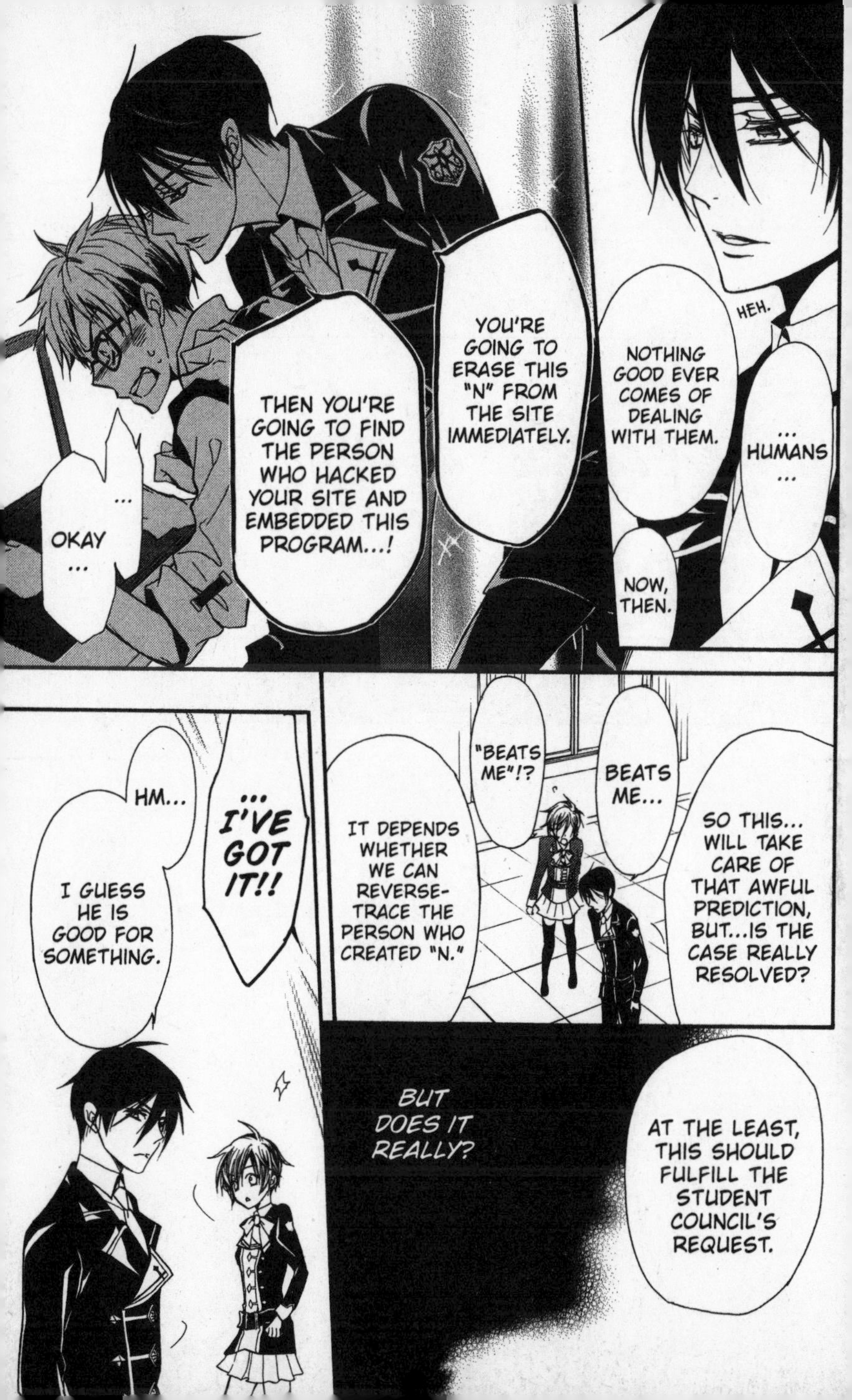
HEH.
...HUMANS...
NOTHING GOOD EVER COMES OF DEALING WITH THEM.
NOW, THEN.
YOU'RE GOING TO ERASE THIS "N" FROM THE SITE IMMEDIATELY.
THEN YOU'RE GOING TO FIND THE PERSON WHO HACKED YOUR SITE AND EMBEDDED THIS PROGRAM...!
...OKAY...
SO THIS... WILL TAKE CARE OF THAT AWFUL PREDICTION, BUT...IS THE CASE REALLY RESOLVED?
BEATS ME...
"BEATS ME"!?
IT DEPENDS WHETHER WE CAN REVERSE-TRACE THE PERSON WHO CREATED "N."
AT THE LEAST, THIS SHOULD FULFILL THE STUDENT COUNCIL'S REQUEST.
BUT DOES IT REALLY?
...I'VE GOT IT!!
HM...
I GUESS HE IS GOOD FOR SOMETHING.

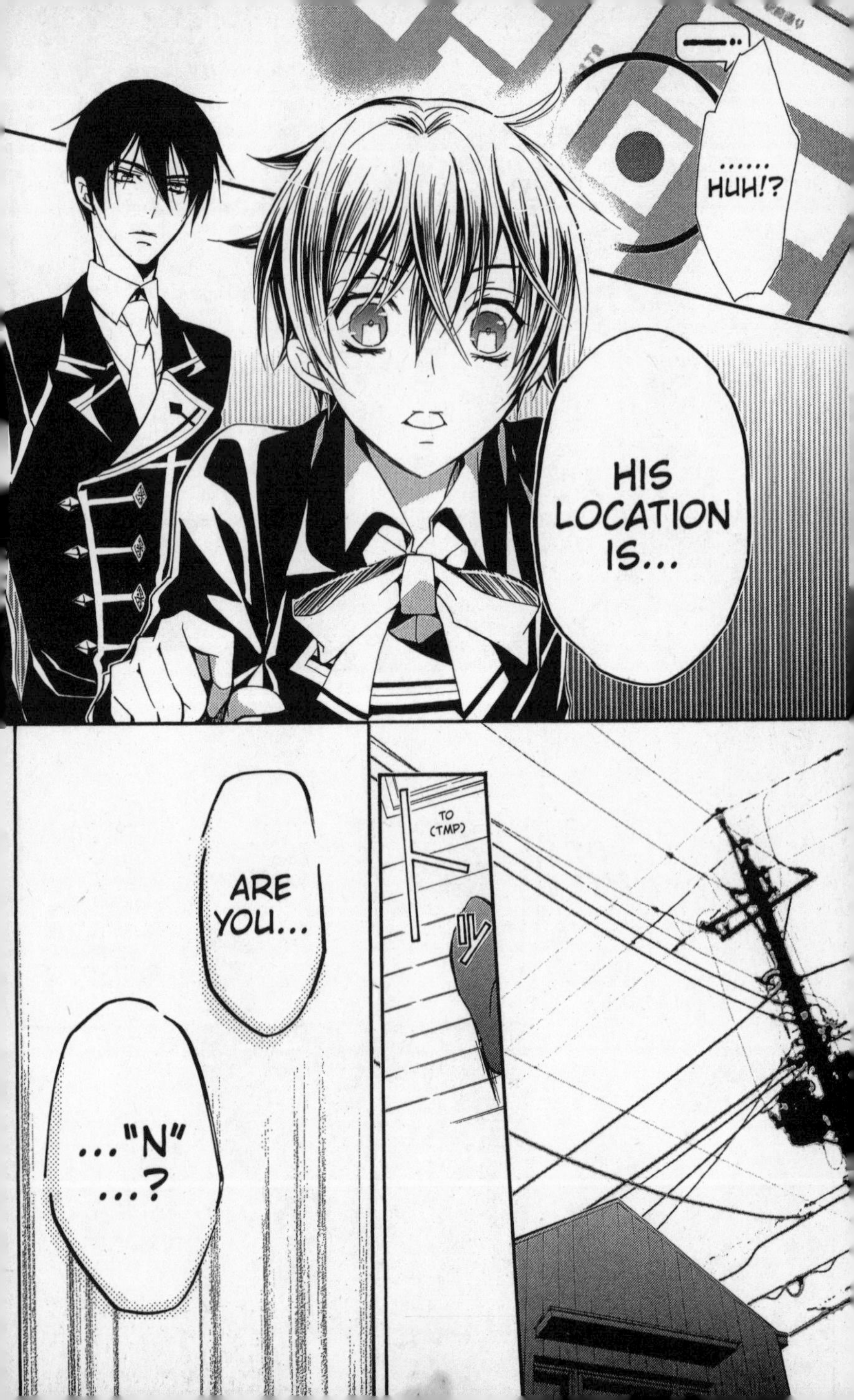
——..
...... HUH!?
HIS LOCATION IS...
TO (TMP)
ARE YOU...
..."N" ...?

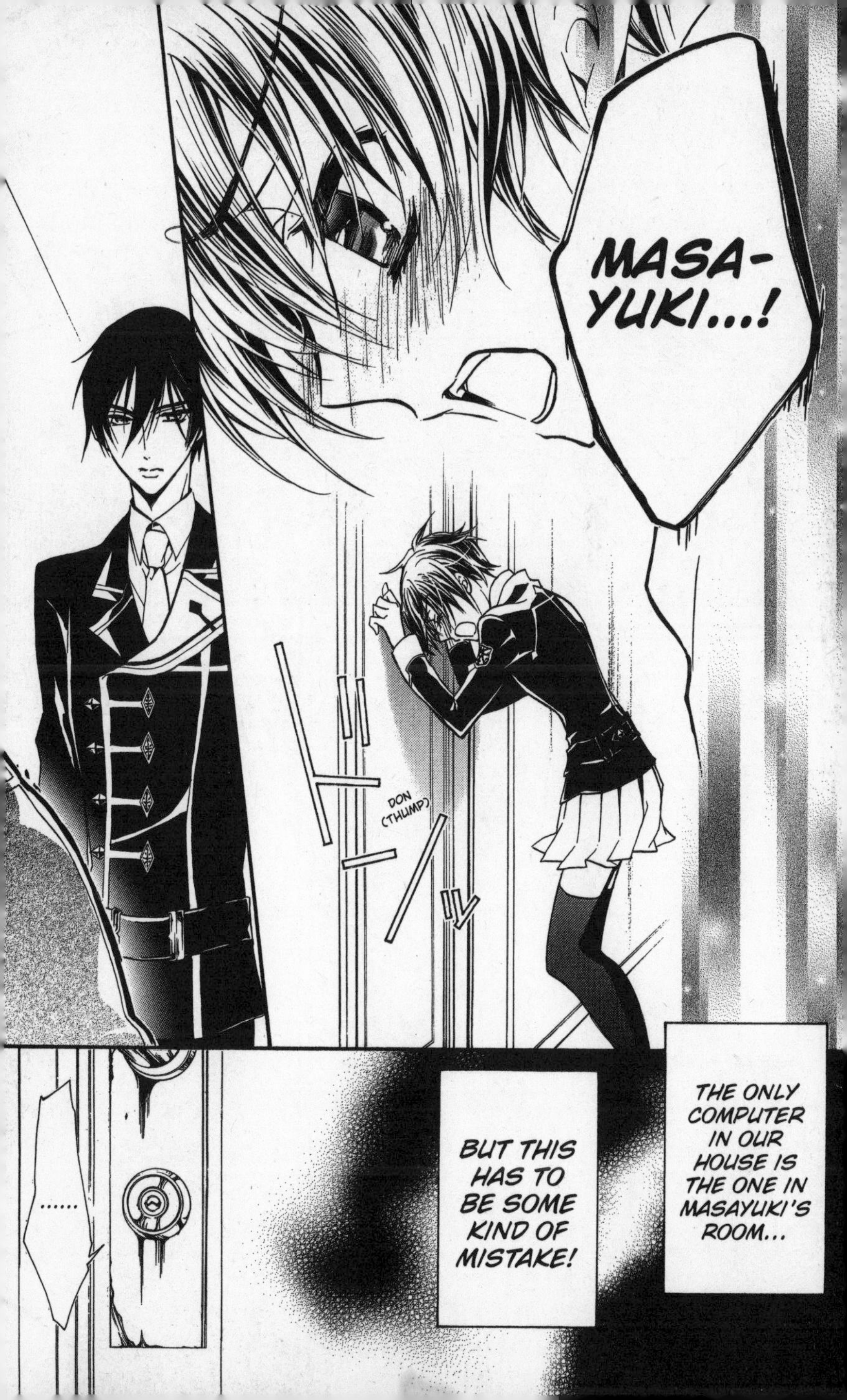
MASA-YUKI...!
DON (THUMP)
THE ONLY COMPUTER IN OUR HOUSE IS THE ONE IN MASAYUKI'S ROOM...
BUT THIS HAS TO BE SOME KIND OF MISTAKE!
......

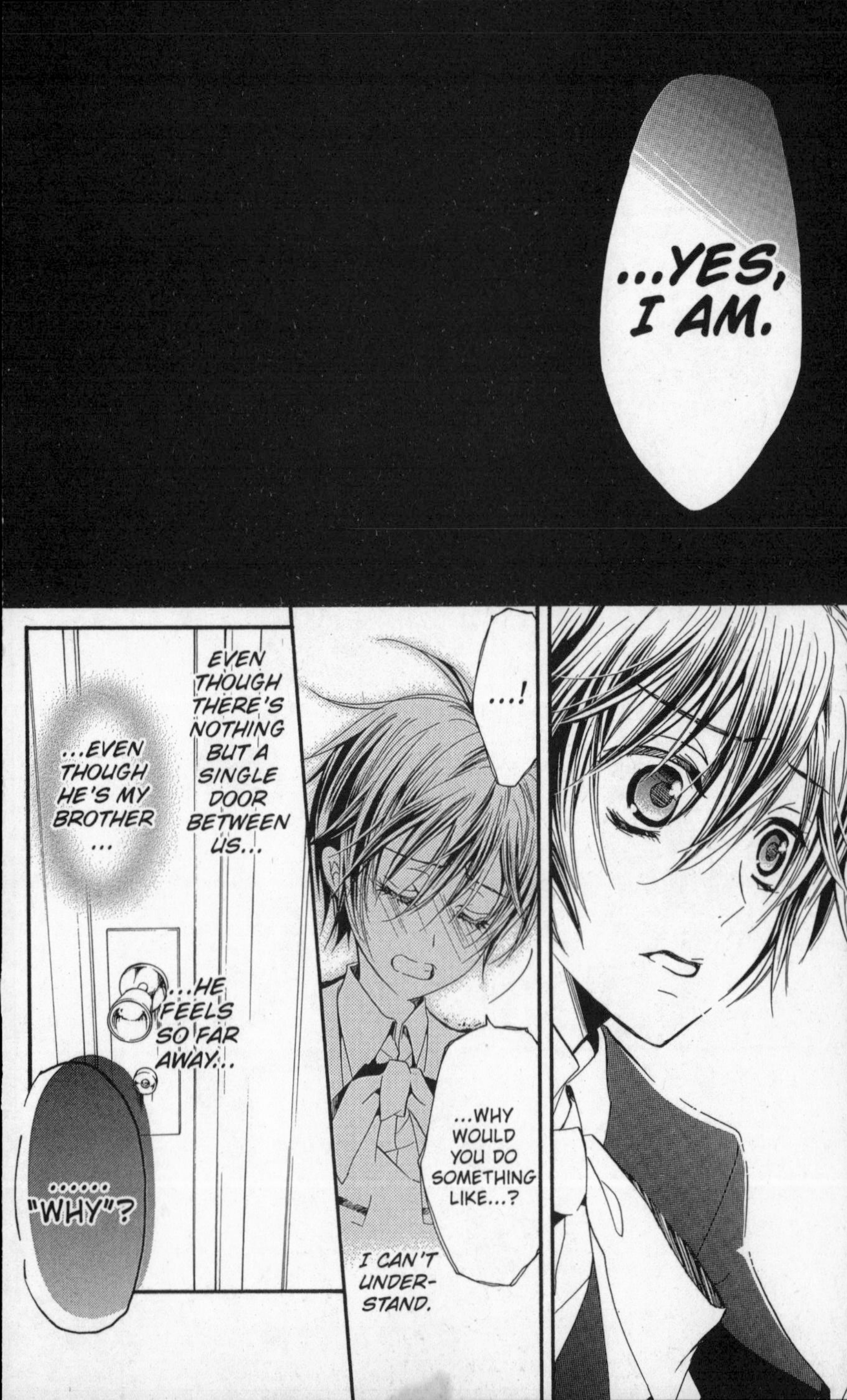
...YES, I AM.
...!
...WHY WOULD YOU DO SOMETHING LIKE...?
I CAN'T UNDER-STAND.
EVEN THOUGH THERE'S NOTHING BUT A SINGLE DOOR BETWEEN US...
...EVEN THOUGH HE'S MY BROTHER...
...HE FEELS SO FAR AWAY...
......"WHY"?

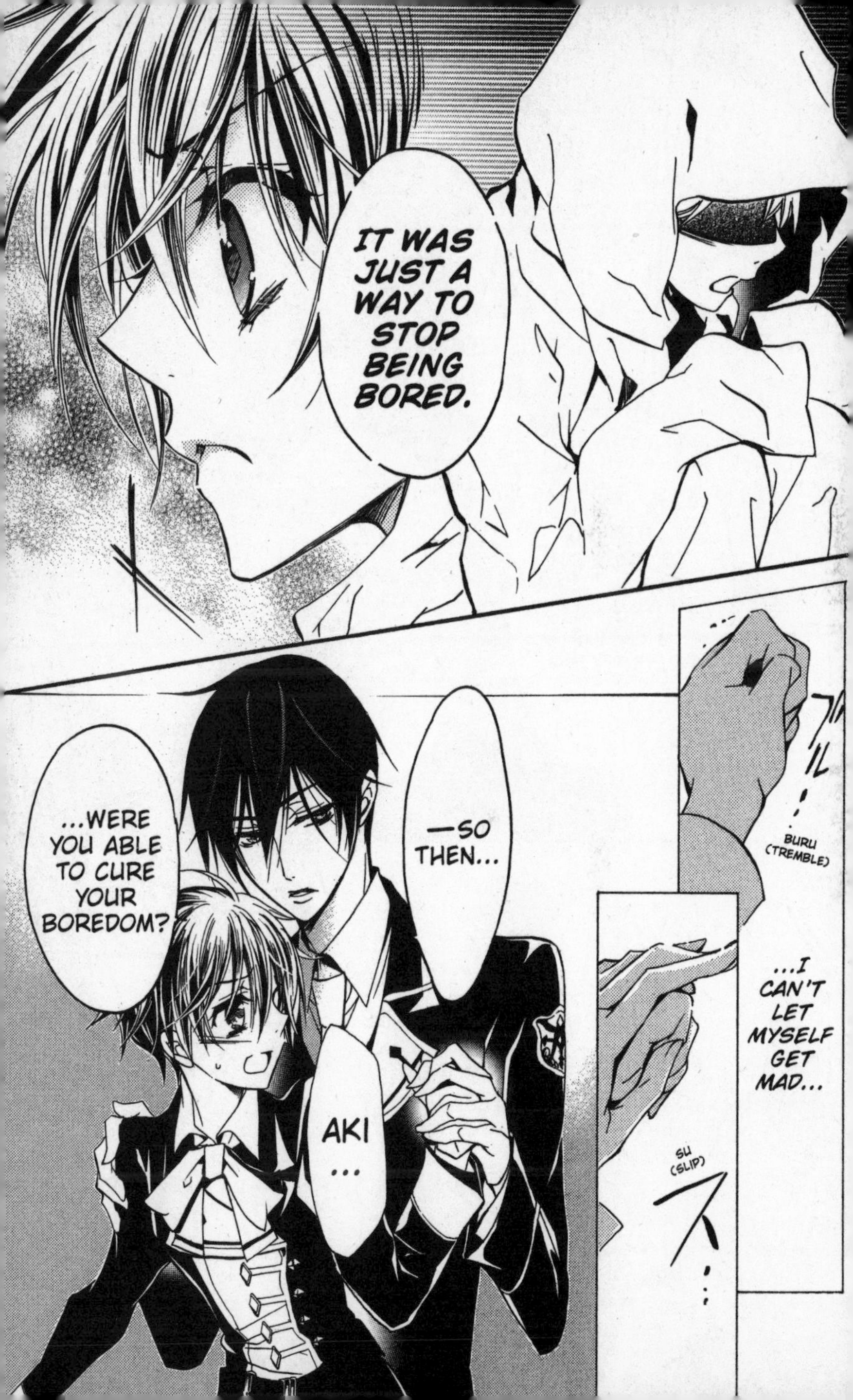
IT WAS JUST A WAY TO STOP BEING BORED.
BURU (TREMBLE)
...I CAN'T LET MYSELF GET MAD...
SU (SLIP)
—SO THEN...
...WERE YOU ABLE TO CURE YOUR BOREDOM?
AKI ...

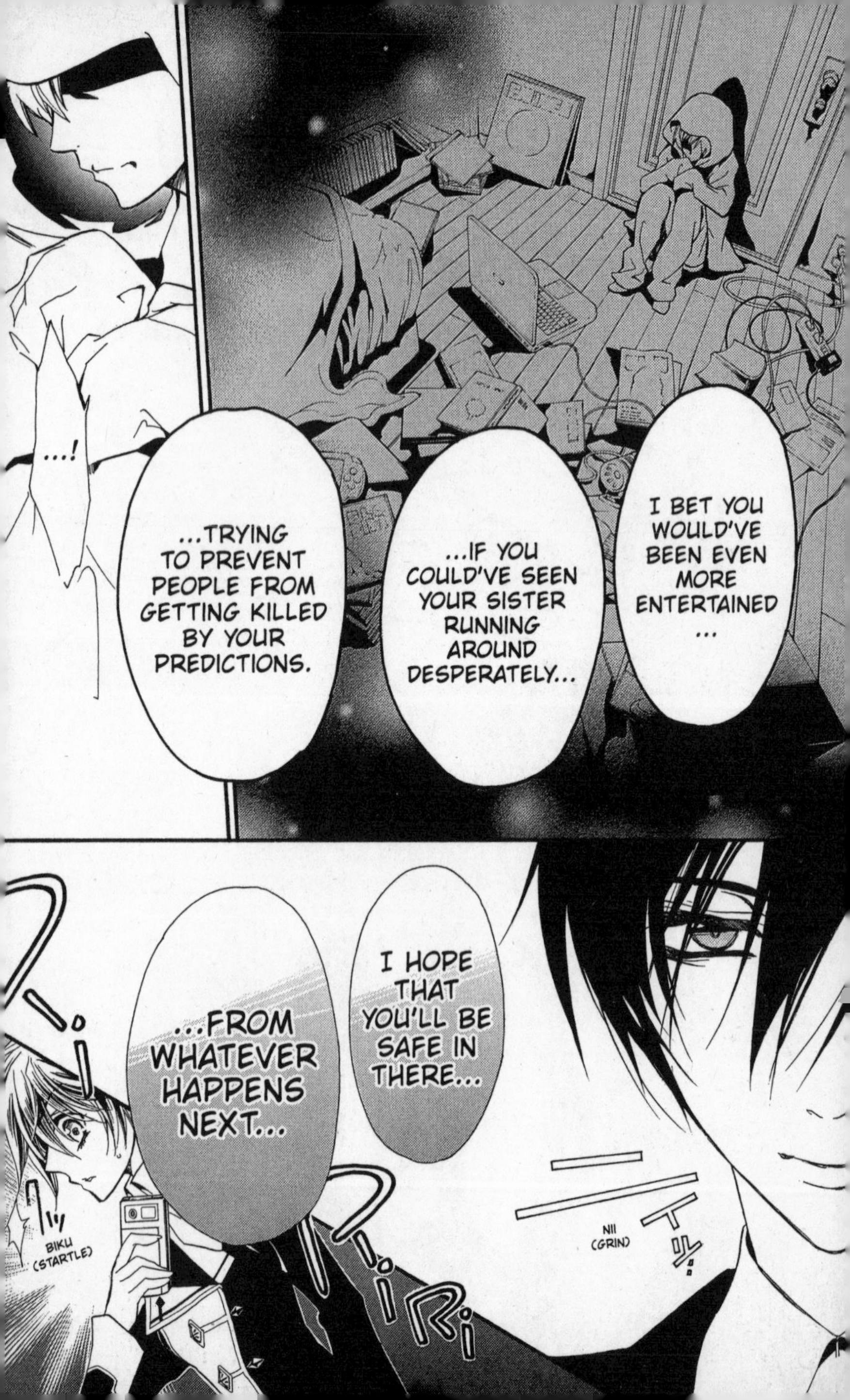
I BET YOU WOULD'VE BEEN EVEN MORE ENTERTAINED...
...IF YOU COULD'VE SEEN YOUR SISTER RUNNING AROUND DESPERATELY...
...TRYING TO PREVENT PEOPLE FROM GETTING KILLED BY YOUR PREDICTIONS.
...!
I HOPE THAT YOU'LL BE SAFE IN THERE...
...FROM WHATEVER HAPPENS NEXT...
NII (GRIN)
BIKU (STARTLE)

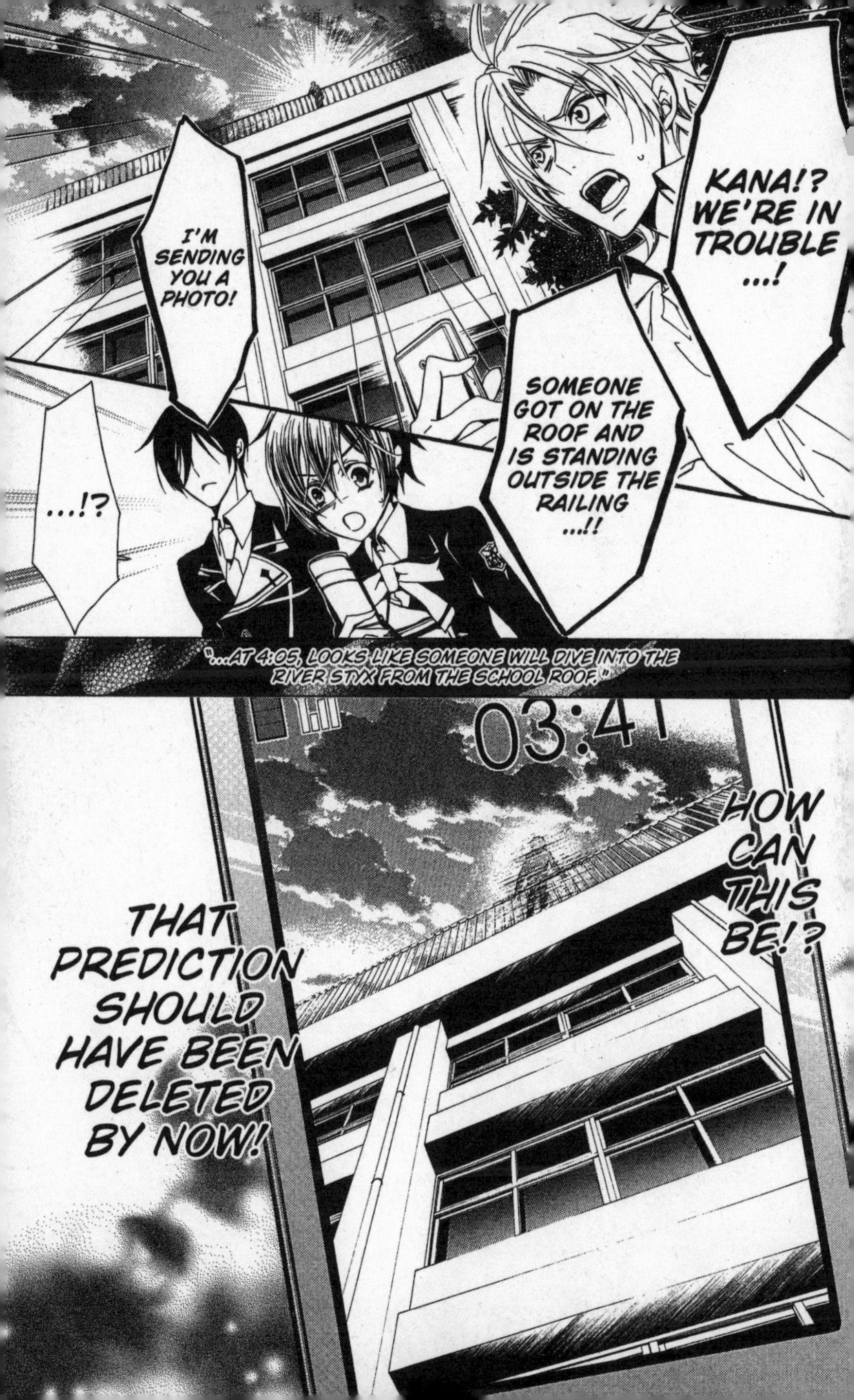
KANA!? WE'RE IN TROUBLE ...!
SOMEONE GOT ON THE ROOF AND IS STANDING OUTSIDE THE RAILING ...!!
I'M SENDING YOU A PHOTO!
...!?
"...AT 4:05, LOOKS LIKE SOMEONE WILL DIVE INTO THE RIVER STYX FROM THE SCHOOL ROOF."
03:41
HOW CAN THIS BE!?
THAT PREDICTION SHOULD HAVE BEEN DELETED BY NOW!

He's my only vampire
Aya Shouoto

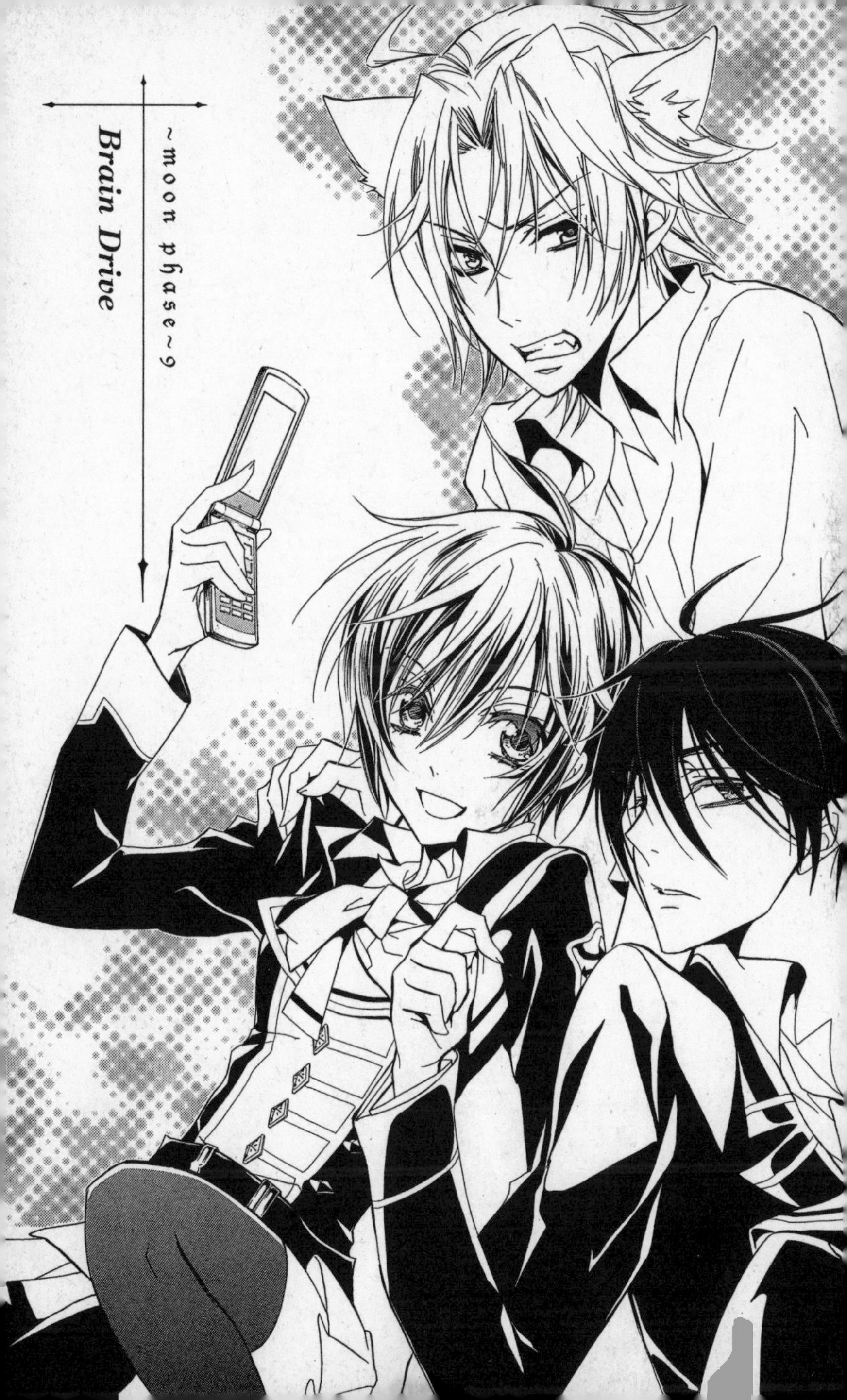
~moon phase~9
Brain Drive

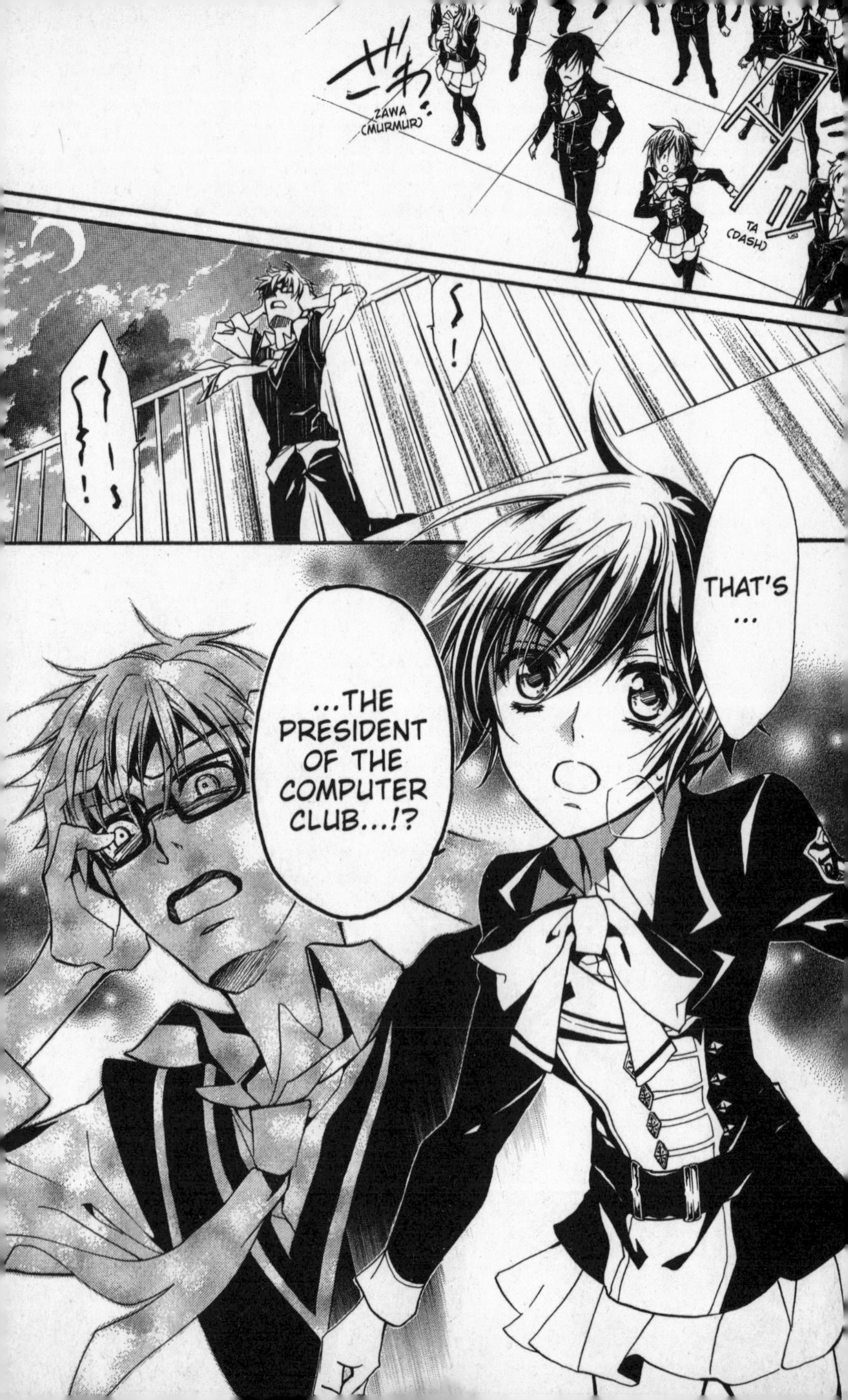

ざわ
ZAWA (MURMUR)
TA (DASH)
THAT'S...
...THE PRESIDENT OF THE COMPUTER CLUB...!?

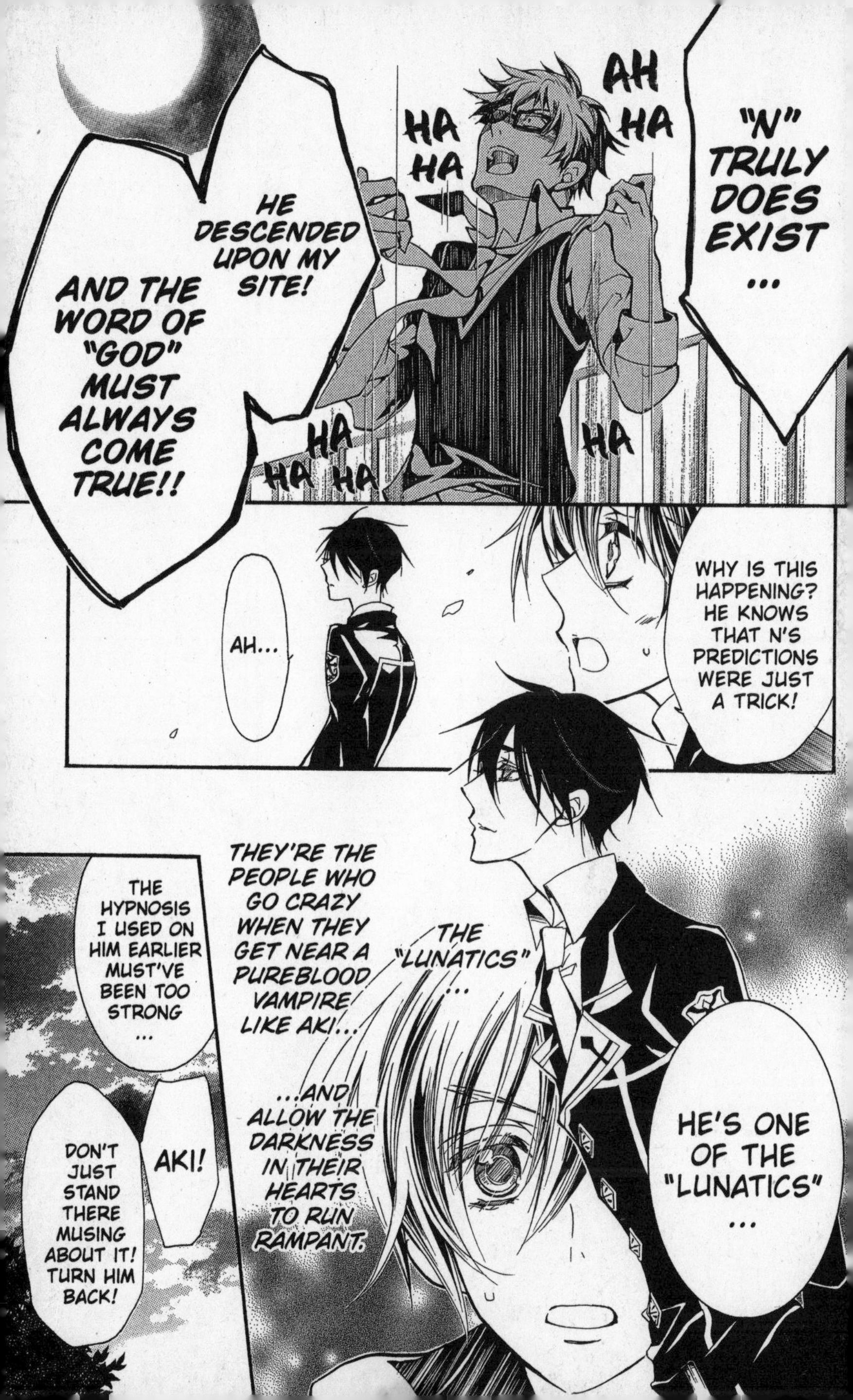
"N" TRULY DOES EXIST...
AH HA
HA HA
HA
HA HA HA
HE DESCENDED UPON MY SITE!
AND THE WORD OF "GOD" MUST ALWAYS COME TRUE!!
WHY IS THIS HAPPENING? HE KNOWS THAT N'S PREDICTIONS WERE JUST A TRICK!
AH...
HE'S ONE OF THE "LUNATICS"...
THE "LUNATICS"...
THEY'RE THE PEOPLE WHO GO CRAZY WHEN THEY GET NEAR A PUREBLOOD VAMPIRE LIKE AKI...
...AND ALLOW THE DARKNESS IN THEIR HEARTS TO RUN RAMPANT.
THE HYPNOSIS I USED ON HIM EARLIER MUST'VE BEEN TOO STRONG...
AKI!
DON'T JUST STAND THERE MUSING ABOUT IT! TURN HIM BACK!

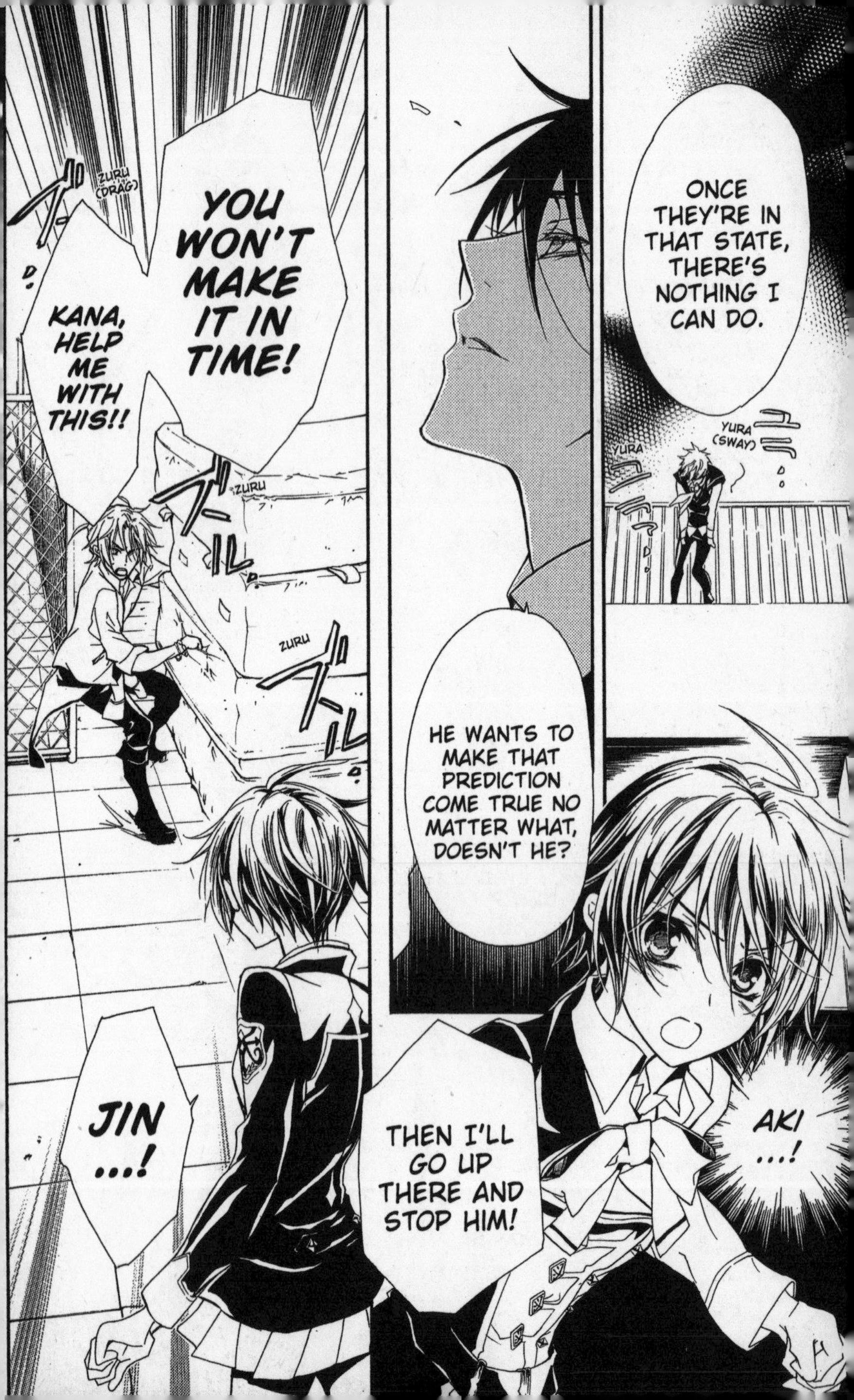
ONCE THEY'RE IN THAT STATE, THERE'S NOTHING I CAN DO.
YURA (SWAY)
YURA
HE WANTS TO MAKE THAT PREDICTION COME TRUE NO MATTER WHAT, DOESN'T HE?
AKI ...!
THEN I'LL GO UP THERE AND STOP HIM!
YOU WON'T MAKE IT IN TIME!
ZURU (DRAG)
KANA, HELP ME WITH THIS!!
ZURU
ZURU
JIN ...!

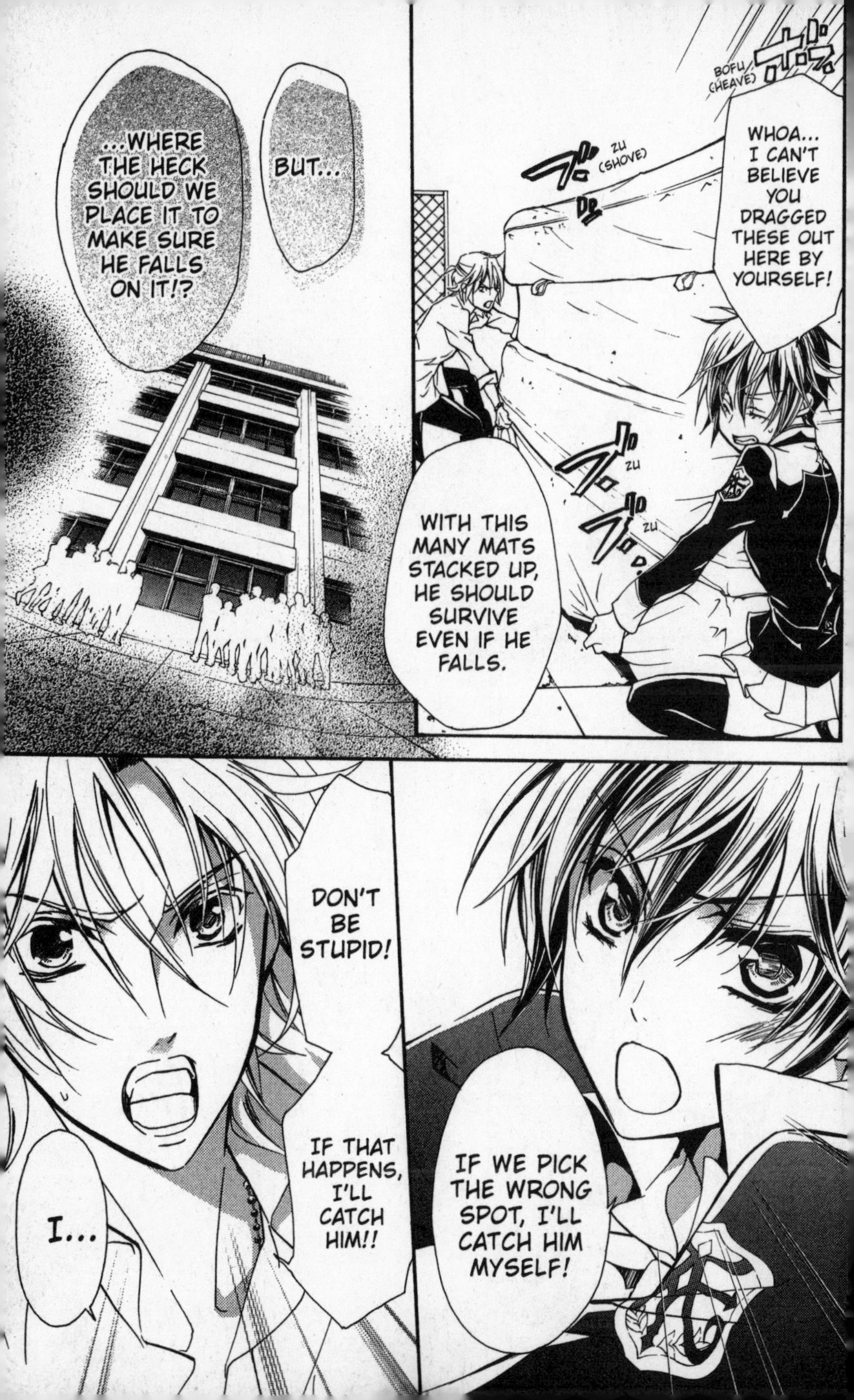
BOFU (HEAVE)
WHOA... I CAN'T BELIEVE YOU DRAGGED THESE OUT HERE BY YOURSELF!
ZU (SHOVE)
ZU
ZU
WITH THIS MANY MATS STACKED UP, HE SHOULD SURVIVE EVEN IF HE FALLS.
BUT...
...WHERE THE HECK SHOULD WE PLACE IT TO MAKE SURE HE FALLS ON IT!?
IF WE PICK THE WRONG SPOT, I'LL CATCH HIM MYSELF!
DON'T BE STUPID!
IF THAT HAPPENS, I'LL CATCH HIM!!
I...

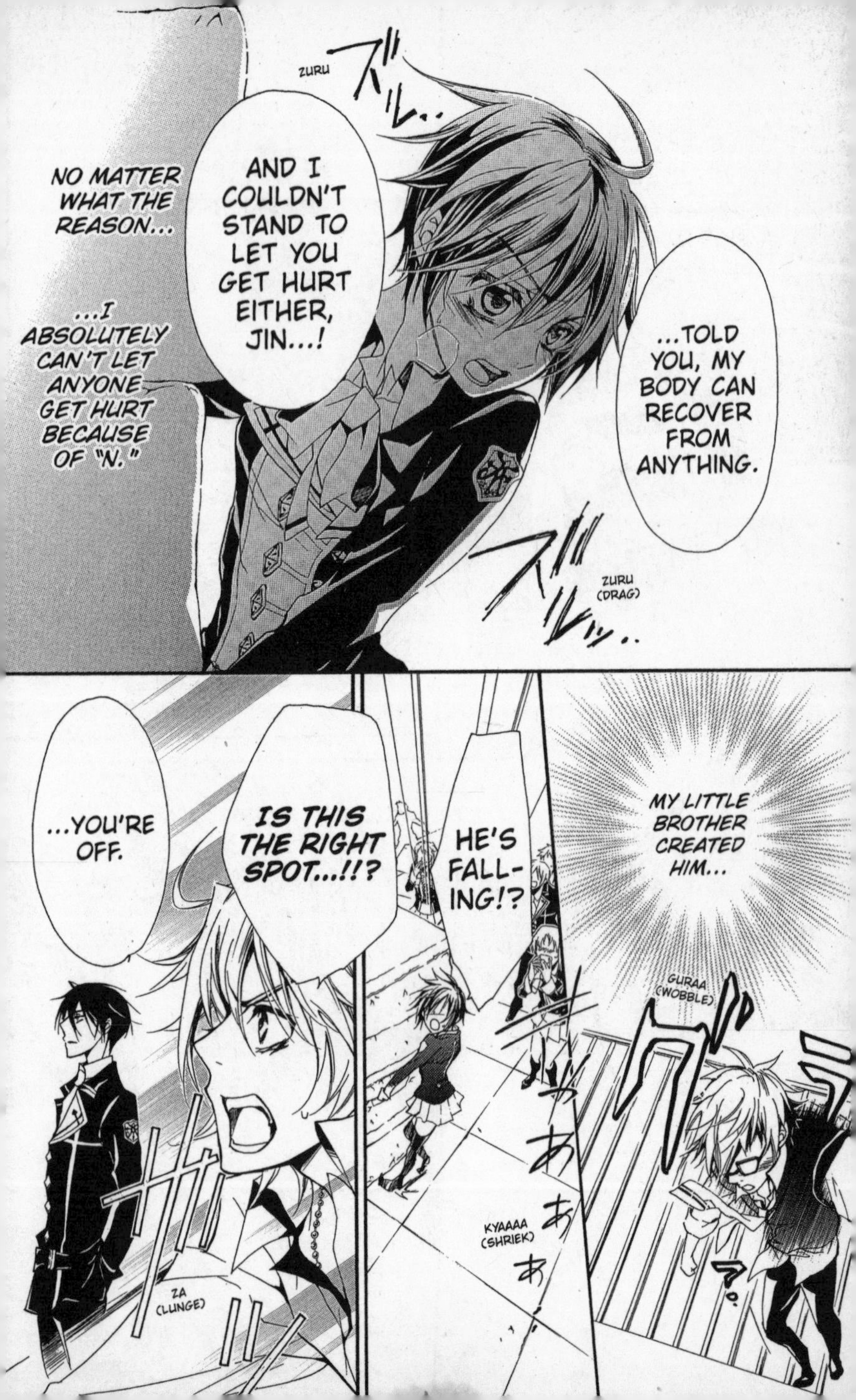
ZURU
...TOLD YOU, MY BODY CAN RECOVER FROM ANYTHING.
AND I COULDN'T STAND TO LET YOU GET HURT EITHER, JIN...!
NO MATTER WHAT THE REASON...
...I ABSOLUTELY CAN'T LET ANYONE GET HURT BECAUSE OF "N."
ZURU (DRAG)
MY LITTLE BROTHER CREATED HIM...
GURAA (WOBBLE)
KYAAAA (SHRIEK)
HE'S FALLING!?
IS THIS THE RIGHT SPOT...!!?
...YOU'RE OFF.
ZA (LUNGE)

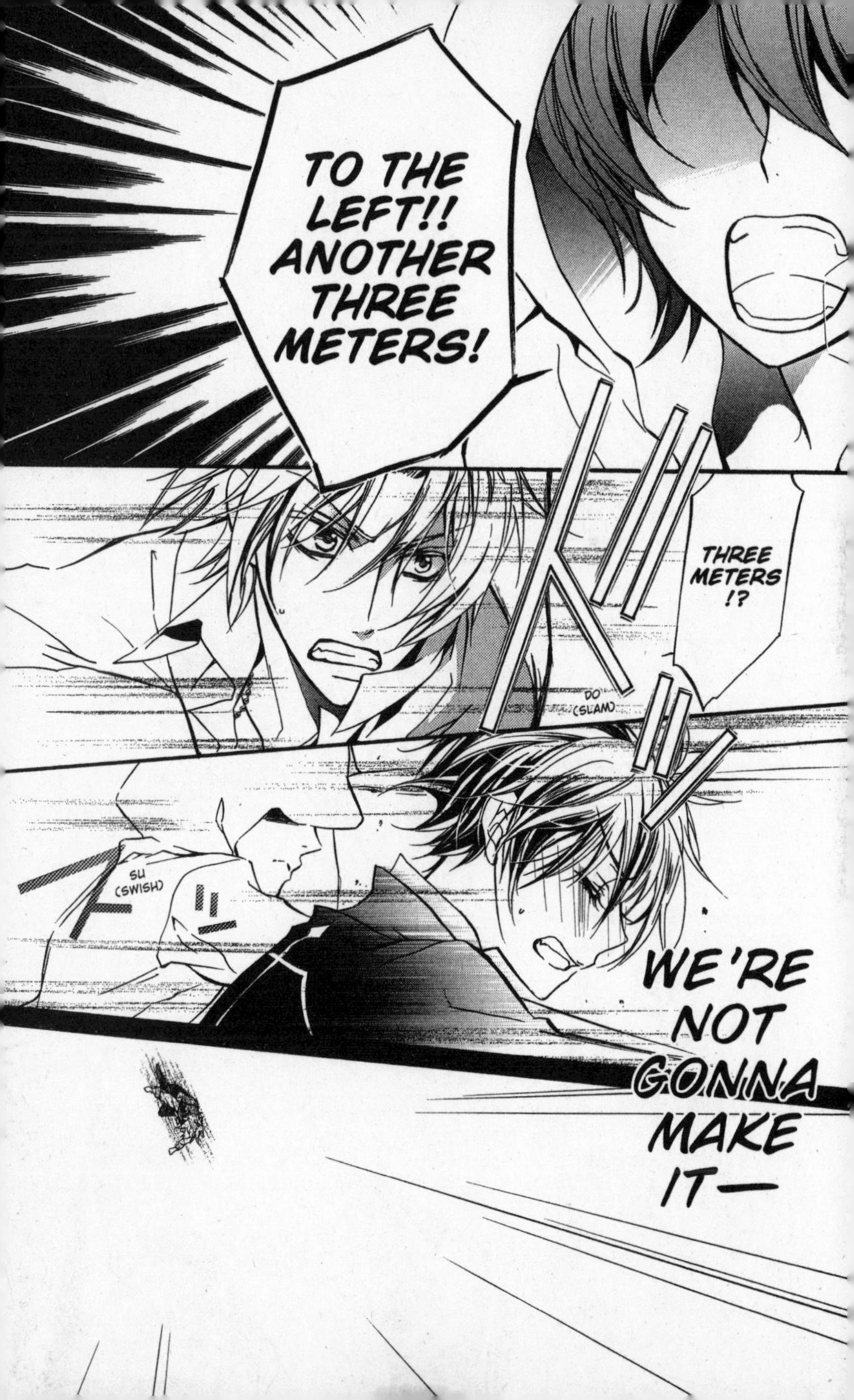
TO THE LEFT!! ANOTHER THREE METERS!
THREE METERS !?
DO (SLAM)
SU (SWISH)
WE'RE NOT GONNA MAKE IT—

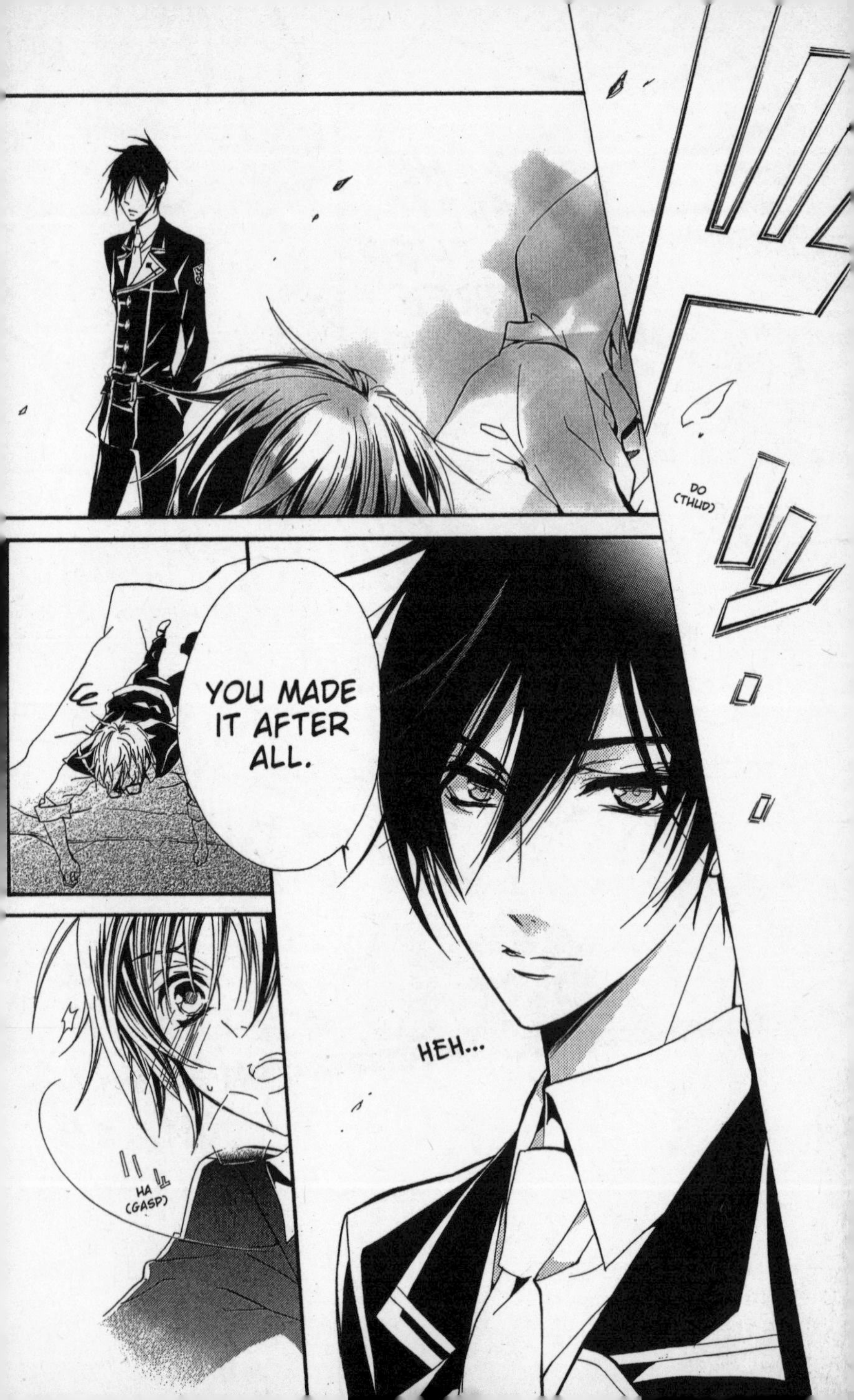
DO (THUD)
YOU MADE IT AFTER ALL.
HEH...
HA (GASP)

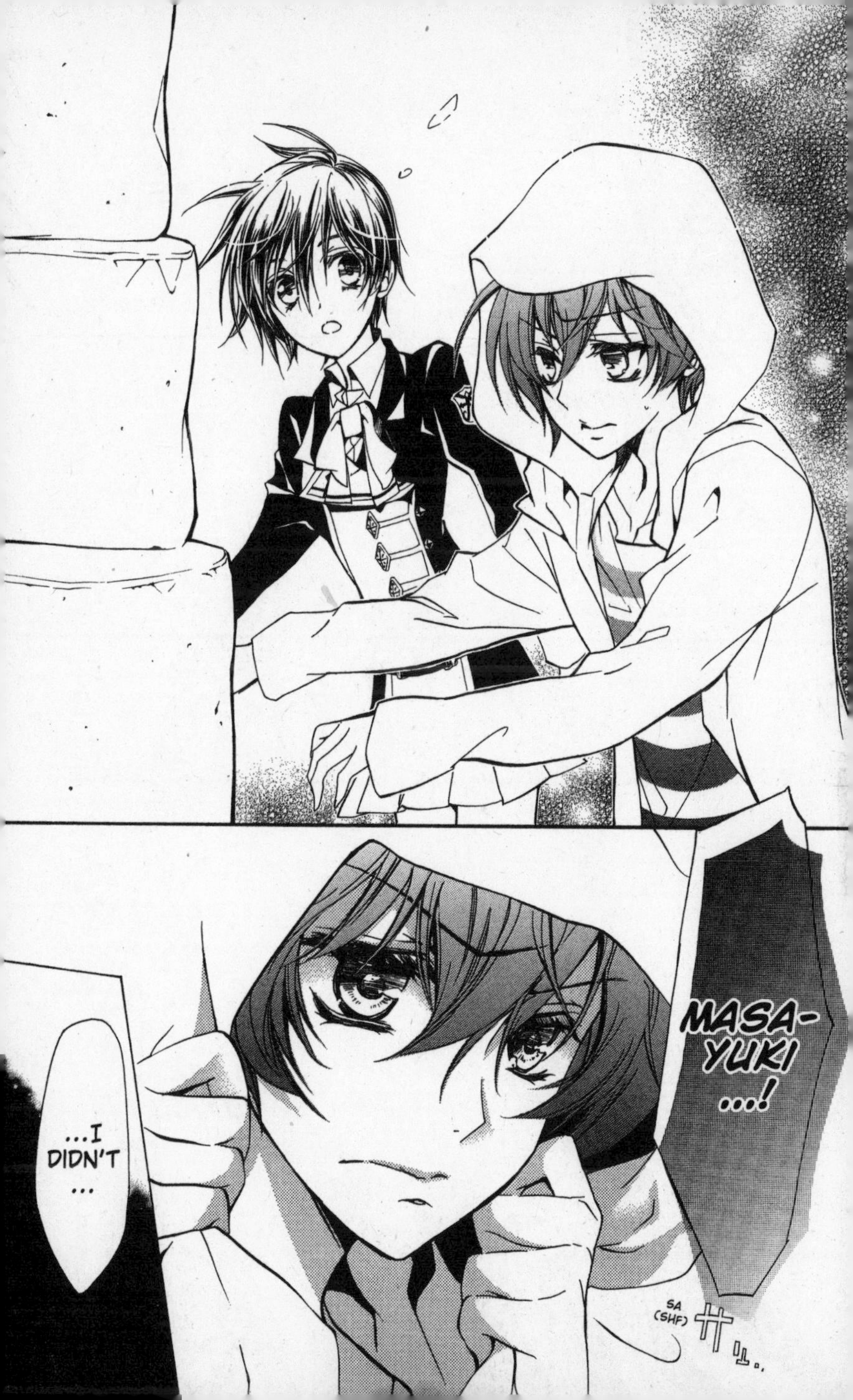
MASA-YUKI ...!
...I DIDN'T ...
SA (SHF)

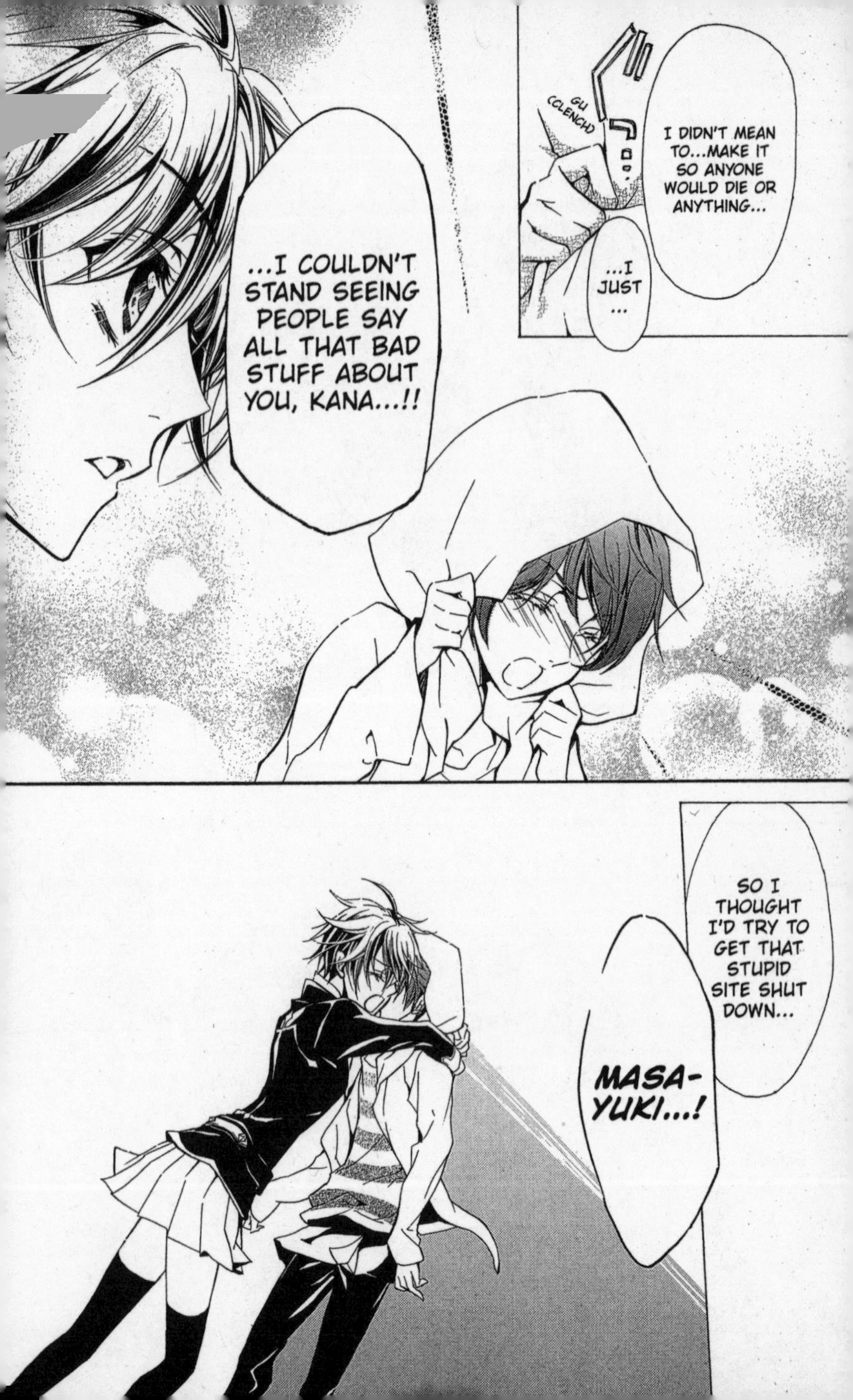
I DIDN'T MEAN TO...MAKE IT SO ANYONE WOULD DIE OR ANYTHING...
GU (CLENCH)
...I JUST ...
...I COULDN'T STAND SEEING PEOPLE SAY ALL THAT BAD STUFF ABOUT YOU, KANA...!!
SO I THOUGHT I'D TRY TO GET THAT STUPID SITE SHUT DOWN...
MASA-YUKI...!

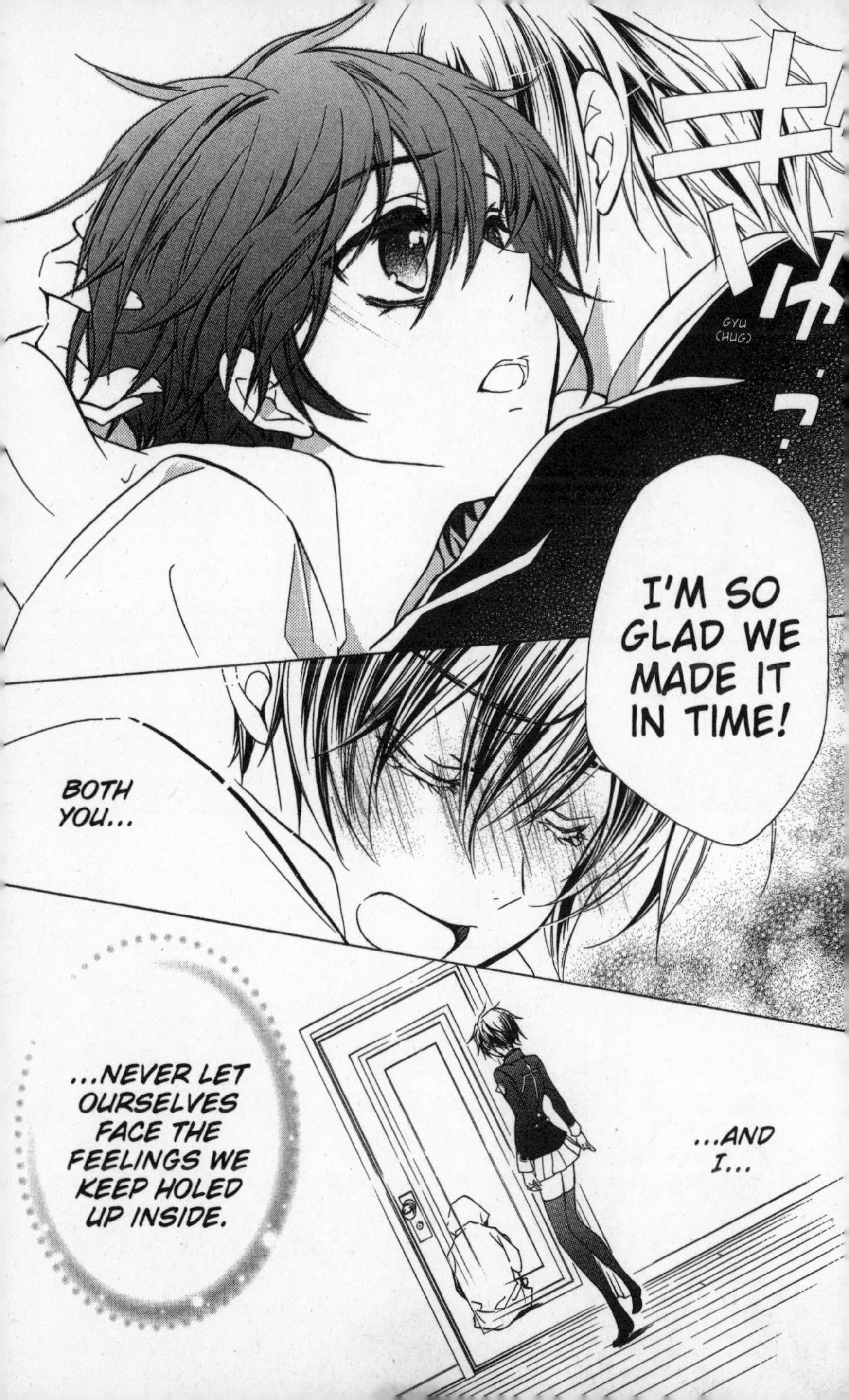
GYU (HUG)
I'M SO GLAD WE MADE IT IN TIME!
BOTH YOU...
...AND I...
...NEVER LET OURSELVES FACE THE FEELINGS WE KEEP HOLED UP INSIDE.

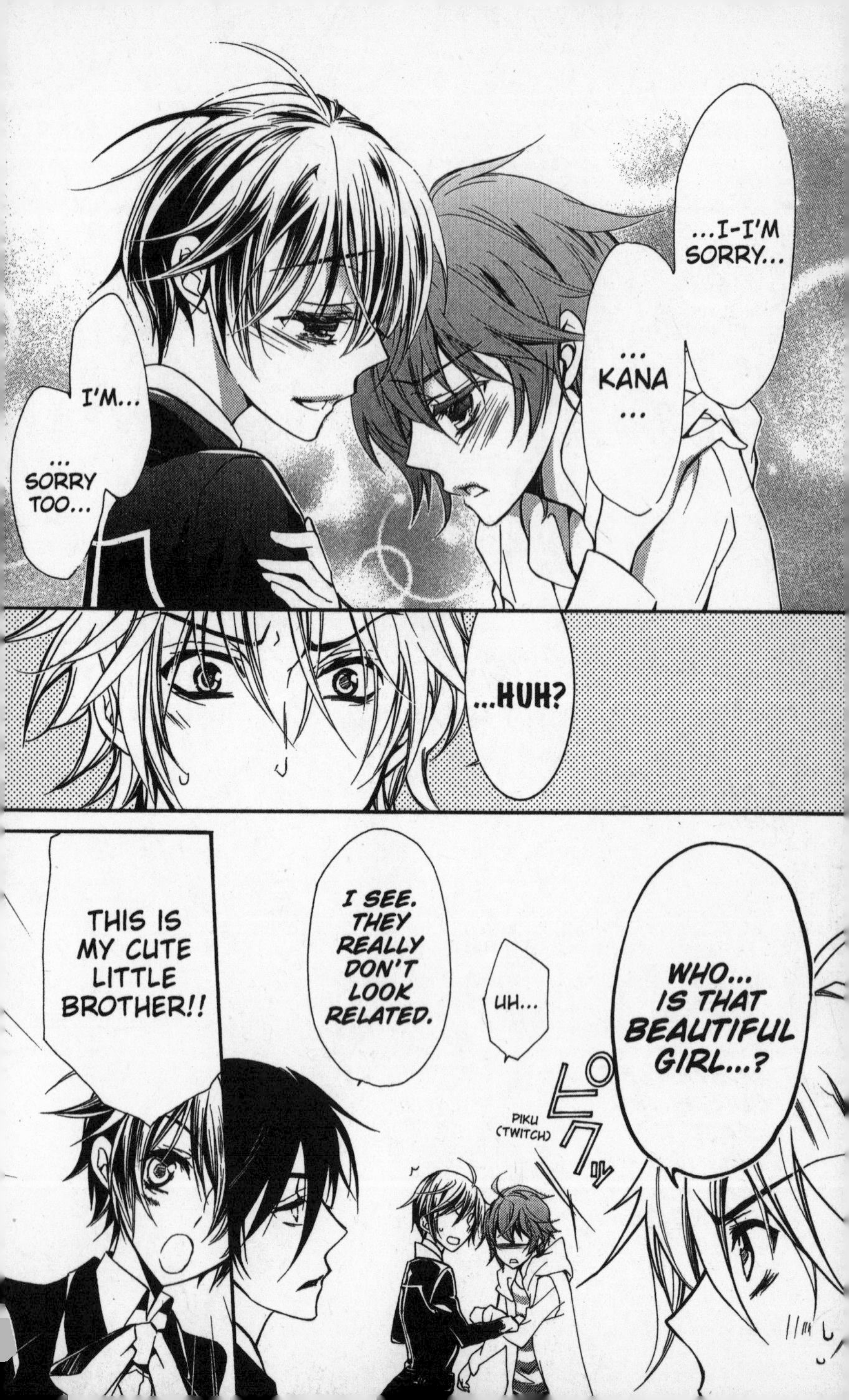
...I-I'M SORRY...
... KANA ...
I'M...
... SORRY TOO...
...HUH?
WHO... IS THAT BEAUTIFUL GIRL...?
PIKU (TWITCH)
UH...
I SEE. THEY REALLY DON'T LOOK RELATED.
THIS IS MY CUTE LITTLE BROTHER!!

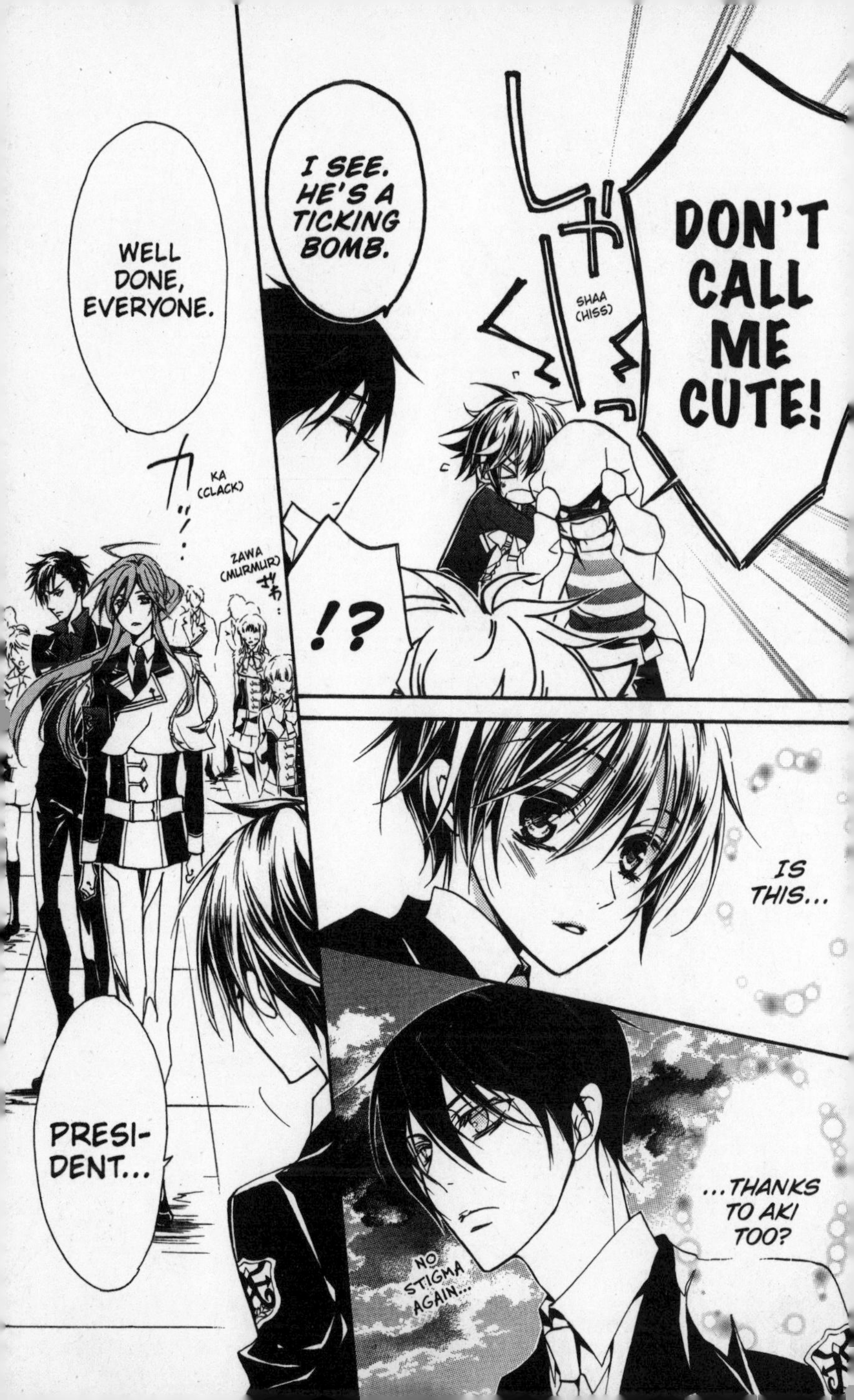

DON'T CALL ME CUTE!
SHAA (HISS)
I SEE. HE'S A TICKING BOMB.
!?
IS THIS...
...THANKS TO AKI TOO?
NO STIGMA AGAIN...
WELL DONE, EVERYONE.
KA (CLACK)
ZAWA (MURMUR)
PRESI-DENT...

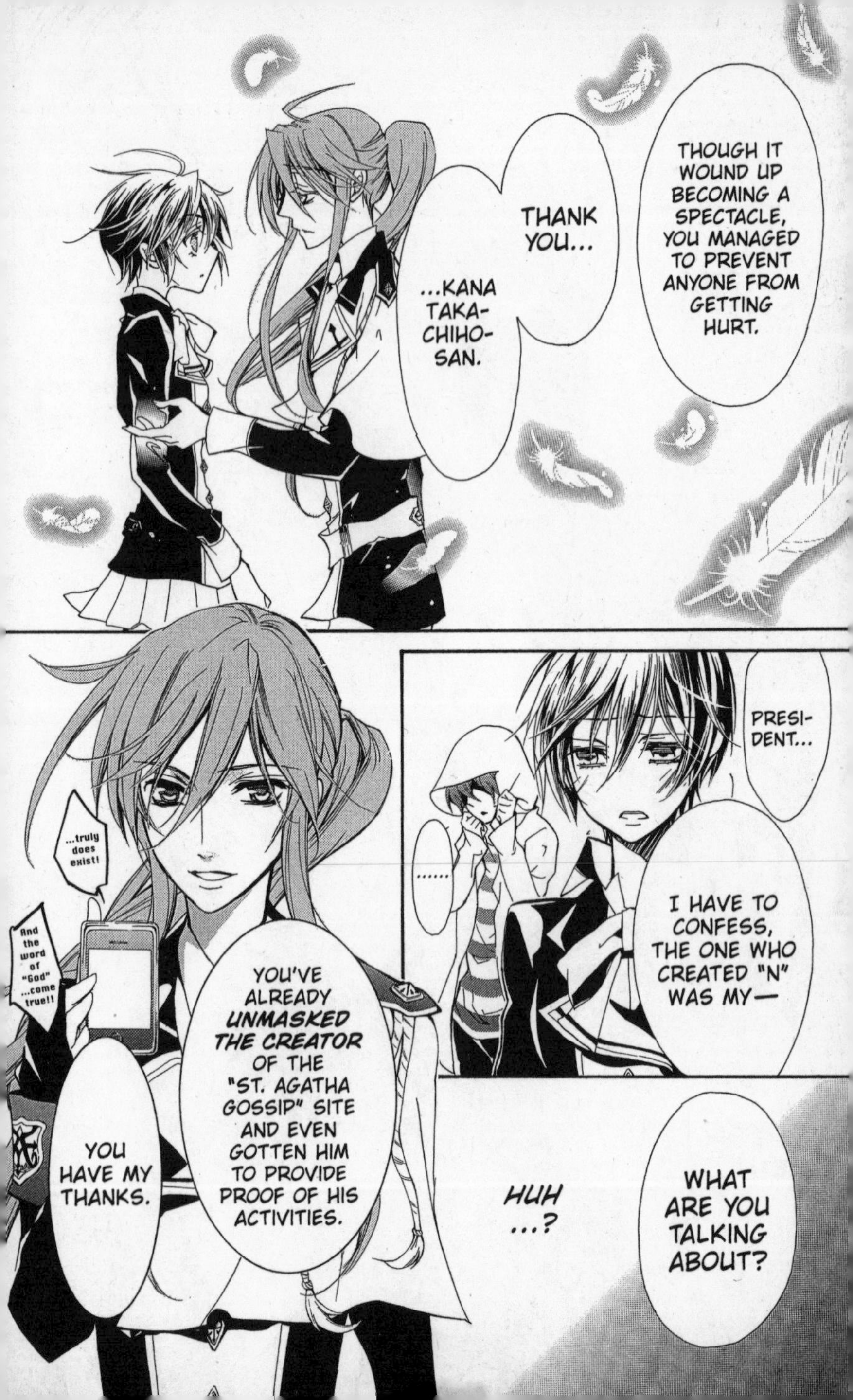
THOUGH IT WOUND UP BECOMING A SPECTACLE, YOU MANAGED TO PREVENT ANYONE FROM GETTING HURT.
THANK YOU...
...KANA TAKA-CHIHO-SAN.
PRESI-DENT...
I HAVE TO CONFESS, THE ONE WHO CREATED "N" WAS MY—
......
WHAT ARE YOU TALKING ABOUT?
HUH ...?
YOU'VE ALREADY UNMASKED THE CREATOR OF THE "ST. AGATHA GOSSIP" SITE AND EVEN GOTTEN HIM TO PROVIDE PROOF OF HIS ACTIVITIES.
YOU HAVE MY THANKS.
...truly does exist!
And the word of "God" ...come true!!

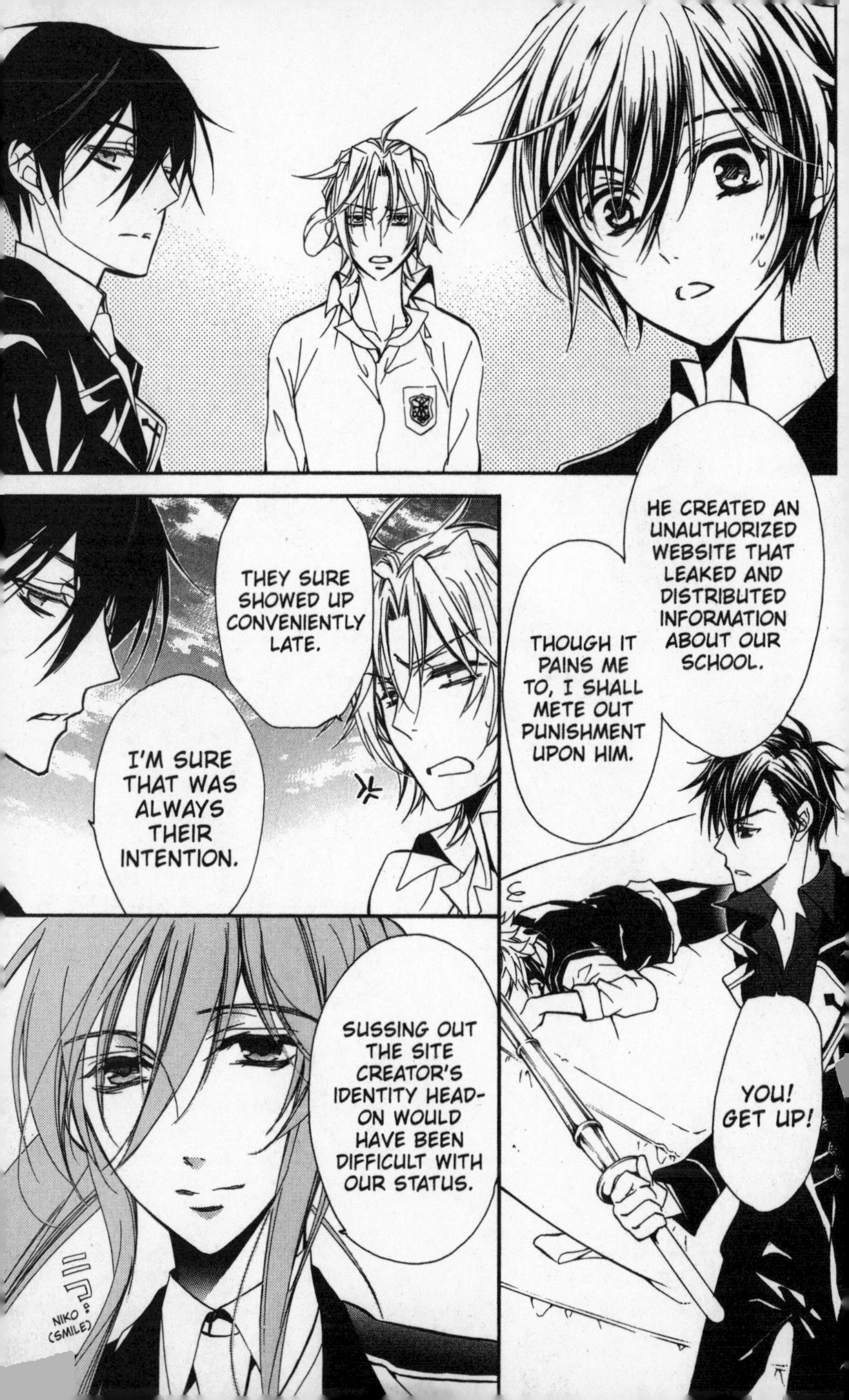
HE CREATED AN UNAUTHORIZED WEBSITE THAT LEAKED AND DISTRIBUTED INFORMATION ABOUT OUR SCHOOL.
THOUGH IT PAINS ME TO, I SHALL METE OUT PUNISHMENT UPON HIM.
YOU! GET UP!
THEY SURE SHOWED UP CONVENIENTLY LATE.
I'M SURE THAT WAS ALWAYS THEIR INTENTION.
SUSSING OUT THE SITE CREATOR'S IDENTITY HEAD-ON WOULD HAVE BEEN DIFFICULT WITH OUR STATUS.
NIKO (SMILE)

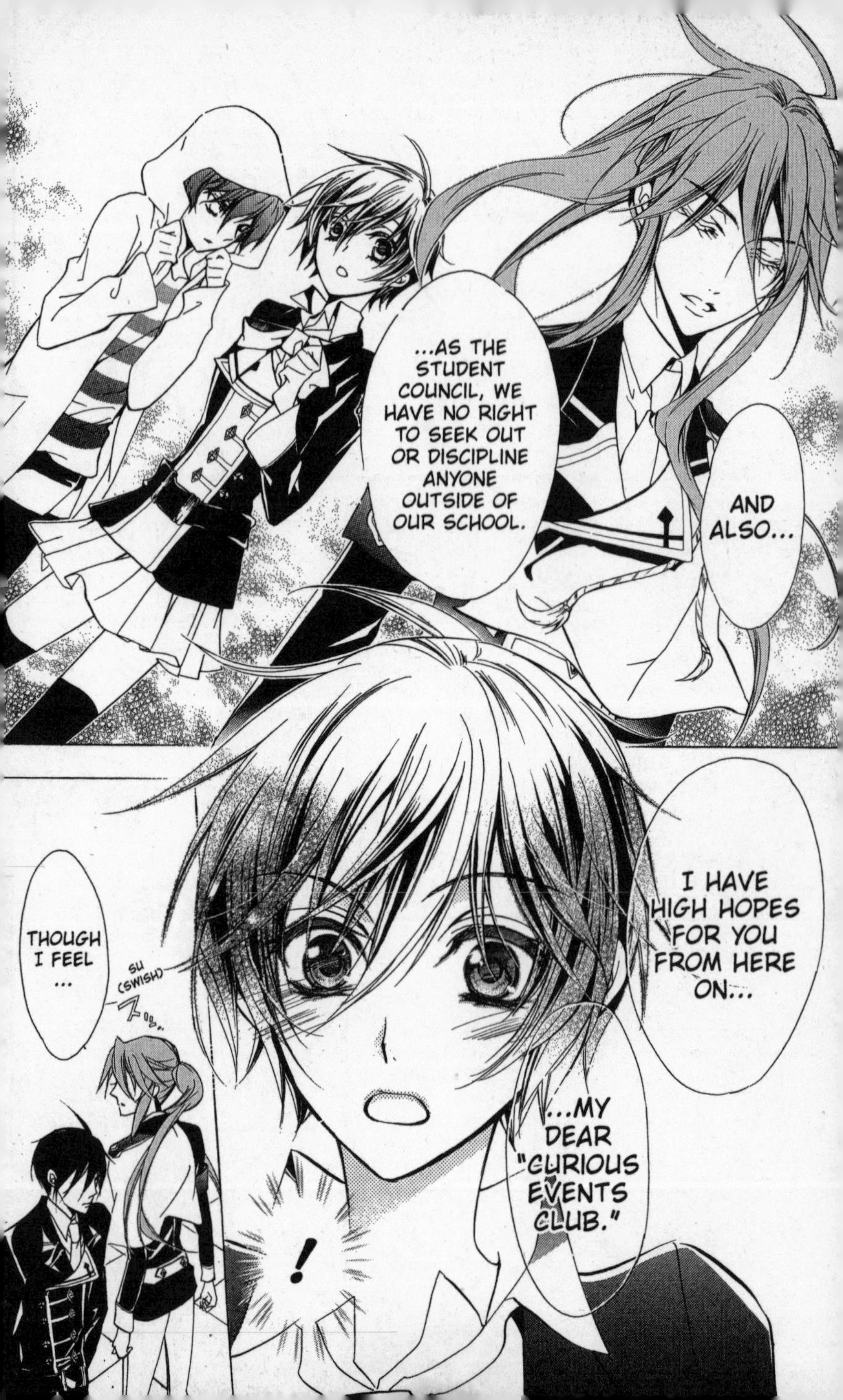
...AS THE STUDENT COUNCIL, WE HAVE NO RIGHT TO SEEK OUT OR DISCIPLINE ANYONE OUTSIDE OF OUR SCHOOL.
AND ALSO...
I HAVE HIGH HOPES FOR YOU FROM HERE ON...
...MY DEAR "CURIOUS EVENTS CLUB."
!
THOUGH I FEEL ...
SU (SWISH)
スッ..

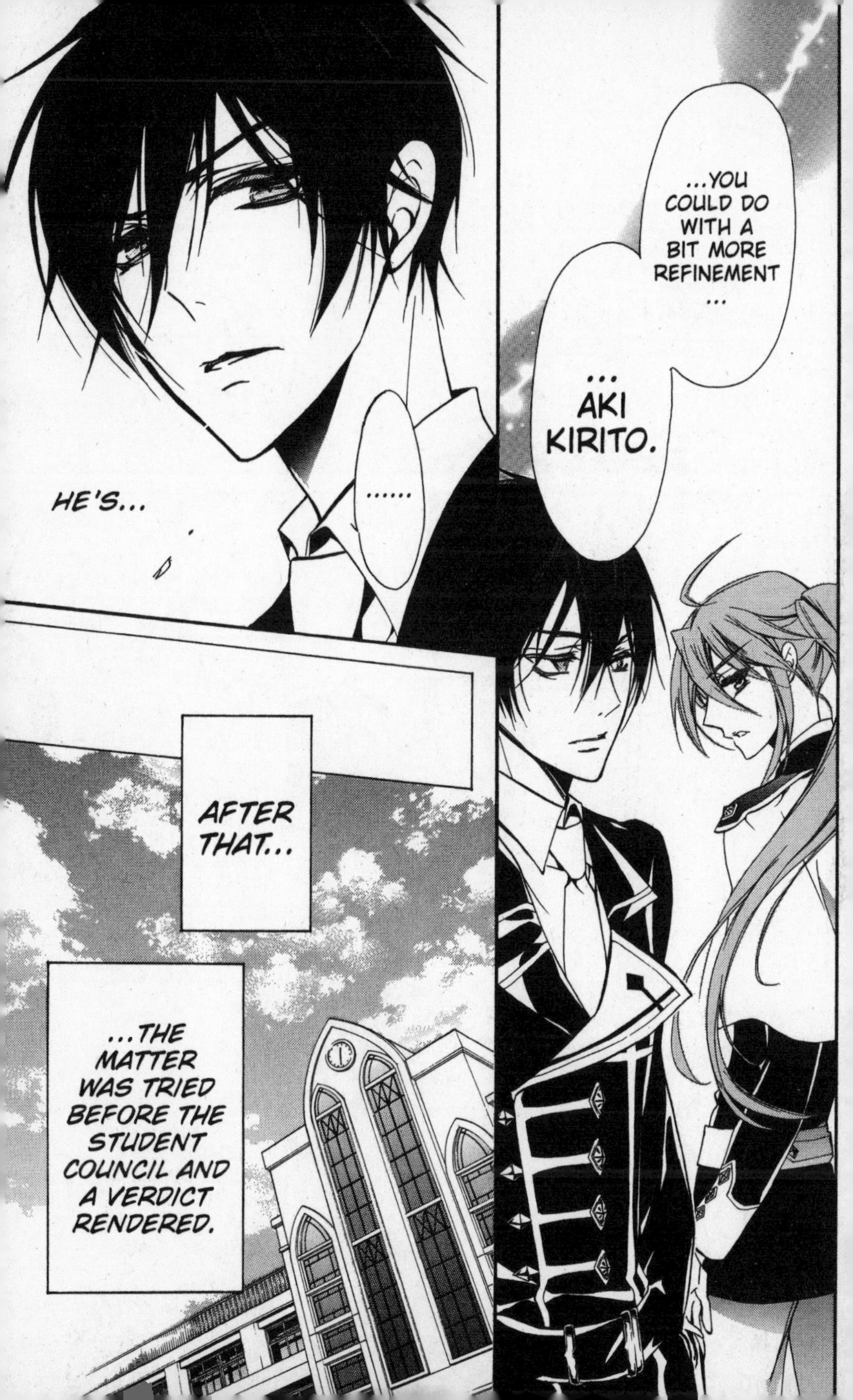
...YOU COULD DO WITH A BIT MORE REFINEMENT...
... AKI KIRITO.
......
HE'S...
AFTER THAT...
...THE MATTER WAS TRIED BEFORE THE STUDENT COUNCIL AND A VERDICT RENDERED.

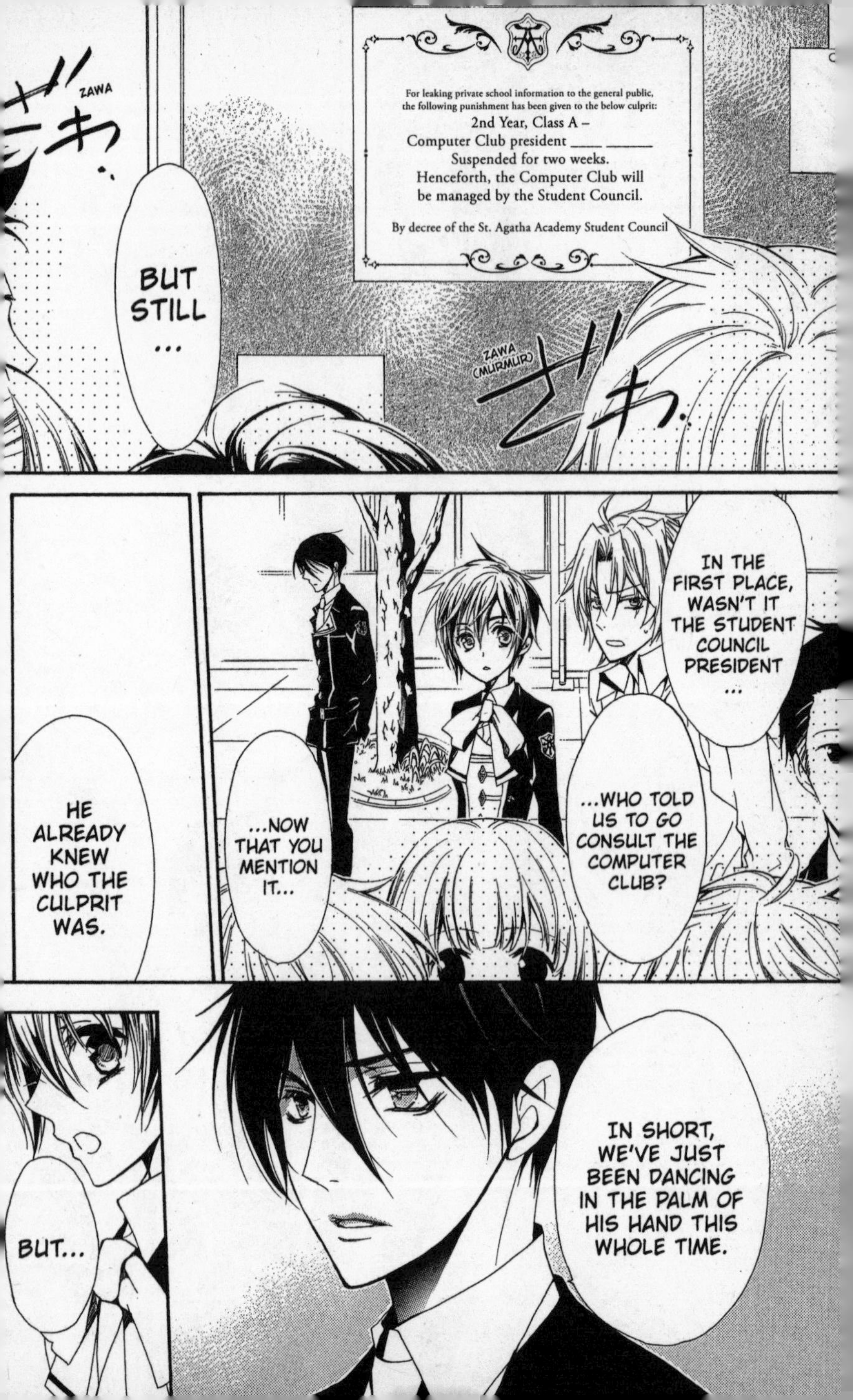
For leaking private school information to the general public,
the following punishment has been given to the below culprit:
2nd Year, Class A –
Computer Club president ____ ______
Suspended for two weeks.
Henceforth, the Computer Club will
be managed by the Student Council.
By decree of the St. Agatha Academy Student Council
ZAWA (MURMUR)
ZAWA
BUT STILL...
IN THE FIRST PLACE, WASN'T IT THE STUDENT COUNCIL PRESIDENT...
...WHO TOLD US TO GO CONSULT THE COMPUTER CLUB?
...NOW THAT YOU MENTION IT...
HE ALREADY KNEW WHO THE CULPRIT WAS.
IN SHORT, WE'VE JUST BEEN DANCING IN THE PALM OF HIS HAND THIS WHOLE TIME.
BUT...

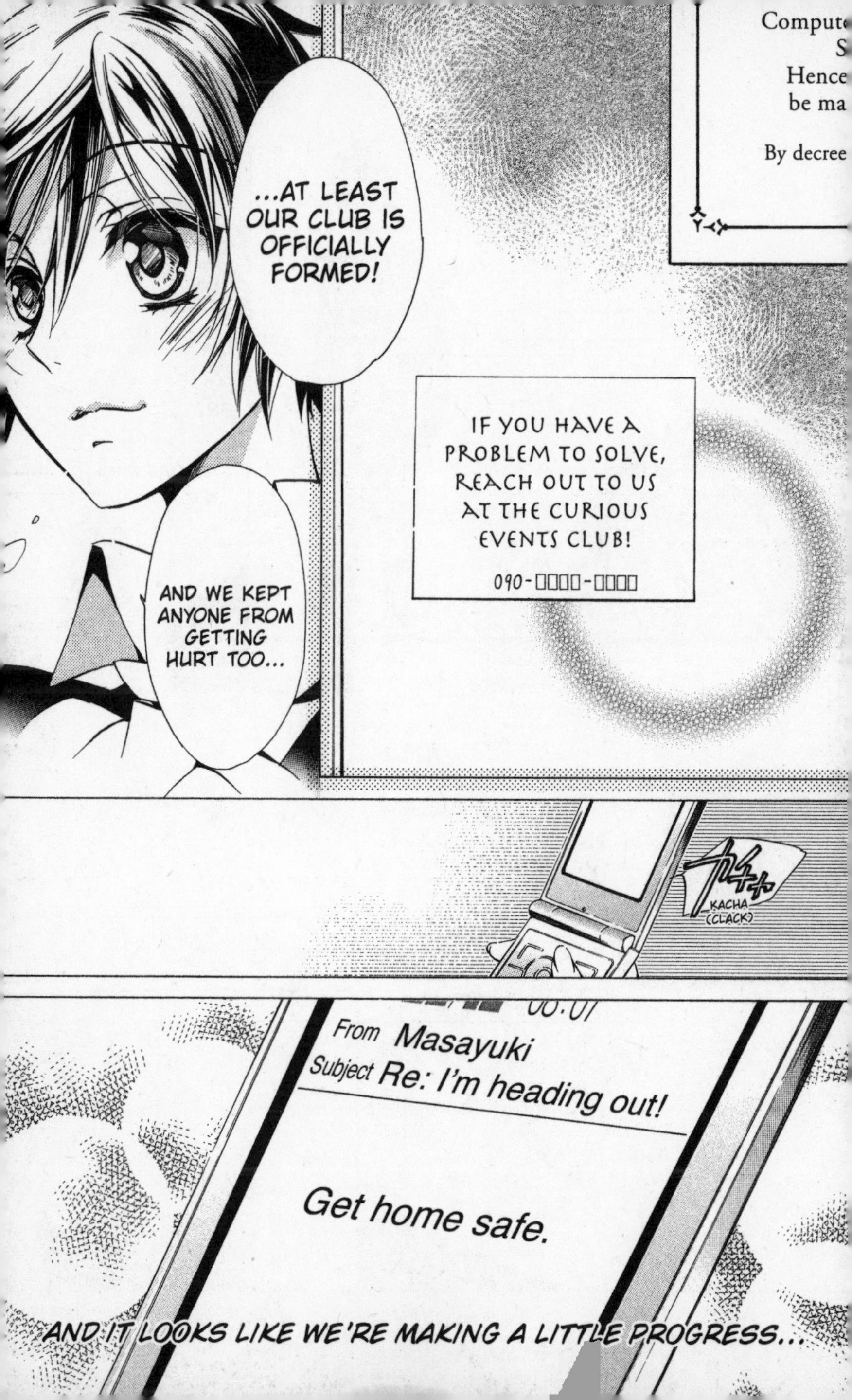
Comput
S
Hence
be ma
By decree
...AT LEAST OUR CLUB IS OFFICIALLY FORMED!
IF YOU HAVE A PROBLEM TO SOLVE, REACH OUT TO US AT THE CURIOUS EVENTS CLUB!
090-□□□□-□□□□
AND WE KEPT ANYONE FROM GETTING HURT TOO...
KACHA (CLACK)
From Masayuki
Subject Re: I'm heading out!
Get home safe.
AND IT LOOKS LIKE WE'RE MAKING A LITTLE PROGRESS...

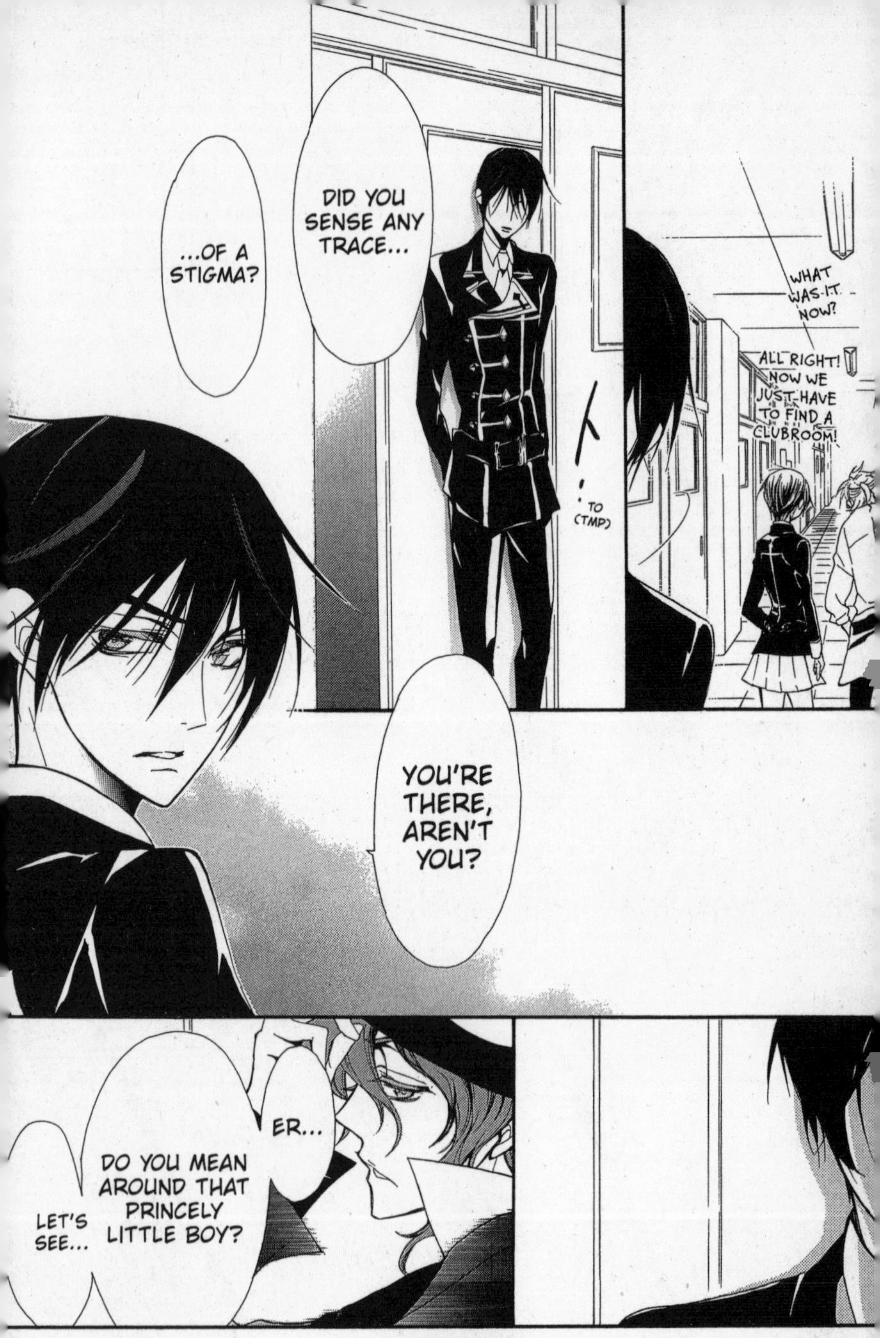
WHAT WAS IT NOW?
ALL RIGHT! NOW WE JUST HAVE TO FIND A CLUBROOM!
TO (TMP)
DID YOU SENSE ANY TRACE...
...OF A STIGMA?
YOU'RE THERE, AREN'T YOU?
ER...
DO YOU MEAN AROUND THAT PRINCELY LITTLE BOY?
LET'S SEE...

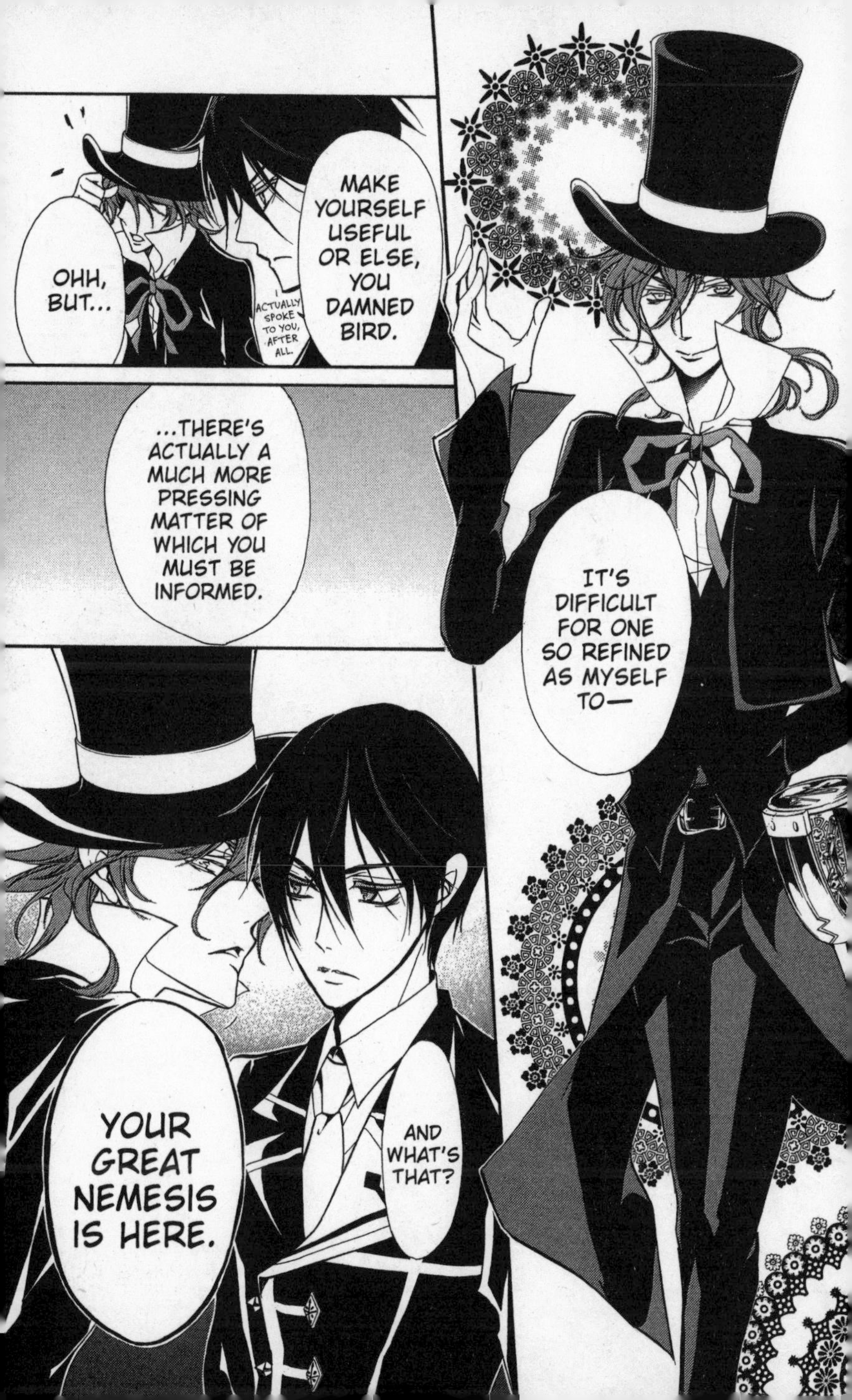
IT'S DIFFICULT FOR ONE SO REFINED AS MYSELF TO—
MAKE YOURSELF USEFUL OR ELSE, YOU DAMNED BIRD.
I ACTUALLY SPOKE TO YOU, AFTER ALL.
OHH, BUT...
...THERE'S ACTUALLY A MUCH MORE PRESSING MATTER OF WHICH YOU MUST BE INFORMED.
AND WHAT'S THAT?
YOUR GREAT NEMESIS IS HERE.

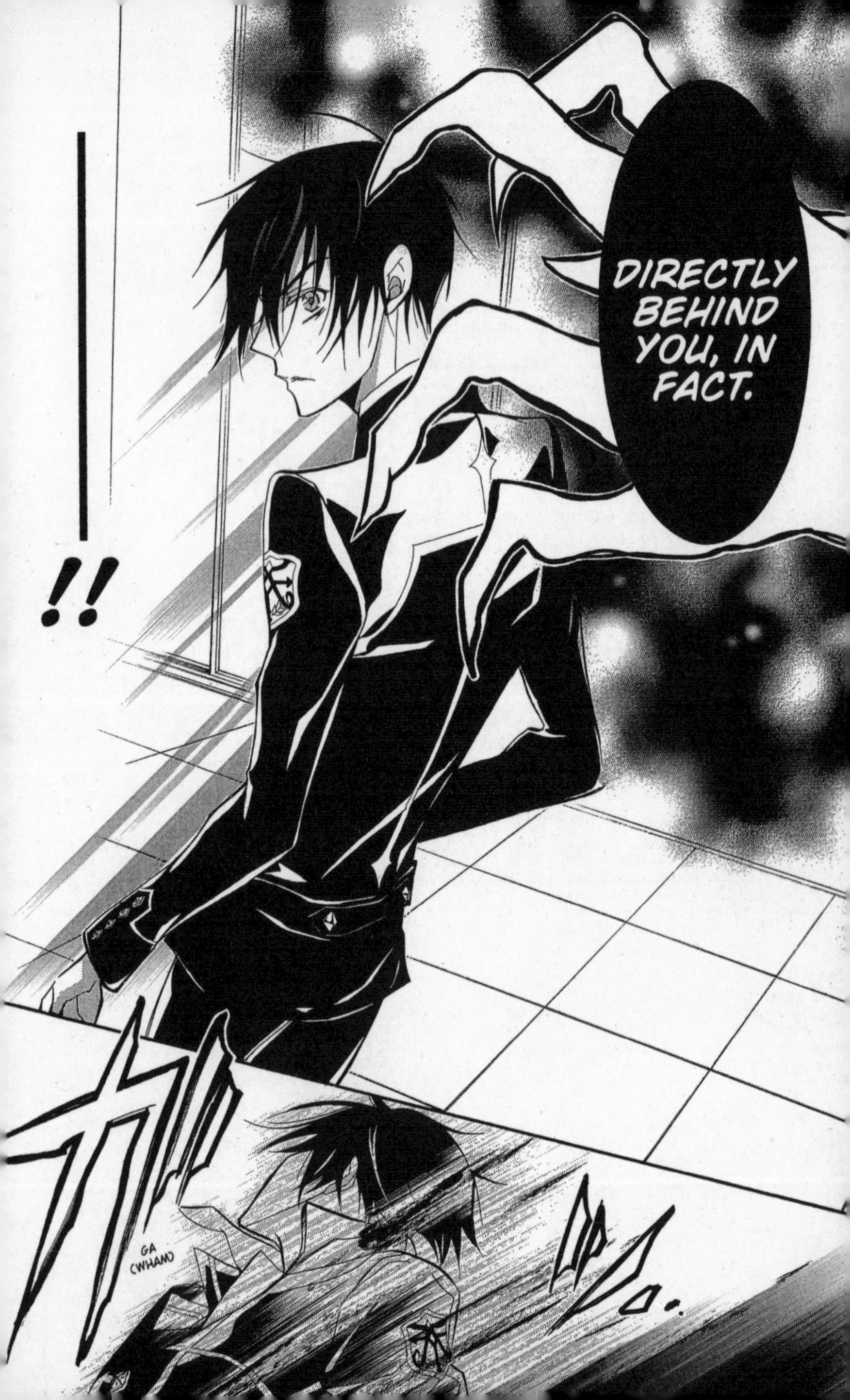
DIRECTLY BEHIND YOU, IN FACT.
!!
GA (WHAM)

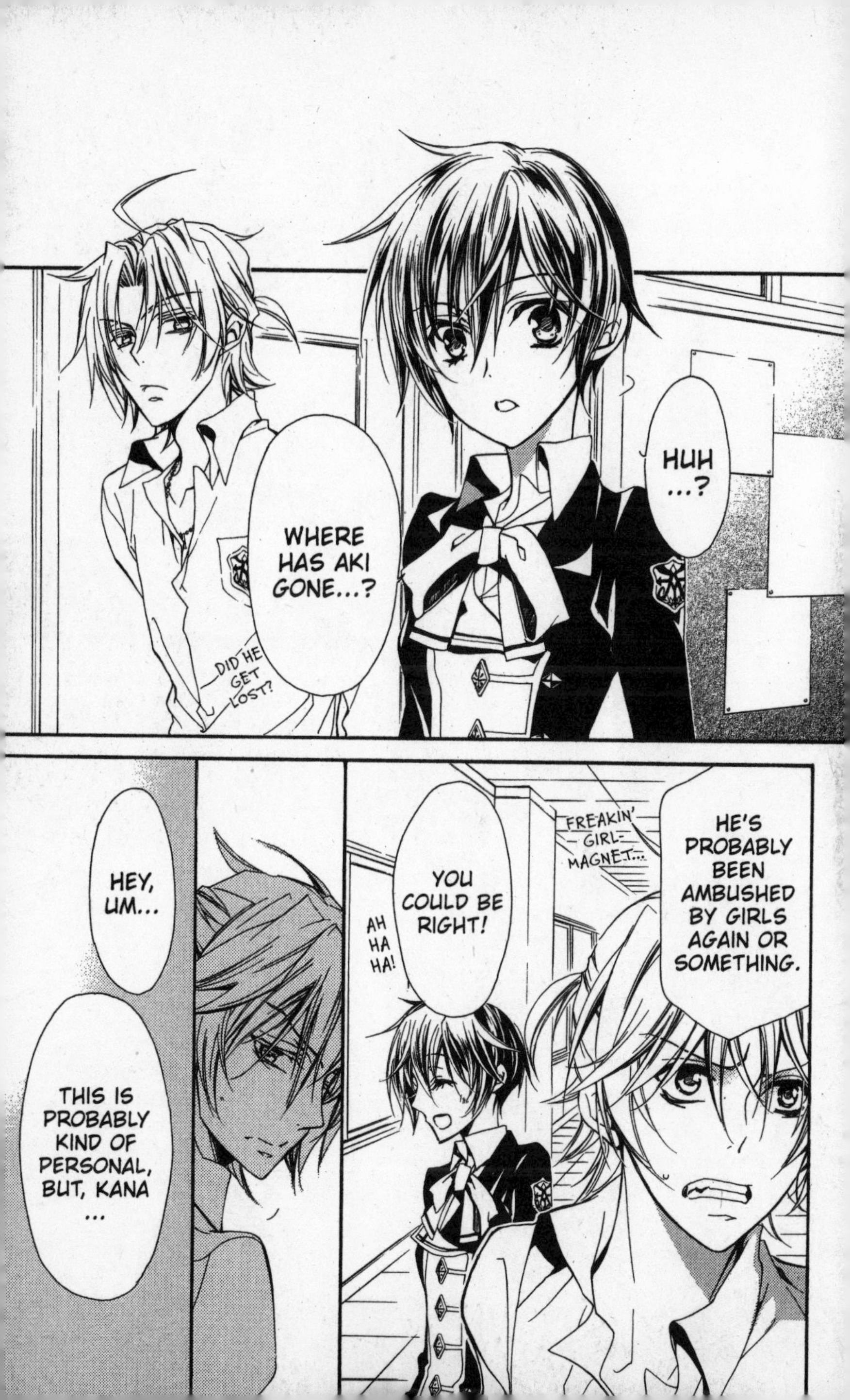
HUH ...?
WHERE HAS AKI GONE...?
DID HE GET LOST?
HE'S PROBABLY BEEN AMBUSHED BY GIRLS AGAIN OR SOMETHING.
FREAKIN' GIRL MAGNET...
YOU COULD BE RIGHT!
AH HA HA!
HEY, UM...
THIS IS PROBABLY KIND OF PERSONAL, BUT, KANA ...

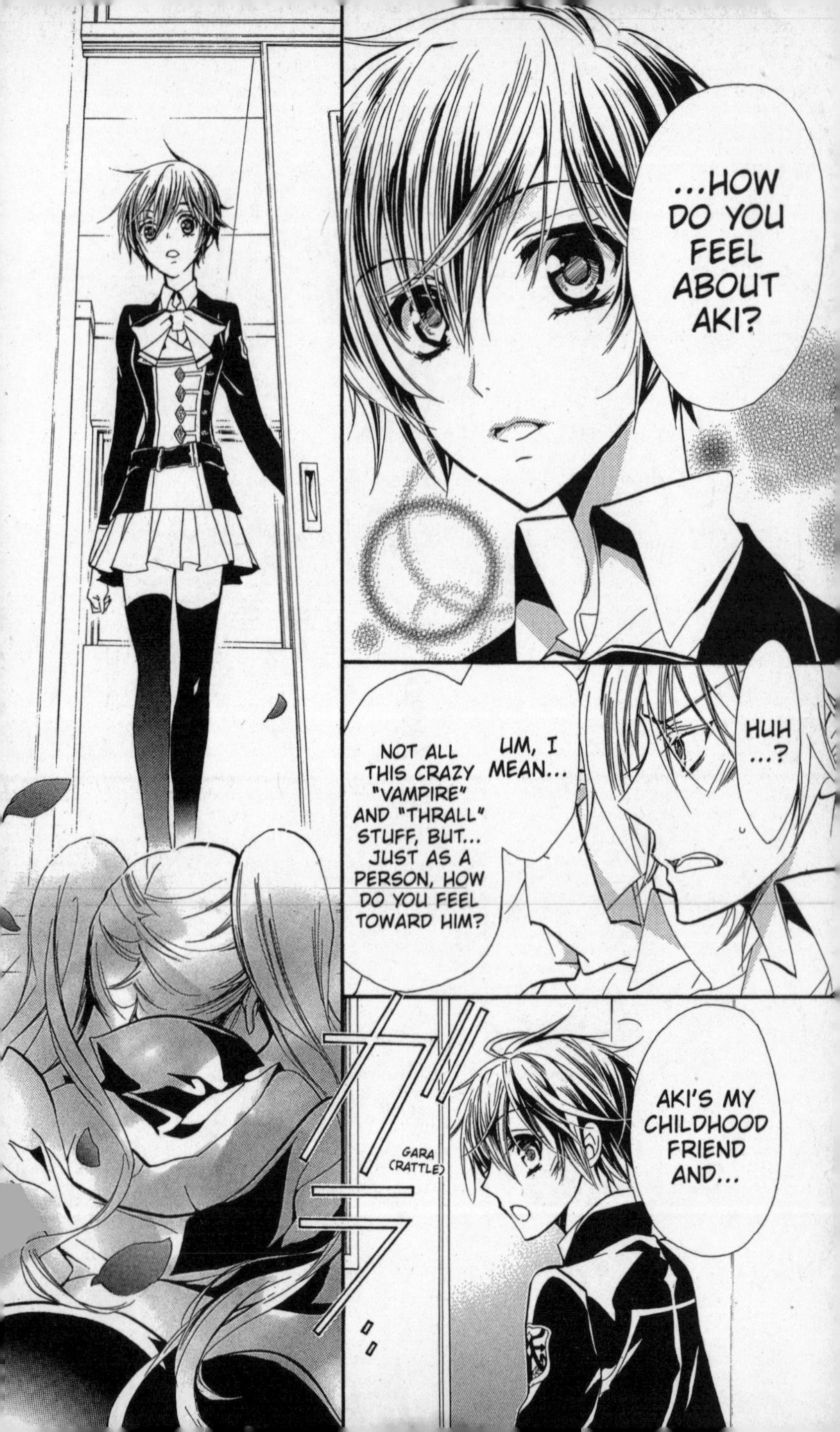
...HOW DO YOU FEEL ABOUT AKI?
HUH ...?
UM, I MEAN...
NOT ALL THIS CRAZY "VAMPIRE" AND "THRALL" STUFF, BUT... JUST AS A PERSON, HOW DO YOU FEEL TOWARD HIM?
AKI'S MY CHILDHOOD FRIEND AND...
GARA (RATTLE)

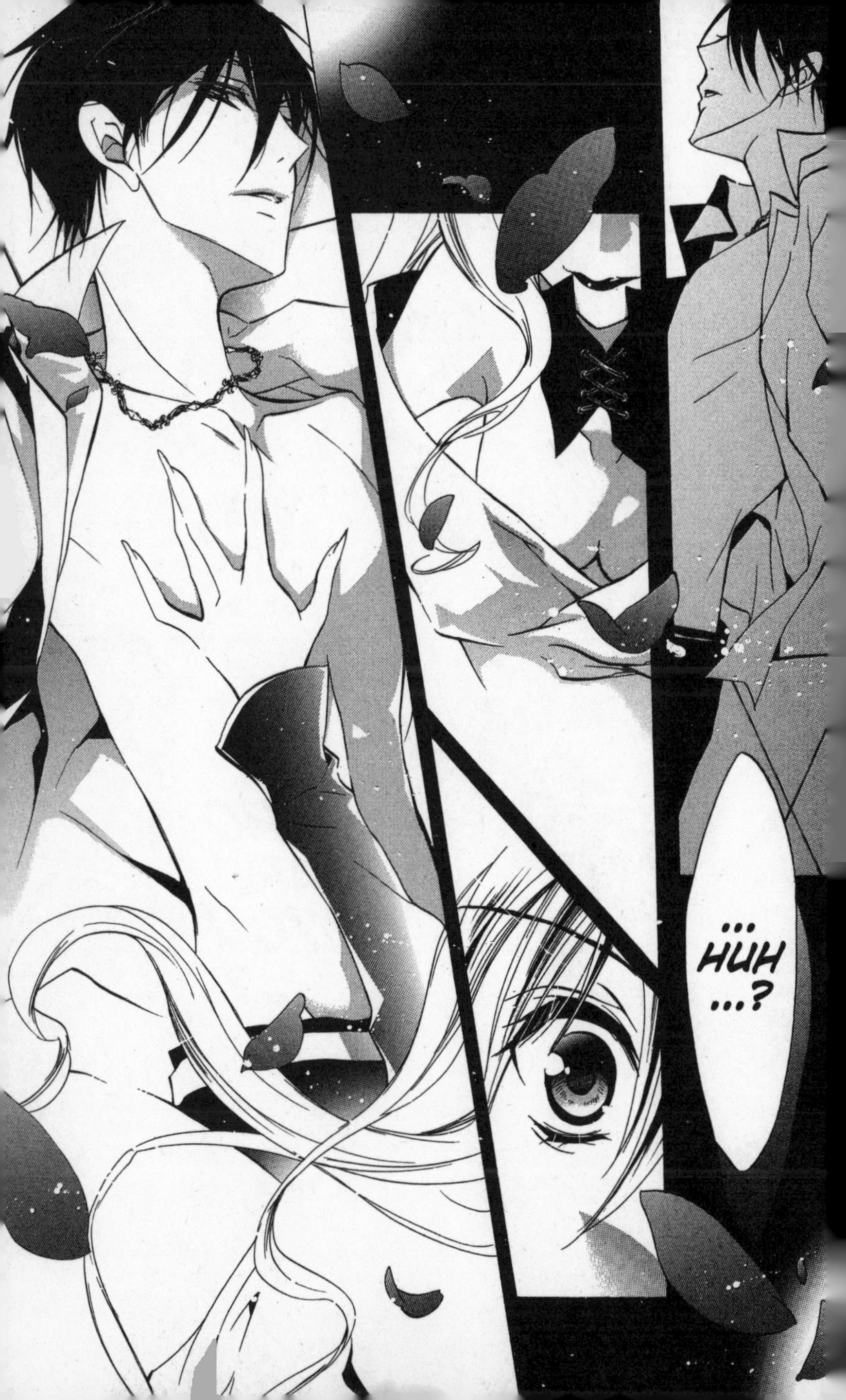
...HUH ...?

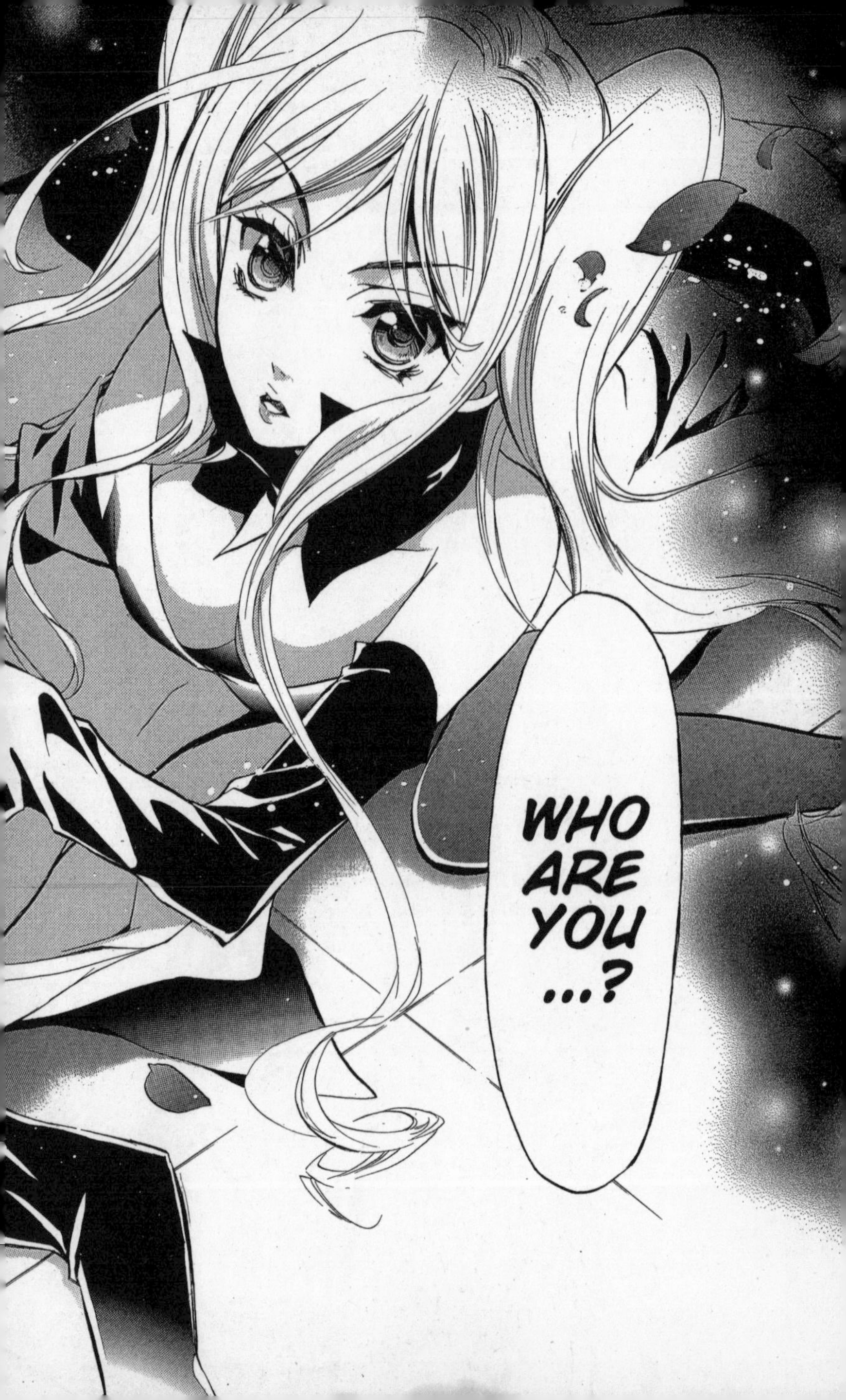
WHO ARE YOU ...?

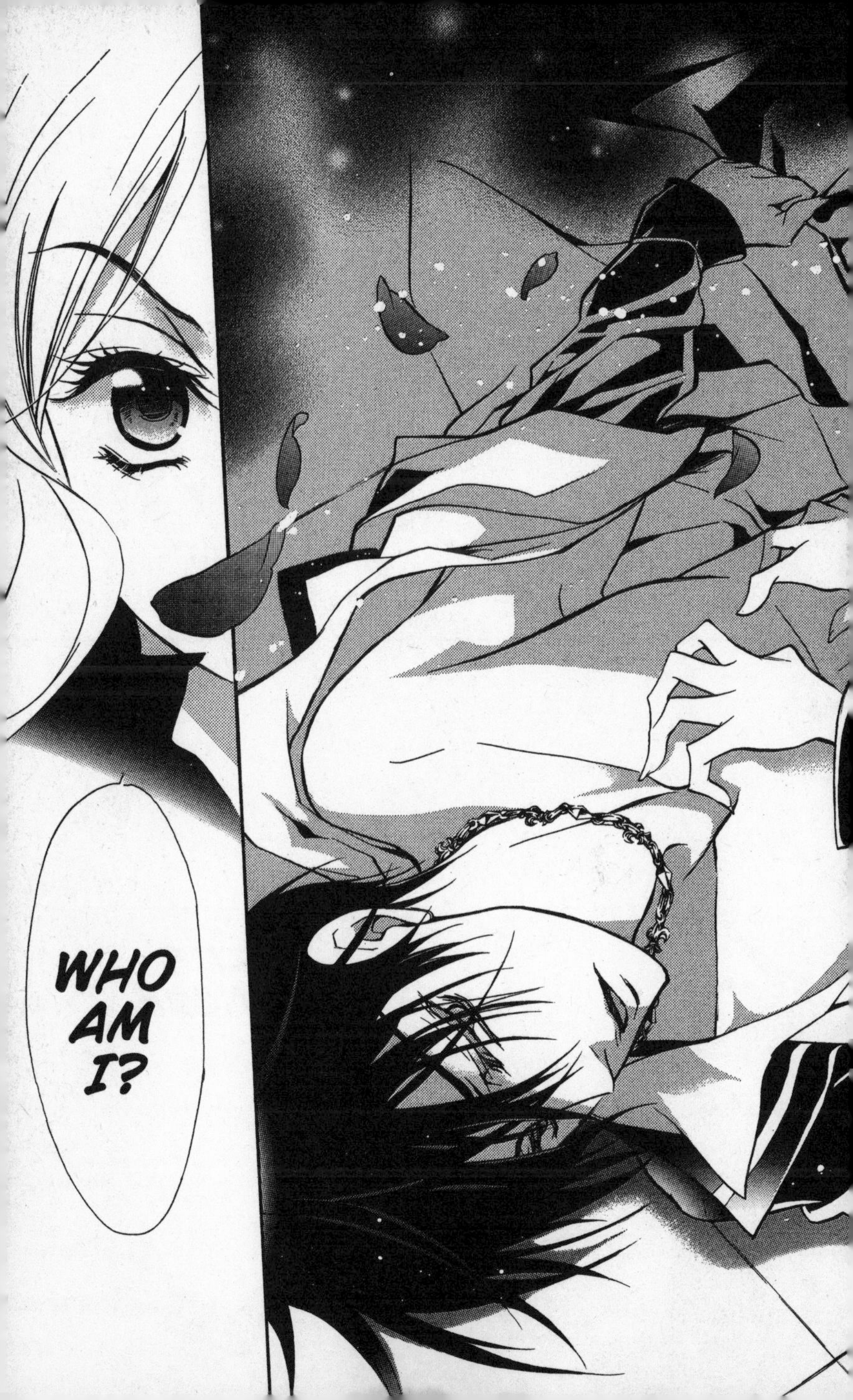
WHO AM I?

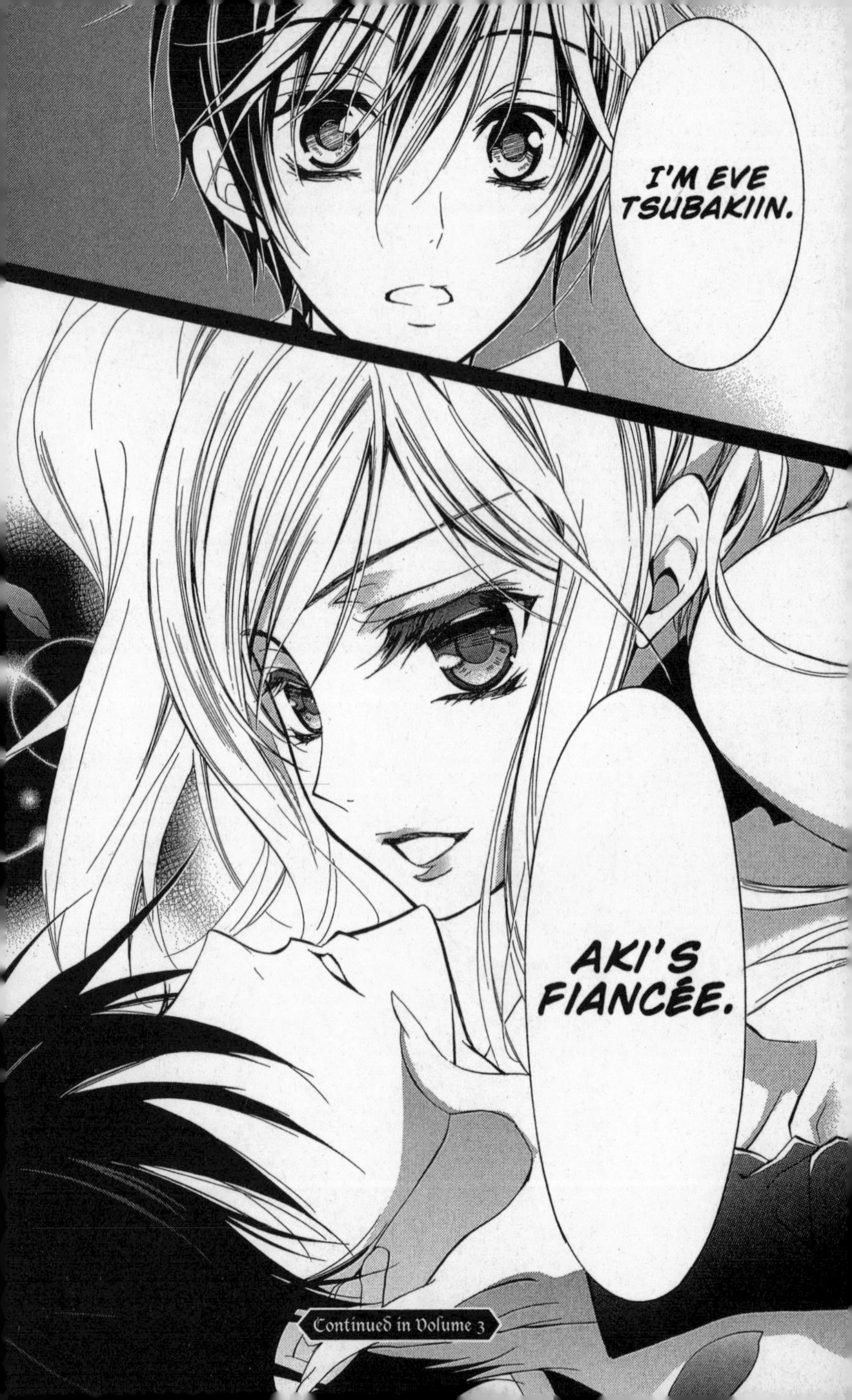
I'M EVE TSUBAKIIN.
AKI'S FIANCÉE.
Continued in Volume 3

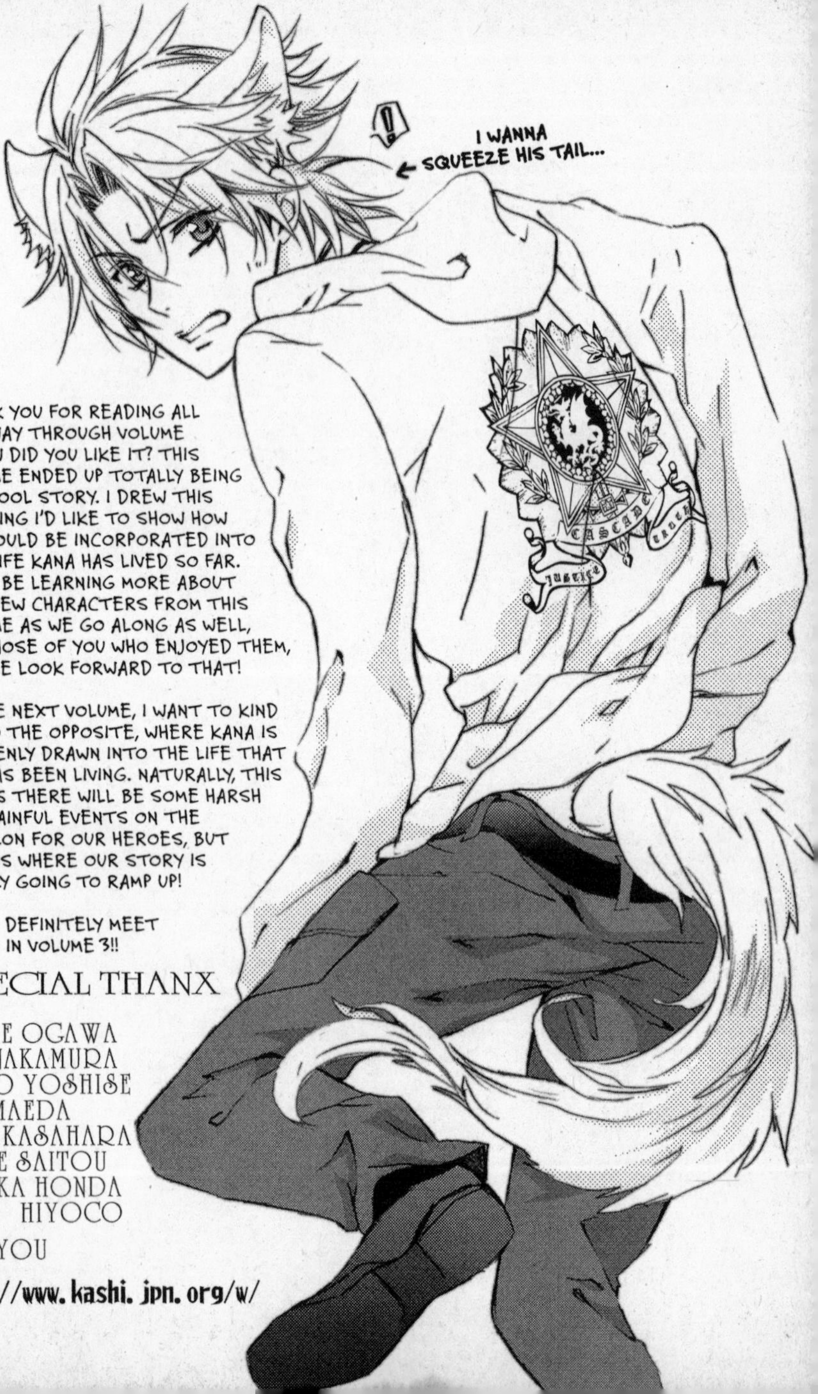
!
I WANNA
SQUEEZE HIS TAIL...

THANK YOU FOR READING ALL THE WAY THROUGH VOLUME 2! HOW DID YOU LIKE IT? THIS VOLUME ENDED UP TOTALLY BEING A SCHOOL STORY. I DREW THIS THINKING I'D LIKE TO SHOW HOW AKI WOULD BE INCORPORATED INTO THE LIFE KANA HAS LIVED SO FAR. WE'LL BE LEARNING MORE ABOUT THE NEW CHARACTERS FROM THIS VOLUME AS WE GO ALONG AS WELL, SO THOSE OF YOU WHO ENJOYED THEM, PLEASE LOOK FORWARD TO THAT!

IN THE NEXT VOLUME, I WANT TO KIND OF DO THE OPPOSITE, WHERE KANA IS SUDDENLY DRAWN INTO THE LIFE THAT AKI HAS BEEN LIVING. NATURALLY, THIS MEANS THERE WILL BE SOME HARSH AND PAINFUL EVENTS ON THE HORIZON FOR OUR HEROES, BUT THIS IS WHERE OUR STORY IS REALLY GOING TO RAMP UP!

LET'S DEFINITELY MEET AGAIN IN VOLUME 3!!

SPECIAL THANX

ORIE OGAWA
YA NAKAMURA
AIKO YOSHISE
YA MAEDA
IKA KASAHARA
ANAE SAITOU
URIKA HONDA
OU HIYOCO

nd YOU

ttp://www.kashi.jpn.org/w/

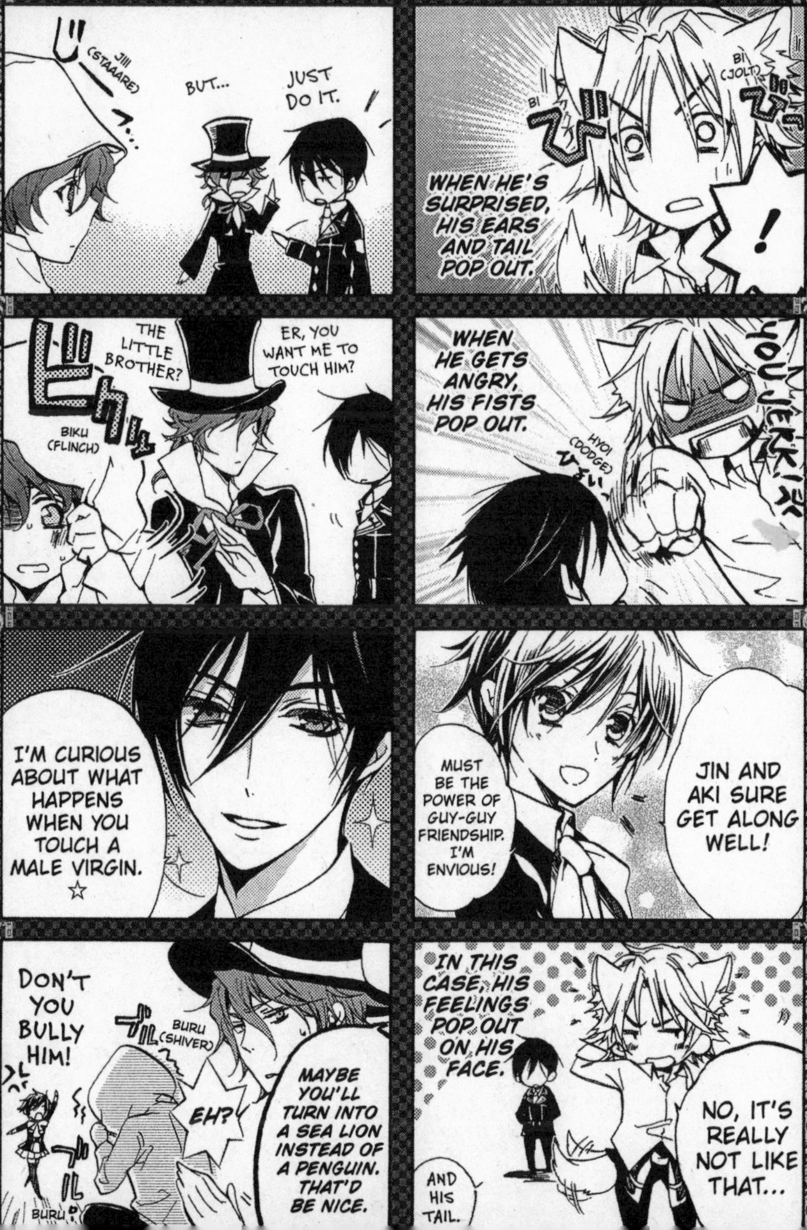
BI (JOLT)
BI
WHEN HE'S SURPRISED, HIS EARS AND TAIL POP OUT.
!
YOU JERK!
WHEN HE GETS ANGRY, HIS FISTS POP OUT.
HYOI (DODGE)
JIN AND AKI SURE GET ALONG WELL!
MUST BE THE POWER OF GUY-GUY FRIENDSHIP. I'M ENVIOUS!
IN THIS CASE, HIS FEELINGS POP OUT ON HIS FACE.
NO, IT'S REALLY NOT LIKE THAT...
AND HIS TAIL.
JUST DO IT.
BUT...
JIII (STAAARE)
ER, YOU WANT ME TO TOUCH HIM?
THE LITTLE BROTHER?
BIKU (FLINCH)
I'M CURIOUS ABOUT WHAT HAPPENS WHEN YOU TOUCH A MALE VIRGIN. ☆
MAYBE YOU'LL TURN INTO A SEA LION INSTEAD OF A PENGUIN. THAT'D BE NICE.
EH?
BURU (SHIVER)
DON'T YOU BULLY HIM!
BURU

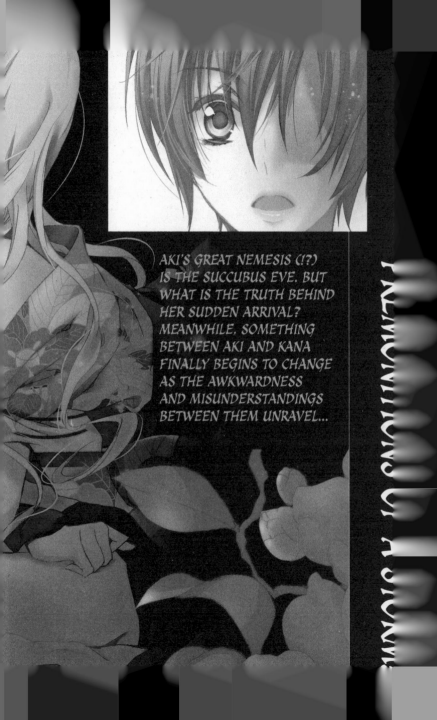

AKI'S GREAT NEMESIS (!?)
IS THE SUCCUBUS EVE. BUT
WHAT IS THE TRUTH BEHIND
HER SUDDEN ARRIVAL?
MEANWHILE, SOMETHING
BETWEEN AKI AND KANA
FINALLY BEGINS TO CHANGE
AS THE AWKWARDNESS
AND MISUNDERSTANDINGS
BETWEEN THEM UNRAVEL...

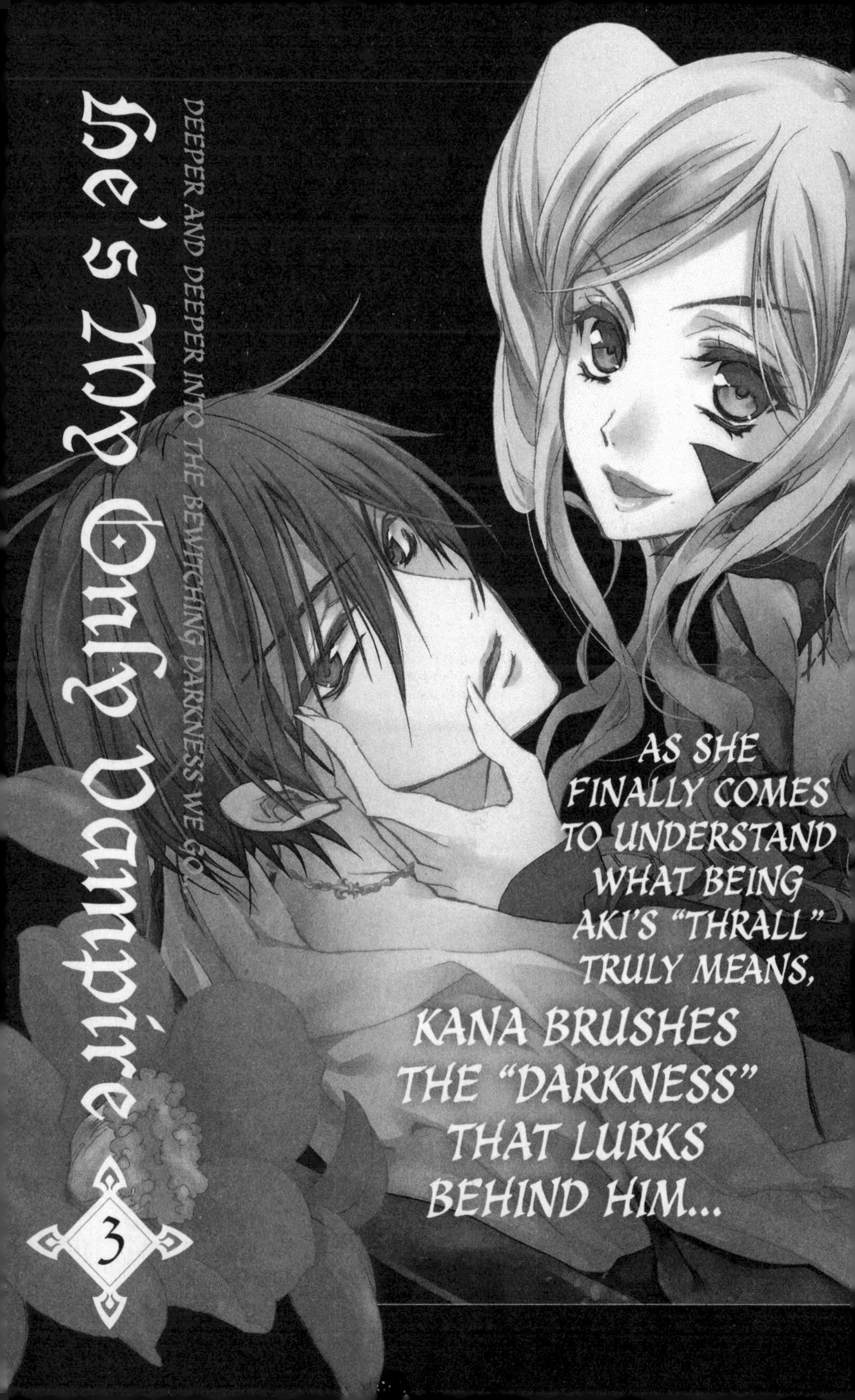
He's My Only Vampire
3
DEEPER AND DEEPER INTO THE BEWITCHING DARKNESS WE GO...
AS SHE FINALLY COMES TO UNDERSTAND WHAT BEING AKI'S "THRALL" TRULY MEANS,
KANA BRUSHES THE "DARKNESS" THAT LURKS BEHIND HIM...

He's My Only Vampire 2

Aya Shouoto

Translation: Su Mon Han † Lettering: Alexis Eckerman

HE'S MY ONLY VAMPIRE Volume 2 © 2011 Aya Shouoto. All rights reserved. First published in Japan in 2011 by Kodansha Ltd., Tokyo. Publication rights for this English edition arranged through Kodansha Ltd., Tokyo.

Translation © 2015 by Hachette Book Group, Inc.

Yen Press
Hachette Book Group
1290 Avenue of the Americas, New York, NY 10104

www.HachetteBookGroup.com
www.YenPress.com

Yen Press is an imprint of Hachette Book Group, Inc. The Yen Press name and logo are trademarks of Hachette Book Group, Inc.

The publisher is not responsible for websites (or their content) that are not owned by the publisher.

First Yen Press Edition: March 2015

ISBN: 978-0-316-38271-7

10 9 8 7 6 5 4 3 2 1

BVG

Printed in the
United States of America